NORMAN VINCENT PEALE

AN INSPIRING COLLECTION OF THREE COMPLETE BOOKS

NORMAN VINCENT PEALE

AN INSPIRING COLLECTION OF THREE COMPLETE BOOKS

HAVE A GREAT DAY

POSITIVE IMAGING

TREASURY OF JOY AND ENTHUSIASM

WINGS BOOKS
New York

Treasury of Joy and Enthusiasm copyright © 1981 by Norman Vincent Peale
Positive Imaging copyright © 1982 by Norman Vincent Peale
Have a Great Day copyright © 1985 by Norman Vincent Peale

This 1997 edition is published by Wings Books,
a division of Random House Value Publishing, Inc.,
210 East 50th Street, New York, New York, 10022,
by arrangement with Baker Book House.

Wings Books and colophon are trademarks of
Random House Value Publishing, Inc.

Random House
New York • Toronto • London • Sydney • Auckland
http://www.randomhouse.com/

Printed and bound in the United States of America

A CIP catalog record for this book is available from the Library of Congress.

Norman Vincent Peale: An Inspiring Collection of Three Complete Books
ISBN 0-517-18661-6

8   7   6   5   4   3   2   1

HAVE A GREAT DAY

CONTENTS

How to Use This Book   9

January   11
February   17
March 1–20   23

SPRING   27

March 21–31   28
April   31
May   37
June 1–20   44

SUMMER   48

June 21–30   49
July   52
August   58
September 1–20   65

AUTUMN   70

September 21–30   71
October   75
November   83
December 1–20   90

WINTER   94

December 21–31   95

With appreciation to
Nancy Dakin
for her help
in preparing
this
manuscript

HOW TO USE THIS BOOK

ALL OF US, IT seems, need something every day to keep us going with full energy and enthusiasm. And perhaps nothing is more effective than a motivating and inspiring thought.

There is an old saying, "An apple a day keeps the doctor away." May it not also be said that an upbeat thought a day will keep the shadows away and let in the bright light of hope and joy?

For many years, I have made it a practice to insert in my mind every day some inspiring thought and visualize it as seeping into my consciousness. My personal experience has been that such thoughts gradually permeate and affect attitudes. Sometimes I have called them "spirit lifters" for they do just that. And spirit lifting is needed by all of us.

At other times, I have called these selected ideas "thought conditioners." Even as the atmosphere of a room can be changed by air conditioning, so the climate of the mind can be changed by "thought conditioning." And a thought can make an enormous difference in how one feels mentally, emotionally, and physically. Certainly, to have a great day every day it helps to think great thoughts and to concentrate on at least one every day.

So, this book presents 366 upbeat and positive thoughts, one for every day in the year, including leap year. It is my hope that you will keep the book readily available on your desk, nightstand, in the kitchen, or perhaps have a copy in each place. If you begin to feel "down," take up the book and read the thought for the day. And if one isn't enough, read a few more of them.

Do not hesitate to mark thoughts that may especially appeal to you; turn down the pages and go back and read them again and again. Rereading helps to sink any helpful thought ever deeper into the mind. And the deeper a thought penetrates, the more powerful will be its effect upon your well-being.

Further, if you want to clip a thought out of the book to carry it in your wallet or pocket or handbag, don't let the notion that a book should not be mutilated stop you. A book is only a tool to be used for one's own good. And if you find you have hacked it up too much, you can always get another copy. The idea is that this book is a kind of medicine chest for healthy thinking. So, take the medicine and become a healthier, happier person.

Let me also suggest what I call the "shirt pocket technique." My shirt pocket is very important to me, for into it I put sayings and quotations written on cards. And, on some cards, I write my goals. Putting the cards into the pocket means placing the quotations over the heart, thus emphasizing the emotional factor. I read these cards repeatedly until, by a process of intellectual osmosis, they pass from the conscious to the subconscious mind and so become determinative.

But, however you use the daily thoughts in this day-by-day book, I truly hope they will help you to have a great day every day.

NORMAN VINCENT PEALE

JANUARY

January 1

At the New Year, we usually resolve to quit something. There is a psychological law of quitting. It's this: The more you keep quitting, the easier quitting becomes. I know, for I've spent a lot of time quitting fattening foods. But I finally discovered how to quit successfully. Quit for one meal, then two, then three. By now it begins to get tough. So you get tougher, quit the next day and the next. After a while, pride enters the picture to help you. You begin to boast about all the things you haven't eaten. Then you point with pride to your belt, for you have tightened it to the last notch. This is called positive quitting and can be applied to anything you want to change in your life.

January 2

Anybody can do just about anything with himself that he really wants to and makes up his mind to do. We all are capable of greater things than we realize. How much one actually achieves depends largely on: 1. Desire. 2. Faith. 3. Persistent effort. 4. Ability. But if you are lacking in the first three factors, your ability will not balance out the lack. So concentrate on the first three and the results will amaze you.

January 3

The way to success: First have a clear goal, not a fuzzy one. Sharpen this goal until it becomes specific and clearly defined in your conscious mind. Hold it there until, by the process of spiritual and intellectual osmosis of which I wrote in my introduction to this book, it seeps into your unconscious. Then you will have it because it has you. Surround this goal constantly with positive thoughts and faith. Give it positive follow-through. That is the way success is achieved.

January 4

To affirm a great day is a pretty sure way to have one. When awakening, get out of bed and stretch to your full height, saying aloud, "This is going to be a great day." What you say strongly is a kind of command, a positive, affirmative attitude that tends to draw good results to you.

January 5

Go forward confidently, energetically attacking problems, expecting favorable outcomes. When obstacles or difficulties arise, the positive thinker takes them as creative opportunities. He welcomes the challenge of a tough problem and looks for ways to turn it to advantage. This attitude is a key factor in impressive careers and great living.

January 6

At Dunkirk, the fate of the British nation hung upon getting the fighting men off the beaches and back to England. During the most difficult hour, a colonel rushed up to General Alexander, crying, "Our position is catastrophic!" The general replied: "Colonel, I don't understand big words. Just get busy and get those men out of here!" That's the kind of thinking needed in crises. Do the simple necessary.

January 7

Fear can infect us early in life until eventually it cuts a deep groove of apprehension in all our thinking. To counteract it, let faith, hope, and courage enter your thinking. Fear is strong, but faith is stronger yet. The Bible tells us, ". . . And he laid his right hand upon me, saying unto me, Fear not . . ." (Revelation 1:17). His hand is always upon you, too.

January 8

As an emotion, anger is always hot. To reduce an emotion, cool it. Some people count to ten, but perhaps the first ten words of the Lord's Prayer will work even better: "Our Father which art in heaven, Hallowed be thy name" (Matthew 6:9). Say that ten times and anger will lose its power.

January 9

Once, when I felt I had done an especially poor job in the pulpit on a Sunday morning, forgetting the best things I had to say and saying the poorest things, I was pretty discouraged. An old preacher, a polished orator in his day, patted me on the back. "Don't let it bother you, son," he said consolingly. "Forget it. The congregation will, and you might as well make it unanimous."

January 10

I shall never forget Ralph Rockwell. He was the farmer on our place in the country. Ralph was a New Englander of the old school, always caring for the place as though it were his own. He said to me once, when I was presuming to give him advice: "Tell you what, Dr. Peale, you do the preaching. I'll do the farming." It is good to remember to take advice as well as give it.

January 11

George Reeves was a huge man, 6 feet 2, weighing 240 pounds. He was my teacher in the fifth grade. In class, he would suddenly shout, "Silence." Then he would print in big letters on the blackboard the word CAN'T. Turning to the class, he would demand, "And now what shall I do?" Knowing what he wanted, we chanted back, "Knock the T off the CAN'T." With a sweeping gesture, he would erase it, leaving the word CAN. Dusting the chalk from his fingers, he would say, "Let that be a lesson to you—you *can* if you think you can."

January 12

The place was Korea, the hour midnight. It was bitter cold, the temperature below zero. A big battle was building for the morning. A burly U.S. marine was leaning against a tank eating cold beans out of a can with a penknife. A newspaper correspondent watching him was moved to propound a philosophical question: "Look," he said, "if I were God and could give you what you wanted most, what would you ask for?" The marine dug out another penknife of beans, thought reflectively, then said, "I would ask for tomorrow." Perhaps so would we all—a great tomorrow.

January 13

My college classmate Judson Sayre started with nothing and became one of the most successful salesmen in our country. At dinner, in his apartment on Lake Shore Drive in Chicago, we got to talking about having a great day—for he was expert at it. "Come look at my mirror," he said. He had pasted a sign there which read:

Want a great day?
Believe a great day.
Pray a great day.
Deserve a great day.
Take God with you for a great day.
Get going and make it a great day.

January 14

At one time I lived in upstate New York, where the winters are quite cold. And the roads would freeze and melt and freeze again. Come springtime, they were pretty badly broken up and rutted. One early April day, I came to a bad stretch of road where someone had put up a hand-made sign: "Choose your rut well. You'll be in it for the next twenty-five miles." Pretty good idea to get into the right rut, isn't it?

January 15

Obviously, he was a happy man. He was Joe of Joe's Place, a little lunch counter I found one night. There were about a dozen stools occupied, for the most part by elderly men and a couple of old women from the neighborhood. He set a steaming bowl of soup before an old man whose hands shook. "Mamie made it special for you, Mr. Jones." One elderly and rather stumbling lady started to go out the door. "Be careful, Mrs. Hudson, the cars go pretty fast out there. And, oh yes, look at the full moon over the river. It's mighty pretty tonight." I sat there thinking that Joe was happy because he really loves people.

January 16

The "as if" principle works. Act "as if" you were not afraid and you will become courageous, "as if" you could and you'll find that you can. Act "as if" you like a person and you'll find a friendship.

January 17

Attitudes are more important than facts. Certainly, you can't ignore a fact, but the attitude with which you approach it is all-important. The secret of life isn't what happens to you but what you do with what happens to you.

January 18

You can do amazing things if you have strong faith, deep desire, and just hang in there.

January 19

The best of all ways to get your mind off your own troubles is to try to help someone else with theirs. As an old Chinese proverb says, "When I dig another out of trouble, the hole from which I lift him is the place where I bury my own."

January 20

Said William James, "Believe that you possess significant reserves of health, energy, and endurance, and your belief will help create the fact."

January 21

A man who had suffered a succession of devastating blows said something I liked: "I came through because I discovered a comeback quality had been built into me."

January 22

A whimsical old preacher, speaking on a familiar text, said, "And now abideth faith, hope, and love, these three, but the greatest of these is common sense."

January 23

Don't knock yourself out trying to compete with others. Build yourself up by competing with yourself. Always keep on surpassing yourself.

January 24

Work and live *enthusiastically*. Take successes *gratefully*. Face failures *phlegmatically*—that is, with a "so what?" attitude. And aim to take life as it comes, philosophically.

January 25

Yesterday ended last night. Every day is a new beginning. Learn the skill of forgetting. And move on.

January 26

Self-confidence and courage hinge on the kind of thoughts you think. Nurture negative thoughts over a long period of time and you are going to get negative results. Your subconscious is very accommodating. It will send up to you exactly what you send down to it. Keep on sending it fear and self-inadequacy thoughts and that is what it will feed back to you. Take charge of your mind and begin to fill it with healthy, positive, and courageous thoughts.

January 27

There is a three-point program for doing something with yourself. Find yourself, motivate yourself, commit yourself. These three will produce results.

January 28

The famous Olympic champion Jesse Owens said that four words made him: *Determination. Dedication. Discipline. Attitude.*

January 29

Do not exclusively say your prayers in the form of asking God for something. The prayer of thanksgiving is much more powerful. Name all the fine things you possess, all the wonderful things that have happened to you, and thank God for them. Make that your prayer.

January 30

The controlled person is a powerful person. He who always keeps his head will always get ahead. Edwin Markham said, "At the heart of the cyclone tearing the sky is a place of central calm." The cyclone derives its powers from a calm center. So does a person.

January 31

Theodore Roosevelt, a strong and tough-minded man, said: "I have often been afraid. But I would not give in to it. I simply acted as though I was not afraid and presently the fear disappeared." Fear is afraid itself and backs down when you stand up to it.

FEBRUARY

February 1

It is winter now and the snows can come. It's good to warm yourself before a roaring fire on a winter's night. Lowell Thomas, in persuading me to take up cross-country skiing, said, "To glide quietly on the snow into a grove of great old trees, their bare branches lifted to a cloudless blue sky, and to listen to the palpable silence, is to live in depth." In return, I quoted to him Thomas Carlyle's thoughtful line, "Silence is the element in which great things fashion themselves together."

February 2

I once knew an extraordinarily successful salesman who told me that every morning he says aloud, three times, "I believe, I believe, I believe." "You believe in what?" I asked. "In God, in Jesus, and in the life God gave me," he declared.

February 3

At dinner with some Chinese friends, the conversation turned to the stress and tension so prevalent today. "Bad way to live," said an aged man present. "Tension is foolish. Always take an emergency leisurely." "Who said that?" I asked. "I did," he replied with a smile, "and, if you quote it, just say an old Chinese philosopher said it." Well, it is sound philosophy. "Always take an emergency leisurely."

February 4

To have great days, it helps to be a tough-minded optimist. Tough doesn't mean swaggering, sneering, hard-boiled. The dictionary definition is a masterpiece: "Tough—having the quality of being strong or firm in texture, but flexible; yielding to force without breaking, capable of resisting great strain without coming apart." And Webster defines optimism as "the doctrine that the goods of life overbalance the pain and evil of it, to minimize adverse aspects, conditions, and possibilities, or anticipate the best possible outcome; a cheerful and hopeful temperament."

February 5

My wife, Ruth, and I have a friend, a charming lady down South, who has the typical accent and a big smile. It is her habit every morning, rain or shine, to fling open her front door and say aloud: "Hello there. Good morning." She explains: "Oh, I love the morning. It brings me the most wonderful surprises and gifts and opportunities." Naturally, she has a great day every day.

February 6

Henry Ford was once asked where his ideas came from. There was a saucer on his desk. He flipped it upside down, tapped the bottom, and said: "You know that atmospheric pressure is hitting this object at fourteen pounds per square inch. You can't see it or feel it, but you know it is happening. It's that way with ideas. The air is full of them. They are knocking you on the head. You only have to know what you want, then forget it and go about your business. Suddenly the idea will come through. It was there all the time."

February 7

To maintain a happy spirit, and to do so come what may, is to make sure of a great day every day. Wise old Shakespeare tells us that "a light heart lives long." It seems that a happy spirit is a tonic for long life. Seneca, the old Roman, also a thinker rich in wisdom, sagely observed, "It is indeed foolish to be unhappy now because you may be unhappy at some future time."

February 8

Someone tells the story of when, down in North Carolina, a man asked a weather-beaten mountaineer how he was feeling. "It's like this," drawled the man from the hills after a few seconds of silence. "I'm still kickin', but I ain't raisin' any dust." When you get right down to it, if we just keep on kickin', there is always hope.

February 9

How many unhappy people suffer the mental paralysis of fear, self-doubt, inferiority, and inadequacy! Dark thoughts blind them to the possible outcomes which the mind is well able to produce. But optimism infuses the mind with confidence and builds up belief in oneself. Result? The revitalized mind, newly energized, comes to grips with problems. Keep the paralysis of unhealthy thoughts out of that incomparable instrument, your mind.

February 10

Optimism is a philosophy based on the belief that basically life is good, that, in the long run, the good in life overbalances the evil. Also that, in every difficulty, every pain, there is some inherent good. And the optimist means to find the good. No one ever lived a truly upbeat life without optimism working in his mind.

February 11

In Tokyo I once met another American, an inspiring man, from Pennsylvania. Crippled from some form of paralysis, he was on an around-the-world journey in a wheelchair, getting a huge kick out of all his experiences. I commented that nothing seemed to get him down. His reply was a classic: "It's only my legs that are paralyzed. The paralysis never got into my mind."

February 12

Practice loving people. It is true that this requires effort and continued practice, for some are not very lovable, or so it seems—with emphasis upon "seems." Every person has lovable qualities when you really learn to know him.

February 13

A sure way to a great day is to have enthusiasm. It contains a tremendous power to produce vitality, vigor, joyousness. So great is enthusiasm as a positive motivational force that it surmounts adversity and difficulty and, moreover, if cultivated, does not run down. It keeps one going strong even when the going is tough. It may even slow down the aging process for, as Henry Thoreau said, "None are so old as those who have outlived enthusiasm."

February 14

On Valentine's Day I might call your attention to the law called the law of attraction—like attracts like. If you constantly send out negative thoughts, you tend to draw back negative results to yourself. This is as true as the law that lifts the tide. But a person who sends out positive thoughts activates the world around him positively and draws back to himself positive results.

February 15

A lifetime on this wonderful and exciting earth doesn't last very long. It is here today and gone tomorrow, so thank God every day for it. Life is good when you treat it right. Love life and it will love you back.

February 16

Life is not always gentle—far from it. From time to time, it will hand you disappointment, grief, loss, or formidable difficulty, often when least expected. But never forget you can surmount the worst it brings, keep on going, and make your way up again. You will find that you are stronger and maybe even better off for having had some tough experiences.

February 17

We are so accustomed to being alive that we take it for granted. The thrill and wonder of it doesn't often occur to us. Do you ever get up in the morning and look out the window, or go to the door and breathe in the fresh air, and go back in and say to your spouse, "Isn't it great to be alive?" Life is such a tremendous privilege, so exciting, that it is a cause for constant thanksgiving.

February 18

My old friend and associate, the famous psychiatrist Dr. Smiley Blanton, used to say: "No matter what has happened to a person, that individual still has within vast undamaged areas. Nature always tries to repair, so don't become dismayed, certainly never be discouraged, when you suffer a blow."

February 19

My mother used to tell me: "As you go through life, doors will sometimes shut in your face. But don't let that discourage you. Rather welcome it—for that is the way you are pointed to the open door, the right opening for you."

February 20

Here is a good mental diet:

1. *Think no ill about anyone.*
2. *Put the best possible construction upon everyone's actions.*
3. *Send out a kindly thought toward any person antagonistic to you.*
4. *Think hopefully at all times.*
5. *See only the best happening.*

February 21

When life hands you a lemon, make lemonade. Remember, there is no situation so completely hopeless that something constructive cannot be done about it. When faced with a minus, ask yourself what you can do to make it a plus. A person practicing this attitude will extract undreamed-of outcomes from the most unpromising situations. Realize that there are no hopeless situations; there are only people who take hopeless attitudes.

February 22

I remember a sign I once saw on an office wall: "He who stumbles twice on the same stone deserves to break his neck." That may be rather harshly stated but it emphasizes the truth that a wise person does not get bogged down in a psychology of mistakes or allow errors to accumulate in the mind. When you make a mistake, take corrective action. Once is enough.

February 23

I knew a man who was always saying, "You know, I've half a mind to do this or that." I told him, "Charley, you're a half-a-minder. Everything you think of doing, you have only half a mind to do. No one ever got anywhere with only half a mind." Success requires giving the whole self, the whole mind. Charley became an all-outer and achieved all-out success.

February 24

Success in any business, or for that matter in any kind of undertaking, is determined by six simple words: *find a need and fill it*. In fact, these six words can be equated with practically every successful enterprise or personal career.

February 25

Champions are made by playing their best game today, then tomorrow, and then the next day. Life, too, must be lived well one day at a time every day. And, in both sports and living, success is the result of a succession of more good days than bad ones.

February 26

Start preparing for a happy old age when you are young—for, at seventy, you will be as you are at thirty, only more so. If you are tight with money at thirty, you will be a miser at seventy. If you talk a lot at thirty, you will be a windbag at seventy. If you are kind and thoughtful at thirty, you will be lovable at seventy.

February 27

A lightweight football player used a law of physics to overcome his small size against the giants. Knowing that momentum is the product of mass and velocity, he took to projecting himself at high speed against opponents. This bulletlike human being hurled himself against bigger men. He knocked them over like pins in a bowling alley. This is good strategy to use on big problems.

February 28

If you worry, you are a worrier because your mind is saturated with worry thoughts. To counteract these, mark every passage in your Bible that speaks of faith, hope, and courage. Commit each to memory until these spiritual thoughts saturate the mind.

February 29

This is the extra day we have every four years. Just think, if you live for eighty years, you will have twenty priceless additional days of life. On this one day in Leap Year, God gives us an extra chance at living. Perhaps we should do something special with it, something like making someone's life a bit happier, healing a breach, or offering prayers for persons who are having a hard time of it.

MARCH

March 1

Every month is a new beginning. So is every new day. Perhaps that is why God brings down the curtain of night—to blot out the day that is gone. All of your yesterdays ended last night. It makes no difference how long you've been alive, they're all ended. This day is absolutely new. You've never lived it before. What an opportunity!

March 2

Harry Truman once said, "If you're afraid of getting burned, better stay out of the kitchen." If you are going to fight for principles and convictions, you can hardly avoid a rough time now and then. Never weaken or back down—as all of us feel like doing at times. If we yield to that temptation, life may be easier but it certainly will be less interesting.

March 3

A man said that for years he had been extremely nervous but had finally "practiced" his way out of that condition. The word *practiced* makes sense, for it is certain that no real attainment comes without practice.

March 4

Learn what you can from the beating you have taken. Then move confidently on to the next opportunity. Accept defeat supinely and you're through. Come back at it with all you've got and you've got plenty. You will win with the *never settle for defeat* attitude.

March 5

There is one way to avoid criticism: Never do anything, never amount to anything. Never get your head above the crowd so that the jealous will notice and attack you. Criticism is a sign that your personality has some force.

March 6

Churchgoing can be exciting. A westerner once told me, after a Sunday service, "I came out of church so thrilled, I felt I could throw a lasso around the moon."

March 7

Almighty God freely bestows the good things in this world in proportion to a person's mental readiness to receive. An individual coming to the divine storehouse with a teaspoon, thinking "lack," will receive only a teaspoonful. Another more positive and believing person coming forward confidently with a gallon container will receive a gallon of life's blessing. We can only receive that which we expect according to our faith. So think big.

March 8

Your greatest ability is the power to choose. By the power of choice, you can make your life creative or you can destroy it. Every day we make many choices. Some are seemingly small, but no choice is altogether insignificant, for upon the most seemingly unimportant choice may ultimately depend the outcome of your life. History, they say, often turns on small hinges. That is also true of people's lives.

March 9

The sense of God's presence steadies us, gives us an anchor in the storm, and provides a reservoir of personal power. If you live with God as a friend, He will become so real that He will be your sturdy companion day and night. Then, even when the going is difficult, your heart can be happy within, for you have Him with you.

March 10

"Why can't we have a world that's peaceful and quiet?" a man asked. I told him about an old Irish friend who said there was a tradition in northern Ireland that, when there is trouble on the earth, it means there's movement in heaven. And this wise old man told me, "I always rejoice when there's lots of conflict and upset on the earth, because I know that out of this turmoil a movement in heaven will bring something good."

March 11

Don't talk trouble. It only activates more of it. Talk life up, not down. Talking tends to create or destroy, for it puts the immense power of thought to work along the lines indicated by the talk. Always remember Ralph Waldo Emerson's warning that a word is alive. By repeated use, it can either build or tear down.

March 12

A business executive had three boxes on his desk labeled INCOMING, OUTGOING, and UNDECIDED. The latter usually contained the most papers. Then he added a fourth box which he labeled WITH GOD ALL THINGS ARE POSSIBLE. When faced with a particularly tough problem he would prepare a memo and toss it into this box. Then he would go on to other matters, believing that at the proper time he would receive God's guidance. The six-word affirmation on the box positivized the man's attitude and kept reminding him that possibilities existed. Even though a decision was not clear, this thinking challenged him to discern and finally realize those possibilities.

March 13

A formula for self-improvement is to first decide specifically what particular characteristic you desire to possess and then hold that image firmly in consciousness. Second, develop that image by acting as if you actually possessed the desired characteristic. Third, believe and repeatedly affirm that you are in the process of self-creating and the quality you wish to develop.

March 14

People often kill their happiness and their success in life by their tongues. They explode, say a mean thing, write a sharp letter, and the evil is done. And, sadly, the real victim is not the other person but oneself.

March 15

The writer William A. Ward formulated a plan for successful achievement. He called it the "8 P Plan" and it goes like this: Plan Purposefully, Prepare Prayerfully, Proceed Positively, Pursue Persistently.

March 16

The biblical advice "Do not let the sun go down on your anger" is psychologically sound. Anger can accumulate to the exploding point and must be emptied out every night. Drain off the anger content that may be seething in your mind by forgiving everybody. And practice the art of forgetting.

March 17

We love those who make us believe in ourselves. "This above all," Shakespeare wrote, "to thine own self be true, And it must follow, as the night the day, Thou canst not then be false to any man."

March 18

There is only one person with whom to compete and that is yourself. Keep aiming to surpass your own best performance and ever strive to reach higher levels. If you are always measuring yourself against some other person, resentment and antipathy are bound to develop within your mind. Then tension mounts, you are thrown off your timing, and poorer performance results. Remember Thomas Edison's challenge: "There is a better way. Find it."

March 19

The average person uses only a small fraction of his potential abilities. Some authorities estimate that this is somewhere around ten percent of capacity. One reason is that we do not devote enough attention and time to deliberate, systematic development of our personalities. And another is that we frustrate ourselves with self-imposed limitations. Try to reach your full potential.

March 20

After a heated struggle in the U.S. House of Representatives over an important bill, an older congressman, Madden, approached a junior representative whose support of the bill had obviously been gained by questionable means. "Son," he asked, "why did you vote as you did?" "I had to," the young man answered. "I was under very great pressure." The older man put his hand on his younger colleague's shoulder. "But boy," he asked, "where are your inner braces?" Faith can brace us against pressure.

DURING LATE MARCH, SPRING is supposed to appear, at least tentatively. Officially, March 21 is the first day of spring, but it just could be that, on this date, the great March winds are blowing and sighing around the house and snow is in the air. Actually, long experience indicates that spring comes when it comes and only then.

Crocuses are usually up by late March. On our place, we have planted them around the base of our huge and ancient maples as well as along the driveways. They are optimistic, as flowers go, for they will push up from the ground in what seems a most inauspicious climate, and, if the cold is as sometimes occurs, more January-like, they hang their heads disconsolately. But, at the first opportunity, they are sprightly again and add great charm to springtime over the several weeks that they are in bloom.

Then along come hyacinths, jonquils, and daffodils. I like them because they are not only optimistic that spring has really come but they also reveal an indomitability that humans might well emulate.

One spring, all was bright and beautiful. The balmy air, so definitely associated with springlike days, was softly engaging. The flowers exuded the confidence that finally they had it made. Spring was here at last. But, during an April night, someone must have gotten the calendar mixed up. There was a throwback to the wild and gusty winds of March. Then the snow began falling thick and fast. Big winter flakes they were and, when chilly morning came, a real winter snow lay six inches deep upon the ground, including the flower beds. The hyacinths stood pretty straight, considering the weight of the snow, but the jonquils and daffodils bent over as if it was all too much for them.

But, having lived through many a springtime in our part of the country, we were not too much concerned. And, sure enough, the next day came a warm wind, the snow melted and, behold, the flowers perked up, took a wondering look around, then stood tall and straight and went about their business of blooming and being beautiful. All of which was a reminder of the rebound quality built into nature. I wonder if it is not also built into human nature. Perhaps one function of flowers and trees is to remind us that we, too, have a comeback quality.

I've seen trees devastated by winter storms—branches broken and hurled to the ground, tops apparently ruined. Then comes spring with God's healing touch; a multitude of leaves hides the hurt and, after a couple of springtimes, it is hard to find the damage, so great is a tree's repair power. Similarly, people are hurt. Some never recover but perhaps most do for they, like the trees, have an astounding ability to repair their hurts. They do, after all, have the same Healer.

March 21

At long last, every one of us draws to himself exactly what he is. If you want to know what life is going to bring you, all you need to do is to analyze yourself.

March 22

An incredible goodness is operating in your behalf. Confidently receive God's abundant blessings. Think abundance, prosperity, and the best of everything. Expect great things to happen. God wants to give you every good thing. Do not hinder His generosity by disbelief.

March 23

Standing by my mother's tombstone, I saw it for what it was—a place where only mortal remains lay. Her mortal body was only a coat laid aside because the wearer needed it no longer. But she, that gloriously lovely spirit, was not there. I walked out of the cemetery and rarely return—for she is not there. She is with her loved ones for always. "Why seek ye the living among the dead?" (Luke 24:5). You can depend upon the reliability of Christ. He would not let us believe and hold convictions so sacred unless they were true.

March 24

If you want a desirable quality in your life, let me remind you to use the "as if" principle—act *as if* you already have it. As you act and persevere in acting, so you tend to become. Try it—it's powerful and it works. If one acts as if God were with him, if he talks to God as if God were listening to him, in due course, he becomes very sure of God. You then know that God is with you always as He said He would be. And you know He is listening to your prayers.

March 25

Every human being needs to have a quiet center within his mind. You don't need to worry about confusion if you have inner quietness from which to handle it. And you can achieve this. You can learn to have a bit of God's great silence in your mind and heart.

March 26

We human beings often engage in the tragic process of mentally building up difficulties to overwhelming size and thus become afraid of them. We convince ourselves that we are defeated before we start and build a case for not trying. This is the time to release the sleeping giant within you. Then you become the great person you have it in you to be. You win victories instead of suffering defeats.

March 27

Most of us have no adequate conception of our inherent powers and abilities. At heart, we underestimate ourselves. We do not really believe in ourselves and for that reason remain weak, ineffectual, even impotent, when we could be strong, dominant, victorious. An old cobbler in Edinburgh was in the habit of beginning each day with the prayer, "O Lord, give me a high opinion of myself." Not a bad idea!

March 28

Be yourself. Being a slave to conformity is one of the most fundamental of all dishonesties. When we reject our specialness, water down our God-given individuality and uniqueness, we begin to lose our freedom. The conformist is in no way a free man. He has to follow the herd. We need more "characters" among us, who do not weakly conform to standardized ways of behaving, people not afraid to be "different." Men and women who accomplish the most in this world are almost always "characters" in the sense that they are not afraid to be themselves regardless of what fashion or the "in" attitude dictates.

March 29

Talk, actually speak, to the health forces within yourself. Summon them to your aid. Every day, strongly encourage God's health forces; restimulate them to creative action within your total being. Standing straight and tall, say: "I affirm the presence within me of God's recreative forces. I hereby yield myself in confidence to their health-giving effects. I affirm that the life force is renewing me now. I thank God, the Creator, but also the Re-Creator, now making me new."

March 30

Make no mistake about it: any kind of dishonesty cripples, and the first thing you lose is freedom. One has to lie to cover up and soon becomes entangled in lies. An entangled person cannot be free. The honest person is the free person.

March 31

At some time during every day, I find it good to observe a period of absolute quiet, for there is healing power in silence. To find this power, do not talk; do not do anything; throw the mind into neutral; keep the body still; maintain complete silence. This is the practice of creative quiet.

APRIL

April 1

"Whether you *think* you can or *think* you can't—you are right," said Henry Ford.

April 2

That which we constantly affirm has the tendency to take over in our thoughts and to produce changed attitudes. A simple affirmation repeated three times every morning—such as "I am alive. Life is good. God is with me. I am going to have a wonderful day"—produces the results imaged.

April 3

The Bible puts it this way: "For as he thinketh in his heart, so is he" (Proverbs 23:7). Perhaps it might also be put this way: Think right to make things go right.

April 4

Workmen building the Panama Canal had been digging and excavating the big ditch for a long time. Just as they thought it was finished, there was a huge landslide and much of the dirt taken out fell back in again. The man in charge dashed up to the boss, General Goethals, and exclaimed: "It's terrible! Terrible! All the dirt's back in again! What shall we do?" Goethals said calmly, "Dig it out again." What else was there to do?

April 5

Louisa May Alcott was told by an editor that she would never be able to write anything that would have popular appeal. A music teacher told

Enrico Caruso: "You can't sing. You have no voice at all." And a teacher warned a boy named Thomas A. Edison that he was too stupid to pursue a scientific education! Never let anyone shunt you off from the main line of your aspirations.

April 6

A fair amount of caution is sensible. Only a fool would be without it. But to listen to one's fears when seeking guidance is quite another matter. Consider cautiously, but take counsel from your beliefs, not your fears—and you will average out a lot better in life.

April 7

It isn't necessary or perhaps even good to have everyone like you. That idea can make you the worst kind of a mollycoddle. You will be spineless, uninteresting, lacking in character. Perhaps the greatest compliment ever paid President Grover Cleveland was when he was put in nomination before the Democratic Convention and the orator who presented his name said, "We love him for the enemies he has made."

April 8

One of the problems of our day is how to counteract the effects on the younger generation of a civilization dedicated to the pursuit of luxury and the avoidance of effort. A hundred years ago, there was kindling to be chopped, water to be carried, animals to be fed. But not anymore. We are in danger of robbing our children of one of their greatest heritages: that of struggle.

April 9

You never need to settle for what you are. You can be a new person. I've seen people change—defeated people become victorious, dull people become excited, real people experience marvelous change. We were not merely created: we can be re-created.

April 10

The more I see of people the more I'm impressed by their astounding ability to meet tough situations. And their ability to rebound is fantastic. There is a built-in comeback power in you that should never be underestimated.

April 11

In my youth, I heard a great speaker say, "You can become strongest in your weakest place." As in welding, the broken point becomes strongest when heat is applied. So thought and intensity of faith can weld the weak spots in personality into great strength. It's amazing what a person can creatively do with his own self.

April 12

Never run yourself down. Believe in yourself, esteem yourself not with egotism but with humble, realistic self-confidence. Stop brooding over the past. Drop the post-mortems. Live enthusiastically. Starting today, make the best you can of it. Give it all you've got and you will find that to be plenty.

April 13

When you have failed, your first step is to forget. The second is never to settle for it; never accept a failure. Then go right back at it again. Extract what know-how you can. Never say: "Well, I failed. That means I can't do it. I'll not try it anymore." That will develop the failure psychology in you so that you will become a failure person. Ask God's guidance about how to do the thing better the next time and keep right at it until you become a success person.

April 14

Many people suffering from unresolved fear find release and relief through the practice of courage and confidence. These two positive mental attitudes—courage and confidence—banish fear; they make wonderful things happen. Yet all three—confidence, courage, fear—result from the kind of thoughts we think. The mental climate a person creates determines whether he will have confidence even when things seem hopeless and have courage even when apprehensive factors appear. Think courage, act with courage. Image yourself as confident. Act with confidence. As you think, act, and image, so shall you become.

April 15

When asked to explain his calm indifference to criticism a friend asked: "What happens when someone points a finger at you? Point your finger at me now." Nonplussed, I leveled my forefinger at him. "Now, who are your other three fingers pointing at?" "Why, they are pointing at me!" I exclaimed. "That's right," he concluded triumphantly. "So I win over a critic three to one!"

April 16

Waking up creatively every morning is an important skill in having a good day. It can be cultivated and developed so effectively that you can guarantee to yourself a good day, all day every day. As you arise in the morning, mentally picture the good day you want and confidently expect it. Picture it clearly in your mind. Strongly affirm the good day ahead. Then proceed to make it so.

April 17

Inscribed on a sundial on the Mount Holyoke College campus are these words: "To larger sight, the rim of shadow is the line of light." Perhaps death is only a momentary rim of shadow. Behind it, waiting, is the radiance of eternal life, the greatest days of all.

April 18

Watch out for defeat psychology. An experience in which you don't make out too well can shake your confidence in yourself; and, if you do not promptly make another try, defeat psychology can take hold and freeze you mentally. So, when you fall flat, pick yourself up fast and go right on to the next challenge. Don't give failure time to develop in your consciousness.

April 19

The most vital, creative, and positive thoughts are those stated in the Bible. Its words are alive and form powerful thought processes. The Bible itself states what its inspired words will do: "If ye abide in me, and my words abide in you, ye shall ask what ye will, and it shall be done unto you" (John 15:7).

April 20

Difficulties can be and often are blessings in disguise. Horace, the great Roman, said, "Difficulties elicit talents that in more fortunate circumstances would lie dormant." And Disraeli wrote, "Difficulties constitute the best education in this life."

April 21

When faced with great difficulties, hold clearly and tenaciously in your mind the thought that, with God's help, you can marshal your powers of concentration, reason, self-discipline, and imagination. And keep on believing that you actually do have the power to beat back circumstance. In so doing, you are bound to win.

April 22

A successful businesswoman commits every day to God. As a result of this practice, she says that nothing can be a disappointment because whatever happens is according to His plan and will. It changes disappointment to *His* appointment.

April 23

I have watched many star athletes. Looking back at the men who were consistently good—Ty Cobb, Lou Gehrig, Joe DiMaggio, Roger Hornsby, Duke Snyder—there was one quality possessed by all of them: *enthusiasm*. That spirit helped these men boost their batting averages to become the greatest performers in baseball history. It can help you.

April 24

On a classroom wall of my boyhood hung a picture showing a lonely beach with the tide out and a boat stranded on the sand. Few things look more depressing than a boat left high and dry by receding water. The inscription under the picture said, "Remember, the tide always comes back." There is ebb and flow in the vicissitudes of human life. When everything goes against you and it seems you can hold on no longer, never give up. The tide will turn.

April 25

In Kyoto there is a shrine famous for its stone garden. For centuries, fifteen stones of different shapes and sizes have been resting in a garden of carefully raked sand. By tradition, the stones represent the fifteen basic problems of mankind—every person names his or her own. But all the stones cannot be seen at the same time. The message I take away from the enigmatic stones at Kyoto is that no one can or should try to contemplate, much less solve, all his problems at once. People should instead make a deliberate mental effort to block out all their problems except one, and concentrate on solving that one—this way there is more mental strength to apply.

April 26

All actions, good or bad, start somewhere. They are best controlled at the start. If you stop the thought that leads to a dishonest action, you will block off the action itself.

April 27

The Kingdom of God is within you—within every man. It is God's gift to all humanity—available for the asking.

April 28

Twice he had failed in business—once during a depression and again when a partner ruined him. Twice he started over. Twice he was forced to sell out and work his way out of debt. But did it faze him? Not at all. "A failure is just the reverse side of success," he said. "With God's help, I find you can always turn things around. I have faith in God and faith in myself."

April 29

If you do not like a person, or he you, and you do something for him, it can sometimes increase his dislike because it puts him under obligation to you. He may even regard your action as patronizing. But if you encourage him to do something for you, he will feel complimented despite himself and his good opinion of you will increase, for you have shown that you respect his ability. You have treated his ego with esteem.

April 30

A friend, Harry, loved dogs, especially a favorite, "Whiskers," who always went everywhere with him. Once Harry had to go to a nearby town on some business. He wrote to a hotel asking if he could bring his dog with him. The reply was:

> *Dear Sir:*
> *By all means bring your dog Whiskers along. Dogs rate high in this hotel. Never have I had to eject an unruly dog in the middle of the night. Never has a dog gotten drunk and messed up my furniture. I have never had a dog go to sleep and set the mattress on fire with a lighted cigarette. Never has a dog made drinking-glass rings on my dressers. I have never yet found a towel or an ashtray in a dog's suitcase. So bring your dog along.*
>
> *P.S. You can come, too, if the dog will vouch for you.*

MAY

May 1

I had made a speech to a large and friendly crowd. My cousin Philip Henderson heard me. Afterwards, he said: "You were not up to your best. It just wasn't good enough. You didn't give it all you've got. You coasted, you only wanted to get by. You must always do your top best, nothing else." It was a wise appraisal from one who loved me with the kind of love that gives it to you straight to make you be your best self.

May 2

A friend has six gems of wisdom which he repeats almost every day. The first is from Cicero: "To live long, live slowly." The second is from Confucius: "The way of a superior man is threefold: virtuous, he is therefore free from anxiety; wise, he is therefore free from perplexity; bold, he is therefore free from fear." The third is from Robert Louis Stevenson: "Sit loosely in the saddle of life." The fourth, Saint Theresa's famous words: "Let nothing disturb you; let nothing frighten you. Everything passes except God; God alone is sufficient." And from Isaiah, ". . . in quietness and in confidence shall be your strength" (Isaiah 30:15). Then finally, and most importantly, the words of Jesus: ". . . my peace I give unto you: not as the world giveth, give I unto you. Let not your heart be troubled, neither let it be afraid" (John 14:27).

May 3

Charles F. Kettering, the famous engineer, said: "I am not interested in the past. I am only interested in the future, for that is where I expect to spend the rest of my life!"

May 4

Once, in a restaurant, Henry Ford was asked, "Who is your best friend?" Ford thought for a moment, then took out his pen and wrote in large letters on the tablecloth, "He is your best friend who brings out of you the best that is in you."

May 5

Built into you is the inner fortitude and strength to stand up to things— to anything. The best lightning rod for your own protection is your own spine. That means, stand up straight and handle difficulties with faith in yourself.

May 6

A family holds a yearly "unhappy-thought burning." Each person drops into an urn pieces of paper on which they have written things they want to forget. They watch their unhappy thoughts burn and curl into ashes. This act helps them forget.

May 7

General Stonewall Jackson was approached by a timorous subordinate general who admitted grave doubts about a planned military sortie. "General Jackson," he said, "I'm afraid of this. I fear we can't quite carry it off." Jackson replied, "General, never take counsel of your fears."

May 8

A physician tells of a patient who died of "grudgitis"—a long-held hatred of another person. It is healthy to get rid of grudges; they seldom hurt the other person but they can make the holder sick.

May 9

My father, Charles Clifford Peale, often said to me, and indeed it was one of the last things he said: "I have always believed in you. You have never failed me. Remember, the Peales never quit." While I have not always lived up to my father's statement, one thing is sure—it has always helped when I begin to weaken.

May 10

There is only one power greater than fear, and that is faith. When fear comes to your mind, immediately counter it with an affirmation of faith. Think positively, visualize achievement. Never doubt. Always think faith.

May 11

Never settle for a failure. To do so is a serious blow to self-confidence. When an acrobat fails, he tries again, and, in fact, will keep the audience waiting for minutes, if necessary, until he completes his stunt successfully. He will not leave the stage until he has performed it. Otherwise he accepts into his consciousness the fact of failure so that the next time he performs he is afraid, is not sure he can do it and is, indeed, likely to fail.

May 12

The key phrase of failure is "if only." If only this hadn't happened! If only I had done differently. If only . . . if only! Shift the key words. Take "if only" out of the mental slot. Slide in a new phrase, image it locked into place in your mind. It can cancel out failure thinking. Instead of "if only," say "next time . . . next time . . . next time."

May 13

A man said: "I've been afraid, but not anymore, for now I've got the five Gs going for me: *Guidance:* God guides me in everything. *Grace:* God does for me what I cannot do for myself. *Guts:* Just plain man-sized courage. *Gumption:* Good old American common sense. And the greatest of all: *God.*"

May 14

In his book *The Unobstructed Universe*, Stewart Edward White suggests that when the blades of an electric fan are at rest, or moving slowly, you can't see through them. But when the fan is revolving at top speed you can see through all the points of the circle in which the blades are revolving, because they have been stepped up to a higher frequency. Is it not conceivable that around us now in this mysterious universe are those whom we have loved and lost for a while, and that we get glimpses through the barrier in rare moments when our spiritual frequency is at one with the higher frequency?

May 15

A friend, a famous baseball player, hit regularly in the neighborhood of
.315. Early in the season I had listened on the radio through two innings
of a game and was dismayed when he struck out. Meeting him later that
day, I told him how sorry I was he had struck out. "Oh," he said, "I
struck out again in the eighth inning." "Twice? What's happening to
you?" I asked anxiously. "Nothing at all," he responded with unconcern.
"I take comfort in the law of averages. To bat an average of .315 as I have
been doing, one will strike out about ninety times a season. So today,
when I fanned twice, it means I have only eighty-eight times more to
strike out this season."

May 16

Some people feel they can change and improve their situation merely by
moving from one place to another. "I'm tired of this job. My talent isn't
being used. I'm not appreciated here. Think I'll look around." These
statements are often born of illusion. People sometimes make them primarily because they are tired not only of the job but of themselves.
Nothing is likely to change for them unless they first change their attitude. Then they won't require escape.

May 17

Empty pockets never held anyone back; it's only empty heads and empty
hearts that do that.

May 18

Do the best you can, trust the Lord, serve Him, walk with God, love
people, do your duty, be honorable and upright, live right, think right,
and you will live at peace with yourself.

May 19

Every day, preferably about midafternoon, when energy lag usually
comes, try repeating: "... in him we live, and move, and have our
being ..." (Acts 17:28), meanwhile visualizing yourself as plugged into
the spiritual power line. Affirm that God's recreative energy is restoring
strength and power and health to every part of your body, mind, and
soul.

May 20

You can be made tired by your thoughts—thoughts of weariness, fear, anxiety, or resentment. But when you hold thoughts of hopefulness, confidence, positiveness, and good will, a constant flow of energy develops. Do not think tired thoughts. Think lively ones.

May 21

It is difficult to sustain concentrated, creative thinking. But we have the capacity to do so. As we keep thinking, never give up—solutions to problems will come. But the effort must be made and continued. As Leonardo da Vinci observed, God gives us everything "at the price of an effort."

May 22

I once asked President Dwight D. Eisenhower who was the greatest of all the great men he had known. His instant reply: "It wasn't a man. It was a woman—my mother. She had little schooling, but her educated mind, her wisdom, came from a lifelong study of the Bible. Often I have wished I could consult her. One night we were playing a card game, mother, my brothers, and I. Not with playing cards. It was Flinch—mother was straightlaced. But hands were dealt and I drew a bad one. I began to complain. " 'Put your cards down, boys,' Mother said. 'Dwight, this is just a friendly game in your home where you are loved. But, out in the world where there isn't so much love, you will be dealt many a bad hand. So you've got to learn to take the hands life deals you without complaining. Just play them out.' "

May 23

The controlled person is a powerful person. He who always keeps his head will get ahead. The number of people whose careers have been ruined through lack of emotional control is astonishing.

May 24

The mental and spiritual heat created by enthusiasm can burn off the apathy-failure factor in any personality and release hitherto unused, even unsuspected, personal power qualities. The president of a large corporation states: "If I am trying to decide between two men of fairly equal ability and one man has enthusiasm, I know he will go further than the other man, for enthusiasm acts as a self-releasing force." Enthusiasm is infectious. It carries all before it.

May 25

Physical death is a transitional step in the total life process. The soul, which does not die, having finished with the earthly body, moves to a higher level of life, where it grows under greatly enhanced circumstances.

May 26

Imagine yourself looking at all of your difficulties lined up like an army before you. As you face this army of discouragement, frustration, disappointment, hostility, and weakness, affirm, "If God be for us, who can be against us?" (Romans 8:31). Know that God is for you and His power is greater than all opposition. Visualize these enemies of your peace and happiness as retreating, giving way before God's power.

May 27

By always expecting the best, you are putting your whole heart and mind into what you want to accomplish. People are defeated in life not because of lack of ability but for lack of sustained expectation and wholeheartedness.

May 28

It is always well to remember that a lost battle or two or three does not mean the war is lost. With God's help, you can take any setback or defeat, muster your forces, and win out in the end.

May 29

In time of discouragement, it helps to take paper and pencil and add up all your assets—all that you have going for you. You will be astonished by what you have as you stop thinking about what you have not.

May 30

A physician told me he had seen people die, not because of organic trouble but because they had lost their enthusiasm, their will to live. Had they continued to possess the zest for life that enthusiasm gives, they could have overcome the physical problems that took their lives. Enthusiasm is an elixir of life.

May 31

So you've made a mistake. Who hasn't? But perhaps you feel it's a pretty serious one. I have always liked the following quotation from Grove Patterson, a famous editor:

A boy . . . leaned against the railing of a bridge and watched the current of the river below. . . . Sometimes the current went more swiftly and again quite slowly, but always the river flowed on under the bridge. Watching the river that day, the boy made a discovery. It was not the discovery of a material thing, something he might put his hand upon. He could not even see it. He had discovered an idea. Quite suddenly, and yet quietly, he knew that everything in his life would someday pass under the bridge and be gone like water. . . . And he didn't worry unduly about his mistakes after that and he certainly didn't let them get him down, because it was water under the bridge.

JUNE

June 1

The big heart of faith can push the crushing circumstances of life wide apart. The positive mind is not limited. It has extra problem-solving power. People who have big hearts and big minds need not be afraid of what may come, for those hearts and minds determine the quality of the future.

June 2

God, who created us in the first place, continually recreates. If we cooperate He will constantly fill us with new life, increased strength, and adequate power. You can have energy that never runs down if you image yourself as being constantly recreated.

June 3

One thing is sure—to live your life successfully you will need to overcome proneness to error or the mistake tendency. It is error that gets us into trouble. All of our failures and mistakes have been due to the mistake tendency. But rightness leads to right results and rightness is cultivatable.

June 4

A. Harry Moore, a poor boy who became governor of New Jersey for three terms, had an early struggle to make a career. He often became discouraged and would say to his mother: "Mom, I'm discouraged. I want to do something and be somebody, but I just haven't got it in me. Besides, we have no money or influence." His mother's reply was blunt: "You've got plenty in you. All you need is God and gumption." It's a good formula: "God and gumption."

June 5

When your feelings are hurt, what then? Immediately put some healing balm on that sore spot. Forgiveness is the best medicine. Open your mind completely and empty out all the grievances. Pour them out until not a vestige remains in your thoughts. Your hurts will heal quickly.

June 6

To make the day good, visualize or image it in your mind as good. We become what we think. Our life's events, good or bad, are governed by our thoughts. Develop the habit of thinking good days and you will go a long way toward having good days.

June 7

Henry Thoreau, the American philosopher, upon awakening in the morning would lie abed telling himself all the good news he could think of: that he had a healthy body, that his mind was alert, that his work was interesting, that the future looked bright, that people trusted him. Presently, he arose to meet the day in a world filled with good things, good people, good opportunities.

June 8

Not every day can be an easy one, nor every day fully happy; but even a day of tough going and difficulty can be a good day. Robert Browning knew this when he wrote: "Meanwhile as the day wore on the trouble grew, Wherefrom I guessed there would be born a star."

June 9

Mentally picture your body as being perfect both in condition and in function. Do not visualize it as in decline or as deteriorating. Train yourself to stop looking for something to go wrong. Think positively about your physical self. Think health, not sickness. This is important, for mental images tend to reproduce themselves in fact.

June 10

On the dining room wall of a four-hundred-year-old inn in Saint Moritz, I read this inscription: "Just when you think everything is hopeless, a little ray of light comes from somewhere." Your mind may seem to be dark and hopeless. But Almighty God, the Creator, established hope in you, an unshatterable hope deep within yourself. If darkness has settled deeply in your mind, just open up your thoughts and let in that "little ray of light [that] comes from somewhere."

June 11

When Henry Ford, whom I like to quote, was seventy-five years old, he was asked the secret of his health and calm spirit. "Three rules," he answered. "I do not eat too much; I do not worry too much; and, if I do my best, I believe that what happens, happens for the best."

June 12

Members of a service club in one city went out to give a dollar to every person on the streets who looked happy. At the day's end, they had been able to give away only thirty-three dollars. Perhaps life in our cities is getting so impersonal that people feel insignificant and retreat into their shells and glare rather than smile. But a peaceful, happy face is a blessing to passersby and to oneself!

June 13

Ernest Hemingway wrote of a commander in the Spanish Civil War who "never knew when everything was lost and if it was, he would fight out of it." That is the way with people who have the quality of determination. They keep on going, no matter what. The hang-in-there attitude gives courage, strength, vitality, power. Somehow such people always seem to win through anything and everything.

June 14

Patient understanding is the secret of all human relationships.

June 15

The business card of a friend gives his name, company, address—all the usual information. On the reverse side is this message:

> *The Way to Happiness: Keep your heart free of hate. Keep your mind from worry. Live simply, expect little, give much. Fill your life with love. Scatter sunshine. Forget self, think of others. Do as you would be done by. Try this for a week and you will be surprised.*

June 16

We do not believe in immortality because we can prove it, but we try to prove it because we cannot help believing it. Indeed, the instinctive feeling that it is true is one of the deepest proofs of its truth. When God wishes to carry a point with His children, He plants the idea in their instincts. The instinct for immortality is of such universality that it can hardly be met with indifference by the universe. What we deeply long for, what we deeply feel, must surely reflect a basic fact of existence.

June 17

In a twisting little street in Kowloon, I passed a shop where tattooing was done. Pictured in the window were some suggestions: a mermaid, a flag, and the motto "Born to lose." I was so astonished by the latter that I entered the shop and asked the man if anyone ever had those words actually tattooed into his skin. "A few," he replied. But then he added a wise insight in broken English: "Before tattoo on body, tattoo on mind."

June 18

"We are saved by hope." This fragment of a passage from Romans 8:24 could mean many things. If we have hope in God, we are saved to eternity. If we have hope in life, we are saved from many a defeat and many a weakness. Nestle that passage up against your mind: "We are saved by hope."

June 19

When I joined the ranks of the grandfathers, I noted how times have changed. When I was a boy, grandfathers, to my young eyes, had one foot in the grave. But just take a look at grandfathers nowadays. They are a pretty sprightly lot. Indeed, they have to be to keep up with grandmothers.

June 20

Think joy, talk joy, practice joy, share joy, saturate your mind with joy, and you will have the time of your life today and every day all your life.

NOW COMES THE GOOD old summertime. It is that time of
year when nature, quietly but impressively, demonstrates its
growing power. Trees have completed the old but ever amazing process
of putting forth their thousands of leaves. I've always wondered how a
tree knows when to adorn itself with leaves and how it does it. From the
stark, bare branches of winter to the green leaves of summer is one of the
astonishing miracles by which nature adds charm and beauty to our lives.

Flowers everywhere are adding to summer's festive character and the
songs of birds joyously fill the air. Nests are in the trees and other nooks
which father and mother birds have carefully selected. Balmy breezes
blow softly and golden sunshine filters down through branches to fall
gently upon clipped green grass. Corn is coming up in the fields. As
the old saying goes, "It will be knee-high by the Fourth of July." Wind
ripples caressingly over the growing wheat. At such times we may find
ourselves repeating those familiar and famous lines from *The Vision of Sir
Launfal* by James Russell Lowell:

> And what is so rare as a day in June?
> Then, if ever, come perfect days;
> Then Heaven tries earth if it be in tune,
> And over it softly her warm ear lays;
> Whether we look, or whether we listen,
> We hear life murmur, or see it glisten;
> Every clod feels a stir of might,
> An instinct within it that reaches and towers,
> And, groping blindly above it for light,
> Climbs to a soul in grass and flowers.

Everything is perfection since good God, the Creator, designed and
made it all. And He never did anything badly. But, with all respectful
deference, I cannot help wondering, come every summer, just why
the Lord thought it necessary to make mosquitoes and flying insects.
Oh, I know it has to do with nature's balance and all that; still I must
confess those creatures surely interfere with the perfect pleasures of
summertime.

A few years ago, I purchased two old-fashioned rocking chairs from a
firm down in Georgia that has been making them since before the Civil
War, or if you're reading this down South, the "War Between the
States." We have an 1830 house in Duchess County, New York, just
over the Connecticut line. It stands on a hill overlooking a great valley,
its white pillars marking the wide front porch, which looks west toward
the Hudson River.

Around the corner is a side porch looking over a valley southward. And the back porch off the kitchen looks over another valley into Connecticut. Here were placed these great rocking chairs. From this peaceful vantage, we look over a wide sweep of land, through great maples, across the valley to hills beyond.

On a warm summer afternoon or in the cool of twilight, I like to sit here with my wife, Ruth, rocking in perfect enjoyment until the mosquitoes surge in to attack all exposed parts and the gnats come en masse, buzzing and stinging. So, finally, I retreat inside the house thinking not the most kindly thoughts about summer. But actually, not even that affects the joy and glory of summer, the beautiful season at the fullness of the year.

Sometimes on a peaceful and lovely summer day I find myself reciting these lines of Robert W. Service:

> *The summer—no sweeter was ever;*
> *The sunshiny woods all athrill;*
> *The grayling aleap in the river;*
> *The bighorn asleep on the hill.*
>
> *The strong life that never knows harness;*
> *The wilds where the caribou call;*
> *The freshness, the freedom, the farness—*
> *O God! how I'm stuck on it all.*

From childhood to old age we love it, the good old summertime.

June 21

How can a person gain promotion in a job? I suggest seven rules:

1. *Be intent only on doing your present job well.*
2. *Don't think about being promoted; think only of being efficient now.*
3. *Work hard.*
4. *Work early and late.*
5. *Study, study, study until you learn real know-how.*
6. *Work your head off.*
7. *Try not to have a heart attack.*

June 22

During the Civil War, a man once stayed overnight at the White House in Washington. In the middle of the night he awakened suddenly and thought he heard Lincoln's voice, as though in pain, somewhere nearby. He jumped up, and went out into the dimly lit hall and, walking slowly in the direction of the voice, came to a door left ajar. Peering in, he beheld the lanky form of Lincoln prostrate on the floor in prayer, arms outstretched. Lincoln was humbly beseeching God to strengthen him against his sense of inadequacy. Lincoln knew he needed the great gift of God—"My peace I give unto you"—so he sought and prayed for it with all his mind and heart.

June 23

You have vast undamaged areas within yourself! No matter what life has done, no matter what you have done; the renewal power is there within you. If you bring spiritual power to bear upon those undamaged areas, you can rebuild life, no matter what has happened to it.

June 24

Talking with Herbert Hoover in his later years, I asked him how he had been able to endure all the hostile criticism and hate that was heaped upon him during his last months in the White House. He said, "I'm a Quaker, you know . . ." and reminded me that Quakers are taught from childhood to practice and develop inner calm. "When you have peace at the center, the trying experiences cannot overwhelm you."

June 25

God must surely be interested in our having good, strong, sound bodies—for does not the Bible tell us the body is the temple of the soul?

June 26

When you have done your best and something frustrating happens, instead of being discouraged, examine the interference. It may mean improvement. Thorvaldsen, the famous Danish sculptor, looked with satisfaction on a finished figure of Christ he had made out of clay, with face looking toward heaven and arms extended upward. It was the imperious figure of a conqueror. That night, sea mist seeped into the studio, the clay relaxed, the head and arms dropped. Thorvaldsen was bitterly disappointed. But, as he studied the figure, something about it moved him deeply. Now Christ looked down with love and compassion. This was a greater conception. That statue, *Come Unto Me*, became immortal.

June 27

Brother Lawrence, a saintly character of the Middle Ages, was a humble man, a cook and a great spiritual discoverer. His secret of the good life was the practice of the presence of God. He believed that always, at any hour of the day or night, in whatever circumstances or condition, the Lord is actually present.

June 28

The only way you can rid yourself of a thought or thought pattern is by displacement—by putting another thought in, by substitution or thought-switching. If you entertain in mind a defeat thought, a discouragement thought, a frustration thought, or any negative thought, practice thought substitution. Deliberately open the mind and substitute the contrary thought pattern, one positive in nature. Such thought conditioning can change your life.

June 29

Gloom drives prosperity away. Prosperity shies away from dark and negative thoughts, veering off from minds filled with pessimism and doubts. So think bright thoughts and attract prosperity. Note that the word *scarcity* is built upon the word *scare*. Be careful not to think scarcity and so scare prosperity away. Think plenty and stimulate abundance.

June 30

Here is a five-day mental diet. It's good for healthy-mindedness. It will help give you a great day every day.

FIRST DAY: *Think no ill about anybody—only good about everybody.*

SECOND DAY: *Put the best possible construction, the most favorable interpretation, on the behavior of everybody you encounter or have dealings with.*

THIRD DAY: *Send out kindly thoughts toward every person you contact or think of.*

FOURTH DAY: *Think hopefully about everything. Immediately cancel out any discouraging thought that comes to mind.*

FIFTH DAY: *Think of God's presence all day long.*

JULY

July 1

What is hope? Hope is wishing for a thing to come true—faith is believing that it will come true. Hope is wanting something so eagerly that, in spite of all evidence that you're not going to get it, you go right on expecting it. And the remarkable thing is that this very act of hoping produces a strength of its own.

July 2

There is a spiritual giant within each of us telling us we need not remain enslaved by weakness or victimized by frustrating limitations. The giant within you is always struggling to burst his way out of the prison you have made for him. Why not set him free today?

July 3

Thomas Edison is supposed to have made a curious remark which is fascinating: "The chief function of the body is to carry the brain around." That is to say, you are what you think and your life is determined by what goes on in your brain. The brain is the center of thought, memory, feeling, emotion, dreams, prayer, faith; in short, it is the creative and directing center of the entire person. The body may become old, feeble, suffer disability; but so long as the brain is clear and in working order, so long do you really live.

July 4

Winston Churchill once gave a talk to the boys of Harrow, his old school. He stressed the importance of believing they could win. "Never, never, never, never give in," he told them. Four times he said "never." Churchill gave those boys the basis of success: Never quit.

July 5

A positive thinker does not refuse to recognize the negative; he refuses to dwell on it. Positive thinking is a form of thought which habitually looks for the best results from the worst conditions.

July 6

The head of a university hospital once said, "When a person becomes ill he should send for his minister, priest, or rabbi as he sends for his doctor." That is to say, the sick may be helped in two ways: through the science of medicine and surgery, and through the effective use of faith and prayer.

July 7

There is no circumstance in your life where God will not stand with you and help you, no matter what the trouble may be. He understands all your problems, all your frustrations and disappointments. He sympathizes in your weaknesses. He loves you.

July 8

An old man appeared on a popular television program. He had received a prize for having won a contest. He stole the show with his exuberant spirit and quick wit. "It's easy to see," remarked the admiring master of ceremonies, "that you are a very happy man. What's the secret of being as happy as you are? Let us in on it." "Why, son," the old man answered, "it's as plain as the nose on your face. When I wake up in the morning, I have two choices. One is to be unhappy; the other is to be happy. And I want you to know, son, that I'm not as dumb as I may look. I'm smart enough to choose happiness. I just make up my mind to be happy . . . that's all there is to it."

July 9

A friend once had a problem that had been agitating his mind for days and to which he could not get an answer. He decided to practice "creative spiritual quietness." He went alone into a church and sat for an extended period in absolute silence. Presently, he began to be conditioned to quietness. Finally, he "dropped" his problem into a deep pool of mental and spiritual silence. He meditated upon God's peace rather than upon the specific details of the problem. This seemed to clarify his thinking and, before leaving that quiet place, an answer began to emerge which proved to be the right one.

July 10

A physician tells me that 35 to 50 percent of the ill are sick because they are basically unhappy. "Joy has significant therapeutic or healing value," he says, "whereas gloom and depression militate against creative life processes." Learn to live the joy way, for "a merry heart doeth good like a medicine" (Proverbs 17:22).

July 11

In this life, we must learn to develop the quality of urbane imperturbability. This is the ability to accept people as they are, and not let their annoying actions get under your skin. It will, in time, even get you to loving people.

July 12

The late Mrs. Thomas A. Edison told me that when her husband was dying he whispered to his physician, "It is very beautiful over there." Edison was a scientist, with a factual cast of mind. He never reported anything as fact until he saw it work. He would never have reported, "It is very beautiful over there," unless, having seen, he knew it to be true.

July 13

If a person habitually thinks optimistically and hopefully he activates life around him positively and thereby attracts to himself positive results. What you mentally project reproduces in kind. Positive thinking sets in motion positive and creative forces and success flows toward you.

July 14

Don't be an *if* thinker; be a *how* thinker. The *if* thinker mouths, "If only I'd had a break." The *how* thinker emphasizes the hows: "How do I compensate for this shortcoming?" or "How do I accomplish it?"

July 15

What are the essential factors in creative and exciting successful living? Number one is to be chief executive officer over your life and over yourself. When you feel life is pushing you around, or you are being pushed around by a variable self, you are not happy or effective. But when you become supervisor of your life, there is no joy in the world equal to it or to the excitement and satisfaction you will feel.

July 16

Deep within the individual is a vast reservoir of untapped power waiting to be used. No person can have the use of all this potential until he learns to know his or her own self. The trouble with many people who fail is that they go through life thinking and writing themselves off as ordinary, commonplace persons. Having no proper belief in themselves, they fail to utilize their talents. They live aimless and erratic lives very largely because they never realize what their lives really can be or what they can become.

July 17

One of the greatest things you will ever be able to say in your lifetime is this: "I have realized the potential that Almighty God put into me."

July 18

Life for most of us contains many tough and difficult problems; we need all the confidence and reassurance we can get. Nothing builds confidence and reassurance like a word of praise. Nothing restores our self-esteem and recharges our batteries like a little admiration. Why, then, needing appreciation ourselves so badly, do we deny it so often to others?

July 19

Practice changing critical attitudes toward your fellowmen. Get in the habit of looking for something to praise, something good to say. Once you start picking at people critically, you will find yourself criticizing everything they do. Reverse this mental attitude by finding something, however small, to praise in everyone. It will greatly add to your own happiness.

July 20

God answers prayer in three ways: *yes*, *no*, and *wait awhile*. If you receive a *no* answer, look for the lesson the *no* answer teaches. God sometimes shuts doors to lead you to the right open door. If you experience difficulty and hardship, perhaps it is because God wants to do something for you other than you expected or have yet experienced.

July 21

"Don't you know the world is full of problems?" asked the negative thinker. "But the world is also full of the overcoming of problems," replied the positive thinker.

July 22

Every last one of us possesses the power to live a truly wonderful life; yet we settle for being unhappy, when it isn't necessary. We should ask ourselves what we have done with the talents and abilities which God built into us. Every human being ought to look inside himself and thank the good Lord that he has unused strength he has never drawn on—and then start drawing on it.

July 23

Help others to overcome fear and worry and you gain greater power over these problems yourself. Every day think of yourself as living in companionship with Jesus Christ. If he actually walked by your side, you would not be worried or afraid. Say, "He is with me now." Repeat it every time you feel fear or begin to worry. Recommend the practice to others as I do to you. It works.

July 24

The world needs millions of acts of forgiveness and repentance to flush out hate, resentment, and bitterness.

July 25

What's wrong with having problems? The only people who have no problems are in cemeteries. Problems are a sign of life. So be glad you've got them. It means you are alive. The more problems you have, the more alive you are. If you have no problems, better get down on your knees and ask: "Lord, don't You trust me anymore? Give me some problems."

July 26

You need not fear if you know an action is right. Pray about it to be sure it's right, for if it isn't right it's wrong, and nothing wrong can turn out right. Knowing you are right, there is nothing in this world that can defeat you. It may go hard; you may receive blows. But God will not let you down. He will see you through. Know you are right, then fearlessly go ahead.

July 27

Having asked God for forgiveness, accept release, then truly forgive yourself and turn your back definitely on the matter. Fill your mind with hopeful, helpful, and positive thoughts. Have faith and go forward. "Forgetting those things which are behind, and reaching forth unto those things which are before" (Philippians 3:13).

July 28

The best way to deal with a problem is this: Write it down on a piece of paper. Study its component parts. Think it through. Then put it aside and think of God. Forget the problem. Think of God. The more you think of Him, the more He will put ideas into your mind when you pick up the problem again. You will get your answer. God answers. If you don't get it that first time, you will the second or the third. *Shift from the problem to God.*

July 29

Many of the world's finest Oriental rugs come from little villages in the Middle East, China, or India. These rugs are hand-produced by crews of men and boys under the direction of a master weaver. They work from the underside of the rug-to-be. It frequently happens that a weaver absentmindedly makes a mistake and introduces a color that is not according to the pattern. When this occurs, the master weaver, instead of having the work pulled out in order to correct the color sequence, will find some way to incorporate the mistake harmoniously into the overall pattern. In weaving our lives, we can learn to take unexpected difficulties and mistakes and weave them advantageously into the greater overall patterns of our lives. There is an inherent good in most difficulties.

July 30

If you will set aside a few minutes, ten or even five, to think about God and Christ, to confess your sins, to pray for those who have done wrong against you, and to ask for strength—and if you do this consistently day after day—a true faith will begin to send spiritual health and power through your personality.

July 31

Positive thinking is how you *think* about a problem. Enthusiasm is how you *feel* about a problem. The two together determine what you *do* about a problem.

AUGUST

August 1

Say to yourself every day, especially when things get dark and trouble stares you in the face, "I am a child of God." Asserting and affirming your divine origin will strengthen you and you will realize that whatsoever comes you have Someone watching over you and helping you. This practice will help you to have a great day every day.

August 2

My method for awakening is this: When I return to at least a semiconscious state after a night of sleep, while still lying in bed, I repeat this phrase from Psalm 139: "When I awake, I am still with thee" (verse 18). These words emphasize the greatest truth known to man—that we are not alone. Then, just before getting out of bed, I repeat that glorious old passage from Psalm 118: "This is the day which the Lord hath made; we will rejoice and be glad in it" (verse 24). He made this day to be a precious thing full of opportunity; He gives it to us. We must do something good with this day.

August 3

A prominent businessman whose daily schedule is packed to the limit, his responsibilities many and his activities widely diverse, always handles himself with impressive quietness. "I have learned to begin and end each day calmly," he says. "I repeat to myself this line from Isaiah: 'In quietness and in confidence shall be your strength' [Isaiah 30:15]. That is my secret."

August 4

Enthusiasm is no Pollyannish, sweetness-and-light, inborn and fortuitous concept. It is a strong, rugged mental attitude that is perhaps hard to achieve, difficult to maintain, but powerful—so powerful!

August 5

How do some people rise above calamities that leave others crushed in spirit, bitter and defeated? In the Book of Job we find a clue: "When he [God] giveth quietness, who then can make trouble?" (Job 34:29). The first essential for meeting misfortune sturdily is to achieve quietness, calmness, serenity at the center of yourself. Out of such quietness at the center arises simple gratitude—for the gift of life, for present blessings, for advantages and possibilities you do have. This thankfulness, in turn, opens doors to happiness and opportunity which otherwise remain closed.

August 6

A prayer for energy: Dear Lord, I need more energy and strength. I seem drained and tired. I do not seem to possess what it takes to do all that I must do. I know that the wrong kind of thoughts can make one tired. Change my thoughts that they may be in harmony with Your power. Keep me in close contact with You who are the Source of energy, energy that never runs down. I accept this strength and energy now. I thank you. Amen.

August 7

A long while ago, there was a man who had to hook up his wife's long dresses every day. They used to hook from top to bottom and he got tired of the job. It was most exasperating. He nearly lost his religion every time he did it. He is the fellow who developed the zipper. He met a situation with creativity.

August 8

To cure worry, spend fifteen minutes daily filling your mind full of God. Worry is just a very bad mental habit. You can change any habit with God's help. Start practicing faith, the number-one enemy of worry. Every morning say, "I believe, " out loud, three times. Pray: "I place my life, my loved ones, my work in the Lord's hands. There is only good in Your hands. Amen."

August 9

While driving your car, if you become annoyed by impolite and careless actions on the part of another driver, instead of reacting in kind, remain affable and send up a sincere prayer for him. You can never know what pressures motivate him. Perhaps your prayer may reach his problem. One thing is sure, it will reach you.

August 10

Beneath the tension-agitated surface of our minds is the profound peace of the deeper mental levels. As the water beneath the surface of the ocean is deep and quiet, no matter how stormy the surface, so the mind is peaceful in its depths. Silence, practiced until you grow expert in its use, has the power to penetrate to that inner center of mind and soul where God's healing quietness may actually be experienced.

August 11

When you get discouraged, when you cannot seem to make it, there is one thing you cannot do without. It is that priceless ingredient of success called relentless effort. You just never give up, never quit.

August 12

"Let your requests be made known to God," says the Bible (Philippians 4:6). But it also says, "Your Father knows what you need before you ask Him" (Matthew 6:8). Ask for what you want but always be willing to take what God gives. It may prove better than what you ask for.

August 13

Have you ever noticed how people who master words and use them well, bringing out their beauty and employing their persuasiveness, are those who go far in life? One does not need be a great platform speaker. The fine choice of vocabulary in daily speech will mark one as different and of extra quality and in a quiet way that person will become a leader. Just think what wonderment is inherent in a combination of words.

August 14

You can reach any goal . . .

IF *you know what the goal is;*
IF *you really want it;*

IF *it is a good goal;*
IF *you believe you can reach it;*
IF *you work to achieve it;*
IF *you think positively.*

August 15

God has confidence in us. He gives us the power of private judgment. He makes us free moral agents so that we can do what we want to do—even contrary to His will. That is a big God. If God were a little God, He would tell us exactly what to do. But He leaves us free. Still He hopes we are smart enough to do right.

August 16

There's a story about a rusty pickax found in the old Colorado gold country. The handle had long since deteriorated, but the rusted pick remained driven into the ground a hundred years or more. The manner in which it was driven hard into the earth revealed the defeat felt by some frustrated prospector. It seemed to say: "Oh, what's the use? I'm through." The pathetic fact—which this unknown defeated prospector never learned—was that a few yards farther on was a rich vein of gold that later produced millions. If only he had persisted.

August 17

A homing pigeon, released in the air, instinctively heads for home. Birds in migration over thousands of miles unerringly return to the same place from which they came. Every rivulet is pulled by the lure of the sea. We come from God; He is our home. Every human life feels the tug of God. The instinct is to return to Him and love Him always.

August 18

Hope is like a pointing finger painted on a door that is closed to you. It points, directing you to another door further on that will open to your big opportunity. Look for that other door—that open door.

August 19

Some people shrink from going to places that remind them of their departed loved ones; others shrink from doing things that they once did together with others, especially as husband and wife. This is understandable, because it can sharpen the sense of physical loss. The antidote is to remind yourself that the loved person is not only still with you in a spiritual sense but is far more constantly with you than was possible when he or she was alive. When my wife, Ruth, telephoned to tell me my mother had died, she said: "I know you will find this hard to believe right now, Norman, but your mother is going to be with you and nearer to you from now on to a far greater degree than she ever was before. In the past, you have always made plane trips to be with her for a few days or even a few hours. Now she can be with you always." This was true and, once I was able to grasp it, my sense of grief and loss was vastly diminished.

August 20

Storms bring out the eagles; little birds take to cover. Little people try to run from storms and are sometimes smashed by them. But big persons ride storms to better things.

August 21

Many people suffer poor health not because of what they eat but from what is eating them. Emotional ills turn inward, sapping energy, reducing efficiency, causing deterioration in health. And, of course, they siphon off happiness. This situation can be improved by a big daily dose of faith and positive thinking.

August 22

To have friends, be friendly and kindly to everyone. Be happy and out-going. Get a lot of fun out of everything. Act so that people will have a good opinion of you. Have a spirit-lifting and inspiring personality. Like people. Help those who are having it rough. This is the way to real happiness.

August 23

There is one certain way to decide whether you are old: What is your attitude when you arise in the morning? The person who is young awakens with a strange feeling of excitement, a feeling which he may not be able to explain but which is as if to say, "This is a great day; this is the day on which the wonderful thing will happen." The individual who is old, regardless of age, arises with the spirit unresponsive, not expecting any great thing to happen. This day will be just about like all the rest. The person may hope it will be no worse. Some people retain the spirit of expectation at threescore and ten; some lose it early in life. The measure of one's age is actually how well he retains the romance of youth.

August 24

What a stupendous framework God provides as a setting for our lives! The endless galaxies of innumerable stars; the tempestuous, enormous oceans; the great sighing, surging winds; rolling, reverberating thunder; dashing rain; the drama, mystery, and diversity of the recurring seasons; the thrill of the rising sun and the glory of its going down; the romance of silver moonlight—these are wonders round about us all our lives for us to get thrilled about.

August 25

Be a tough-minded optimist. That is one who does not break apart in the thought processes or attitudes, whatever the stresses. It is one who continues hopefully and cheerfully to expect the good, no matter what the apparent situation. This optimist stays right in there, everlastingly slugging away.

August 26

When tension begins rising in my mind, I often find one technique effective. I practice remembered peacefulness, returning mentally to and imaging the most peaceful scenes I have known. I affirm, "The peace of God, which passeth all understanding . . ." (Philippians 4:7).

August 27

With faith and patience and sound thinking, you can do many things that "can't be done." Things once thought impossible become possible. As the U.S. Army Corps of Engineers claims: "The difficult we do immediately. The impossible takes a little longer."

August 28

When energy runs low and discouragement creeps in, when you have to force yourself to keep going or when some unexpected obstacle throws you and you find it hard to pick yourself up and get going again, it is a time of crisis when the vital factor is simply good old perseverance. Have you got what it takes to stand up and go at it again—and still again? That's the question. Of course you have.

August 29

There is pollution of the mind. If we harbor hate, prejudice, and negativism, we destroy our best thinking potential. We frustrate our highest achievements.

August 30

If you traveled the world over, you would never find another person quite like yourself. Geneticists say if it were possible for one couple to have millions of children, no two would be exactly alike. Because you are different from everyone, there is something which only you can do in this world. The only way you may live a truly creative life, or know the highest happiness, is by being yourself—developing your own unique potential.

August 31

I do not believe that you can ever be loved unless you truly love other people. Even a dog knows when you love him. I bought an old dog along with my house in the country. I bought him because he came up and put his paw on me and nudged me, looking at me with those beautiful eyes as if to say, "I'm here."

SEPTEMBER

September 1

A person who dislikes himself because of guilt or inferiority feelings will often try to escape painful awareness of this condition by "taking it out on other people." He projects his self-dislike upon others. It is significant that the commandment which begins, "Thou shalt love thy neighbor," concludes with "as thyself" (Leviticus 19:18). If you do not have a normal measure of esteem for yourself, you cannot genuinely like other people. Self-dislike is an enormous obstacle in developing or maintaining good relationships.

September 2

The tough-minded optimist takes a positive attitude toward a fact. He sees it realistically, just as it is, but he sees something more. He views it as a challenge to his intelligence, to his ingenuity and faith. He seeks insight and guidance in dealing with the hard fact. He keeps on thinking. He knows there is an answer and finally he finds it. Perhaps he changes the fact, maybe he just bypasses it, or perhaps he learns to live with it. But in any case his attitude toward the fact has proved more important than the fact itself.

September 3

Prescription: Until condition improves, every day

1. *Take two minutes to think about God.*
2. *Read a psalm.*
3. *Read a chapter from the Gospels.*
4. *Do something kind for someone.*
5. *Get outside yourself by joining some human-betterment effort.*
6. *Go to church every Sunday and get into an atmosphere of faith.*
7. *Become a believer—in God, in life, in yourself.*

September 4

Stronger than willpower is imagination. The word might be pronounced *image-ing*. This means the projection of mental images or pictures of a desired outcome. A basic fact of human nature is the tendency to become like that which we habitually imagine (image) ourselves as being. The deeply held mental image tends to realize itself in fact. If you visualize a goal and hold it firmly in consciousness, the mind has a tendency to complete the image.

September 5

The process of tranquilizing the mind is important in assuring a condition of body, mind, and spirit that will induce perfect rest. Deliberately conceive of the mind as completely quiet, like the surface of a pond on which there is not even a ripple. Picture the mind as motionless and filled with deep quietness. Think silence until an atmosphere of silence seems to surround you. Suggest tranquil ideas to the mind, remembering that your thoughts respond to suggestion. Slowly, deliberately image peace at the center.

September 6

Before this day is out, do something specific and concrete that will demonstrate your determination to change yourself and your life for the better. Pay a debt. Heal a broken relationship. End a quarrel. Offer an apology. Pray for someone. Visit someone who is sick. Restrain yourself from buying something you had planned to buy for yourself and give the money to charity instead. Do whatever you do quietly, without ostentation. And do it, not in hope of reward, but simply because you want to do it, because you prefer to be an inner-directed person.

September 7

On the morning of our thirty-fourth anniversary, Ruth and I went into the church in Syracuse where we were married. How well I remember the day when I first saw her. I was holding a committee meeting following the church service. The door opened and in burst a girl. I had never before seen her but said to myself, *That is the girl for me.* Of course, I had a little job persuading her, but that was the start of a romance that now covers over fifty years. When she and I went into the church on our anniversary, there was no one there. So I said, "Ruth, please go back and burst through that door again." She did. Believe me, I would do it all over again! And she says she would, too.

September 8

The average man usually empties his pockets onto his dresser or desk before retiring. Personally, I rather enjoy standing over a wastebasket during this process to see how many things I can throw away: notes, memos, scraps of paper, completed self-directions, even knicknacks which I have picked up. With relief, I deposit all items possible in the wastebasket. It is perhaps more important to empty the mind as one empties pockets. During the day we pick up mental odds and ends: a little worry, a little resentment, a few annoyances, some irritations, perhaps even some guilt reactions. Every night, these should be thrown out for, unless eliminated, they accumulate and subtract from the joy of life.

September 9

A critic is an asset, though perhaps an unpleasant one. Consider criticism objectively and ask whether it is justified. If it is, then try to profit by it, even when it is unfriendly. If it isn't valid, then forget it. Don't criticize in return, just keep on doing your job to the best of your ability. Sure, it hurts, but we are not intended to go through life without some hurt. We are supposed to make strong people of ourselves.

September 10

An old Chinese farmer was walking along the road with a stick across his shoulder. Hanging from the stick was a pot filled with soybean soup. He stumbled and the jar fell off and broke into pieces. The old farmer kept going, unperturbed. A man rushed up and said excitedly, "Don't you know that your jar broke?" "Yes," the old farmer answered, "I know. I heard it fall." "Why didn't you turn around and do something about it?" "It's broken; the soup is gone—what can I do about it?" he asked.

September 11

Here is a good way to end a day and get ready for a great day tomorrow: Do not carry the day into the night. Let it rest while you rest. Before you go to sleep, run over your personal world mentally and thank God for everyone and everything. Count your blessings; name them one by one. Then say to yourself, "God watches over me, over my house, over all my loved ones." Then go to sleep in peace. Let go and let God.

September 12

On the plains, winter storms can take a heavy toll of cattle. The temperature drops below zero. Freezing rain and howling winds whip across the prairie. Snow piles into drifts. In the maelstrom, some cattle, I'm told, turn their backs to the icy blasts and slowly drift downward, finally coming to a boundary fence barring their way. There they pile against it and many die. But other cattle react differently. They head into the wind, slowly working their way forward against it until they come to a fence. Here they stand, shoulder to shoulder, facing the storm. "We 'most always find them alive and well," said an old cowboy. "That's the greatest lesson I ever learned on the prairie: to attack difficulties head-on and not turn and run."

September 13

Captain Eddie Rickenbacker once gave me an exercise for relaxing: Sit loosely in a chair, making yourself limp. Imagine yourself a burlap bag filled with potatoes. Mentally cut the string, allowing the potatoes to roll out. Be like the bag that remains. Lift your arms one at a time, letting them fall limply. Do the same with your legs and eyelids. Conceive of all your muscles as relaxing. Say, "All tension is subsiding, all stress is leaving me. I am at ease. I am at peace with God, with the world, with myself."

September 14

Think negative thoughts and you thereby activate negative forces and tend to draw back to yourself negative results. Like attracts like. Send out hate and you get back hate. Send out fear and you get back fear. Send out defeat and you draw defeat to yourself. Conversely, send out positive thoughts and positive results will come to you. We defeat ourselves, or gain victories, by the thoughts we think.

September 15

Some persons simply refuse to grow old. I like that eighty-year-old man who told me:

> What's wrong with being eighty years old? It isn't how long you've been around; it's what you've done while you've been around. Sure, I've been in the world eighty years. But I don't have an old philosophy. I do not think old thoughts. I happen to own the business I run. But I can still run it all right. When I find some bright young fellow who is as smart as I am, I'll step down. Don't think because I have a

game leg that I can't handle the business. You don't run a business with your leg but with your head. And my head is okay. I don't intend ever to get old. I know there will come a time when my obituary will be in the paper, but I will have had the time of my life all my life.

September 16

Rufus Jones, Quaker educator and philospher, pointed out that the word *individual* implies a being who resists being divided. When you muster yourself on the side of the real you, you come alive, accomplish more, gain a sense of greater worth—and live with joy. The effort it takes to be your own individual really pays off in satisfaction.

September 17

Changing one's thought pattern may be a long and difficult process. But it can be accomplished by the practice of displacing unhealthy thoughts with healthy ones. You can pray out hate, for example. A man told me he had to pray 142 times to get rid of a certain hate but then, like a fever, it broke and he became a well man spiritually and emotionally. Don't knock yourself out disliking or hating or resenting. It isn't easy to shift from that habit to the love habit. But the person who does just that is in for a lot of happiness.

September 18

If your predicament looks hopeless, remember there is no situation so completely dark that something constructive cannot be done about it. When faced with a minus, ask what you can do to make it a plus. Reject hopelessness; substitute faith; use intelligent, persevering effort and you can lift yourself out of hopelessness.

September 19

A salesman who from being a loser became a winner, told how he did it:

I went to church one Sunday in a small town where I had to wait over until Monday. In the sermon, the pastor came up with this idea: "You are never going to get the most out of life until you give living all you've got. Don't wait for living to give something to you; you give something to living." This was a new idea to me, exactly what I was not doing. It was as if a door opened in my mind. I had an entire new image of myself and decided I would give living everything I had. So, first thing next morning, I got up earlier than usual, took out the list of people I was going to see that day, and prayed for every one of them. I got to the first store before it opened. I helped the man open up and made my first sale before I would normally even have been up. And I had a wonderful day all day long. It was like magic! All along I had been expecting life to give me something and it hadn't been doing it. Now I was giving something to life and it was giving wonderful things back.

September 20

One of professional golf's outstanding players once told me: "One secret of a good shot is 'seeing' the ball going where you want it to go before you hit it." And pianists have told me it is possible to practice a number in one's mind without being near a keyboard. You need only visualize the notes with your inner eye and hear them with your inner ear. Whatever your goal, to reach it, fix in your mind a definite and successful outcome. Hold that image and go to work, for you have set in motion a realizable force.

*. . . there is a harmony
In autumn, and a lustre in its sky,
Which through the summer is not heard or seen,
As if it could not be, as if it had not been.*

SO WROTE PERCY BYSSHE Shelley. "Harmony" and "lustre" are true of autumn. But I also see it as an exciting time of year. Another powerful adjective to associate with autumn is "glorious." "Sensational" and "incredible" go well with it also. For surely woods, aflame with colors that make description difficult, and hills and valleys spread afar like an oriental rug, can hardly be depressing.

Oh, I know where the sadness concept comes from: the dying year, the early twilights, the passing of the fullness of summer, and all that. The last leaf clinging to the moldering wall brings long thoughts tinged with melancholy.

But enough of that. Let's wander, on a late September day or one in crisp October, down a quiet country road in New England or New York or Ohio or Pennsylvania or wherever we can smell autumn. The aroma of burning leaves perfumes the air. Perhaps they contribute something to that "haze on the far horizon, The infinite, tender sky, The ripe rich tint of the cornfields, And the wild geese sailing high." Yes, indeed, as W. H. Carruth says, some of us call it autumn, but others call it God.

Hand in hand, down a winding country road with all this indescribable beauty all about and, at every turn, deep thoughts of home and memories of old days—this is the mystic gift of autumn.

Indian summer it is sometimes called in America, for in bygone years it was said that the haze lingering over the landscape was caused by the fires from the Indian wigwams and tepees. The Indians who peopled the country are long gone, but the old-time autumn haze endures. Could it be that the spirits of the warriors once again come trooping over storied hills and along river valleys famed in song and story in autumn time? Who knows? Many an American, immersed in history and lore, can sense them in the gathering dusk of an October evening. As long as our country endures, the Indian tribes will surely come riding out of the past, down the silvery moon spread of autumn. So it is the mystic time, the romantic interval, the long dream time laced with history still with us, that is called the fall of the year.

And with it comes the music of the falling leaves. Silently they float downward, red, yellow, russet, piling up in windrows until one walks through them ankle deep. Strange about that sound. We became acquainted with it as childhood toddlers. But, at eighty years and beyond, it sounds exactly as it did on long-vanished October days—the rustling of the leaves.

The katydids, who dolefully warned us on September nights that summer was ended and fall had come, are silent now. The nights are still. The big, round harvest moon rides high. The air is cool and crisp. Inside the snug house, the fire burns brightly on the hearth. Apples and walnuts are ready at hand; cider is poured from the jug. It's autumn, it's October, it's America, it's home. There is nothing quite like it in all the world, an American autumn.

September 21

Keep the mouth lines up. Smile and be happy. William James claimed that we are happy because we smile rather than we smile because we are happy. The smile comes first. It is also a fact that happiness in the heart puts a smile on the lips. Cultivate optimism, always looking on the bright side, and you will develop a happy state of life.

September 22

Your mind will give you back exactly what you put into it. If, over a long period of time, you put defeat into your mind, your mind will give you back defeat. But if, over a long period, you put great faith into your mind, your mind will give faith results back.

September 23

Sing at least one song every day. This may not add to the enjoyment of your family or friends, but it will be a wonderful tonic for you. Actually, a hymn is best—a hymn with the morning shower will wash your mind on the inside as soap and water do on the outside.

September 24

Quiet and activity are the opposite sides of creative energy. I doubt that anyone can ever be a creative activist who is not at the same time a creative quietist.

September 25

"Do you ever try talking about God?" I asked a woman whose marriage was not going well. "No," she answered, "my husband talks a great deal about God, but not in the way you mean. When we talk, we argue and quarrel about bills and every unpleasant thing you can think of." I suggested she try returning thanks at the table, for a start. Usually, her husband would sit down and glumly pull up his napkin. Finally, one night, she interrupted softly, "I'm going to return thanks." She did the same the next night, and the next, and the next, until, finally, he said: "Okay, it's my turn. I am going to return thanks!" After that, it was easier to talk about things sanely. They tell me that now their marriage is "in good shape."

September 26

Always start the day with prayer. It is the greatest of all mind conditioners. Even if you do not have the time, pray. It is that important. Always begin the day with the thought of God, His love and care, and with the thought of your responsibility for serving Him. An old friend of mine said it well: "Fill the mind full of God and the whole day will be full of happiness, even if the going gets hard."

September 27

While talking with a physician, I asked what he thought were the physiological advantages of optimism over depression. He told me: Depression in the mind increases the possibility of infection at least tenfold. Optimism actually may help as a force burning out infection. People who maintain a confident attitude have a strange power over sickness. I recommend an attitude of optimism and faith as one of the greatest aids to health.

September 28

Here is one week's treatment for tension, uptightness, and stress. Begin it today and continue for the next seven days:

FIRST DAY: *"Peace I leave with you, my peace I give unto you. . . . Let not your heart be troubled, neither let it be afraid"* (John 14:27).

SECOND DAY: *"Thou wilt keep him in perfect peace, whose mind is stayed on thee: because he trusteth in thee"* (Isaiah 26:3).

THIRD DAY: *"My presence shall go with thee, and I will give thee rest"* (Exodus 33:14).

FOURTH DAY: *"Rest in the Lord, and wait patiently for him: fret not thyself . . ."* (Psalms 37:7).

FIFTH DAY: *"Come unto me, all ye that labour and are heavy laden, and I will give you rest"* (Matthew 11:28).

SIXTH DAY: *"Let the peace of God rule in your hearts . . ."* (Colossians 3:15).

SEVENTH DAY: *"He maketh me to lie down in green pastures: he leadeth me beside the still waters. He restoreth my soul"* (Psalms 23:2, 3).

September 29

To combat that "overwhelmed" feeling, use the old military maxim: Concentrate your forces and attack at the point where you may achieve a breakthrough. Don't sit around wringing your hands because so many problems and difficulties beset you. Pick out one, break it down into manageable parts, and go after each part in turn.

September 30

Along in September, up our way, the "line storms" come. High winds of gale force were driving across the ridge on our farm. I heard something groaning and found it was a huge maple tree, 150 years old. But it wasn't groaning; actually it was laughing. It was having the time of its life with that wind. *Maybe it's going to come down*, I thought. "Don't worry," it seemed to say, "I was here before you and I'll be here after you're gone." Oh, trees do go down sometimes, but then what happens? A little shoot comes up and a new tree is started. Human beings are of the same breed. They are absolutely undefeatable when they know they are. But they've got to know it.

OCTOBER

October 1

Fear is the strongest thought pattern, save one. Faith is always stronger than fear. Where faith is, fear cannot live. Faith withers fear. You can crowd fear out by filling your mind with faith. It is an absolute, demonstrable fact that the person who practices faith, real faith in God, rises so high above fear that it can no longer affect that individual.

October 2

Real forgiveness involves no holding back at all. One must go the whole distance in restoring relationships. If one says, "I will forgive you the wrong you have done me, but I can never forget it," that is only qualified forgiveness. To make it real forgiveness, forgetting must be added.

October 3

A businessman told me he was going to fire a certain employee because the man was slow, dull, and sleepy. "Instead of firing him *out* of the business, why not fire him *into* the business?" I asked. "You mean build a fire under him?" he demanded. "No," I said, "build a fire *in* him. Get him excited. Get him motivated." The employer did just that and now he reports of the same employee, "The man is a ball of fire."

October 4

The Bible gives a tremendous statement which, in the softness of these days, is scarcely ever quoted, at least not often enough. I heard it frequently in the sturdier days of my boyhood: "Quit you like men, be strong" (1 Corinthians 16:13). We simply have to develop sturdiness of will if the tough, hard problems of life are to be handled effectively. Every person has a will. If it is soft, exercise will strengthen it. Think of your will as a "muscle" of the spirit. Like any muscle, if not exercised, it becomes flabby. But, with repeated use, it toughens up, acquiring tone and resiliency.

October 5

A tornado swept through a southwestern city doing great damage. A mother there, confined to her bed because of infantile paralysis, paralyzed from the waist down, at the height of the tornado became alarmed for her two children in the next room. There was no one to help; the tornado was striking the house with force. Her limbs were assumed to be without power, but concern for the safety of her children was stronger than her limitations. Slowly she got out of bed and painfully made her way into the adjoining room. Taking her babies in her arms, she walked with them out of the house. Love proved more powerful than the paralysis from which she had been told she might never recover. Some people become paralyzed, not in their limbs, but in their thoughts. They accept limitations by saying, "This is all I can do." But that depreciating self-appraisal is not the truth. You are greater than you think you are.

October 6

One of Thomas Jefferson's rules of personal conduct was, "Always take hold of things by the smooth handle." Go at a job or at a difficulty or at a personal-relationship problem by a method that will encounter the least resistance. The less resistance, the faster things move.

October 7

The secret of a successful life is to reduce the error and increase the truth. It is because of the error in us that we make so many mistakes, do so many stupid things, get ourselves into so much trouble, and have things turn out wrong so much of the time. The opposite of error is truth. Jesus Christ said, "I am the way, the truth, and the life" (John 14:6). When we follow Him we follow the truth. The more truth, the fewer errors. It is just that simple.

October 8

Heart is the essence of creative activity. Fire the heart with where you want to go and what you want to be. Get that goal so deeply fixed in your unconscious that you will not take no for an answer. Then your entire personality, your total mentality, will follow where your heart leads. You will go where you want to go, be what you want to be.

October 9

The important fact isn't that we have problems. It is rather our attitude toward problems. There is a small sign in my office that states a big truth: "Attitudes are more important than facts." Of course you cannot ignore a fact, but the attitude of mind with which you approach that fact is all-important.

October 10

Perhaps we have wanted to reach some goal still unattained and to be something which we have not yet accomplished. Let's determine that before this year ends, goals will be reached and dreams come true. Then we will dream new dreams and set higher goals for the years yet to come.

October 11

How do you go about being a happy person? One way is to get into God's rhythm. The heavenly bodies are in rhythm. The internal system of blood and heart and organs are in rhythm. And rhythm is a kind of synonym of harmony, as harmony is one for joy. Therefore, when you are joyful you are in rhythm, and when you are in harmony with God, you are a happy person.

October 12

Five words from the Bible can determine the success of any person or any enterprise: "Seek, and ye shall find" (Matthew 7:7). Seek a need—the world has many. Find a need you can fill and you are on the way to success in life.

October 13

A champion golfer says, "What you think while playing golf is probably the most important single part of your game." He stresses the importance of concentration and the practice of visualizing what you want to achieve. The champion confidently projects in his mind the exact direction of flight designed to take the ball where he wants it to go. This principle of imagining also works in determining and reaching goals in life. One must know precisely where he or she wants to go. By firmly visualizing that goal, you force a focus on it and then you can reach it.

October 14

It's good to keep our dreams of the future and the thrill of going somewhere ever luring us on. When I was a newspaper reporter, my editor wrote a piece I've kept for years:

> *As a boy of fourteen I stopped Old Bess in the furrow where I was trying to cultivate my father's cornfield. The field was near the railroad track which crossed a trestle. I took off my cap, wiped my brow, and looked up at the fast train of the Baltimore & Ohio Railroad. At every window, as the train sped on, was someone going somewhere. I had never been anywhere, but then and there I made up my mind that someday I would be on my way. I have been on my way ever since, but there are still so many places to go, so many fascinating things to see and do. The train went around the bend. But the dreams of a boy, as the twilight came down, are the dreams I have today. The future beckons with the same mystic allure. It was so in the cornfield; it is so now.*

October 15

A young woman successfully achieved a considerable weight loss—here is what she did: She pictured explicitly the weight she wanted to reach by a certain age. Each time she was tempted, she estimated how long it would take her to eat the gooey desserts, chocolates, or other rich food. Then she thought how happy she would feel after those few minutes had she not eaten it. For the first time she began to experience the thrill of self-mastery. At bedtime, she ran over her temptations mentally and added up all the fattening things she had *not* eaten that day. Eagerly, she looked forward to topping her record the next day. She achieved her weight goal. And she held it, too.

October 16

I have not the slightest doubt concerning the truth and validity of immortality. I believe absolutely and certainly that, when you die, you will meet your loved ones and know them and be reunited with them, never to be separated again. I believe that identity of personality will continue in that greater sphere of life in which there will be no suffering or sorrow as we know them here in the physical sense. I hope there will be struggle, for struggle is good. Certainly there will be ongoing development, for life with no upward effort of the spirit would be incredibly dull. In the teachings of Jesus Christ, death does not refer to the body but rather to the soul: "The soul that sinneth, it shall die" (Ezekiel 18:20). But the soul that is in God will live forever.

October 17

It is never necessary for any individual to live a dull, uninteresting and lackluster life. If one does so, it is because of just letting life become that way. No one needs to live in frustration or allow oneself to become old, worn, and tired. Everyone has the opportunity to open wide the mind and heart, to live a life that is dynamic and exciting. Becoming a positive thinker will help you to have a good day.

October 18

I rode with a man who had the following prayer taped to his instrument panel:

> *Dear Lord, this is Your car. Put Your hands on the steering wheel along with mine and guide me through busy streets and highways. Protect this car from all danger and accident. Give us a safe and pleasant journey. Keep me from getting angry at other drivers. Help me to be polite and observe the rules of the road. Let my driving be a pleasure and not a strain. Amen.*

October 19

One of the greatest blessings in this world is to have good, sound healthy-mindedness. The person who possesses it is most fortunate. Healthy-mindedness is to be a normal, well-balanced, integrated, well-organized human being. It means a mind devoid of inner conflicts and obsessive reactions. The emotional aspect of your nature is under the control of your reason or mind. When you achieve such healthy-mindedness you are free of abnormal fear, free of hate; you are not motivated by resentments; you are free of sulkiness, gloominess, and depressiveness. And such a condition makes for a life that is good every day.

October 20

A good man who had always walked with God approached death. The light was on in his room. Suddenly, a look of surprise crossed the dying man's face. "Turn out the light, the sun is up," he said—and was gone. Apparently it is always light and beautiful over there. But it can be the same here as well when we think it so.

October 21

He lives today no less than long ago. He is alive, not merely as Caesar and Napoleon and Lincoln, for example, are alive—as memories of great men. Jesus is not a memory. He is an actual, contemporary, reachable Person. He is the living Christ, who has the power to enter into people's lives and change and lift them up. Every day the very much alive Lord Jesus is at work among us.

October 22

Here is a prayer to start this day, to help you make it a great day:

Dear Lord, thank You for the night's rest You so graciously gave me. I am grateful for renewed energy and enthusiasm. I accept this new day as a wonderful opportunity. May I use it minute by minute to do Thy will. Guide me in every problem, every decision I shall make this day. Help me to treat everyone kindly and to be fair and just and thoughtful in everything today. And if I should forget Thee during this day, O Lord, please do not forget me. Amen.

October 23

A basic fact about every individual is the craving to be appreciated. One can find happiness by looking for the best in other people, and that will help bring the best out of them. And it also helps when we put the best possible connotation on everyone and everything. Faith in people and a positive attitude can release these tremendous resources that are resident in everyone.

October 24

I continually advocate that you be a true optimist, rugged mentally, a real believer. No doubt-thinking person can be an optimist, for an optimist is a person who believes in good outcomes even when he can't yet see them. That is also the Bible's definition of *faith* as "the substance of things hoped for, the evidence of things not seen." So the real believer is a person who believes in better things when there is yet no evidence to confirm his expectation. He is one who believes in his own future even when he cannot see much possibility in it.

October 25

Get worked up about your job and you will work your job up. Get fired up about it and you will put fire into it. Any human occupation has excitement in it if you have excitement in you. And how do you find this excitement? A famous French writer answered with these words: "Faith is an excitement and an enthusiasm: it is a condition of intellectual magnificence to which we must cling as a treasure."

October 26

Here are five simple and workable rules for overcoming inadequacy attitudes and for learning to believe in yourself:

1. *Formulate and stamp indelibly on your mind a mental picture of yourself as succeeding. Hold this picture tenaciously. Never permit it to fade. Your mind will seek to develop this picture as fact. Never think of yourself as failing; never doubt the reality of the mental image.*
2. *Whenever a negative thought concerning your ability comes to mind, deliberately voice a positive thought to cancel it out.*
3. *Do not build obstacles in your imagination. Depreciate every so-called obstacle. Minimize them. Difficulties must be studied and efficiently dealt with, but they must be seen only for what they are. They must not be inflated by fear thoughts.*
4. *Do not be awestruck by other people or try to copy them. Nobody can be you as efficiently as you can.*
5. *Ten times a day repeat these words:* "If God be for me, who can be against me?" (*see Romans 8:31*).

October 27

Experience bears out the thesis that things go wrong because we are wrong. If we resolutely seek to understand where we're wrong and make changes, we are on our way to better things. "Most of the shadows of this life," said Ralph Waldo Emerson, "are caused by standing in our own sunshine." When we get busy changing attitudes that have been casting shadows and making things go wrong, then things start going right. A changed person changes situations and conditions.

October 28

We are continuously building up or breaking down the self. Through the years, every thought, every emotion, every experience contributes to the quality of self. No matter how old or how set we become, self is in the making. Everything contributes to its greatness or littleness, its stagnation or growth. What will *your* contribution be today?

October 29

When you attain a sense of undefeatableness, you will always be high-spirited and confident. Spirit is taken out of you when you allow yourself to be overwhelmed, nonplussed, and stymied by circumstances and conditions. An important secret of success is to get yourself firmly based in spiritual understanding, in faith and positive thinking. Then nothing, no matter what, can defeat you. You will have attained indomitability.

October 30

Basic in living creatively is to accept pain and difficulty as a challenge. God, who made this universe, gives us difficulties for our own best interest. He wants to make something of us and people do not grow strong in soft and fortuitous circumstances. Struggle toughens personality.

October 31

Ever practice remembered peacefulness? I think of a favorite spot in Switzerland, remembering how, at evening time, the snows on the mountains change coloring from brilliant gold to mystic purple and then fade into the dark. I think of a night on the China Sea when mists veiling the face of the moon were blown aside by a gentle breeze to allow long, silvery shafts of moonlight to fall on limpid waters. I think of a night at Srinagar in the Vale of Kashmir, where the sound of singing boatmen came across the lake on the surface of which water lilies floated. Once in my doctor's office, my pulse and blood pressure readings were taken. "Well!" he said, "that's fine. You have learned to live calmly." I told him the technique of remembered beauty to help promote tranquility. He nodded. "Good, that helps in keeping healthy."

NOVEMBER

November 1

You and I, ten years from now, will be mostly what we think during that period. You can think yourself to failure and unhappiness, or you can think your way to success and real happiness. Better give your thoughts a good overhauling once in a while. Think good days today and you'll have them tomorrow as well.

November 2

An uptight man once said to me, speaking of New York, "The very air of this city is filled with tension." "Not so," I said. "If you were to take a sampling of this air to a laboratory for analysis, you wouldn't find a trace of tension in the air. You see, tension is in the minds of people who breathe the air."

November 3

One man's rules for making a success in life are:

1. *Practice the affirmation of God's presence daily.*
2. *Pray for those with whom you work and deal.*
3. *Image success not only for yourself but also for your competitors.*
4. *Try to live by faith.*

November 4

George Cullum, Sr., Dallas construction executive, had a formula for himself and his men. He used to say: "When the job gets tough, get as tough as the job. When the rock gets hard, get as hard as the rock." Life can be tough, really tough. But God built something in human nature that is tougher still. Draw on it.

November 5

Take minute vacations during the day. Sit back in your office chair. Close your eyes and, in memory, go away to some place that means a lot to you, such as where you like to fish or play golf, or swim. Letting the mind go away, if only for a moment, tones up the body with an infusion of fresh energy.

November 6

A successful businessman told me what had turned the tide for him when he was doing poorly. It was a picture of a boat stuck in the sand, the tide out. The title of that picture was *The Tide Always Comes Back*. Don't ever accept defeat. Never even think, *I can't*. Instead, say to yourself, "The tide always comes back." It will, if you will it so.

November 7

As a boy I had an enormous inferiority complex and, believe me, it was no fun. I used to go around thinking negatively: "I don't amount to anything. I have few brains and no ability." I became aware, after a while, that others were agreeing with me. They always will—for, unconsciously, people will take you at your own self-appraisal.

November 8

The world offers so much fun and pleasure. It is pathetic how little of it many people find. Thousands live in what might be called "pleasure poverty" despite the available wealth of fun opportunities. They keep their noses to the grindstone and develop a sad crop of neuroses and tensions. Work is good but, when it's mixed with fun, it's a lot better. Don't be a fun pauper! Revel in the delights a good God has put into the world!

November 9

How to relax? Repeat slowly and quietly, bringing out the melody in each, a series of words which express quietness and peace, as, for example, tranquility (say it very deliberately and in a tranquil manner), serenity, quietness, imperturbability. Say the following, which has an amazing power to quiet the mind and relax the body: "Thou wilt keep him in perfect peace, whose mind is stayed on thee" (Isaiah 26:3). Repeat this several times during the day and you will find relaxation.

November 10

A salesman was having trouble making sales, always afraid, forever whistling in the dark. An older salesman gave him a three-sentence prayer. The results were miraculous and his percentage of sales rose steadily. This is the prayer he used: "I believe I am always divinely guided. I believe I will be led always to take the right turn of the road. I believe that God will always make a way where there is no way."

November 11

An important question for anyone is: What am I doing to my own self? Am I making myself big to equate with the power potential in me? Or am I accepting smallness as all I am capable of? To think yourself smaller than you are is a violation of your real nature. Think big.

November 12

Rural wisdom: On the platform of a small-town railroad station years ago, two men and a dog watched the express train streak past. The dog went racing after it—and was still chasing and barking at it when the last car vanished in the distance. "Crazy fool dog! Does he think he can catch the Empire State Express?" snorted the stationmaster. After a reflective silence, his friend observed, "And what would he do with it if he did?"

November 13

There are rules to follow if you wish to get along with others:

1. *Know the names of all with whom you associate and speak to them by name.*
2. *Be quick with praise.*
3. *Always be constructive if it is necessary to criticize.*
4. *Keep your temper under control.*
5. *Always be ready to lend a helping hand.*
6. *Readily admit your own mistakes and never hesitate to say, "I'm sorry."*
7. *Take a real interest in the organization which employs you.*
8. *Seek no acclaim for achievement but always give someone else the credit due him or her.*
9. *Assume that other people like you.*
10. *Try to like and esteem other people as you would have them like and esteem you.*

November 14

An old Oriental maxim says, "What you think upon grows." You tend to become what you think of yourself as being. Raise your appraisal of yourself. Affirm that you have greater possibilities than have ever yet appeared. Don't self-limit yourself, even in your private thoughts. Always see yourself as greater than you have ever been.

November 15

Want to give up smoking or, for that matter, anything else? The desire to smoke is basically one of thought, plus a nervous impulse to do something with the hands. Also involved is the infantile tendency to put something in the mouth. To quit, decide you really want to quit. Intense desire is always basic in achieving or quitting. Then, decide you are really going to quit. Finally, picture yourself as being released from the habit. Hold that picture firmly and tenaciously until your subconscious mind accepts it. Do not try to taper off—stop entirely. Ask God to help you and believe that He will. The desire is primarily in your mind— think victory thoughts and images. To cure the nervous movement of the hands, practice control of muscle tension. Believe you can—and you can.

November 16

Repeat these four statements when tense and uptight:

> *From Confucius:* "*The way of a superior man is threefold: virtuous, therefore free from anxiety; wise, therefore free from perplexity; bold, therefore free from fear.*"

> *From Robert Louis Stevenson:* "*Sit loosely in the saddle of life.*"

> *From Saint Theresa, a sixteenth-century mystic:* "*Let nothing disturb you; let nothing frighten you. Everything passes except God; God alone is sufficient.*"

> *From Isaiah:* "*. . . in quietness and in confidence shall be your strength*" (*Isaiah 30:15*).

November 17

The word *resentment* means to re-feel—to feel again. Someone wrongs or wounds you; in resenting it, you re-feel the injury. And you re-hurt yourself. The Hebrew Talmud says that a person who bears a grudge is "like one who, having cut one hand while handling a knife, avenges himself by stabbing the other hand." The best way to avoid this self-inflicted suffering is to apply "spiritual iodine" the moment anybody hurts you. Get your resentment healed at once, before it starts to fester.

November 18

The more we apply mental power against seemingly hopeless difficulties and follow the flashes of insight which come from real thinking, the surer our accomplishment. Thinking gives one the daring to do the unusual when a situation calls for it: a readiness to shift thinking quickly when problems turn out differently than anticipated.

November 19

Problems are a normal and essential part of all of life. Strength develops from standing up to them, thinking them through, and mastering them. By approaching problems in a positive frame of mind, you can always derive good from them, no matter how difficult they may be.

November 20

No matter how dark things become, someone is always with you—and that someone is God. He helps by giving you peace and a positive mental attitude. With these, you can start real creative thinking and, as a result, will be able to take a hopeful and not a negative view. Such dynamic thinking will start things coming your way and presently you will find yourself on top of trouble.

November 21

Thanksgiving is a grateful recognition of past benefits and the activator of blessings yet to come. Thankfulness stimulates a continuous flow of blessings. If, in your life, there is a paucity of blessings, it may be that your practice of thankfulness has grown weak and inactive. The attitude of gratitude is important in achieving wholeness in life. Only by enumerating the many blessings bestowed upon us can we fully appreciate the generous bounty of God.

November 22

Really, there is one thing that you must never do. You must never, as long as you live, stop believing in yourself! You were made by God, the Creator, and He never made anything badly. When He made you, He made you good, very good. And, therefore, you have the right to hold a high opinion of yourself. A good, healthy self-respect is normal and right. So have a great day today and a great life always.

November 23

Fear lurks among shadows and thrives in darkness. A spiritually darkened mind is a breeding ground for terrifying fears. But, when the mind is filled with the Lord's presence, it is automatically also filled with light. Intelligent thinking follows and fears are driven off. "The Lord is my light . . . whom shall I fear?" (Psalms 27:1).

November 24

To have mental health and live successfully, every person must move away from past failures and mistakes and go forward without letting them weigh upon the mind. Never dwell upon the "ifs" but rather upon the "hows." Forgetting is absolutely necessary to a successful future. Every night, when you lie down to sleep, practice dropping all failures and mistakes into the past. They are over, finished. Look confidently to the future. Go to sleep in peace. God gives you new opportunities every morning.

November 25

Here is a prayer to help you to forgive: Lord, You tell us to forgive our enemies. This I want to do—or do I, really? But Lord, I do not know how to forgive—or is it that I just haven't the moral strength to do so?

Deliver me from nursing a grudge. Help me to want to forgive.

Fill my mind with magnanimous thoughts. Make me bigger than I've been acting. Let me know the joy of forgiveness and reconciliation. The Bible says, "For if ye forgive men their trespasses, your heavenly Father will also forgive you" (Matthew 6:14). So please take my enemy off my hands. And I thank You that I find it in my heart to say, "Be good to him or her." Amen.

November 26

Many factors determine the way we go and how we go and where we arrive in life. But one thing is for sure: If you forget those things which are behind, as the Bible teaches, and reach forward toward those things which are ahead, pressing "toward the mark for the prize of the high calling of God in Christ Jesus" (Philippians 3:14), you have a future that will be full of achievement and joy.

November 27

The Bible tells us that the sins of the fathers are passed on to succeeding generations. The virtues of the fathers can be passed along, too. If a father is an honest and upright man, and if he establishes any sort of adequate relationship with his sons and daughters, it is going to be very hard for those children to get off the track, or getting off, not to get back on. The desire to emulate and imitate is too strong.

November 28

Prayer of a distracted parent: Dear Lord, I love my children but they are driving me to distraction. I have lost my self-control. I need help. I realize, dear Lord, that I can never direct them in their young lives if I am disorganized. Help me not to be angry and not to shout at them. Give me a sense of humor. Help me to know that their restless energy is a sign of vitality and part of their development. Don't let me be tired and upset but rather enter joyfully into my relationship with them.

Thank You for my children, Lord, but, don't let them get me down. Amen.

November 29

My brother, Bob, and I used to fight each other occasionally, but if any other boy attacked either of us, he had both of us to contend with. We have been inseparable all our lives; our fighting ended a long time ago. Our love is lifelong—and even beyond. The love of our brothers and sisters is a gift for which we should be grateful.

November 30

In one sense, the big issue of our personal life is the competition between error and truth. When error is in the saddle and rides us, we do dumb things and spend a lot of time regretting them. When truth is in control, we stay on the beam and handle life's problems masterfully.

DECEMBER

December 1

Two words—*deny yourself*—are important to self-control. They may relate to success or to failure. Refuse the candy, skip second helpings, don't buy the dress, don't goof off—where will *you* start to say no to yourself? Don't consider it a decision *against* some form of fun but a decision *for* a desired goal in your life. This makes it a positive, not a negative step. This isn't taking the joy out of life. Actually it's putting the joy into life. The more we give up to concentrate on an important goal, the stronger we become. Self-denial in the present, to gain greater benefits in the future, is the hallmark of a rational human being.

December 2

My wife, Ruth, was at a church dinner out west and was seated across from a farmer. His hands and windblown look showed how he had toiled. She asked, "How are the crops this year?" "Ma'am," he replied, "we had a long drought, then came the grasshoppers. I lost ninety percent of my crop. But my brother lost all of his." Appalled, Ruth asked, "But what did your brother do?" Quietly, he answered, "We just aimed to forget it." Next year offers a new beginning.

December 3

On an airplane in the Far East, in typhoon season, I asked the pilot how he handled those strong winds. "Oh," he replied, "I turn typhoons into tailwinds!" In life there are many troubles, some seemingly as big as typhoons. With faith in God and by using the mind He gave you, you can learn the laws that govern trouble. Then you can turn difficulty into opportunity and make it speed you on your way with a strong tailwind to achievement.

December 4

How do you draw on a higher power? Practice living with God. Live with Him every day. Be with Jesus Christ. Talk to Him. Have conversation with Him as a friend. Pray to Him. Think about Him. Do not do anything, however seemingly small or insignificant, without bringing Him into it. The more you do this, the more you will identify with divine forces, and the power flow from them to you will increase.

December 5

By dwelling too much upon mistakes you can keep yourself in an error groove. Mistakes can be teachers—but they can also be leeches, clinging to your thinking, conditioning you to make the same mistakes again. It is all too easy to let yesterday's mistakes ruin today. Train your mind to learn from your successes.

December 6

At any point in our lives each of us is standing on a kind of moral ladder. There are rungs above us and rungs below. We can climb up or we can step down. Or we can simply stand still, which is the easiest thing to do, because it requires no effort and involves no risk. What we really have to do if we are interested in self-development is make up our minds to move up a rung and then another and another on the moral ladder.

December 7

One man checks on the rightness or wrongness of a proposed action this way: He visualizes his role reported in big black headlines in tomorrow's newspaper. If something in him winces at the thought, he tells himself he had better censor that action.

December 8

Never laugh off anyone who has an evangelical zeal for or against anything. A single individual with strong and zealous determination can stimulate amazing forces which may become dominant, even when a vast majority disagrees. A fat, sleepy majority can be pushed around by a few persons aflame with positive conviction or negative destructiveness. Both are powerful motivators. Fortunately, positive convictions are more powerful than negative ones.

December 9

When trouble strikes, what you want is not only comfort and sympathy. You want strength to stand up to it and meet it. You can have both. Remind yourself that God is with you, that He will never fail you, that you can count upon Him. Say these words: "God is with me, helping me" and "God is our refuge and strength, a very present help in trouble." This will give you a sense of comfort. New hope will flood your mind. Emotional reaction will give way to rational thinking. New ideas will come. A new sense of strength will be yours. Result—you will rise above your trouble.

December 10

A pilot told me that some of the big jet airplanes have a series of blades extending down the wings which cause air to swirl toward the rear of the plane. This provides the necessary turbulence for directional accuracy in flight. If the air is too smooth, some roughness has to be added to improve flight conditions. Perhaps suffering and hardship serve the same purpose for a human being. Maybe we need "turbulence" to help us develop a sense of direction so that we may ultimately reach the destination intended for us in life.

December 11

Arve Hatcher tells how, after a heavy blizzard, his car was stuck in a snow pile, and his efforts to get it moving only dug its wheels in deeper and deeper. Down the street came a muscular teenager carrying a shovel. When he saw the problem he promptly got to work and set the car free. "Many thanks," Hatcher said gratefully, and reached to hand him some folded bills. "No way," the teenager said with a smile. "I belong to the DUO Club." "Never heard of it," Hatcher replied. "Sure you have," the boy grinned. "It's the do-unto-others-as-you-would-have-them-do-unto-you club." And with a wave of his hand and another big smile, he was on his way.

December 12

To have courage, think courage. We become what we think. As you think courage, courage will fill your thoughts and displace fear. The more courageous your thinking, the greater the courage you will have. Act courageously. Practice the "as if" principle. Act as if you are courageous and you will become as you think and act. A person should pray for courage as he prays for his daily bread. And your prayer for courage will enable you to think and act with courage.

December 13

Set apart a regular time to deliberately still your thoughts and emotions so that you may commune with your deeper self. When the mind is agitated by the noise, hurry, and confusion of modern life, you cannot truly consult the creative depths within yourself where lie answers to your perplexing problems. Remember Thomas Carlyle's words: "Silence is the element in which great things fashion themselves together."

December 14

Dare to be what you ought to be; dare to be what you dream to be; dare to be the finest you can be. The more you dare, the surer you will be of gaining just what you dare. But if you go at things timorously, telling yourself, "I'm afraid I'll never make it" or "I just know I can't do it" or "I haven't got what it takes," then you will get a result in kind. Dream great dreams; dare great dreams. Have great hopes; dare great hopes. Have great expectations, dare great expectations. ". . . the Lord is the strength of my life . . . in this will I be confident" (Psalms 27:1, 3).

December 15

An enemy of worry is reason. Hit your anxiety hard with reason. Worry is an emotion; reason is a sound mental process. No emotion can stand long against cool, factual, reasoned analysis. Spread your worry out and apply reason to it. Take it apart and see how its constituent elements fade in the presence of reason.

December 16

Christianity is not only a philosophy; it not only a theology. It is also a science. A science is any body of truth that is based on demonstrable formulas. Jesus gives us such formulas. If you love, you will get loving results; if you hate, you will get hateful results. He tells us that, if we live a good life, we will experience inner joy. Christianity works for all who try it.

December 17

Our taxi made about two blocks in fifteen minutes that Christmas season. "This traffic is terrible," my companion growled. "It draws off what little Christmas spirit I've got." My other companion was more philosophical. "It sure is something," he mused, "really something. Just think of it. A baby born more than nineteen hundred years ago, over five thousand miles away, causes a traffic jam on Fifth Avenue. Yep, that sure is something!"

December 18

I often think of my grandmother, how she would talk with God and about God, as simply as with her next-door neighbor. She talked to me when I was a lad, about God as a kindly Father, about Christ as the Head of the house. She had a framed placard hung up which read, "Christ is the head of this house, the Unseen Listener to every conversation. . . ." Christ was around about at all times. He was very near because Grandma and Grandpa practiced religious conversations. In those days they shared their spiritual experiences and talked about the deep things of life. Sharing God brings you closer to Him.

December 19

Everyone has both a best and a worst side. A poet once said, "There is an unseen battlefield in every human breast where two opposing forces meet and where they seldom rest." For every human being the great issue is which of the two shall triumph and prevail in him, the worst or the best? You must pray for the best.

December 20

"This is the refreshing . . ." said the prophet Isaiah (28:12). These few words remind us of a spring of cool water. They have a renewing quality. The frequent use of this text has an invigorating effect. After a busy day or in the midst of tiring details, as in Christmas activities, stop and say these words over to yourself and note how they dissipate weariness and refresh the body, mind, and spirit. Say them slowly, emphasizing their soft and quiet melody. At the same time, conceive of peace, rest, and renewal as coming to you. They will.

WINTER! SOME DO NOT like it much, but endure it. Others go away from it to warmer climates and sojourn among palm trees and on sandy beaches warmed by a golden sun. Followers of perennial summer and devotees of higher temperatures, they have long since lost acquaintance with winter's rugged delights.

But some of us are devoted lovers of the four seasons. Having lived among them for so long, the changing of the seasons is our inherited life-style. And while, now and then, we grumble at the ice and snow, we really don't mind winter all that much and, believe it or not, we like it most of the time.

A summer night in June or July can be of entrancing beauty and charm, but the same may be said of many a winter evening in December or January. It is a time of snow crunching underfoot, the night clear and cold, brilliant stars in the sky, moonlight so bright it rivals noonday. The glorious colors of warmer areas are beautiful beyond the ability to describe them, especially when one tries to convey the exotic fragrances of tropical or semitropical flowers. But then, black and white can be beautiful, too, either separately or in combination.

Only recently, returning from a winter afternoon's walk on our farm on Quaker Hill, Ruth and I simultaneously stopped, arrested by the beauty of the scene before us. Our house atop a hill stood etched in white against a blue sky, its stately Corinthian columns gleaming in the early setting of the sun in the west. Snow lay deep upon the ground, festooned on bushes and trees. The long white fences ran off into the distance, lined by gigantic maples, stark and black against the white-clad hills. Long shafts of golden sunlight lay across the snow-covered lawns as the winter evening came down cold and stern. This beauty was of black and white to which gold was added. Ruth enthusiastically agreed when I exclaimed, "In its own glorious way, this just has to be as beautiful as that lovely southland."

"Yes," she replied, "but isn't all of God's great world beautiful, north or south or wherever?"

Winter silences have their meaningful appeal to the reflective mind. Gliding cross-country on skis into a lonely grove of trees, then standing still and quiet until the palpable silence makes itself felt is, in a deep sense, to be at one with the essence of life. I have been alone in the same grove of trees in midsummer, but nature is not so silent then—for aliveness is all around. In winter, nature's utter and incredible stillness steals upon one, though at either time the healing of her gentle touch is felt.

But whether it is the tentative change of nature's springtime, or the fullness of her summer, or the flaming glory of autumn, or finally, the disciplinary cold of winter, the good God made them all for us.

December 21

Perhaps courage is a basic life quality which God gives us. It builds up the spirit in crises. Moments may come when courage alone stands between us and disaster. In the long pull, across the years, there will be times when we need dogged courage to keep us going when the going is hard. And what is the source of such rugged courage? It is surely that sense of God's presence when we hear Him say, "I am with you always."

December 22

Our children are the citizens of the future who must be taught not to lie and cheat but to be honest people like the sturdy and decent forefathers who forged our great country. Dishonest living is a blow at the United States itself, for a free land can survive only through men and women of integrity. Tell them that the Child of Bethlehem came to make people good.

December 23

What greater happiness can come to a family than the arrival of a baby! Surely it is a sign that God has blessed that marriage and that home. A baby is God's masterpiece—a wonderful creation of His infinite mind. The arrival of baby Jesus brought a great and exciting happiness into the world.

December 24

The poet James Russell Lowell wrote in "A Christmas Carol":

> *And they who do their souls no wrong,*
> *But keep at eve the faith of morn,*
> *Shall daily hear the angel-song,*
> *"Today the Prince of Peace is born!"*

There's a lifelong glory to the Christmas season, from wide-eyed childhood to old age. It's an inexpressible glory. Keep it that way always.

December 25

The Christmas story is ushered in with a song, ". . . and on earth peace, good will toward men" (Luke 2:14). Everyone was joyful, for something wonderful had happened. A great Teacher had come to earth to tell the simple secret of peace and joy. And what a secret it is. When we have peace in our hearts, we also have love in our hearts and good will toward all men. Who but our Lord could have thought of such a simple way to happiness? And our Saviour, whose birth we celebrate this Christmas day, saves us from our sins and receives us to eternal life. No wonder we happily say to each other today, "Merry Christmas!"

December 26

We are much disturbed by antagonisms held by other people toward us but usually little concerned by the unfriendly feelings we have for them. We think the other man ought to change, but give little consideration to the possibility that we ourselves ought to change. To get changed spiritually ourselves—that is the real solution. The spirit of Christmas can help us to do that.

December 27

A physician says that 70 percent of his patients reveal resentment in their case histories. "Ill will and grudges help to make people sick. Forgiveness," he says, "will do more toward getting them well than many pills." So it is healthy to forgive, to say nothing of its being the right way to live. Develop the habit of looking for people's good points. Everybody has them. This thought may help you get ready for great days in the upcoming new year.

December 28

Marcus Aurelius, the Roman emperor, said: "Life is what our thoughts make it." Saint Paul said substantially the same thing: ". . . be ye transformed by the renewing of your mind . . ." (Romans 12:2). This is the great secret that Christianity has given people across the centuries, changing them from desultory to vital, from dead to alive, from weak to strong, from dull to alert. "I live; yet not I, but Christ liveth in me" (Galatians 2:20).

December 29

As the old year runs out, one of the most important skills you can cultivate is the ability to forget. If you really want to move away from failures and unpleasant experiences, you've got to be able to say, "Okay, I've had it—now I'll forget it." Then do just that. ". . . forgetting those things which are behind, and reaching forth . . . I press toward the mark . . ." (Philippians 3:13, 14).

December 30

To start your new year right, I suggest finding a deeper spiritual life. Something happens deep within you and thereafter you are filled with joy and warmth and beauty. This may happen quickly and dramatically. It could happen today. On the other hand, it may be a developing experience, unfolding as a rose, beginning with a bud and ending with full flowering. But, however it happens, this is the greatest experience possible to a human being.

December 31

Here is a New Year's Eve thought to ensure a great day every day beginning now. Saint Paul says, ". . . walk in newness of life" (Romans 6:4). What does that mean? It simply means to get rid of all these old barnacles that have encrusted you for so long: resentments, dishonesties, rationalizations, fears, weaknesses, and so on. These must all go, so that you may "walk in newness of life." When you're new, you *feel* like walking, head up, standing tall, for you have fresh new power. That God may reactivate your life so that you may "walk in newness of life," why not just be done with some things. Get so tired of the old, so fed up with it, that you are done with it. If you've been full of fear, be done with being full of fear. If you've been full of error and defeat, be done with it. Say, "By God's grace, I'm done with it," and take charge of yourself like never before. And, for certain, it will be a Happy New Year for you.

POSITIVE IMAGING

Scripture quotations in this volume are from the King James Version of the Bible.

Material on Peggy Paul is reprinted courtesy of the Tampa *Tribune*.

Material on Steve Stone is reprinted courtesy of *The Evening Sun*, Baltimore, Maryland.

Several of the stories in this volume originally appeared in *Guideposts* magazine.

This book was formerly published under the title *Dynamic Imaging*.

*Gratefully and affectionately
dedicated to longtime friend
and associate Arthur Gordon,
skilled editor and writer,
with thanks for the helpful
assistance he has given in the
preparation of this book*

CONTENTS

INTRODUCTION 103
1 IMAGING: WHAT IT IS AND HOW IT WORKS 105
2 HOW THE IMAGING IDEA GREW 113
3 THE CONCEPT THAT CONQUERS PROBLEMS 121
4 HOW IMAGING HELPS TO BOLSTER A
SHAKY EGO 129
5 HOW TO MANAGE MONEY PROBLEMS 136
6 USE IMAGING TO OUTWIT WORRY 145
7 IMAGE YOURSELF NO LONGER LONELY 153
8 THE THREE BIGGEST STEPS ON THE ROAD TO
SUCCESS 158
9 IMAGING: KEY TO HEALTH? 169
10 THE WORD THAT UNDERMINES MARRIAGE 180
11 THE HEALING POWER OF FORGIVENESS 191
12 IMAGING THE TENSENESS OUT OF TENSION 199
13 HOW TO DEEPEN YOUR FAITH 208
14 IMAGING IN EVERYDAY LIFE 217
15 THE IMAGING PROCESS IN MAKING AND KEEPING
FRIENDS 226
16 THE MOST IMPORTANT IMAGE OF ALL 234

A Special Note to the Reader

The pages that follow are written in the first person because to have a single narrator is said to lend clarity and unity to a book. But it is misleading because this book is the product of two minds, one masculine and one feminine. My wife, Ruth, and I have worked together for so long that neither of us can function without the other. This is as much her book as mine. It is a team effort all the way through, and I hope the reader will be conscious of that and bestow credit where it is due.

NORMAN VINCENT PEALE

Your sons and your daughters shall prophesy, your old men shall dream dreams, your young men shall see visions.

JOEL 2:28

INTRODUCTION

SUPPOSE A TRUSTED FRIEND came to you and said, "There's a powerful new-old idea that people are talking about, one I think you should be aware of. It's a concept available to all of us that can shape and change human lives for the better in an astonishing way." What would you say?

You'd say, "Tell me about it!" wouldn't you?

That's what I want to do in this book—tell you about it.

The concept is a form of mental activity called imaging. It consists of vividly picturing, in your conscious mind, a desired goal or objective, and holding that image until it sinks into your unconscious mind, where it releases great, untapped energies. It works best when it is combined with a strong religious faith, backed by prayer and the seemingly illogical technique of giving thanks for benefits before they are received. When the imaging concept is applied steadily and systematically, it solves problems, strengthens personalities, improves health, and greatly enhances the chances for success in any kind of endeavor.

The idea of imaging has been around for a long time, and it has been implicit in all the speaking and writing I have done in the past. But only recently has it begun to emerge clearly and be recognized by scientists and medical authorities as additional proof that mind and body and spirit are one indivisible unit, as the Bible has been telling us all along.

Jesus Christ Himself said, "What things soever ye desire, when ye pray, believe that ye receive them, and ye shall have them" (Mark 11:24). That is the great promise that lies behind the theme of this book. Please keep it in mind as you turn the page and start reading *Positive Imaging*.

1

IMAGING: WHAT IT IS AND HOW IT WORKS

THERE IS A POWERFUL and mysterious force in human nature that is capable of bringing about dramatic improvement in our lives. It is a kind of mental engineering that works best when supported by a strong religious faith. It's not difficult to practice; anyone can do it. Recently it has caught the attention of doctors, psychologists, and thinkers everywhere, and a new word has been coined to describe it. That word is *imaging*, derived from *imagination*.

Imaging, the forming of mental pictures or images, is based on the principle that there is a deep tendency in human nature to ultimately become precisely like that which we imagine or image ourselves as being. An image formed and held tenaciously in the conscious mind will pass presently, by a process of mental osmosis, into the unconscious mind. And when it is accepted firmly in the unconscious, the individual will strongly tend to have it, for then it has you. So powerful is the imaging effect on thought and performance that a long-held visualization of an objective or goal can become determinative.

Imaging is positive thinking carried one step further. In imaging, one does not merely think about a hoped-for goal; one "sees" or visualizes it with tremendous intensity, reinforced by prayer. Imaging is a kind of laser beam of the imagination, a shaft of mental energy in which the desired goal or outcome is pictured so vividly by the conscious mind that the unconscious mind accepts it and is activated by it. This releases powerful internal forces that can bring about astonishing changes in the life of the person who is doing the imaging.

To illustrate, right here at the beginning, let me tell you four true stories. As you read them, I think you'll see very clearly the imaging principle at work. Here is the first one:

It's wintertime in Cincinnati a generation ago. A cold wind chills the crowds hurrying along the busy street. A young boy—maybe eleven, maybe twelve—has stopped outside the building that houses the city's newspaper, the powerful and respected Cincinnati *Enquirer*. The youngster is not too warmly dressed; his clothes are obviously hand-me-downs. Shivering a bit, he is staring through the big plate-glass window, watching the feverish journalistic activity inside.

One figure in particular has caught his eye: a burly man in shirt-sleeves seated at a central desk. A green eyeshade shields his eyes from the glare of a light bulb dangling above his head. An unlighted cigar is clamped between his teeth. His desk bristles with scraps of typescript impaled on spikes. Papers overflow from wire baskets. The black headlines of various editions spill onto the floor around him. Activity. Confusion. Chaos. But power emanates from that desk, and the boy in the street can sense it. He knows that this man is in command.

The man spins around in his swivel chair, twists a sheet of yellowish paper into an ancient typewriter, hammers out a few staccato lines. He rips it out, stares at it, takes a black copy pencil from behind his ear, makes a few lightning-swift corrections. He raises his head, barks an order. A copyboy darts forward, snatches the paper, disappears. The shivering witness in the street watches, transfixed.

A huge policeman saunters past, twirling his nightstick. Impulsively, the boy turns to him. "Officer, who is that man in there—the one with the eyeshade and the cigar?"

"Him?" The blue giant looks down indulgently. "He's the editor, sonny. The editor of the Cincinnati *Enquirer*, that's who he is."

The policeman moves on. Finally the boy goes down the street, looking just as he did before. But he is not the same as before. He is changed. He's no longer aware of the cold wind or the hurrying crowds around him. Inside his head a scene is forming—not just a vague or casual daydream, but a vision of the future that has all the reality, all the intensity of the present. Intuitively, the boy knows that sooner or later what he is visualizing will come to pass. He is sure of it. The scene in his head is a replica of the scene he has just witnessed behind the plate-glass window, with one all-important change. The occupant of the editor's chair, thirty years hence, is himself. Himself, Roger Ferger, a poor youngster with no connections, no advantages, nothing except an image so powerful that it will bend all the laws of probability until they conform to an even stronger, though hidden law.

He goes home with that image fixed in his head. When he says his prayers that night, he relives his dream and asks for help in achieving it. Night after night he does this, unaware that by imaging himself so intensely in that editorial chair, and by reinforcing that image with prayer, he is touching the kingdom of God within himself and releasing forces more powerful than he knows.

How do I know this story? I know because Roger Ferger related it to me years after that memorable day in his childhood. He told me when he was not merely the editor but also the publisher and the owner of the Cincinnati *Enquirer*.

The Image of Her Future

Now for the second story. Again we go back through the years. We are in one of the poorer sections of an Ohio town. A young girl is bending over a metal washtub. She is one of eight children, the daughter of a miner. She is washing her father's overalls.

As she washes her father's overalls, staring now and then out the grimy window at the bleak, familiar symbols of poverty that surround her, an image comes to her. She has had daydreams about her future before, but this is more than a daydream. Diamond clear in her mind is the picture of a college campus, tranquil green lawns, ivy-colored buildings. Graduation ceremonies are in progress, and she sees herself in cap and gown receiving a parchment scroll. She feels the soaring happiness, the sense of achievement, the pride.

But what kind of impossible dream is this? No member of her family has ever gone to college. Mary Crowe has prayed for the chance to go, it is true, but there is no money for such things. The Great Depression has the country by the throat. There is barely enough food on the Crowe family table. Her strange vision must be just a young girl's wistful fantasy, nothing more. And yet, the image of herself receiving the parchment scroll was so vivid, so real.

Consider, now, what happens next. Mary Crowe receives a summons; her parish priest would like to see her. Puzzled, she goes to the rectory, where the good father opens a desk drawer and takes out an envelope. "Mary," he says, "quite a while ago one of our parishioners gave me some money to be used to educate some deserving young person. I've been watching you, and I've decided you are the one. These funds will make it possible for you to have a four-year scholarship at Saint Mary-of-the-Springs. I know you'll make a wonderful record there."

Again, passionate dream into concrete reality. Burning image into tangible substance. Just coincidence? No, because Mary Crowe told me that—incredibly—when she went to Saint Mary-of-the-Springs and saw the campus for the first time, she recognized it. It was the campus she had seen in the vision that came to her while she was sloshing her father's overalls in the battered tin tub in the Crowe family kitchen.

I can't explain that; Mary Crowe couldn't, either. But she did go to college there. She studied hard and got top grades. As graduation approached, she began to think about a career. She knew of a case in her own run-down neighborhood where a life-insurance policy had stood between a poor family and total disaster. So she decided she would like to become an insurance salesperson.

In those days there were almost no women selling insurance. It just wasn't done. It was a man's world. But Mary Crowe "saw" herself as a successful producer. She visualized buyers whose lives would be protected and helped by the insurance they bought. She fixed all this in her mind with tremendous clarity and vividness. Then she went to look for a job as an agent for one of the largest insurance agencies in the city.

The man in charge of hiring turned her down. Flat. Women on his staff? "Go away," he said to Mary Crowe, "you're wasting your time. And mine."

Mary Crowe went away, but the next day she came back. Again she was refused. Again she came back. Again she was turned down. Day after day this went on. Night after night, on her knees, Mary Crowe prayed for patience and persistence and the strength to follow her dream. She closed her mind to doubt. She would not let it in.

Finally the man in charge of hiring was impressed with her dogged determination. "All right," he said. "We'll take you on. But no salary. No drawing account. Commissions only. So go on out and starve."

Mary Crowe went out and started selling, door to door. People listened, because she made them feel that she was primarily interested in helping *them*—as indeed she was. And she didn't starve. Far from it. She became the number-one salesperson for that company. She became a member of the Million Dollar Round Table—the exclusive group of insurance agents who sell more than a million dollars' worth of insurance in a single year. She became a legend in the insurance business. She became, in other words, just what she had *imaged* herself to be—a stunning success.

Well, you may say, those are interesting stories, but they happened years ago. What about the modern world? What about the present day? Let me tell you about Harry DeCamp.

Imaging Helps Heal Harry DeCamp

Harry was also in the insurance business. Quite successful at it, too. But the day came when that success meant little because he was told that he had cancer of the bladder. Inoperable cancer. When he asked how much time he had to live, the doctors couldn't tell him. They gave him some painkillers and sent him home to die.

Harry had never been a very religious man. As he put it, "I had only a nodding acquaintance with God." He thought about praying, but he didn't know how. "I knew God was there," he said later, "but He was some mystical Being, far away. It didn't seem right to start begging after ignoring Him for so many years."

Then two things happened in rapid succession. Someone sent Harry a get-well card and wrote on it, "With God all things are possible" (Matthew 19:26). Somehow that phrase stuck in Harry's mind. It kept coming back to him. Then he picked up an inspirational magazine and read two stories in it. One was about a seriously injured soldier who recovered from near-fatal wounds by creating mental pictures of himself as a healthy, whole individual. The other story was by a cancer victim who claimed that total believing and total faith were the keys to answered prayer, that Christ meant exactly what He said when He told His followers, *"What things soever ye desire, when ye pray, believe that ye receive them, and ye shall have them"* (Mark 11:24, my italics).

Harry DeCamp was not a churchgoer, though he was a nominal believer. After much thought, he decided to believe with total conviction that God could do anything, and that constant prayer backed by real faith could put him in touch with the enormous healing power of the Almighty. In addition to that, he decided to visualize the healing process taking place in the most dramatic form that his imagination could supply.

He began to image armies of healing white blood cells in his body cascading down from his shoulders, sweeping through his veins, attacking the malignant cells and destroying them. A hundred times a day, two hundred, three hundred, he went through this imaging process. He worked at it constantly, day and night. "The images," he said later, "were just as clear as if they were coming in on our TV screen. I could see an army of white blood cells cascading down from my shoulders into my stomach, swirling around in my bladder, battling their way into my liver, my heart. Regiment after regiment they came, endlessly, the white corpuscles moving relentlessly on the cancer cells, moving in and devouring them! On and on the victorious white army swept, down into my legs and feet and toes, then to the top of my body, mopping up stray cancer cells as they went, until at last the battle was over. Day after day I replayed that battle scene in my mind. It made me feel terrific."

Harry DeCamp also kept on with his chemotherapy, although he was convinced he didn't need it. Six months later, when he went back for a checkup, the malignant mass was gone.

Which was responsible for Harry DeCamp's dramatic recovery—the chemotherapy or his intense imaging effort? Some modern physicians would say both. A noted cancer specialist, Dr. Carl Simonton, in conjunction with Dr. Stephanie Matthews-Simonton, has written a book called *Getting Well Again*, in which he expresses his conviction, based on experience with hundreds of cases, that we all participate, whether consciously or unconsciously, in determining our own health. Dr. Simonton is convinced that imaging is a powerful and effective tool available to victims of cancer or any other illness.

I Discover Imaging

Now I would like to tell you about a personal experience that happened to me many years ago. It was through this experience that I first came upon the powerful concept of imaging. And it happened in an unexpected manner.

Ruth and I had started a magazine called *Guideposts*, a spiritual, motivational publication. Beginning with only seven hundred dollars in working capital, the subscription list had risen to approximately forty thousand, but the financial situation had become difficult, in fact almost hopeless.

At this juncture, a meeting of the directors of the magazine was called as we were in imminent danger of being forced to discontinue the project. Present at this meeting was a wonderful lady named Tessie Durlack, from whom we received a dynamic and creative idea, one that changed the entire course of events. And, I might add, that same idea can change your life, too, as it did ours.

Tessie listened to our glum and dismal appraisal of the situation. We had hoped that she might follow an earlier substantial contribution with another monetary gift. But she quickly said she was going to give something much better than money, namely, a vital idea which in turn would lead to prosperity. "The situation," she said, "is that you lack everything—subscribers, equipment, capital. And why do you lack? Simply because you have been thinking in terms of lack. You have been imaging lack so, therefore, you have accordingly created a condition of lack. What you must do now, at once, is to firmly tell these lack thoughts or images to get out of your minds. You must start imaging prosperity instead."

Some of the directors objected that to mount a frontal attack on an unhealthy or negative thought pattern would not exorcise such thoughts but on the contrary would only serve to drive them more deeply into consciousness. Other directors added their opinion that we do not control our thoughts, but they control us. Seemingly disgusted by these expressions, Tessie snapped, "Don't you remember what the great Plato said?" I hadn't the slightest idea what the great Plato had said, but not wishing to reveal my ignorance I asked brightly, "To which of the many familiar statements of Plato do you refer?"

"To one you never heard of," she declared, and forthwith gave a quotation which she attributed to Plato. As I recall, it went something like this: " 'Take charge of your thoughts. You can do what you will with them.' So flush out these lack thoughts and do it now," she said. So then and there, we flushed them out, actually "seeing" them troop out of our minds.

She then explained that those lack ideas or visualizations were hanging around in the expectation that they would return soon to the perch in our minds where they had been hospitably entertained for so long. She declared that the only way they could be kept out permanently was by substituting a more powerful prosperity thought to displace them, an abundance or prosperity mental picture. She then asked how many subscribers were needed to guarantee a continuance of publishing and we agreed that one hundred thousand would do it. "All right," she said, "I want you to look out there mentally and see or visualize one hundred thousand persons as subscribers to *Guideposts*, people who have paid for their subscriptions."

Our visualizing was imperfect, to say the least, but she "saw" them, and so powerful was her imaging that we began to visualize them, too. Then, to our surprise, Tessie declared, "Now that we see them, we have them. Let us pray and thank the Lord that He has given us one hundred thousand subscribers." Rather astonished, we joined her in a prayer in which she asked the Lord for nothing, but instead thanked Him for everything in advance, including our one hundred thousand subscribers. In the course of her prayer she quoted that great Scripture, "What things soever ye desire, when ye pray, believe that ye receive them, and ye shall have them" (Mark 11:24).

She had no sooner said "Amen" than Ruth and I, now tremendously excited, looked to where a stack of unpaid bills had been put in front of our directors, fully expecting they would have disappeared. Apparently we thought the Lord might send down some sweet chariot to whisk them all away. But the Lord, when He wants to change a situation, has a better method. He changes people, and changed people change situations.

And that is precisely what happened in this instance. Our hitherto discouraged directors came alive and began to come up with new ideas at a lively rate. Of course, 90 percent of them were not workable, but 10 percent were valid, and in no time at all the bills began to melt away and subscriptions poured in. Today *Guideposts* has not 100,000 subscribers but 3,600,000, and is read monthly by 12 million persons, making it the fourteenth largest magazine in the United States.

This incident and the demonstration of the projected image as a basic law of mind was one of the highlights of our learning experience. Ruth and I at once became aware of the incredible possibilities in the imaging process. We realized the truth that if a person persistently images failure, life will try its best to develop that picture as fact. But if one images success, it will similarly strongly tend to develop that image as fact. From that time until the present, we have studied the principle of imaging and worked with it, testing it in many demonstrations of actual experience under varied circumstances. We have come to the conclusion that this technique is effective in just about all the important areas of living. It is one of the great principles of creative living and is the theme of this book. It must be kept in mind, however, that imaging is not a magic formula that simply, by some kind of mental trick, brings desired results. In an amazing way, it does open doors to problem solving and to goal achievement. But once those doors are open there must be discipline, determination, patience, and persistence if the problem is to be solved or the dream is to become reality. In this way you will find, as we have, that what you can image you can be.

2

HOW THE IMAGING IDEA GREW

IMAGING SURROUNDS US EVERY moment of our lives; we're exposed to its power from the moment we're born. If a parent is a doctor or a lawyer or a soldier and wants a child to follow in his footsteps, that parental image or dream is bound to have some effect on the growing child. Not a decisive influence, perhaps, because at first the image is only in the mind of the parent. But an influence, nevertheless.

In my own case, my decision to leave the newspaper field after a year as a reporter and study for the ministry was a reflection of my mother's imaging that some day I would become a preacher, like my father. As intensely as only a mother can, she *imaged* me as a *preacher*. She reinforced that image with fervent prayer, and a minister is what I became.

So the images that other people hold of us do impinge on our lives. But the images that affect us most strongly are the *self*-images that we develop as we move through the years. Sometimes these images are positive and strong; sometimes they're negative and weak. I know that as a youngster in various small midwestern towns, I had some pretty negative self-images, only I didn't call them that. I'm not sure the term "inferiority complex" had been invented yet, but if an inferiority complex means a whole nest of inadequacy feelings, that is what I had.

Where did they come from? I'm not at all sure. My father and mother were both unusually able, strong-minded, outspoken individuals. Maybe somehow I felt that I'd never quite measure up to them, or to their ambitions for me. Or maybe it had something to do with my physique, which was slender and lightweight. I was almost frail compared to my younger brother Bob, who was a rough, tough football player. Perhaps I equated being skinny with being inadequate in other ways. Anyway, it bothered me a great deal, and no matter how hard I tried to gain weight, nothing seemed to help.

Another thing bothered me, as it has bothered the children of clergymen from time immemorial, was the fact that I was a "preacher's kid." Growing up in those small towns, as I did, I resented this label. I had the feeling that people expected me to be a goody-goody, that adults would condemn me if I wasn't and my friends would despise me if I was. So this left me tense and overconcerned about the impression I made on other people.

There was still another thing that may have reinforced my image of myself as an inadequate person. If a guest came to the house or a minister came to call, as was the custom among church families, it was the duty of the children of the family to play the piano or recite a poem or otherwise "perform" for the visitors. This ordeal filled me with absolute horror. Whenever I saw guests arriving, I would try to hide. On one occasion, my Uncle Will removed me from the woodshed, where I had taken refuge, and dragged me to the front parlor where, like an early Christian martyr being thrown to the lions, I was compelled to recite "The boy stood on the burning deck," or as much of it as my state of near paralysis would permit.

The result of all these factors was that when I got to college and had to get up occasionally in class and give answers, I acted like what I was: the possessor of a huge inferiority complex.

This self-image of inadequacy might have gone on indefinitely had it not been for something a professor—Ben Arnesson was his name—said to me during my sophomore year. One day after I had made a miserable showing, he told me to wait after class. Then, when we were alone, he said some things that were tough and true and to the point.

He said that I had a reasonably good mind, but that I was not making adequate use of it by being so hesitant and bashful. "How long are you going to be like this," he demanded, "a scared rabbit afraid of the sound of your own voice? You probably excuse yourself by thinking that you're just naturally shy. Well, you'd better change the way you think about yourself, Peale, and you'd better do it now, before it's too late. If you're not able to do it by yourself, if you need help—well, you're a minister's son. You ought to know where to turn. That's all. You may go now."

To this day I remember the emotions that roared through me as I left that classroom and went out into the sunshine that lay like a golden rug across the quiet campus. I was angry, I was resentful, I was hurt, but most of all I was frightened because I knew that what the professor had said was true. A scared rabbit! How far would I get in life if I kept on seeing myself as a scared rabbit?

Life-Changing Experience

I sat down on the steps of the chapel and prayed the deepest, most desperate prayer of my whole life. "Please help me," I prayed. "Please change me. I know You can do it because I've seen You make drunkards sober and turn thieves into honest men. Please take away these inferiority feelings that are holding me back. Take away this awful shyness and self-consciousness. Let me see myself, not as a scared rabbit, but as someone who can do great things in my life because You are with me, giving me the strength and confidence I need."

I don't know how long I sat there on the chapel steps, but when I got up something had changed. Of course the inferiority feelings weren't all gone; I still have some of them to this day. But the *image* I had had of myself was changed—and with it the course of my whole life.

As the years went by, I began using imaging techniques whenever I wanted to achieve a certain goal. In my second little church, located in Brooklyn, New York, attendance was low; in fact one day I found the sexton dragging one of the back pews out of the building. When I asked him why, he said he was going to chop it up for firewood. "No one sits in it anyway," he explained.

"Put it back," I told him grimly. "Somebody is going to sit in it!" I visualized that pew full, and all the other pews full, and the church filled to capacity. I held that image in my mind. I worked for it with every ounce of strength I had. I made it part of my innovative thinking. And the day came when the image became a reality.

Now and then my old feelings of being inadequate would come back to haunt me, but usually I was lucky enough to discover an image of success that was stronger than my image of failure. One Memorial Day, I remember there was a mass meeting sponsored by the American Legion. Fifty thousand people crowded into Brooklyn's Prospect Park, where the guest of honor was General Theodore Roosevelt, Jr. I had been invited, I thought, merely to open the meeting with a prayer. But when I got there I found that my name was listed on the program as the main speaker.

A wave of panic swept over me. I had no speech prepared. The thought of standing there before fifty thousand people and disappointing them terrified me. I went to the sponsors of the gathering and told them that I couldn't do it. I wouldn't do it. They would have to find somebody else.

General Roosevelt overheard my lamentations. "Son," he said to me, "stop focusing on failure. You're a minister, aren't you? Here you have a chance to minister to all these grieving mothers. You can tell them how much we love them for the sacrifice they've made. You can tell them how proud this country is of the sons and husbands they lost. So get up there and talk, and I'm going to sit right behind you and visualize you loving these people and helping them and holding them spellbound for the next twenty minutes. I have a picture of this in my mind, and it's so strong that I know it's going to happen!"

So, shamed into it, I tried to do as he said. And his image of my succeeding must have been stronger than mine of failure, because the talk went pretty well. Afterward, I remember, General Roosevelt said to me, "Now, you see, if you think you can, or somebody who believes in you thinks you can, why, then you can!"

Perhaps the idea of the power of positive thinking was conveyed to me right then and there. But behind that idea, and in it, and beyond it was the concept of imaging—holding the *image* of yourself succeeding, visualizing it so vividly that when the desired success comes, it seems to be merely echoing a reality that has already existed in your mind.

I didn't grasp that concept fully then, but I kept on using it. In 1927, when I was called to a big church in Syracuse, New York, I met the same problems I had encountered in Brooklyn. Church debts. Low attendance. The sexton actually kept a tall ladder stretched across some of the empty pews in the balcony because it was the easiest place to store it. "Take it away," I told him. "I see that balcony filled with people, not ladders." And in time, it was.

Imaging was involved in our solution to the church-debt problem, too. The debt was fifty-five thousand dollars. It seems small by present standards, but it was a large sum for those days, and it had been on the books for quite a while. I didn't think we could raise enough money to pay off the whole debt; that seemed too optimistic. But I thought we might raise perhaps twenty thousand dollars. And with this in mind I went to see a member of our congregation, a colorful old gentleman named Harlowe B. Andrews.

Brother Andrews, as we called him, was the wholesale grocer who had the reputation of being the smartest businessman in Syracuse. He had the Midas touch; whenever he put out his hand, money just sprang into it. I figured Brother Andrews would contribute something and might tell me how to get the rest.

Brother Andrews lived all alone in an old-fashioned house in the country. So I drove out and told him we were trying to raise twenty thousand dollars to reduce the debt. I also hopefully asked him how much he might care to contribute.

Brother Andrews looked at me over the half-moon glasses that he wore far down on his nose. "Why," he said, "that's easy. Since you are not going to raise the whole debt I will give nothing. Not a nickel. Not a cent." He studied my face for a minute. Then he said, "But I'll tell you what I will do. I'll pray with you."

That didn't fill me with any burning enthusiasm. It wasn't prayer I was after. It was cold, hard cash. But we got down on our knees, and Brother Andrews spoke very freely to the Lord.

An Unforgettable Prayer

This was his prayer: "Lord, here we are. We have to raise some money. Lord, this young minister means well, but he doesn't know the first thing about business or how to do things in a big way. He has little faith. He doesn't really believe in himself or in his ministry. Now, Lord, if he is only going to try to raise twenty thousand dollars, I won't give him a nickel, but if he will believe he can raise the whole fifty-five thousand dollars, I'll give him the first five thousand. Amen."

As that prayer ended, I was pretty excited. I said to Brother Andrews, "Where are we going to get the rest of it?"

He said, "Where you just got the first five thousand. You prayed for it and you got it. Now let's get down to business. There's a doctor downtown who will tell you that he hasn't any money, but I'm on the finance committee at the bank and I know exactly how much he's got. So we're going to pray that he will give you the next five thousand dollars. We'll not only pray, we'll visualize him doing it. The Bible says that if you have faith even as a grain of mustard seed, nothing is impossible for you. So go downtown and see that doctor and ask for that money and get it!"

I went downtown full of qualms and saw the doctor and asked him for a contribution of five thousand dollars. He looked at me and said, "Why, that's preposterous! That's absurd!" Then he was silent for a while. Finally he said, "Well, I can't explain it, but something comes over me as we're sitting here. I'll give you the five thousand dollars."

I jumped in my car, drove back to Brother Andrews's house, and burst in on him. "He did it! He did it!" I cried.

"Why, sure he did," said Brother Andrews. "Listen, son, I sat here all the time you were driving downtown *not* believing he would do it and I just sent a thought hovering over you all the way down there that he *would* do it, and my thought hit him right between the eyes."

I exclaimed, "You know, I saw it hit him!"

He said, "It penetrated his brain and it changed his thinking. But this should change your thinking, too. Just remember, when you want to achieve something, hold in your mind the picture of yourself achieving it. Paint in all the details. Make it as real as you possibly can. And remember this, too: You're never defeated by anything until you accept in your mind the thought that you are defeated. You are never defeated until you accept the image of defeat."

Brother Andrews, you see, understood the difference between positive and negative imaging. He was telling me that you can image victory, or you can image defeat. You can program yourself one way or the other.

In years gone by, a few people had grasped the concept of imaging and were talking or writing about it, although no one seemed to call it by that name. A French psychologist named Coué advised people to say to themselves constantly, "Every day in every way I'm getting better and better." Some people considered this a silly form of mental gymnastics— lifting yourself by your own bootstraps—nothing more. But there was something to it. I, myself, once heard Coué lecture. To illustrate the power of imagination, he asked the audience to visualize a plank six inches wide and twenty feet long laid across the living-room floor.

Anyone could walk it with ease and confidence. Then he asked us to imagine the same plank stretched between two buildings one hundred feet in the air. Imagination—in this case the image of falling—would make walking it almost impossible.

A woman named Dorothea Brande wrote a best-seller called *Wake Up and Live*. In it she gave a formula for successful living that she had stumbled upon almost by accident. The formula was this: In whatever you attempt, *act as if it were impossible to fail*. This was just another way of saying *image yourself succeeding*.

When I moved from Syracuse, New York, to the Marble Collegiate Church in New York City, this grand old center of worship, with a history going back to 1628, had fallen upon difficult times. The gloom and fear of the Great Depression of the 1930s were everywhere. Only a handful of worshipers were in the pews. It wasn't easy to create and hold an image of a dynamic church filled to capacity with enthusiastic people. But I knew that was what I had to do.

The night I was installed as minister there was a ceremony of great dignity and solemnity. My parents were there, of course. Later, when we walked out into the rainy night, my mother stopped suddenly, put her hand against one of the great marble buttresses of the church, and began to weep. "This old church is so solid," she said, "so strong. You've got to keep it that way, Norman. Tonight it was filled with people hungry for love, searching for guidance. You've got to give them those things, meet those needs. If you do, your church will always be full."

I was deeply moved, and never forgot those words. I took them then as a reminder of a responsibility, which of course they were. But what my mother also did was implant in me a strong subliminal picture of people seeking something, of people coming to the church to find it. She gave me a vivid picture of a church filled with warmth and joy and vitality. That's what I "saw" with my inner eye and that's what I have tried ever since to bring to reality.

There have been moments of discouragement, of course. But it's odd how, almost always, someone steps forward to renew the image of better results. I remember one night when I gave what I thought was a really terrible sermon. Nobody told me it was bad, but they didn't have to—I knew it was a flop. I slunk out of the church and walked along Fifth Avenue in a state of total despondency. I didn't even want to go home, because I knew my wife, Ruth, would try to cheer me up and I felt I didn't deserve it.

I Apply for a Job

On lower Fifth Avenue near Twelfth Street was a drugstore run by a man named A.E. Russ, a member of the church and a good friend of mine. The lights were still on, and through the window I could see my friend behind the soda fountain. So I went inside and slumped down on one of the stools, looking as dejected as I felt. When Mr. Russ asked what was bothering me, I told him. "I'm in the wrong profession," I said. "I'll never be a decent preacher. How about a job as soda jerk?"

"Mix me a strawberry soda," said A.E., smiling. "Maybe I'll give you a job."

So, in an effort to lighten my gloom, I went behind the counter, squirted strawberry syrup into a glass as I had seen him do, added ice cream and soda, and handed it to him. He took a sip and made a face. "Better stick to preaching!" he said.

But then he grew serious. "Time to close up," he said. "Why don't you come home with me and talk for a while?"

I went along with him because he was one of those people who project warmth and caring spontaneously, and I needed him. He told me not to worry about one bad sermon, or two, or three, or four. "They'll happen sometimes," he said. "Nothing to get despondent about. Don't focus on that. Focus on people and the needs they have."

There was a photograph of his wife on the table and he nodded toward it. "It was rough when I lost her, but some of the things you've said in church helped me a lot. You've helped in other ways, too, maybe without even knowing it. You've pulled me through some trying times. And that's what it's all about, Norman. Meeting needs. Helping people. So you just keep on trying. Don't worry if a sermon goes sour now and then. Just reach out and help people, and that church will always be full."

So there it was again, the image of a great church actualizing itself. Full of people trying to find a wonderful way of life.

I remember one other time when the imaging process worked in a dramatic fashion. It was a stormy Sunday night in Manhattan. Wind howled around the corners of the skyscrapers, sending sheets of rain mixed with sleet swirling along the streets. I was scheduled to talk, as usual, at the evening service. As Ruth and I drove slowly down to Twenty-ninth from Eighty-fourth Street, I became more and more agitated because I was convinced I would be talking to nothing but empty pews.

"This is awful," I said to Ruth. "Terrible. Nobody in their right mind will come out in this weather." I kept on in this negative fashion for block after block. Finally, Ruth could stand it no longer. She pulled the car over to the curb and parked in the drumming rain. "What's the matter with you?" she demanded. "You're always preaching optimism and positive thinking. Now you're just thinking about yourself and whether or not you'll have a large audience." She pointed at the tall apartment houses around us, gray in the rain, the yellow lights of windows shining dully. "Why don't you think about all the people in those apartment houses? Lonely people, hurting people, people who need the message you have to give them? Why don't you visualize them streaming into the church, filling every pew, bringing their needs and their problems, finding solutions? Let's pray about this right now, right here. Let's ask for the church to be full, not to buttress your pride, but so you have people to help. Let's *see* it full, and give thanks that it will be full!"

Somewhat abashed, I nodded. So we sat and held hands and prayed and imaged, visualized. Then we drove on down to the church and—what do you know—we couldn't find a parking space. "Wouldn't you think," I complained to Ruth, "that the pastor of a church could at least have a parking space?"

We finally found one, walked back two blocks through the rain, and the church was jammed, wall to wall, with people still coming, just the way my mother and A.E. Russ had imaged it so many years earlier—and as we had imaged it, reinforcing our image with prayer.

Can it be argued that the church would have been full anyway that night? Of course it can. But who knows how many people who were hesitant or dubious about going felt a sudden impulse to go? Remember what old Harlowe B. Andrews said of that doctor up in Syracuse: "I saw the idea fly in there and penetrate his head and lodge right there in his mind!"

Let the skeptics have their doubts. I prefer to believe that ideas do have wings!

3

THE CONCEPT THAT CONQUERS PROBLEMS

IN MY POCKET AS I write these words is a card I always carry with me. It came to me many years ago, and I have it retyped occasionally because it gets ragged and worn. On it are five lines, as follows:

The light of God surrounds me
The love of God enfolds me
The power of God protects me
The presence of God watches over me
Wherever I am, God is!

Why do I carry this card? Because the image that it evokes of a loving, caring God is the perfect antidote to fear, to worry, to anxiety, to just about every problem under the sun. Whenever I'm troubled, I take that card out and let it remind me that there is an all-powerful Being in the universe who loves me and who is only a prayer away.

This is the greatest concept that the human mind can hold. The more intensely you image it, the happier you are going to be, because you will never feel abandoned or alone. That's what religion is all about, that's what churches are all about, that's what Christ came to teach us—that the love of God is available to us uncertain, groping, unsure human beings, all the time, no matter where we may be.

Sometimes, of course, people refuse to accept this wonderful message of reassurance and hope. I have in my library a book entitled *God Is Able* by a former New York City colleague of mine, Dr. John Ellis Large, who was for some years rector of the Church of the Heavenly Rest on upper Fifth Avenue. Dr. Large is a man of much experience in the healing ministry, and in his book he tells of the case of a man named George. This man's wife, Sarah, was one of Dr. Large's parishioners, although she never came to church or had anything to do with the religious life of the church except when she got into trouble.

One day she came to see him and said, "Dr. Large, I shouldn't take your time. I've been on your church rolls, but I'm what is commonly known as 'dead wood.' But," she said, "I have a real problem. It's my husband. He isn't well. He's irritable, he's irascible, he's full of tension, he's on edge all the time. He's a disappointed, frustrated, unhappy man, and he's developed all sorts of symptoms of poor health. He has gone to the doctor, and the doctor says there isn't anything really wrong with him that wouldn't be straightened out if he got his life in order.

"I've tried to talk to him about it," she continued, "but he just ignores me. It's very difficult. He misses one promotion after another at the office. All the men he started out with in his company have moved ahead faster than he. And this fills him with indignation and resentment. I talked with his boss. He said, 'George is contentious, he is not cooperative, he doesn't play ball, he has no enthusiasm and at times he's full of downright meanness.' "

So Dr. Large suggested to this troubled wife, "Why don't you bring your husband to see me?"

"He would never come," she replied. "He has no use for you or any minister or for the church. I can't even get him to pray with me. He says he is fed up with God. He says he doubts there really is a God."

"Well then," said Dr. Large, "let's give him some treatment at home." And he asked her this unexpected question: "What are your husband's sleeping habits?"

"He tosses most of the night," she said, "wears himself out groaning and moaning, but by about five o'clock in the morning he is in deep sleep. I have to wake him up to get him to the office."

"All right," the rector said, "I'll tell you what to do. At five o'clock every morning you get up and sit by your husband and pray for him. Believe that Jesus Christ is there by your husband's side, actually present with you and with him. Image your husband as a whole man—happy, controlled, organized and well. Hold that thought intensely. Think of your prayers as reaching his unconscious mind. At that time in the morning his conscious mind is not resisting and you can get an idea into his unconscious. Visualize him as kindly, cooperative, happy, creative and enthusiastic."

"Why," she exclaimed, "I never heard anything like that before!"

"Well, it's time you did," he told her. "Now go and do it."

She said afterward that she soon got so she didn't need an alarm clock. She would wake up promptly at 5:00 A.M. and hover over her husband in the company of Christ, projecting these thoughts and prayers into his unconscious. For many weeks nothing seemed to happen, but finally George said to her one day, "You know, it's strange how nice everybody has become—people I used to think were hating me and double-crossing me. What's come over them? They're all so nice. Everything is so different."

Some days later he came to her when he got home from work and said, "What do you know! The boss told me today that he is making me a division manager. I asked him why in the world he would do that. And he said, 'Because of the great change in you. You're happy, you're cooperative, you play ball, you're enthusiastic—you're becoming one of the best men we have.' "

His wife never did tell him how he was reached. But the disorder left him. The power of Jesus Christ is very subtle and very skillful. No wonder the multitudes two thousand years ago sought to touch Him, because the power that came out of Him healed them. And today, twenty centuries later, He is still the greatest healer among all the great healers of the world.

Whenever some deeply troubled person comes to me, I try to plant in his or her mind this image of a loving God who, in the Person of Jesus Christ, is a constant companion. "Picture Jesus sitting there beside you in the pew," I sometimes say to the members of my congregation. "When you leave the church, visualize Him walking out with you, strong, compassionate, protective, understanding. Take Him with you into your home. Take Him with you when you go to work tomorrow. And don't think this is some romantic daydream or pious flight of fancy, because He *is* there. He said He would be with us unto the end of the world, and He meant exactly what He said."

Frightened or unhappy people almost always respond to this message. I remember a night years ago—it was during the Korean War— when a phone call awakened me from a sound sleep. It was from a young woman obviously in great distress. She said her soldier husband was overseas in an area where there was heavy fighting. She was afraid he wouldn't survive and come back to her. Her fears had crowded in on her in the dead of night until they seemed overwhelming. "I called you," she sobbed, "because I go to your church sometimes. I don't know where to turn. I don't know what to do."

When something unexpected like this happens, I always say a quick, silent prayer, asking for guidance in what I'm about to say. This time, as I said my prayer, I thought I heard, through the telephone, sounds made by a small baby. So the dialogue between us went something like this:

"Is that your baby that I hear?"

"Yes."

"Is it a boy or a girl?"

"It's a girl."

"Is your baby frightened?"

"No, I'm the one who's afraid."

"Why isn't your baby frightened?"

"I don't know."

"It's because you're with her, isn't it? You love her. The baby knows it. You're there with her."

"But the baby doesn't know what's going on."

"Perhaps not. But she can feel your arms around her, and that makes her feel safe. And that's what you have to do: become like a little child yourself. You have a loving Father, you know. He's with you right now. Picture His arms around you, protective, strong. Be like that baby of yours. Relax—and trust. Do you think you can do that?"

"Well, I can try," she said, and she did sound calmer.

"And one more thing," I said to her. "Thoughts can influence events in ways that no one fully understands. So instead of sending out these fear thoughts, pray for your husband's safe return, with love and hope and confidence. And strongly image him returning safe and sound. Thank God in advance for keeping him safe and bringing him back to you. See him coming through the door, smiling, happy and home again. Hold that image, day and night. We'll say a prayer together now. Then go back to sleep, picturing yourself cradled in the peace and security of the everlasting arms."

Months later that young couple came up to me at the church and introduced themselves. The young soldier thanked me for helping his wife through that midnight crisis. And the young woman told me that she had never really known or felt the nearness of her Heavenly Father until then.

That young woman's problem was the most basic of all problems— fear that threatened her emotional stability until it was driven out by a concept even more powerful: faith in the goodness and nearness of a loving God. As the old saying puts it:

> Fear knocked at the door.
> Faith answered.
> No one was there.

The Biggest Problems Can Be Solved

You are greater than anything that can happen to you. This is a basic fact about human beings and their problems. In big and terrifying crises, people find within themselves a power and a strength and also a wisdom they had no idea they possessed. Of course we believe that these resources come from God, who created every person and who is resident in human nature as well as in the natural world. We also believe that since the Kingdom of God is within all of us, the solutions to problems are also within us. The assumption makes sense.

A woman named Peggy Paul, in her early forties, faced a problem—a really tough problem. Terminal cancer, they called it. But she won a victory over it, according to her story in the Tampa *Tribune* of March 8, 1981, in an article by Tom Berndt. Since a successful application of imaging is documented in this remarkable article, we will give a brief rundown on her handling of the difficult problem that was hers. We follow the newspaper story closely in relating this woman's experience.

There is a striking similarity with that of Harry DeCamp mentioned in chapter 1, except that the use of imaging by Mr. DeCamp was instinctive and without any previous knowledge that any such technique existed. Also in the case of Mr. DeCamp there was a strong spiritual factor. This is not mentioned in that of Peggy Paul, so we must assume the religious element was not involved in her cure. Nor had Harry DeCamp ever heard at that time of the work of the Doctors Simonton.

Ms. Paul was, and is, so we understand, under the care of distinguished physicians, who employed chemotherapy, but as her condition deteriorated and she became fatalistic in outlook, a small incident, the gift of a tray on which were inscribed the words "Don't Quit," coupled with a statement by a nurse that she did not have to die simply because she was told that she was terminal, stirred up her will to live and her will to fight. It was then that she came upon the self-help techniques suggested in the Simonton book *Getting Well Again*. The Simontons, as we understand their viewpoint, believe that psychological forces such as unhappiness and emotional despair are prominent in the development of cancer and conversely the elimination of these factors is important in the cure of the disease.

The immune system or the immunity power of the body seems to be greatly affected by the mental level of unhappiness and emotional distress. The Simontons apparently hold this view and their effort is to develop a joyous and positive life-style to counteract the deleterious effect of negative emotions. Relaxation and visualization are evidently basic in their method. The patient is encouraged to image the white cells in the immune system of the body along with administered drugs, chemotherapy, and other forms of medical treatment involved in the effort, as destroying the malignant cells.

According to the article, Ms. Paul adopted the routine of relaxation and an untensing procedure, meanwhile imaging the progressive destruction of the unhealthy cells by the healthy and powerful white cells. Instead of Mr. DeCamp's method of imaging an army of white cells doing battle with the unhealthy cancer cells, Peggy Paul has her own technique, but one that has also proved effective. She begins by picture the drug she is receiving in chemotherapy as having the power to break off cancer cells from any tumor and turn them into highly visible orange food, which is then swallowed up by her white blood cells, which she envisions as being rabbits.

She envisions rabbits for a good reason, says Peggy Paul. Rabbits reproduce freely, so there are always lots of them around. And they are always very hungry so they naturally eat lots of their favorite food, the orange-colored cancer cells.

Since the cancer cells can be anywhere in her body, this patient visualizes her hungry rabbits/white blood cells going through her blood-stream everywhere, seeking out and eating the orange food/cancer cells until no more food can be found.

"I need to make sure that there aren't any cancer cells coming to rest in my chest or anywhere else. So I have my rabbits/white blood cells going up and down my arms and through my whole body, my brain and everywhere. But when they get to my liver area, they really concentrate," she says.

She is said to have also reorganized her positive goals and life priorities. She visualized the battle for health as being gradually won, mean-while continuing under regular medical treatment. "Finally," says the article, "twenty-two months after her liver cancer was diagnosed, a fourth liver scan confirmed what Ms. Paul had imaged for so long, the tumor in her liver had indeed shrunk. The scan came back with normal results."

It is significant that this patient, rescued from death, thinks that, in the total process of recovery from a malignant condition, her new under-standing and control of problems is an important factor. She is quoted as saying, "Today I can tell you that I think the fact that I had this disas-trous disease was fortuitous for me. It made me look at myself, it has given me an opportunity to reassess my life's direction and to make goals I have never thought about making before. It also settled a lot of resent-ment and anger that I had. I was able to resolve those problems and to feel much more secure about who I am in the universe and where I stand. I'm delighted about that."

Peggy Paul, so we are told, gives to all who show an interest a card on which are printed the words "Whatever your mind can conceive and believe, and your heart desire, you can achieve."

And so imaging gave new life to one who could indeed conceive and believe. This is a powerful process but it doesn't have to be a compli-cated process. Sometimes a simple mental picture can help you get rid of your troubles. I had a letter the other day from a man who said his life had been plagued by all sorts of worries and fears. Then one evening he heard me on the radio giving a talk on the importance of emptying the mind of doubts and apprehensions and negative thoughts. It happened that at that particular moment he was holding in his hand a glass filled with a popular soft drink, clear and carbonated and cold. As he listened to my talk he looked at the glass and noticed the bubbles rising from the bottom, one by one, moving up through the liquid, reaching the surface, then breaking and disappearing into nothingness.

He said that the parallel struck him so forcibly that he decided then and there that this was the image he would hold in his mind during the day, and especially at night before falling asleep: the image of his worries and fears, like the bubbles, coming from deep within him, rising to the surface and breaking into nothingness. He added that he had tried this technique and "already it is working wonders."

Not a bad idea! If worries make you sleepless, image them as nothing but insubstantial bubbles, and let trust float them away.

Ruth and I feel that trying to help people solve their difficulties is perhaps the most exciting and rewarding thing we do. Day after day the phones ring and the mail pours into our offices from people with every kind of problem under the sun: health problems, money problems, personality problems. Each call, each letter reveals some negative aspect of life that is holding someone back from happiness. "I have a boss who doesn't like me." Or a wife who nags me. Or a husband who is unfaithful. Or a conscience that troubles me. Or a child who defies me. Or a weight problem. Or a drinking problem. On and on. Everywhere, problems. Everywhere, people struggling to solve them.

Half a century of trying to relieve people in distress has left Ruth and me convinced of three things.

1. *Every human being has an enormous problem-solving potential built into him or her*. It's only when that potential is blocked or weakened by defeatist attitudes or negative emotions that problems seem unsolvable or overwhelming.

2. *Problems are an essential and necessary ingredient of life*. They can actually be good for you, although they may be painful at the time. All worthwhile achievements are the result of problem solving. Problem solvers are strong people *because* they struggle to overcome difficulties or adversities. And the reverse is true: People who never have to face problems get soft, mentally and spiritually, just as people who never exercise get flabby physically. When I hear some troubled person cry, "Why does God let this happen to me?" I often feel like saying, "Because He knows you'll grow and be strengthened if you grapple with your difficulty; He *made* you that way!"

3. *The basic tools of problem solving are available to anyone*. One of the most effective is this technique of imaging. Anybody can experiment with it. There's nothing very difficult about it. And, as I hope to show in subsequent chapters, it can be applied to just about any problem under the sun.

One cautionary word, though, right here at the start. Make the Lord a silent partner in all forms of imaging, because He is the touchstone that will keep your desires on the high plane of morality where they belong. Imaging can be applied to unworthy goals as well as worthy ones. Praying about goals is essential, because if there are any selfish aims or sinful motives, they will appear as you pray. Pray to be sure your goal is right, for if it isn't right it is wrong, and nothing that is wrong ever turned out right.

A wise man once said, "Be very careful what you wish for, because you may get it." That applies to imaging even more forcefully: if you image something long enough and hard enough, you *will* get it.

I remember a somber story of misused imaging that my psychiatrist friend Dr. Smiley Blanton once told me without mentioning any names. A famous Hollywood producer came to him, Smiley said, because things were going so badly in his life. He said he had lost his grip, his career had fallen apart, he couldn't sleep, he was miserably unhappy, and so on.

Finally the inner story emerged. The producer had met an attractive young actress who was trying to get started in films. It was the old story. Although he was married, he decided to have an affair with her. The girl had scruples and resisted, but the producer was a persuasive and determined man, willing to use the power of his position. Also, he was aware of the power of imaging, and he used it to visualize the whole course of the seduction: buildup, timing, setting—he planned it like one of his scenarios. The outcome was just as he imaged it.

But then the girl came to him and told him that she was pregnant. She thought he loved her, perhaps enough to get a divorce and marry her. Instead, he told her to go and have an abortion. She went back to her apartment and took a fatal dose of sleeping pills, leaving a note that implicated the producer. Even in jaded Hollywood, it was a scandal. The man's career was ruined.

So never fail to hold your imaging goals up to the light before you set about achieving them.

In the remaining sections of this book, which we have worked on together, Ruth and I plan to take some of the most common problems that plague and challenge human beings and show how imaging can be used to help solve them. Before you move on to those sections, here's a simple imaging technique that you may find helpful if some stubborn problem is harassing you or troubling you. Take thirty seconds right now and picture yourself taking command over that problem. See yourself solving it, overcoming it, moving beyond it into a realm of confidence where other problems will be met and mastered as they arise.

Then take three long, deep breaths and exhale slowly after each one.

As you take the first one, say to yourself, "I'm breathing in confidence; I'm breathing out fear."

With the second: "I'm breathing in power; I'm breathing out weakness."

With the third: "I'm breathing in victory over my problem (name it); I'm breathing out defeat."

Then as you turn the page, visualize new confidence and determination flowing into you. You *can* take control of your problems. You *can* take command of your life. This book about imaging is designed to help you do it—and it will!

4

HOW IMAGING HELPS TO BOLSTER A SHAKY EGO

DR. SMILEY BLANTON, FAMOUS psychiatrist and one of the wisest men I've ever known, used to say that day in and day out the most common problem he was called upon to deal with in his patients was lack of self-esteem. Most of the people who consulted him, Smiley said, were deficient in self-love. They had a poor opinion—that is to say, a poor image—of themselves. And this great doctor, who knew the Bible backward and forward, always referred such people to the second great commandment: "Thou shalt love thy neighbor *as thyself*" (Matthew 22:39, my italics).

"There it is," Dr. Smiley Blanton would say. "Plain as the nose on your face. Love is the answer to all human ills. But the Bible says here"—and he would thrust the Book right into the patient's hands—"that you can't love anyone properly as long as you despise or downgrade yourself. Look! There it is, right there. See? Right there!"

Inferiority complex: how would you define it? I think I'd say it was timidity in the presence of life. And Smiley was right: it is very common. I have found in my own counseling experience that often the most outwardly confident and aggressive people are using that apparent confidence as a mask for deep doubts about themselves and their ability to cope with the challenges and problems of living.

It's a paradox, really. God made a masterpiece when He created human beings. The Bible says we rank just a little lower than the angels, which is pretty high on the scale of things. It says He crowned us with glory and honor. Now you'd think that a creature made in God's image would be pretty sure of himself, wouldn't you? But all too often he's not. Something holds him back from the belief in himself that makes for happiness. And—as anyone who suffers from a sense of inferiority will tell you—when a person's inner image of himself drops below a certain level, the result is pure misery.

It's almost as if there were two separate, warring entities inside each of us: the strong and the weak, the bold and the fearful, the large and the small. Each of us has a "big me" and a "little me" inside, and many times the "little me" frustrates and paralyzes the "big me."

I remember reading some years ago about the famous Italian tenor Enrico Caruso, surely one of the greatest masters of song ever to step onto a stage. In later life, his confidence was enormous, but at the beginning of his career he was unsure and uncertain.

One opening night at the opera, Caruso was standing in the wings waiting to go on when he was seized by an overwhelming attack of stage fright. His throat became constricted. Perspiration poured from him. He was actually shaking with fear.

Then the stagehands nearby were astonished to hear him say, in a whispered command. "Out! You miserable 'little me,' get out of my way! Out! Out!"

By a tremendous effort of will, Caruso was changing his self-image. He was saying to the fearful, timid element inside of him that the strong, positive element inside him must prevail, would prevail, and in the face of this fierce counterattack, the "little me" shrank away. He went onstage, where he sang with the beauty and power that were characteristic of the great Caruso. At the end, the audience surged up, shouting "Bravo!" Were they applauding the skill of a great artist? Yes, but perhaps intuitively they were acclaiming something more—the man who brought the "big me" out of himself by overcoming the fears and frustrations of the "little me."

I told that story one time to a young wife who came to consult me. She was upset and frightened. Her husband was under consideration for a promotion, an important one. But it was the custom of that particular company to have a party at which top executives had a chance to observe the employee under social conditions. Wives were always asked to this affair, because the company believed, quite rightly, that a man and his wife are an inseparable team—when you deal with one you are dealing with the other.

I said to this young woman, "Why are you so concerned? You are able to handle yourself."

"Oh, Dr. Peale," she said, and her eyes were actually full of tears, "all those other wives have been to colleges like Smith or Vassar or Wellesley. I never got past high school. They'll talk about things I'm not familiar with. I just know I'll be so tense I'll say or do something dumb and ruin Jim's chances for this promotion. I can't bring myself to go, and yet I can't refuse to go. Oh, what shall I do?"

Timidity, you see, timidity even in the presence of a routine situation.

I said to her, "Look, you're a very pretty girl; you dress well; you have honesty and your own quiet charm. Don't worry about those wives from Wellesley. They don't know all that much, anyway. Just be yourself. The trouble with a lot of people is that they always try to copy somebody else. If the Creator wanted us all to be alike, He would have made us that way.

You are the only person in the world like you. Think of that: millions of people and only one like you! You are unique and very special. So you just walk into that party and be yourself, your own attractive self. Mix right in with those people and you will shake off this inferiority complex. Go among them saying to yourself, 'I can do all things through Christ who strengthens me.' Just image yourself as charming, natural, and likable and you will come off okay."

Then I told her the Caruso story, and finally she went away a little less frightened, a little less tense, a little more hopeful, and later I heard that the party went very well. Her husband got the promotion.

But there are millions of people who don't know how to shake off doubts and fears, millions who crawl through life on their hands and knees instead of standing tall and proud. I sympathize with them from the bottom of my heart, because I know what psychic pain is like.

Bolstering Your Ego

So what can you do if you have an ego that needs bolstering? How can you stop imaging yourself as an inadequate person—an attitude that just perpetuates the state of affairs you want to avoid?

The first thing is, examine your entire life and see if you can pinpoint some specific cause for these inferiority feelings. Often the cause goes back to childhood. Certainly we're not born with inferiority feelings; a healthy baby has a strong ego and—so far as one can tell—a high opinion of himself. But even so, that self-confidence can be damaged, sometimes by a harsh or hypercritical parent, sometimes by other children who tease or ridicule, sometimes by siblings who outshine or overshadow a sensitive brother or sister.

I remember one man who came to the Institutes of Religion and Health, a counseling service founded by Dr. Blanton and me some thirty years ago. He was seeking help because he felt so wretchedly inadequate most of the time. He just felt that he couldn't cope. And believe me, the "I can't cope" feeling is widespread. Finally, after long discussion and probing, it was found that as a small boy he had nearly drowned in a swimming pool. His frantic mother forbade him ever to go in the water again. He would stand by the pool watching the other boys swim, and gradually the idea took hold of him that he couldn't do what the others did. Thus his disbelief in himself began to grow.

He grew up filled with fear, and when we saw him his talk was full of symbolic references. "This is over my head," he would say. Or, "This is too deep for me." Or, "If I try that, I'll be sunk." This man struggled so hard against a constant conviction of inadequacy that he was close to a nervous breakdown. I told him, as I tell everyone who has an inferiority complex, that the basic answer to the problem is to get a deep sense of the presence of God in your life. Image yourself walking alongside the Power that created the tiniest flower and holds the constellations in their places. This is the surest way to cast out all fear and shrinking and sense of failure. No matter how fearful you think you are, I will guarantee that if you get your consciousness filled to overflowing with God, you will not be afraid of anything in this world. You will walk through life erect, head held high, unafraid.

How do you do it? Well, the answers have been given so often that they sound hackneyed and trite, but they are eternally true. You pray—which is conversation with God. You go where God is talked about and thought about and focused on—and that is usually in church or some good spiritual group, of which there are many. You read the Bible and apply what you read to yourself. There is no great benefit in reading the Bible just because somebody says you ought to. The Bible only comes to your rescue when you take its message and diligently apply it to yourself and your problems and to the image you have of yourself.

Take the story of David and Goliath, for instance. Everyone knows how the slender shepherd boy went out against the great armored giant of the Philistines. Where were his weapons? A sling and five smooth stones, you say? True enough, but that was only *part* of his armament, indeed the smallest part. Listen to the words of David himself as he went out to face what everyone else thought was certain death: "Thou [Goliath] comest to me with a sword, and with a spear, and with a shield: but I come to thee in the name of the Lord of hosts . . ." (1 Samuel 17:45).

In other words, David went to battle supported by a God-saturated mind. That was his powerful armament. Therefore he knew no fear. And therefore he was victorious.

Now, don't just read that famous Bible passage as an old story, as an exciting bit of ancient history. The idea is to apply its truth to yourself. What are the fearsome problems that confront you, that frighten you, that give you a sense of inadequacy? Stand up to them, as the story says, in the name of the Lord. Almighty God meant us to walk the earth as men and women made in His image, not to crawl through life on our hands and knees.

Select one of those problems that loom so large in your mind and take some action against it. Remember what Emerson said: "Do the thing you fear, and the death of fear is certain." Suppose you're afraid to ask the boss for a raise. Summon up your courage and ask him if you honestly think you deserve it. You may not get it, but you will have done wonders for yourself anyway, because you will have broken through the fear barrier. And that is of more value than a larger paycheck.

Once we had in this country a great psychologist named William James. He pointed out that there is in all of us a psychological barrier that he called the first layer of fatigue. He said that most of us work and struggle until we come to this point and then we say, "I'm so tired. I haven't any more energy. I'll have to stop." But James said that beyond this barrier of fatigue there is tremendous power and energy waiting for us, if we will just force ourselves through it. "The people who really do great things in this world," said William James, "are those who drive past the first layer of fatigue."

Self-doubt is like that, too. It sets up a barrier and timid people turn back when they encounter it. They keep turning back until it becomes a habit—a bad habit. But if you crash through it, if you *make* yourself ask the boss for that raise, if you *do* the thing you fear—just once—the barrier will be broken and your image of yourself will be upgraded. Confidence will begin to flood into your mind and drive out the doubts and the feelings of inadequacy.

There is another thing you can do, too. Examine the life-style you are leading and, if necessary, clean it up. One big cause of inferiority feelings—perhaps the greatest—is wrongdoing, being off the beam from a moral standpoint. People do things that are morally wrong, sometimes because they are tempted, sometimes simply because they want to and think they can get away with it. To use the old-fashioned hard-hitting term, they commit sin. And this is one of the stupidest things you can do, because once you commit a sin it will never let up on you. You can try to ignore it. You can try to put it out of your mind. But it's like putting erroneous information into a computer. It's there. It is not going to disappear. It is going to cause the computer to give wrong answers because it is *programmed* wrong.

A Splinter in the Unconscious

I've never understood why the consequences of sin aren't glaringly obvious to everyone. A moral transgression is like a splinter in the unconscious mind. Unless that splinter is removed, it is going to fester. And what form does this festering take? First of all, it damages the self-esteem of the individual. He knows he has done something wrong, and so he doesn't like himself quite as much as he did before. Next it begins to affect his performance in subtle but unmistakable ways. A deep, unacknowledged sense of guilt, a built-in censor, will tell that person that so far he may have been doing pretty well, but now, because he has done wrong, he doesn't deserve to do so well anymore. The voice of conscience, the censor within the mind, will say, "You are a wrongdoer, my friend, you are a sinner." It may even get inelegant and say, "You are a dirty dog and you deserve to be punished ... and if no one else will punish you, I hereby order you to punish yourself."

Sometimes the punishment is quite subtle in that it takes the form of inefficiency or loss of creativity. Sometimes it appears as ill health. Most often it reveals itself as a growing feeling of inadequacy and inferiority. So if such feelings trouble you, perhaps it would be a good idea to take a ruthless moral inventory of yourself and if necessary change some area of your life that you may find is not as it should be.

One last suggestion: If you feel inadequate, sometimes it is a good idea to ask yourself, "Inadequate compared to what?" I've known people who were despondent and downcast because they allowed themselves to become victims of too-great expectations. A young man about to enter college sought me out to talk about his inferiority feelings. It didn't take much perception to see that the trouble lay in his relationship with his father, or rather, with his father's memory, since the parent had died some years before. The father had been a great athlete, an all-American fullback, in fact, and foolishly the boy's mother was forever reminding him of this. The boy himself simply didn't have the physique to be a football player, or an outstanding athlete of any kind. But instead of accepting this fact, he was letting it make him miserable.

"Look," I said to him after I had asked a few questions. "You're a good student—probably better than your father was. You're a fine chess player. You've been the editor of your high school yearbook. You're not an inferior person; you're a superior one. You're just using the wrong yardstick, that's all! Be proud of your father, sure. But also be proud of yourself, because you deserve to be!"

Nine times out of ten, as was the case with this youngster, a feeling of inferiority is nothing but a state of mind. It was Milton who wrote:

> The mind is its own place, and in itself
> Can make a Heav'n of Hell, a hell of Heav'n.

Image yourself as a worthwhile person; *act as if* you were someone worthy of admiration and respect—and gradually that is what you will come to be. What you can image, you will be, in the long run.

To sum up, then, here are some specific things to do if you need to bolster a shaky ego: Hold in your mind the image of the kind of person you want to be: confident, assured, competent, calm. Break through the "fear barrier" by deliberately doing something that has been causing you apprehension. Say to yourself, "I can do all things through Christ who strengthens me, and I *will* do this thing that I have been flinching from."

When feelings of inadequacy get you down, remind yourself that God made you and that He does not do poor work. Get rid of such thoughts by seeing yourself as opening up your mind and letting the clean winds of faith blow through. Vividly visualize those winds sweeping away all the cobwebs of self-doubt and self-distrust.

Try to find the root cause of your feelings of inadequacy. Once you bring it into the open, it will lose much of its power to dominate you.

Invite the good Lord into your everyday experience. Ask Him to go back into your past, to find the hurtful memories and heal them. He stands ready, always, to aid you.

Turn your sense of inadequacy into a plus by letting it act as a spur, as a motivator. Something in you is yearning and straining to dominate and eliminate weakness. Let the "big you" brush aside the "little you." Visualize the "big you" wielding a big broom and doing just that.

Be realistic; accept some limitations as natural and inevitable. Nobody is "the best" at everything. But image yourself as the best at something.

Stop telling yourself that you can't. Image yourself succeeding in the area where you wish most completely for success. Imagine a television screen on the wall in front of you. In that screen, see yourself as the principal actor doing the thing you long to do. Run this "film" over and over again in your mind. This is the technique that Roger Ferger used, that Mary Crowe used, that Harry DeCamp used, and it is the technique Ruth and I learned in the formation of *Guideposts* magazine.

It is called imaging. It worked for them. It worked for us. It can work for you.

5

HOW TO MANAGE
MONEY PROBLEMS

A T A BUSINESS CONVENTION, after I had given a talk that included some of these ideas about the importance and effectiveness of imaging, a man came up and confronted me with a certain truculence. "Well, doctor," he said, "all that stuff about imaging is interesting, but I don't see how it can solve my problem."

Naturally, I asked him what his problem was.

"Money!" he said, "Or rather, lack of money. I'm up to my ears in debt. I have two notes coming due at the bank and I don't know how I'm going to meet either one of them. Will imaging put twenty thousand dollars into my checking account by next Monday? Will imaging take care of my mortgage payments and my insurance payments? Will imaging pay for my wife's new car or my daughter's debut? Come on, be honest now. Yes or no!"

"That's easy," I said. "The answer is no. Imaging isn't some kind of Aladdin's lamp that you can rub and have a genie appear and bring you instant riches."

"Then what good is it to me?" he demanded triumphantly.

"It could do you a lot of good," I told him. "From what you say, being in debt is a way of life with you. But obviously it's not a way of life that makes you happy. If you would picture yourself debt free with intensity and sincerity, if you would visualize vividly the happiness and peace of mind that solvency would bring you, if you would really make that your aim and give it top priority, you'd move toward that goal and finally achieve it. And *that* would be the result of imaging."

He gave me a strange look, half-skeptical, half-wistful. "You mean," he said, "I should try to see myself managing these money problems— *and* my extravagant wife, *and* my spoiled daughter—instead of having them manage me?"

"Something like that," I told him.

"Thanks," he said. "Maybe I'll give it a try." And he was gone.

I don't know whether that man will be able to upgrade his life-control factor and straighten out his situation, but I do know this: With the possible exception of health problems, money problems weigh more heavily on people's minds than any other form of anxiety. Ruth and I are constantly made aware of this by the mail that reaches us. Despairing letters from elderly people whose fixed incomes are being eroded by inflation. Frantic letters from young people caught in the quicksand of installment buying or credit-card spending. Panicky letters from people staggering under mountainous debts. Fear-filled letters from people who have lost their jobs. The list goes on and on.

Tremendous emotional currents often swirl around money problems. A letter came in the other day from a young woman who said bitterly that she hated money. She hated it for what it did to people like herself who didn't have enough (she'd been laid off from her automotive-company job). She hated it for what she claimed it often did to people who had too much. She said that America had become a materialistic, money-grubbing, dollar-worshiping society, and she blamed money for that. She even misquoted the Bible. "Money is the root of all evil," she wrote, underscoring every word. (Actually, the Bible says that the *love* of money is the root of all evil, quite a different thing.)

As is our custom, Ruth and I discussed the letter and how to reply to it. Often we turn to the Bible as a guide, or play a kind of game in which each of us reminds the other of a passage that may be pertinent. In this case, we recalled various New Testament references to money, such as the widow's mite, or the thirty pieces of silver paid to Judas.

"It's easy to think of the widow's mite as being good money," Ruth said, "or the money paid to Judas as bad money. But actually money itself is neither good nor bad. It's what people do with it that counts."

"It can symbolize things, though," I said. "In the parable of the talents, for instance, it symbolizes both energetic risk taking and timorous overcaution."

"The *people* in the parable were either energetic or overcautious," my practical wife said. "Not the money. So hating money, as this woman does, makes about as much sense as hating a stick or a rock!"

In the end I wrote to the young woman and urged her to try to change her image of herself. "Stop seeing yourself as the helpless victim of an imaginary villain called money," I wrote. "If you personalize money so vehemently and hate it so intensely, you certainly won't ever attract it, because your unconscious mind will be programmed to repel and reject it."

I urged her to create and focus on the self-image of a well-balanced, intelligent person whose mind was able to take charge of her emotions. "Calm down," I wrote. "Be objective. Stop all this hate business. Hold the image of yourself as someone determined to remove all these churning, turbulent, conflicting, confusing emotions from your mind. Nothing is going to go right for you until you do."

Anger is just one emotion that money problems can generate.

Another is fear. Not long ago I was on a radio show, a call-in program where listeners could pick up the phone and ask questions of the person on the show. One woman who called said to me, "I wish you'd tell me what to do about bill collectors. I'm terrified of them. When a bill collector comes around, I get so nervous and full of fear that I can barely talk to him."

Bill Collectors Are Human, Too

"Well," I said to her, "I happen to know a couple of bill collectors and both have told me how nervous *they* are when they come to a home to talk about nonpayment of bills. They say they get tense and tongue-tied and hot and cold all over."

The woman said, "I can't believe it!"

"It's true," I told her. "A bill collector is also a human being and is not trying to harass you or be mean to you or put you in jail. He's just representing a man or woman in business who has to get money to keep on selling merchandise to people like yourself. He wants you to continue to be a paying customer, so he wants you to stay solvent. His main objective is to get you to work out a payment plan.

"So here's a suggestion. The next time a bill collector comes to your door, change the picture you have in your mind of what the interview is going to be like. Instead of seeing yourself as embarrassed and angry and evasive, and him as hostile and threatening, visualize a meeting between a nice person who has a job to do and a nice person who happens to have some unpaid bills. See both of you working out a solution together in a friendly way. And here's another suggestion: Before you open the door, say a quick prayer for the poor fellow, because he's probably just as nervous as you are."

"Well," she said, "I certainly never thought of praying for a bill collector. But if you say so, I'll try."

In trying to solve life's problems, imaging is only one of the many techniques. Through the years, trying to help people in financial difficulty, Ruth and I have worked out half a dozen simple suggestions that seem to be effective.

The first is simply this: *don't panic*. If you find anxiety getting the upper hand, go to work imaging peace of mind. The simple act of praying creates an image of your problems being brought to the Source of all wisdom, and that is tremendously reassuring and comforting. Then read the Twenty-third Psalm. When you come to those marvelous words ". . . I will fear no evil: for thou art with me . . ." (verse 4), run them through your mind at least twenty times. Repeat them to yourself during the day if you feel your anxiety returning. Write them on a piece of paper and tape it on your bathroom mirror, where you will see it first thing every morning. Saturate yourself with this idea.

Then, when you have your emotions under control, the next step is to *get organized*. This is Ruth's favorite bit of advice because she is a highly organized person herself. Make a complete list of all your debts, everything you owe. Make another list of essential expenses. Add up all sources of income and see what you can count on. It's amazing how many people really don't know exactly how much they owe or what their basic expenses are. Visualize yourself living within your income with a fraction left over for debt reduction. Paint that image vividly in your mind.

Next, *be disciplined*. You have to learn to ignore that sly little destructive demon named Instant Gratification who lurks in all of us and whispers, "That's pretty; get it!" or "That's a bargain; grab it!"

The demon is happiest when you don't know the true state of your finances, because then he knows you are less likely to apply the brakes. I must confess that's one of the problems Ruth and I had to work through in the early years of our marriage. Soon after we moved to New York, I decided that we had to have a new car. The old one was falling apart and beginning to cost a lot of money in repairs. So I went to a car showroom, picked out one I liked, and told the salesman to hold it for me.

When I told Ruth about it that night, she shook her head. "No," she said.

"What do you mean, 'No'?" I asked her.

She said, "I mean, we can't afford it. Our budget barely takes care of things now. There's no money for new-car payments. So forget it!"

Well, naturally, this reduced me to a state of gloom, especially when I had to call up and disappoint the eager salesman. But Ruth was applying precisely the ingredient—discipline—that fends off money problems before they can get started.

A fourth suggestion we sometimes offer is blunt and to the point: *think*. If you'll just sit down and really think, you may come up with an idea or an insight that can change everything.

I've always liked William Saroyan's story about the time when, as a struggling young writer, discouraged and almost broke, he decided to ask a rich uncle in a nearby city for a loan. With his last bit of cash, Saroyan sent his uncle a telegram. Back came a reply of just three words: HAVE HEAD EXAMINED.

Once he got over the shock of this seemingly sardonic refusal, Saroyan pondered the message. Gradually he began to see what his uncle was saying: You don't need a loan. Look inside your head. That's where you'll find a solution in a new idea.

Thus challenged, Saroyan sat down, thought up a plot for a short story, wrote it, sold it, and was on his way to a brilliant career as playwright and novelist.

There's Always an Answer

Remember my druggist friend, A.E. Russ, who told me not to worry about an occasional inept sermon? He had a niece who was living in upstate New York when the crash of the big depression came. Her husband lost his business. Things went from bad to worse. Finally Russ decided to go up to Utica and see if he could be of any help to them.

He found his niece and her husband dejected and disheartened. All they could talk about was the depression and the grim things that had happened to them. But Uncle Alfred refused to join them in their gloomy postmortems. "Let's focus on the future," he said. "Find something to build on. Let's go over *everything* with the future in mind. Forget the past. Think of the future!"

As they talked, he noticed that his niece was sewing something, and he asked her what it was. She told him that it was just a pot holder.

"Very pretty," he said. "Do you have any more?"

She said she had made a dozen or so.

"Well," said Uncle Alfred, "they're *good* pot holders—a lot better than most. So why don't you take them down to Woolworth's tomorrow and see their buyer. He might order some."

The niece was hesitant and her husband skeptical, but Uncle Alfred was firm. "Let's do some practical imaging. There is going to be a factory someday," he said. "A factory making pot holders and all sorts of other useful things. I can see it right now in my mind: tall chimneys, employees streaming through a gate in a big fence, an enormous sign with your name on it. Now you just go down to Woolworth's, keeping that thought in mind, and see what happens!"

Years later, I happened to be in a Pullman car early one morning on my way back to New York from a speaking engagement. Approaching Utica, I pulled up the shade in my lower berth and looked out. The train was passing a sizable textile factory with a tall fence and a sign at least twenty feet high. And you can guess whose name was on the sign! Why? Because in this case someone, Uncle Alfred, "had his head examined," did some creative imaging, and found a simple solution to a massive problem.

One more example. Soon after World War II a young man named Hal LeMaster went to Florida to seek his fortune. Nothing much happened until one day when he was alone, fishing for trout. Nearby was a boat with an old man who kept hauling in fish while LeMaster had no bites at all. When LeMaster asked plaintively how he did it, the old fellow explained that he was using live sardines, little silvery minnows, for bait. "The trout see 'em flash," he said. "They can't see the bait you're using."

LeMaster went home, shaped an artificial minnow out of transparent plastic, added hooks, and put a strip of shiny metal inside. Result: the famed "Mirro-lure" that became a national favorite and made LeMaster a rich man—all because he "had his head examined"—by himself!

Opportunities for moneymaking surround us all the time; it just takes an inquisitive, lively mind to see them. It also takes an optimistic mind, one that expects good things to happen in the future.

It's not easy to stay optimistic these days because pessimism is so rampant. Newspapers are full of it. So are the airwaves. One night Ruth and I were watching a television program about the troubles of a young farmer and his family. This man had a small farm with a few cows and some chickens. But he had run out of cash and stumbled into debt, and now his creditors were going to take away his cows as payment for those debts. He was probably going to lose his house, too, we were told. He wasn't eligible for welfare, apparently, because he still owned some livestock. His three children were reduced to eating sandwiches, and the gloomy thought was introduced that pretty soon there might be no more sandwiches.

Now here was a genuine case of economic hardship, but the whole thrust of that presentation was to tell millions of viewers that the way to handle a money problem is to add up and focus on and dwell upon all the difficulties involved.

Ruth said impatiently, "This is all so downbeat! Why doesn't someone tell those people to make a list of their remaining assets? That might give them the kind of lift they need."

"What assets would you list?" I asked, just to see what she would say.

"Well," she said, "the man seems healthy and strong, a vigorous person. That's asset number one. Next, he has a wife who seems intelligent, who obviously loves him and is loyal to him. That's asset number two. The kids are not crippled or sick or handicapped in any way; they're normal, healthy kids. So that's asset number three. He hasn't lost his house yet; they still have a roof over their heads. That's asset number four. Their plight is being brought to the attention of millions of sympathetic Americans, some of whom will undoubtedly try to help them. That's asset number five. But nobody even mentions these things!"

On the contrary, while we continued to watch, the commentator went on to say dolefully that the young farmer had been reduced to taking on odd jobs.

"Reduced?" I said to Ruth. "What is so reducing about an odd job? Remember Michael Cardone?"

Michael Cardone is a friend of ours who in middle age found himself out of work. But he didn't let it get him down. One day he saw a pile of discarded, worn-out windshield-wiper motors in a garage, and he began to wonder why they couldn't be fixed and sold more cheaply than new ones. So he began to fix them and sell them—a pretty odd job because there was no demand for rebuilt wiper motors and no one had ever bothered to do it before. But he kept on, and today Michael Cardone is the head of an enormous plant in Philadelphia that makes all sorts of automotive supplies. Why? Because he had a dream, an image of being his own boss, of running his own show, of finding automotive needs and filling them—and an odd job was the springboard that started him on his way. And what he was able to image, he became.

Michael Cardone is an intensely religious man. He and the top executives in his company begin every business day with prayer. They're convinced that if they have God as their senior partner, and make all decisions in the light of His teachings, they cannot go wrong. Michael himself is sure that there is a spiritual side to every great success story, and his own accomplishments seem to prove him right.

Ruth and I agree with Michael in believing that there is a spiritual force in all this, something that goes beyond the reach of reason. A woman once said to me, a bit snappishly, when I was trying to help her overcome her fears about money problems, "What do you know about what I'm going through? You're a successful minister, a well-known personality, a writer of books, publisher of *Guideposts*, a popular magazine. You don't have any debts. You don't owe anybody anything. You're not afraid somebody may show up any minute to turn off your electricity or repossess your secondhand car. So how can you understand what I'm going through?"

I said to her, "I can understand it because I've been through it, too. You're too young to remember the Great Depression, but I do, and believe me, it makes all these recent 'recessions' look like Sunday-school picnics."

I told her that back in 1930 I was a young minister, recently married, in Syracuse, New York. My salary, which had been a handsome (for those days) six thousand dollars a year, was cut twice—first to five thousand, then to four thousand. We had no manse or home supplied by the church. Everyone was frightened and depressed. Businesses were failing. Nobody could borrow money; there was no money to be had. Men used to greet one another grimly by saying, "Have you had your pay cut yet?" Everyone had to take several cuts before that depression ended, and many people lost their jobs altogether.

At four thousand dollars a year, I just didn't see how we could get by. My salary was the only income we had. I was helping my younger brother with college expenses and I knew he had to count on that. The pressure got worse and worse. I hated to burden Ruth with my fears. One night I went out alone and walked through Walnut Park near our little apartment, and for the first time in my life I felt icy terror clutching at my mind and heart. I wasn't just worried; I was terrified. When I finally went home, I could keep it to myself no longer. I said to Ruth,

"We're in a desperate situation. We can't pay the bills. What are we going to do?" And her answer really startled me. She said, "We're going to start tithing."

Our Financial Problem Solved

"Tithing?" I echoed. "Tithing with what? We can't do it. It's impossible!"

"No," Ruth said. "Not impossible. Essential. You know what the Bible promises to those who give ten percent of everything to the Lord." I can see her yet, standing right there in the kitchen and quoting Malachi 3:10 to me: "Bring ye all the tithes into the storehouse . . . and prove me now herewith, saith the Lord of hosts, if I will not open you the windows of heaven, and pour you out a blessing, that there shall not be room enough to receive it."

"We're going to do that," she said stoutly, "and we're not going to starve, either. We're not going to be evicted. We are going to get by on ninety percent of your twice-cut salary because tithing is an act of faith, and the Bible says that if we have faith even as small as a grain of mustard seed, nothing will be impossible for us. We have to start imaging God's prosperity."

So we did it. And Ruth was right, we did get by. Money certainly didn't pour in, but there always was just enough. Furthermore, the act of tithing seemed to calm my fears and stimulate my mind so that I began thinking. I started imaging. I knew I had one small talent: public speaking. And so I decided to try to capitalize on that. I offered myself as a public speaker wherever one was needed. I spoke at civic clubs and garden clubs and graduations and community gatherings. Sometimes I was paid five or ten dollars, sometimes nothing at all. But it helped. What a thrill I felt when I received the first twenty-five dollar fee. Then someone who heard me speak offered me a chance to go on radio. Again, there was no money for this, but the number of speaking invitations increased. So one thing led to another, and gradually we began to get our heads above water.

I am convinced that tithing did it. Anyway, Ruth and I have been tithers ever since, and there is something about this practice of giving that can't be explained in purely rational terms. Tithing seems to put a person in touch with some mysterious force that attracts money. Not a lot of money, necessarily, but enough for the tither's needs. Through the years, in sermons and talks I have recommended tithing to thousands of people, and hundreds have been persuaded to try it. Of those hundreds, not one has ever come back to me and said that the experiment failed, or that he regretted it, or that it was a mistake. Not a single one.

It's almost as if there were an invisible reservoir of abundance in the universe that can be tapped if you will just obey certain spiritual laws.

The word *abundance*, I'm told, comes from a Latin phrase meaning to "rise up in waves." When you tithe, it does seem as if little waves of abundance start rising up all around you.

So if you have financial difficulties, face up to them not just with courage and intelligence but also with warmhearted generosity and concern for others.

Here, then, are the key things to remember where money problems are concerned:

1. *Don't panic.* Fear not only paralyzes the will and the mind but it also seems, in some mysterious way, to scare money away, probably because fearful people are not creative or resourceful people. So try to be calm, be objective, be logical, be hopeful.

2. *Get organized.* Figure out exactly what your income is and what your outlays are. If you can't increase the former, reduce the latter until your budget is in balance. That's the only way to get runaway finances under control.

3. *Be disciplined.* Don't be an impulse buyer. Give up all credit or installment buying until you are debt free.

4. *Think.* Look inside your head for new ideas, new possible sources of income. Money problems can become assets if they force you into creative thinking. You may strike a vein of gold, as Michael Cardone did, that will last for the rest of your life.

5. *Give all you can.* Giving is the best way to put yourself in the great invisible stream of abundance that surges through the universe. Tithing is the surest way to do this, because God Himself has guaranteed the results, and God's promises never fail.

6. *Visualize yourself as debt free.* Imagine vividly the relief, the happiness, the peace of mind you will feel when the last payment is made. Hold that idea in your conscious mind until it sinks down into your unconscious mind. And then you will have it forever, because it will have you.

6

USE IMAGING TO OUTWIT WORRY

ONE NEVER KNOWS EXACTLY what kind of spark will set a man on fire. I once knew a salesman whose life seemed to exhibit a consistent pattern of failure. He was worried, low on cash, and very low in spirit. He would try selling one thing and then another. One season it would be paint and the next cosmetics and the next office supplies and the next lamps and furniture. But no matter what commodity he was offering, he never seemed to make a success of it, and the image of failure became stamped more and more indelibly on his mind.

Then one day someone handed him a piece of paper with a three-line affirmation on it. It went like this:

> I believe that I am always divinely guided.
> I believe that I will always take the right turn in the road.
> I believe that God will make a way where there is no way.

Three lines. Nothing very complicated. No great eloquence. Rather repetitious, in fact. But this salesman began repeating these lines to himself every morning when he first woke up and every night when he went to bed. He memorized them. He let them sink deep into his innermost consciousness. And gradually this man began to change.

He no longer dithered and hesitated over what items he would try to sell. In his simple and unquestioning way he asked God to tell him. Then he listened, believingly, for an answer, meanwhile thanking God in advance for giving him the right answer. When he seemed to feel a nudge in the direction of one item or another, he chose it without hesitation and did not look back. He believed that he was divinely guided, so his choice could not be a mistake. Therefore, when he began to sell the item, he did so with complete conviction that that was the item he *should* be selling—and that his customers would be buying.

If he had to choose between two different cities or two different territories, he went through the same procedure. He asked God to show him the right turn in the road and he thanked God in advance for so guiding him. Then when he felt a nudge in one direction or the other, he followed it without hesitation and without looking back. He was positive that it was the right choice.

If he ran into sales resistance or if a hoped-for sale did not materialize, he didn't become discouraged. He believed that God would make a way where there was no way. His attitude of quiet assurance was so impressive that prospective customers felt it and reacted favorably to it. There was something about the salesman now that inspired great confidence, whereas before he had seemed so uncertain and unsure of himself that prospective customers felt unsure about him.

This dramatic change in personality and approach was accompanied by an equally dramatic change in the image the salesman had of himself. Formerly he had visualized failure and defeat before he even set out on the road. And failure and defeat were what he invariably found. Now he imaged himself succeeding because his conscious mind *and* his unconscious mind had accepted the belief that with God as his ally and partner, he could not fail. Once he began to act as if he could not fail, he did not fail. Before each scheduled road trip was over, he had sold all his stock and had to come home to replenish it. He went on to become one of the best salesman in his part of the country, all because his life had been revolutionized by three simple phrases, each beginning with two magic words: *I believe.*

But there is also such a thing as negative imaging. And the most common name for it is worry. When we worry we are using imaging, all right, but we are pointing it in the wrong direction. When we worry about our health, or our children, or our jobs, or our future, we are giving these fears a degree of reality by allowing them to pervade and color our thinking. And if they dominate our minds, they may also affect our actions. Just as affirmative imaging tends to actualize desirable events sooner or later, so negative imaging, or worry, tends to create conditions in which the unpleasant thing that is worried about has a better chance of coming to pass.

The Bible, that extraordinary Book of Wisdom, clearly recognizes this. In the Book of Job, perhaps the most ancient of all biblical writings, Job cries plaintively: "The thing which I greatly feared is come upon me . . ." (Job 3:25). Of course it did. He imaged this dire happening. He *greatly* feared something, and finally it happened. Haven't you known of cases yourself where people display excessive fears of some misfortune and then that misfortune seems to seek them out? I know I have.

The Bible never mentions a problem without offering a solution. There are constant exhortations to cheerfulness, to hope, to faith—all tested antidotes to worry. "A merry heart doeth good like a medicine" (Proverbs 17:22). "Say to them that are of a fearful heart, Be strong, fear not" (Issaiah 35:4). ". . . my peace I give unto you" (John 14:27). Trust God, the Bible keeps saying, because the more you trust the less you will have to worry about.

Let's be realistic: anyone who has any imagination at all is going to be concerned now and then. A little worry is probably a good thing, if it impels a person to take prudent action. It's chronic worry that is dangerous, the *constant* imaging of undesirable events. The occasional worrier takes affirmative action. The chronic worrier becomes exhausted and confused, like a desert traveler in a swirling sandstorm. His friends may say to him, "Why don't you stop worrying? It's just a waste of time. Doesn't change a thing!" But usually he is unable to follow this cheery advice. And as a matter of fact, that last phrase is dangerously misleading because worry *does* change things—mainly the capacity of the worrier to cope successfully with the thing that is worrying him.

When worry becomes really acute, it can clamp down on the mind like a vise, blotting out all rational thought processes. This is how black magic works. A friend of mine who lives in South Africa once told me how his mother's maid became convinced that a local witch doctor had put a spell on her because she had offended him in some manner. She became unable to eat because all food seemed to have a terrible odor, although actually it didn't. Everything edible became repulsive to her. She was convinced that she was going to die, and although her employers called in doctors and ministers to help her, she finally did die of starvation—so powerful were the negative images that had taken possession of her mind.

A year or two ago, when I was on a national radio program in Australia, a similar situation was brought to my attention. A young girl, a member of one of the aboriginal tribes, was near death because she, too, was convinced that she was the victim of a spell. In this case, when asked if positive thinking might help, I said that the power of faith was stronger than any so-called occult power, and I called upon the radio audience to join me in a massive prayer effort for the girl's deliverance. I suggested that everyone image her as being set free from the deadly idea that was killing her. I think a lot of listeners did, because later I heard that the spell was broken; the girl began to eat again and eventually regained her health.

Few of us ever encounter such dramatic evidences of the power of fear or worry to produce such deadly images, but most of us do have to struggle with worry on a day-to-day basis. And even in relatively mild doses, it can be painful. The word *worry* itself comes from an old Anglo-Saxon term meaning to choke, or strangle, and that is exactly what worry does—it chokes the joy of living right out of its victim. And it chokes off creative power to improve one's condition.

How, then, does one get rid of the clammy, clutching hands of worry about one's neck? How does one let go of worry thoughts, with their bleak images of future problems or disasters lurking just around the next bend in the road?

Believe Worry Can Be Overcome

In the first place, you must believe it can be done. This is the same as saying, picture or image yourself as worry free, and have faith that that picture can become a reality. Worry is a habit. It got into your mind because you *practiced* it, and anything you practice in, you can practice out.

How did you first develop the habit of worrying? It probably began as a thin trickle of negative imaging across your mind. Then, repeated many times, it cut a channel into your consciousness. If this process is not checked, eventually every thought you think may be drained into this channel of worry and come up so tinctured that you see everything in terms that are dark and foreboding.

There is something obscurely satisfying, or shall we say sort of masochistic, about worrying that makes the habit hard to break. Just as some people "enjoy poor health," so some people seem to enjoy worrying in a miserable sort of way. More than once I have suggested to my congregation how wonderful it would be if they could just come forward to the altar, put their worries into a large basket or other receptacle, and leave them there. "But then, you know," I sometimes add, "after the service some of you would creep back down the aisle and fish around in the basket until you found your discarded worry. You'd gotten so fond of it that you couldn't bear to be without it. And you'd go out hugging it tightly to you because you couldn't part with such an old, familiar friend." This always gets a laugh, or at least a chuckle, from my listeners. But there's more than a grain of truth in it, and they know it.

Let me give you a few tips that have helped me outwit worry.

First, if you have something preying on your mind (good phrase; that's exactly what worry does), *think* about it. Stop imaging the worst possible eventuality and reacting with fear and dread and apprehension. Push aside these negative emotions and use your mind positively. Thought is one of the greatest faculties that God gave to us human beings. I'm convinced that we can control almost anything in our lives by thought. Therefore worry, which is an irrational reaction, can be controlled by thinking rationally. Take a worry apart, lay it out, dissect it, analyze it. If you will do this with clear, cool, rational thinking, you'll find that nine times out of ten there won't be much left. There is so much illusionary content in worry that when this is dispelled, the reality that is left will prove to be very small—so small that you can handle it.

When I was a young man, I had a wise old friend, Dr. David Keppel. I used to seek him out when I was struggling with some problem. "Norman," he would say, "let's sit down and take this thing apart." And remarkably, when he got through doing that, as a rule there wasn't much of anything worrisome left. He always said that ninety-five percent of his own worries either never happened or were relatively innocuous when they did happen. "I could always handle that five percent," he used to say. He even wrote a poem about it that, if my memory serves me, went like this:

> Better never trouble Trouble
> Until Trouble troubles you;
> For you only make your trouble
> Double-trouble if you do;
> And the trouble—like a bubble—
> That you're troubling about,
> May be nothing but a cipher
> With its rim rubbed out.

Another useful way to outwit worry is to use symbolism to get rid of it. This is a form of imaging, of course, and it can be very helpful. Once a woman came to me because she was worried—almost literally—out of her senses. Some months previously she had had a slight heart attack. Her doctors told her she had made a good recovery and that her prospects were excellent, but she was obsessed by the fear of dying at any minute. She talked so compulsively and continuously about this fear that I could not get a word into the conversation. Finally I held out my hand, palm upward, and said, "Put it there."

"Put what there?" she asked, bewildered.

"Your problem," I said. "This thing that's worrying you. I know it's invisible, but I also know it's very real. I want you to stretch out your hand and put it into my hand."

Somewhat hesitantly she went through the procedure. I stood up, went to the door, opened it, and made a throwing gesture as if I were casting something out. I closed the door and went back to where she sat. "Now," I said, "the problem is no longer in this room. It's outside that door. We need to deal with it, and we will deal with it. But first we're going to fill the place inside you where that problem was with some thoughts of God and faith and hope. We're going to saturate your mind with the peace that Jesus Christ promised to all of us. And you will find that these thoughts are stronger than worry, stronger than fear."

And eventually she did. But first there had to be the symbolism, or the imaging, that made her receptive.

Many people use this device with good results. A letter came the other day from a woman who said she had been a chronic worrier until she hit upon the device of writing her worries down on slips of paper and putting them in an old teapot that she kept on a high shelf in her kitchen. Every time she put a problem in the pot she said a little prayer, releasing the problem to the Lord. At the end of the year she would take the pot down, read all the slips, and then throw them away. It was amazing, she said, how many of her worries had simply evaporated. And she always felt capable of dealing with the rest.

The late Lord Rank, an outstanding British industrialist, once rather whimsically told me of a little game he played to reduce the impact of worry. He organized what he called the "Wednesday Worry Club." He was the sole member. Instead of worrying every day, whenever a worry cropped up he would write it on a piece of paper and drop it in a box to be worried about on Wednesday afternoon at four o'clock, the meeting time of the "club."

At that time, he would empty all the deposited worries on a table. In going over them, always about 90 percent had solved themselves and no longer needed to be worried about. "But," I asked, "What did you do with the other ten percent?"

"I put them back in the box to be worried about next Wednesday at four o'clock," blandly replied Lord Rank.

This same wise man told me that there were thirteen steps leading from the courtyard to his office. As he mounted them every morning, it was his custom to say a brief prayer on each step, affirming and giving thanks for the goodness of God. He knew how to outwit worry.

A man I know in Chicago is the treasurer and financial genius of a large corporation. He said to me once, "Would you like to know what I do when I've got worries? When it's time to leave the office for the day, I write them on a piece of paper and put it in my pocket. When I get home I put my car in the garage and walk to our front gate, where there is a mailbox. I open it, put the paper in it, close my eyes, and say, 'Dear Lord, I'm giving You my worries. Work on them for me during the night, will You?' I leave them there, and when I come out in the morning, the problem may still be there, but it's no longer on top of me. Rather, I'm on top of it. What was a source of anxiety the night before has now become an exciting intellectual challenge—and it's amazing how often I find the right answer."

Turn Away From Worry

A third way to break the worry pattern is one that is available to all of us: divert yourself. Our word *diversion* comes from two Latin words meaning to "turn away from," and when worry begins to be a problem, that is the sensible thing to do: simply turn away from it.

This is not hard because fortunately the human mind is designed so that it cannot hold more than one idea at a time. You cannot actively worry about something when you are deliberately focusing on something else. So when worry has you by the throat, the simplest way to break its grip is to do something that you enjoy doing. Dig in the garden;

play a game of golf; arrange some flowers; bake a cake; sing a song; (why not a grand old hymn?); take the dog for a run; have lunch with a friend; buy yourself a present; read a good book; go to a decent movie (if you can find one!); plan a trip; browse through a museum; take a child on a picnic. If all else fails, turn on the television! Anything to get your mind off yourself. Robert Louis Stevenson wrote: "The world is so full of a number of things, I'm sure we should all be as happy as kings." The world *is* full of an infinite number of things, but this won't do you much good unless you make a deliberate effort to reach out and include them in your life as worthwhile forms of diversion.

The final and best antidote for worry is simply this: Image Jesus Christ as actually your personal friend. Don't regard Him as some remote, historical, stained-glass kind of figure. Image Him as your constant companion throughout the day. Paint a portrait in your mind of what you think He looks like. Fill in the details: His compassionate eyes, those strong carpenter's hands. How did His voice sound when He talked to people, when He told the story of the Prodigal Son, for example? He must have had a wonderful laugh; can you picture yourself sitting on a hillside in Galilee, hearing it? If you can picture that, why not picture Him sitting alongside of you right now?

The more vivid that image in your mind, the freer from worry you will be. Some years ago a professor of physics from a famous university came to see me. He was a very intelligent man, but haunted by irrational fears and worries that were interfering with his work and making his life miserable. After some discussion, it became evident that the trouble lay in certain immoralities he had committed years earlier. He had asked for forgiveness of those sins, and I was sure it had been granted. But, like many of us, he had not forgiven himself, and his worries and his sense of inferiority and inadequacy came from these deep guilt feelings.

I decided to suggest something that I had used successfully with people of less formidable education. I didn't know how he would react, but my suggestion was that every night, upon going to bed, he place a chair beside his bed and tell himself that Jesus was sitting in that chair all night, watching over him and lifting the burden of worry from his shoulders.

As I expected, he looked uncomfortable. "But that sort of fantasy is for children," he protested.

"The Bible tells us to become like little children," I reminded him. "Maybe that is because they are less likely to be doubters. All you need is a grain of faith—one about the size of a mustard seed will do."

Finally he agreed to try it. At the end of two weeks he called me. "I was about ready to give up on that idea of yours," he said. "But two nights ago—well, I can't exactly explain it, but suddenly I knew in some way much deeper than reason that the Lord actually *was* there beside me.

I'm sure of it. And I believe the grip that guilt and fear and worry and all that depressing stuff had on me is broken. For the first time in years, I actually feel set free."

And subsequently he found that he was, for a fact, free! That was why Christ came into the world, so we are told—to free captives like my physicist friend. And anyone, including you, can be free of worry if you will fill your mind with the factual idea that God is with you and is giving you a normal, steady, intelligent attitude toward the problems of life. When you image yourself as living close to God, you will have the ability to get your mind above the confusion and heat of worry into a place of clarity and calm. Many have found this practice the best way to outwit worry.

Imaging outwits worry. Try it. You'll see.

7

IMAGE YOURSELF NO LONGER LONELY

A<small>N UNHAPPY WOMAN CAME</small> to consult me a few months ago. She was in her mid-fifties, I judged, pleasant looking but with an aura of dejection about her. "Dr. Peale," she said. "I'm in prison, and I can't get out."

"What sort of prison?" I asked her.

"The prison of loneliness," she said. "The prison of isolation from life. And I'm not the only one; there are thousands upon thousands of us—mostly elderly people, but some just middle-aged and widowed, like me. Solitary human beings living in the loneliest solitude of all—the solitude of a big city."

She looked down at the handkerchief she was twisting in her fingers. Finally she went on: "The days crawl by, one just like another. And do you know what the worst time of all is? It's 6:00 P.M. That is when Ralph used to come home from the office, and we would have an hour or so together before I'd get dinner on the table. I used to wait for the sound of his key in the lock of our apartment. Now six o'clock comes, and there is no key in the lock, no familiar face, no one to prepare a meal for. I turn on the six o'clock news and look at it, but I don't really hear it, because I'm so lonely I just want to die."

I did feel sorry for her. I said, "Don't you have some friends or relatives who can partially fill the gap left by your husband's death?"

She shook her head. "No relatives here in the city," she said. "My two daughters are married and live elsewhere. I have a few acquaintances, but they are all busy with their own lives. They don't have time for me, and I don't blame them."

"Why do you say that?" I asked her.

"Well," she said with a wan smile, "I'm not the most scintillating company in the world. I never finished college; I just met Ralph and married him. I don't have much to contribute, I guess. I don't have any skills to get a job with. I'm just a homebody, really. Nobody cares much about homebodies these days."

"You say you're a prisoner," I said to her. "And you want me to help you organize a jailbreak. Well, to begin with, do you know who holds the key to your cell? Do you know who your jailer really is?"

"No," she said, looking puzzled, "not really."

"I think you do know," I told her. "The jailer is you. You're the only person who has the key to your cell. You're the only one who can open the door that leads to freedom. You'll never do it so long as you hold in your mind this image of yourself as a helpless victim of circumstance, a woman who lacks friends because she thinks she has so little to contribute, a person hopelessly trapped in a dungeon of loneliness. If you continue to image yourself that way, that is what you will continue to be. So if we are really going to organize a jailbreak, we will have to begin with you and some of these attitudes that are walling you in."

"Isn't it too late," she said, "to start changing attitudes at my age?"

"That is just the sort of attitude we need to change," I told her. "Of course it's not too late! We can start right now. We are going to do some creative imaging of a fascinating existence for you. You said you see yourself as a prisoner—lonely, almost friendless, living in a drab procession of monotonous days where nothing ever happens. Now I challenge you, this very moment, to throw that tired, old, downbeat, negative image of yourself right out of your mind. In its place visualize a woman—you—with a smile on her face and a song in her heart, inviting a friend over for lunch or a movie or a trip to a museum—and being invited back, taking bridge lessons, perhaps, until she becomes a good player, offering her time and energy as a volunteer at some hospital, buying a new dress or a new coat, going to church on Sunday and meeting new people, taking up a new hobby or two, photography, perhaps, bird-watching, anything. But always image a new life, a vital, interesting life."

I was watching her face as I talked, and I could see hope and doubt simultaneously in her eyes.

Image the New You

"Push those doubts out of your mind, and do it now," I told her. "Pin up this image of the new you that I'm giving you in their place. The doubts will try to come back, and so will a lot of other old, tired attitudes and habits. You just have to practice *dis*placing everything that contributes to a poor self-image and *re*placing those things with realizable goals. What I'm portraying is not beyond your reach. It is a personality change that you can have if you make up your mind to have it, if you desire it with all your heart, if you pray for help in obtaining it. Start every day with a prayer. Prayerize, visualize, actualize—that is the formula for successful imaging. If you carry out the first two steps with all the intensity you can muster, I promise you that the third step will take care of itself."

Twice since then, I've had occasional reports from this woman. She hasn't turned into a complete extrovert overnight, but she is really trying and she is getting somewhere with her new self-image. She is busier and she is happier—and she's stopped thinking of herself as a prisoner. She said that whenever she feels the old insidious chill of loneliness beginning to creep back into her life, she picks up the phone and calls someone who may be lonelier than she is. So I have no doubt that she will conquer her loneliness, because she has discovered the best solution of all: thinking about other people instead of herself.

I've heard it said that loneliness is the great modern plague, that it exists in epidemic proportions. Well, let's take a closer look at this affliction that claims so many victims, and try to list some counter-measures.

First, I think it helps to realize that being alone doesn't necessarily make you lonely. I know quite a few people who actually enjoy solitude because they've mastered the art of living pleasantly with themselves.

Some lucky people seem to be born with this happy faculty. One night when our daughter Margaret was about four years old I heard her laughing and talking to herself long after she should have been asleep. I went into her room and asked her what was going on. "Oh," she said, "I'm just laughing because I have such a good time with me!" And I remember thinking, *What a wonderful way to be*. You have to spend every minute of your life in your own company. If you don't enjoy it, you're going to be miserable. If you do enjoy it, solitude will never bother you.

If the time you spend alone is to be spent pleasantly, you have to know yourself—and you have to like yourself.

Knowing yourself means understanding what makes you happy, what makes you sad, what gives you pleasure, and what bores you. Take myself, for example: I'm a worker. I like to work, I am accustomed to work, I feel happiest when I'm working. Holidays tend to make me restless because I have the uncomfortable feeling that I'm wasting my time. I like the satisfaction that comes from getting things done, so when I have to be alone I'm able to live pleasantly with myself by filling my waking hours with the work I love to do—like writing this book, for example.

Like Yourself

Then there is the question of liking yourself. Most of us think of ourselves quite favorably most of the time. But there are a surprising number of people whose self-esteem is too low. People who have done things they are ashamed of, or suffer from an inferiority complex, or demand too much of themselves and then blame themselves when they fall short. How can other people be attracted to them if they don't like themselves?

The plain truth is, many lonely people are lonely because they turn other people off. They are irritable. Or rude. Or complaining. Or critical. Or self-centered. Or downbeat. Or opinionated. Or just plain dull.

Sometimes they have little mannerisms that drive you up a wall. Many years ago I knew a woman—a good-hearted person, really—who seemed to walk through life in slow motion. She moved deliberately, she talked deliberately, she thought deliberately. Since she was a member of a committee on which I also served, I had to have lunch with her occasionally. When I did, I almost had to grit my teeth to keep from showing impatience as she *slowly* pushed each morsel of food at least six times around her plate, *slowly* raised it to her mouth, *slowly* chewed and chewed. I was able to endure it, due to infrequent meetings, and I always try to take people as they come. But I learned that others fled her in droves.

So if you are lonely, you must face the possibility that something in your own personality is causing that loneliness. And if it is, you have to isolate it and actively do something about it.

Try to see yourself as others may see you. What sort of expression do you habitually wear? Does a smile come easily, or do you feel more at ease with a frown?

How is your posture? Do you stand straight and tall, or do you slump dejectedly?

Do you project an aura of cheerfulness and confidence, or would you make a perceptive observer say, "Here comes bad news!"

How about your dress and your grooming? Are you an attractive-looking person, someone you yourself would like to meet? What about your conversation? Are most of your opinions enthusiastic and optimistic—or are they the reverse? Do the things you find fault with outnumber the things you praise? How many of your sentences begin with a capital "I"?

Do you truly pay attention to what the other person is saying, or are you too busy thinking about what *you* will say next?

Have you learned the basic rule of successful small talk, which is to inquire about other people's interests, or do you rattle incessantly about your own?

Review your attitude about people in general. Ask yourself honestly: Do you really like to be around people? Do you care about them and show them that you care? When you have an outflowing attitude of genuine caring, it creates a state of harmony between you and other people that is irresistible. People feel it instantly, and they always respond.

Another cure for loneliness lies in that old exhortation: Don't just sit there, do something! One of the most common causes of loneliness is inertia and the apathy that comes from not having enough to do.

I remember one day coming out of a Rotary luncheon and seeing a forlorn woman sitting in the lobby of the hotel. She was the widow of a Rotarian who had died some weeks before. When I asked her why she was there, she said that it made her feel less lonely to sit outside the Rotary meeting that had meant so much to her husband.

"If you'll come with me," I told her, "I'll give you a better solution." I took her to my church, where some cheerful women volunteers were stuffing envelopes and having a lot of fun together. "Here is a new helper," I said to them. "Take her in. Make friends with her. Above all, keep her busy." And they did. She told me afterward that having something useful to do, and congenial people to do it with, had rescued her from despair.

But remember this: If you are lonely, you can't just wait for someone to come along and rescue you. You have to be willing to make a move yourself. Form a picture of the interesting life you want to live and of one in which you have many friends and exciting interests. Hold that image and move constantly toward it. The mental picture will reproduce itself as fact.

The truth is, we all need supportive relationships. I once heard a lecture in which the speaker talked about the great redwood trees of California, those magnificent giants of the forest towering as much as three hundred feet in the air. "You'd think such tall trees would require very deep roots," the speaker said. "Actually, redwoods have a very shallow root system, designed to capture all the surface moisture possible. These roots spread out in all directions, and as a result, all the roots of all the trees in a redwood grove are intertwined. They are locked together so that when the wind blows or a storm strikes, all the trees support and sustain one another. That is why you almost never see a redwood standing alone. They need one another to survive."

Most people do, too.

Finally, the best remedy for loneliness is available to each of us, all the time. Not long ago I read about a power failure in a Salt Lake City hotel that left an elevator stuck between floors in total darkness—a frightening situation. Rescue workers, hearing a woman's voice inside, called out, "Are you alone in there?" "I'm by myself," came the calm reply, "but I'm not alone." People soon caught on that she meant God was with her, protecting her, as indeed He was.

You don't have to be trapped in an elevator to practice the presence of God. You can talk to Him anyplace, anytime, about anything, and He will listen and respond.

Jesus said, "I am with you alway, even unto the end of the world" (Matthew 28:20).

Hold fast to that assurance, and the dark shadows of loneliness will fade away.

8

THE THREE BIGGEST STEPS ON THE ROAD TO SUCCESS

WE SOMETIMES TALK AS if imaging were a modern discovery, something that we in our twentieth-century wisdom have brought to light. Maybe in a way our generation *has* rediscovered imaging, but actually it is older than the Pyramids. Much older.

The other night, for example, I was reading an article about the marvelous cave paintings of southern France and northern Spain that are said to be at least twenty-five thousand years old. In those paintings, figures of men armed with spears are shown attacking animals resembling buffalo or bison. The article said that the drawings were part of primitive rituals designed to bring these cave-dwelling hunters good luck in their ceaseless quest for food.

In other words, before the dawn of history men were vividly imaging goals essential to their survival and reinforcing those images by painting them with primitive but lasting colors on the ceilings or walls of the caves that were their homes.

Now, hundreds of centuries later, we don't go forth with sharpened sticks or flint-tipped spears to hunt woolly mammoths or ward off saber-toothed tigers. But modern man still has to make a living in a tough, competitive, sometimes hostile world. The twentieth-century salesman who stalks his customer through the concrete canyons of a modern city is not very different from his remote ancestor in his primary goal, which is to put food on the table for his family. And just as the caveman tried to reinforce the image of himself as a successful hunter, so the modern breadwinner must reinforce and believe in his ability to wrest a living from the world that surrounds him.

I'm convinced that successful people in all walks of life use imaging constantly, whether they know it or not. So in this chapter let us talk a bit about the part it plays in pursuing that often elusive will-o'-the-wisp called success.

Imaging can help in three crucial areas. The first is goal setting. If any endeavor is to succeed, the first thing you must do is choose your goal, visualize it clearly, and fix a specific date for arriving at it.

Several years ago a young man came to me and announced rather

forceful that he wanted to "get somewhere" in life. He seemed to think
that I could help him on his way. "I want to make something of myself,"
he announced. He pounded his fist into his hand. "Yes, sir, I'm determined to get somewhere."

"That's fine," I said to him. "Where do you want to get?"

"I don't know exactly," he told me, a bit taken aback. "I just want to
achieve something worthwhile."

"Well," I said, "when do you want to achieve this ambition?"

"Oh, sooner or later," he said. "The sooner the better."

I tried again. "Tell me," I said, "what, exactly, do you want to do with
yourself?"

He gave me a rather injured look. "If I knew that," he said, "I
wouldn't be here bothering you."

"Look," I said to him, "you must have certain areas of interest or apti-
tude. What sort of thing appeals to you, or comes naturally to you? If
you could wave a wand and have a career happen to you, what would it
be?"

He shook his head sadly. "Those are tough questions. I really don't
have the answers."

"Let me be blunt," I said. "You say you want to get somewhere. Well,
you'll never get anywhere unless you know where that somewhere is.
You have to have a specific goal firmly fixed in your mind, a goal that you
can see as plainly as you see me sitting in front of you right now. Not
only that, you need to have a target date for achieving that goal. Not a
vague point somewhere in the future. An actual date. A deadline. And
once you've set a deadline, you must image yourself meeting it precisely
on the nose. Do you understand what I'm saying to you?"

Somewhat hesitantly he said that he did.

Write Your Goal

"Now, I suggest that you go home and write down what you want to do
with your life. Until you write a goal, it is only a wish; written, it
becomes a focused objective. Put it down on paper. When it is on paper,
boil it down to a single sentence: what you want to do, exactly when you
intend to start (which should be right now), exactly when you plan to
achieve your goal. Nothing fuzzy or hazy. Everything sharp and clear
and definite. No reservations or qualifications. Just one strong, simple,
declarative sentence. Then send me a copy of that life-changing sentence, because that is what it is going to do: change your life!"

"My life?" he echoed.

"Exactly," I told him. "Change you from a fumbling, bumbling, confused drifter and dreamer into a confident, focused, productive, useful
person. I want you to make half a dozen copies of that sentence and put

them where you'll see them at least three times a day. I want that pledge to sink down through all the levels of your conscious mind and deep into your unconscious mind, because that is where it will unlock the energies that you will need to achieve your goal. You will be imaging with power."

He shook his head slowly. "How can you be so sure of all this?" he demanded. "How do you know?"

"I know," I told him, "because when I was about your age, my father made me do just what I'm urging you to do. I was hesitating between two careers, one in journalism, one in the ministry. My father made me think it through and write down my chief goal in life in one sentence. That sentence was: 'Serve the Lord Jesus Christ and spread His Word as far as I possibly can in the course of my lifetime.'

"When I showed my father that sentence, he said, 'All right; that's it. Now if you will print those words on your conscious and subconscious mind, pray without ceasing, and work like the devil, that goal will come to pass.' So that is what I've tried to do. That is what I'm still trying to do with every ounce of strength and energy in me."

My visitor was silent for a while. Finally he said, "All right. I'll go home and do it." And he did. He sent me a copy of the sentence he finally wrote down. It is a large and praiseworthy and difficult objective, but if he does what my father said, if he will print it on his mind, image it, pray about it, and "work like the devil," I know he will achieve it. He has already made significant progress in the imaged direction.

Imaging a goal is a kind of promissory note made out to yourself. And even when these pledges are made casually, or only half-seriously, the unconscious mind can hear them and react to them. I have a novelist friend who told me that when he was a cub reporter on a small newspaper, not much more than a messenger boy, really, his father grew impatient with his apparent lack of progress and wrote him a letter asking him if he thought he would ever amount to anything in his chosen profession.

"I was a little annoyed at his lack of confidence in me," my friend said, "so I sat down and wrote him a note, half-joking and half-serious. I admitted that I seemed to be making little progress, but I added that I was only twenty-one and had a lot of time stretching out before me. Furthermore, I told my father, I knew exactly where I was going and when I would arrive. I said that at age thirty I would be a great newspaper reporter. At forty a great city editor. At fifty a great short-story writer. At sixty a great novelist. At seventy a great grandfather. At eighty a great admirer of pretty women. And at ninety a great loss to the community."

My friend went on to say that his father was much amused. "But you know," he added, "leaving aside the question of greatness or lack of it, my career has followed that predicted pattern to a remarkable degree."

"Of course it has," I told him. "You had a realizable wish, a realizable dream, a realizable image. You pointed the compass of your subconscious mind in the direction of that dream. And that is where it has carried you."

You'll notice that my novelist friend almost instinctively set time limits for each successive stage of his development. "By my thirtieth birthday," he said to himself, "I will be this; by my fortieth I'll be that; by my fiftieth I will have achieved this set of goals," and so on. And his unconscious mind took him quite literally. It will always be obedient to a strong, definite self-image.

This deadline technique is extremely important in major ambitions and in minor ones. A woman approached me one night after I had given a talk in a West Coast city. She had quite a lovely face, but it was supported by a truly massive body. She looked almost as wide as she was high. She said abruptly, "How old do you think I am?" Then, when I hemmed and hawed a bit, she said, "Come on. No evasions. Tell me the truth. How old do you think I am?"

"Well," I said, "I'm no expert in these matters. But I'd say you are forty-eight or forty-nine." (And maybe I was stretching the truth a bit at that.)

She said, "I am thirty-five! Isn't it awful? I'm so fat it is a disgrace. I hate being like this. Every day I look in the mirror and see myself not as an attractive woman, which I used to be, but as an obese female. Have you ever heard a more disgusting description than this?"

"Yes, obese male," I interjected.

"Well," she continued, "I look into the future and see myself getting even heavier and even more unattractive. And I get so discouraged and depressed that life doesn't seem worth living. Can you help me?"

"Well," I said, "perhaps I can help you help yourself. But first we are going to have to change the image you have of yourself, especially when you look into the future."

She Images Her Weight Goal

I found a place where we could talk without interruption, and made her sit down. "Now," I said, "tell me how much you weigh right this moment."

"One hundred eighty-seven pounds," she said sorrowfully.

"And how much do you want to weigh?"

"A lot less than this," she said.

"No," I insisted. "Give me an exact number of pounds."

"All right," she said. "I want to weigh one hundred twenty-eight pounds."

"And what do you want your measurements to be?"

She looked at me as if this were a strange question to be coming from a minister. "I haven't thought about that," she said.

I took a pencil and on the back of an envelope drew a simple outline of a human figure. "Here," I said. "Take this drawing. Add arrows pointing to waist, hips, bust. Put numerals alongside the arrows indicating the number of inches you want to measure in each area."

She took the pencil and wrote down some numbers.

"Good," I said. "Memorize those numbers. Tell your body that is the size it is going to be. Now, when do you want to be this size and weight? Next week?"

She smiled. "I know it won't happen overnight."

"Ah," I said, "but that means you can conceive of its happening, which wasn't the case a few minutes ago. Now, let us pick a target date. How about the first of January? That is eleven months away. If you want to lose fifty-nine pounds, that is only a fraction over five pounds a month—less than two pounds a week. That certainly is obtainable. And if you believe you can, you will do it. You have to visualize the pounds melting away. You have to see yourself fitting into smaller dresses. You have to anticipate the admiration on your husband's face as the girl he married emerges from the prison she has been living in.

"Finally, you have to look into the mirror and image, not an obese female, but a new and vibrant and beautiful woman who has a rendezvous with next New Year's Day. If you hold that image in your mind for one minute every morning when you wake up and one minute every night just before you fall asleep, and if you ask God for spiritual strength to persevere, the dream will actualize itself. I'm sure of it. And I want you to send me a telegram next January first, telling me that I was right."

Well, the telegram didn't come, and I was a bit disappointed. But about a week later, when I was shaking hands with members of the congregation after Sunday service at Marble Collegiate Church, a beautiful, slender woman shook my hand and asked, "How old am I?" I stared at her in amazement. "Oh, it's you!" I exclaimed, because at first I hadn't recognized her as the "obese female" from out west. But here she was, completely transformed. I asked, "One hundred twenty-eight pounds?" She said, "One hundred twenty-seven and a half! Thanks to you!"

"Don't thank me," I said. "Thank the good Lord for working with you all these months. And in particular, thank Him for the power that He put into your unconscious mind through imaging, the power that turns wishes into realities when the wishes are strong enough."

If setting worthy goals is the first step on the road to success, the second is the belief—no, the conviction—that you are capable of achieving those goals. There has to be in your mind the unshakable image of yourself *succeeding* at the goal you have set yourself. The more vivid this image is, the more obtainable the goal becomes.

Great athletes have always known this. The high jumper "sees" himself skimming over the bar; the golfer facing a difficult shot images the ball soaring over the intervening obstacles and landing squarely on the green; the placekicker in football keeps his head down as he kicks, but in his mind's eye he holds the mental picture of what he wants to happen in the next few seconds. He "sees" the great arena full of tense spectators, the onrushing defensive linemen, the blockers holding them off, the ball spiraling back to the holder, the thud as his foot connects with it at precisely the right angle, then its spinning flight squarely between the uprights. The more intensely he images this before it happens, the higher his confidence in himself and the better his chances of making it happen.

Discard the Failure Image

Even people who have a long record of *not* succeeding can be turned into tremendous achievers if they will discard their images of themselves as failures or ne'er-do-wells and become God-trusting individuals whose attainment of desired goals is just a matter of time, and a specific length of time at that.

In Australia a few years ago, I met a remarkable man named John "Bert" Walton. He has since become a close friend. He told me that when he stared out in life he seemed to be caught in a peculiar failure pattern. Whatever he tried would start out well and then end up badly. As a schoolboy he dropped out of several schools for this reason. He became convinced that it was his destiny in life to make good beginnings and then watch them fade away. And naturally, since that was how he saw or imaged himself, that was what always happened.

At one point, he got a job with the Australian division of a famous American company. The same dreary pattern seemed to be unfolding: He started out well and then began to slide. This didn't surprise him much; it was what he expected to happen.

Then the company sent a motivational speaker out to give some talks to their Australian employees, and Bert Walton was in the audience. The visitor told his listeners that they could achieve anything they wanted to, if they would just believe that they could do it. He told them to visualize themselves moving up in the company, receiving promotions, gaining energy and dynamism as they went, right up to the very top. "You can if you think you can," he kept saying. "Most of you are only using ten percent of the powers that are in you. Most of you are letting the fear of failure hold you back. Most of you are living in a dungeon of self-depreciation and negative thinking. All the ingredients of success are right there inside you, if you'll just turn your thinking around. Don't keep telling yourself you can't do this or you can't do that. Knock the *T* off the word *can't*. You can do anything—ANYTHING—if you think you can!"

Bert Walton had never heard anything like this in his whole life. He told me that he walked away from the lecture almost in a state of shock. He realized for the first time that his image of himself as a person who started well and then faded away was all in his head, a state of mind that could be altered any time he made a firm decision to alter it. He said, "I walked past the office of the head of operations for New South Wales, and I visualized myself in that job. I imaged myself sitting at that desk. I said to myself, "I can have that job if I think I can have it, and from now on I do think I can. I know I can. I'm going to have it. I *will* have it. And then I'll move on from there!"

Bert Walton went back to work with tremendous enthusiasm and confidence and energy. He received promotions. He became manager of operations for New South Wales. Finally he became the head of the company for all of Australia. I was told by other Australian friends of mine that he probably could have become the head of the parent company also, but his career took another turn. His father was the owner of a store and wanted his son to come in with him. So Bert Walton built that store into one of the largest merchandising chains in Australia. He was knighted by the queen. Where once he had been dogged by failure, now everything he did was crowned by success. "I'm not an unusual person," he told me. "I really have only an ordinary brain. It was that one talk that changed my self-image by giving it a little twist. It made me see myself differently, and so I was different."

"Well," I told him, "if you have only an ordinary mind, you have certainly used it in an extraordinary manner!" And indeed he has. Sir John Walton is a living example of imaging, of positive thinking and faith.

People who want to succeed in life not only have to build a strong self-image but they also have to get that image across to the people whose goodwill and support they need to get ahead. All successful salesmen know this. When I was a youngster growing up in Bellefontaine, Ohio, there were only two Jewish families in town. One was in the clothing business. Emil Geiger ran the leading men's clothing store. Emil was a good friend of my father—he used to come to our church to hear my father preach because there was no synagogue in town. Everybody liked Emil. If a customer came in and Emil couldn't fit him or supply him with what he needed, Emil would courteously direct him to another store that could. "I'm not just selling clothes," he used to say. "I'm selling the reputation of Emil Geiger as someone who wants to help his fellowman. The secret of success in business is this: Think of the customer's needs, not your own. Create the image of yourself as someone who cares about the customer, not about the customer's money, and you will always do well."

Emil used to give me odd jobs now and then. I remember that one time he had a lot of old marked-down suits that nobody wanted to buy, so he persuaded me to take a friend of mine and go out into the country-side with a horse and wagon and try to sell the suits to farmers. "Tell them these suits are good merchandise even though they are marked down. And the suits will serve them well. Be sure that each customer is happy with his purchase." Emil was pleased with our successful sales campaign.

Years later, Emil came to New York and heard me preach. Afterward, in my study, he said, "Well, Norman, you've come a long way from Bellefontaine, but you are still a salesman, just as I trained you to be. You are offering something that people want and you are thinking about their needs, not your own. What's more, you see yourself as a successful seller of ideas, and so other people accept that image of you, too, and listen to what you have to say. If you just keep on giving people what they know they need, and make them feel you care about them, they will come from miles around to hear you." I shall always cherish Emil's memory, for he cared enough to help me when I was a boy.

Another friend of mine who projects his own self-image into the minds of his customers is Joe Girard, listed in the *Guinness Book of World Records* as the world's greatest automobile salesman. There was a time in Joe Girard's life when he looked like the world's greatest failure. Every-thing he touched went wrong. He was up to his ears in debt. The bank was trying to repossess his house, his car, everything.

One cold night in January he came home, climbing the back fence and sneaking in the back door to avoid bill collectors. When he walked into the kitchen, his wife told him that there was no food in the house. She had nothing to give the children. At that moment the doorbell rang. Another bill collector.

Joe Girard didn't open the front door. Instead, he stooped down in the darkened hallway and prayed a prayer of desperation. He was con-vinced that he was a total failure as a husband, as a provider, as a human being. He asked the Lord to help him, to give him another image of himself, to turn his life around.

The next day he went to an automobile-sales agency where he knew the manager, and begged him for a selling job. The man felt sorry for him and agreed to give him a chance on a commission basis. All that day he dialed people he knew, trying to sell a car by phone, but nothing hap-pened. The timing was unfortunate, just after the Christmas season. It seemed nobody was buying cars.

Making a Sale Gets Him Started

Finally, just before closing time, a man wandered in. Just looking, he said. He had no intention of buying anything. By now, Joe Girard should have been totally discouraged. But somehow, looking at the man, he visualized a warm, friendly encounter that would result in a sale. He imaged himself receiving the commission money, then bringing home bags of groceries to his family. He saw the food steaming on the table, the hungry children enjoying it. He fixed the whole scene in his mind; then he began to talk in a friendly and outgoing spirit to the man, whom he now saw as a promising prospect. In the end, impressed by Joe's sincerity, the man agreed to buy a car. The owner of the agency gave Joe an advance on his commission that enabled him to go out and buy those groceries. He took them home. The whole dream came true.

After that, there was no stopping Joe as a salesman. He never let his customers forget who he was or what he did for a living. He kept records and sent each customer a card on his or her birthday. If they were Irish, he sent them a card on Saint Patrick's Day. If they were Jewish, he sent them one on Jewish holidays. With each sale, his image of himself as the most effective car salesman in the world grew stronger. And he continues to put that image into the thinking of prospective customers to this day.

If the first step on the road to success is to set a goal, and the second is to believe you can reach it, and the third is to image it, the fourth and most important is this: Let God be your partner. God stands ready to help you at all times. I know this, for He has always helped me. And that is for sure. He gives quiet but accurate guidance to those who ask for it. He gives determination to the hesitant, and courage to the fainthearted.

The combination of strong imaging backed by strong faith is irresistible. Years ago, a young woman named Blanche Green, who had always led a sheltered life, married a schoolteacher. Five years later her husband had a serious accident that left him an invalid. It was a frightening situation for the young woman.

But Blanche was a deeply religious woman. She was a believer in God and so in herself. As she prayed for help and guidance, an image came to her. It seemed to involve a company that dealt in women's clothing, and she also seemed to see herself playing an important part in the company. This puzzled her because she had no connection with the clothing industry.

Then she happened to meet two young men who were in the clothing business. The wife of one had designed a new kind of foundation garment for women. The men had the patent for it, but no money with which to launch it. It was still in the idea stage, going nowhere.

But to Blanche this chance meeting was a clear directive from the Lord; she saw it as divine guidance. She told the two young men that she was sure she could sell their new design profitably for them.

Naturally they asked her what selling experience she had had.

"None," she told them. "But I know how it should be done. You get the name of a prospect. Then you pray for that prospect. Then you believe that a helpful and friendly meeting will take place with that prospect. You form a picture in your mind of a successful encounter. You believe that God is always with you. You go out in the name of the Lord, and you meet that prospect, and you sell her the garment."

"Oh, you're crazy!" they said.

"No," she said, "I'm not crazy. If you go out in the name of the Lord, being loving and honest and caring, holding the success picture, the doors will open for you. If you let me try it, you will see."

Reluctantly, they let her try. So this pretty young woman, with no business experience at all but with a positive attitude, went out every day selling door-to-door. As she approached each door, she would affirm to herself, "If God be for me, who [or what] can be against me?" Her manner was so calm and so friendly and so open that people trusted her instinctively. "I'm going to help American women shape up," she used to tell her customers, smiling. And she did. In the end she became the president of a successful corset company and a legend in the garment industry.

The reason for Blanche Green's success was as simple as it was powerful. Faith in God removes tension, fear, worry, and all the negative forces that hold a person back from success. If God be for you (and if your goal is a worthy one, He *will* be for you), then what is there to worry about? If the most powerful force in the universe is on your side, why should you have any fear of failure? A kind of serenity comes over people who have this conviction, and in the center of that serenity more often than not is the sunlit oasis that we call success.

Serenity. That is a most important contribution of religion, isn't it? Religion is a set of beliefs and attitudes that gives calmness and assurance to struggling human beings, gives them the courage and determination they need to get through this life, plus a blueprint that, if followed, will lead them triumphantly into the life to come.

I see this serenity at work in God-trusting people all the time. Not long ago I was in the office of a well-known industrialist, a self-made man in the automotive industry. It was late afternoon, quitting time. I knew he had a tremendously heavy schedule, but his desk was completely clear, not a single piece of unfinished business on it. I complimented him on that. "How do you do it?" I asked him.

"Well," he said, "there was a time when I would finish up a day with papers all over my desk, each one representing an unsolved problem. I tried to figure out what was wrong, and finally I came to the conclusion that I was worrying too much. I hesitated to make decisions because I worried about whether they were the right decisions. I worried about the consequences of the decisions I did make. Worry was acting as a kind of paralysis, slowing me down, holding me back."

"Evidently you got rid of it," I said. "How did you manage that?"

"If you watch as we leave this office," he said, "I think you'll see."

When we did leave a few minutes later, I noticed on the wall near the door a calendar, the kind where each day is indicated on a page that can be torn off and discarded. Underneath the calendar was a scrap basket. My friend paused at the door, tore off the top sheet of the calendar, and slowly crumpled it into a ball. He closed his eyes and his lips moved soundlessly. Finally he opened his hand and let the crumpled piece of paper drop into the scrap basket.

"Great invention, the scrap basket," he said with a smile. "When you want to get rid of something, all you have to do is drop it there and it is gone. So that's what I do with my worries at the end of every day. I ask the Lord to watch over my responsibilities while I am away from this office. I thank Him for His love and His care. Then I open my hand and let the worries and the problems of the day simply disappear." He snapped his fingers. "Just like that! I know there will be new problems the next day, but I don't worry about them. The Lord will help me deal with them. And anyway, the energy I save by not worrying today will be channeled into problem solving tomorrow!

"I ask the Lord to watch over my responsibilities while I'm away from this office." That man had taken the third and crucial step on the road to success by asking God to be his partner in decision making. He asked for support and guidance. He *imaged* the infinite wisdom and sagacity of the Almighty being focused on his problems, untangling them, clarifying them, working out solutions that would appear, when the time was right, in flashes of insight or nudges of intuition in his own mind. He built his house upon the rock, knowing that when the sea of troubles swirled around it, it would still stand.

When you do that, you don't have to worry about pursuing success or happiness. They will come to you.

9

IMAGING: KEY TO HEALTH?

NEAR THE END OF World War II, a young American soldier named Lew Miller was caught in a burst a German machine-gun fire. Five bullets smashed into him: two in his left arm, one in his shoulder, two in his head. He was taken to a military hospital more dead than alive.

Weeks passed, then months. His normal weight of 192 pounds dropped to 90. He was so weak that if he tried to stand, he fell on his face. He was a brave man and he struggled valiantly to regain his strength, but recovery was so slow and painful that it seemed almost hopeless.

He tried praying, but his prayers seemed feeble and futile to him. Doctors did their best, but their best seemed to make little difference.

Sometimes, to make the endless hours pass more quickly, Lew Miller would try to recall happy scenes from the past, athletic triumphs he had had as a boy, or occasions when he had won scholastic prizes or honors. He would picture the applause of the crowds, the pride and happiness on his parents' faces, the satisfaction he had felt. He tried to visualize these events as vividly as possible, because when he did he could forget, momentarily, the hospital bed where he lay.

As he reviewed these memories, Lew Miller began to be aware that most of them seemed to have a common denominator. Each time he had scored a triumph or gained an objective, he had had a mental picture of the success before it actually happened. Whether it was winning a tennis tournament or placing in the first ten runners in a cross-country race, he had "seen" himself doing it in advance, and when he clung to that image with unswerving faith, the actuality seemed in some uncanny way to follow the dream.

Lew Miller had plenty of time to think, and gradually he began to see (just as years later Harry DeCamp would see) a connection between this before-and-after pattern and some of the great promises of the New Testament. He remembered that "what things soever ye desire, when ye pray, believe that ye receive them, and ye shall have them." Was it possible, Lew Miller asked himself, that a strong mental image, backed by intense faith, could actually be a form of silent prayer, prayer unencumbered by words? And if that were so, might he not hasten his own recovery by visualizing it happening and claiming Christ's promise at the same time?

Lew Miller had believed all along in the power of God, but now he began to see that to liberate that power in his own life it was *his* responsibility to create the image of his own recovery and nurture it with faith. And so, with a sudden surge of determination and energy, he began to do just that. He saw himself returning home. He saw himself driving a car, holding down a job, resuming a normal, everyday sort of life. Looking beyond that, he saw himself raising a family, taking part in civic affairs, pursuing a career. Not only did he visualize these things over and over, with all possible intensity, but he almost began to thank God *in advance* for turning these visions into reality.

"We are essentially minds with bodies," Lew Miller told himself, "not the other way around. Therefore our minds can dominate and control our bodies. If I affirm and visualize my recovery, my thoughts will steadily be forming and producing their physical counterparts."

As soon as all these concepts came together in Lew Miller's mind, he felt a remarkable upsurge of hope and well-being. To the doctor's amazement, he began to mend rapidly. Today Lew Miller is a happily married man with two children. He leads the normal, happy, and productive life that he imaged so vividly in that army hospital so many years ago. He is convinced that he groped his way to one of the most powerful healing combinations in the world: intense imaging plus unshakable faith. And it brought him back from the edge of the grave to the land of the living.

What does medical science make of stories like this one? Naturally, there is division of opinion. Some doctors believe that all illness is a reflection of mental or emotional states. Others do not go that far. And certainly a layman like myself cannot pretend to be a judge.

I was interested to read a brochure announcing a course called "Guided Imagery and the Bodymind Approach to Optimum Health," by Jeanne Achterberg, Ph.D., and G. Frank Lawlis, Ph.D. This brochure, in describing the program to be offered, stated:

> Imagery has been the golden thread running through effective medical practice for over 3,000 years. Imagery appears to be the bridge between psyche and soma; it is central to learning biofeedback . . . and may be the basis for understanding and increasing the power of the placebo effect. As such, imagery may well prove to be the single most important technique for modern health care.

Thirty years ago an authority on psychosomatic medicine, Dr. Arnold A. Hutschnecker, wrote, "We, ourselves, choose the time of illness, the kind of illness, the course of illness, and its gravity." And he added, "We are moving toward a recognition that in illness of any kind, from the common cold to cancer, emotional stress plays a part."

Not long ago I came across a newspaper story in which a California physician, Dr. Irving Oyle, was quoted as saying that people could live to be 150 years old if they would just practice a combination of right thinking and prayer. "Positive, beautiful thoughts trigger the release of beneficial hormones in the body and these in turn help the body to heal itself." On the other hand, he said, "If you presume that you live in a hostile universe, the reaction to that presumption is what wears out your body." Then he added, "Prayer is a good way to combat anxiety and promote healing. . . . When you pray, you assume that there is some force in this universe which is on your side—some powerful force. The minute you do that, your body relaxes. And if you really believe that God will respond to you, you have immediately instituted the healing process. Faith itself creates the hormones that make you live longer."

Basic Keys to Healing

Hope, faith, truth—these seem to be the key. When you have them, you can image your own recovery and speed the healing process. When you don't have them, you can't. Dr. Sanford Cohen, Chief of Psychiatry at Boston University School of Medicine, has made some studies that seem to indicate that hopelessness—that is, an image of no recovery—actually kills. If a doctor diagnoses a fatal disease and tells the patient, and if the patient loses hope and gives up, death comes quickly. An autopsy may show the malignancy, all right, but no reason the patient should have died so soon.

I once knew a woman whose elderly father was hit by a taxi as he was crossing a street in Manhattan and died at the age of eighty-seven. When an autopsy was performed, the doctor was amazed. "Your father had all sorts of lesions and ailments that should have caused his death twenty years ago," he said to the woman. "Yet you say he was lively and energetic right up to the end. How do you account for that?"

"I don't know," the woman said, "unless it was his habit of saying to me every single morning, 'Today is going to be a terrific day.' " This daily imaging habit, it seems, paid off.

A doctor friend once showed me X rays of three human hearts. He said, "What do you think of those hearts?"

"Well," I said, "I know nothing about hearts or X rays. Is something wrong with them?"

The doctor said, "You are looking at three damaged hearts. The owners of these hearts were negative people; they all expected to get ill or be ill; two of them expected to die young. On top of that, all three were living irresponsibly. I guess you might say their lives were full of sin."

"Were you able to help them?" I asked.

"In part," he said. "I took over your job. I showed them, with these X rays, how the way they were living and the way they were thinking was affecting their hearts. I told them that if they went on much longer, their hearts would lose the capacity to rebound, but if they changed their attitudes and their habits and their thinking, their hearts could still recover because of the marvelous comeback potential the Creator had built into them." He chuckled. "I guess you could say I scared the hell [sin] out of them. Those people are healthy, vigorous, alive people today because they finally grasped the connection between their minds and their hearts, between moral or immoral living and the functioning of the most important organ in their bodies. You could make a sermon out of this, Norman. If you do, I suggest you tell your congregation that their bodies will take a lot of abuse, but the point finally comes where it won't take anymore—and people had better turn away from downbeat thinking and wrong living before that point is reached, because afterward is too late."

Ruth and I have lived quite a few years now, and both of us have been remarkably free of illness all along the way. Ruth attributes her good health partly to the fact that as a child she ate simple foods, mostly vegetables. Money was scarce in the Stafford family, so there was seldom any meat. Ruth says she never tasted steak or rare roast beef until she went to college. She also thinks there is a strong connection between hard work and good health. "If you keep really busy," she says—and she certainly does—"you don't have time to think about yourself or your health. Or your lack of health."

As for me, I'm convinced that human beings are *supposed* to be healthy; we are *designed* to be healthy; that is what the Creator intended when He made us. I constantly image myself as a disease-free individual. It reminds me of something an airline pilot told me one day when he came back through the plane to visit with us passengers. I said to him, "It always amazes me how these big planes stay up in the air. All this tremendous weight, all this fuel, all of these people, all their baggage. It is astonishing!"

"Not really," the pilot said. "It is the nature of airplanes to stay up in the air. They are designed to fly. They want to stay up in the air. It is very hard for a plane *not* to stay up in the air, because that is the way they are put together."

That is the way God put us together, too. To be healthy, energetic, creative, dynamic people at every age, full of vitality and health. I'm sure of it.

But we have a responsibility, too, not to abuse our bodies with alcohol or drugs or nicotine or other harmful substances, or too much food, for that matter. Nor should we abuse ourselves with overtension. It is hard to persuade people to avoid these things, especially young people, because they have great vitality and think they are immune to trouble and can go on indefinitely. They have to learn the hard way, and that can be unpleasant.

The other night I was reading a book by my friend Art Linkletter, the TV personality. Art doesn't touch tobacco, and in the book he told why. When he was still just a youngster he got a job as a welder. A lot of older welders chewed tobacco or dipped snuff and—wanting to be one of the boys—young Art was ready to try either or both.

But one of the welders, a big, tough fellow, said, "Let me show you something, son. Take off your shoe and sock." When Art did, the man stuck a big wad of tobacco between two of Art's toes. "Now put your shoe and sock back on," he said, "and see what happens."

Within a short time, Art began to feel ill. Before long he was desperately nauseated. The chemicals in the tobacco had invaded his whole system through the skin between his toes. And Art wrote: "At that moment I decided I was never going to smoke." And he never has.

That was pure chemical cause and effect. The interaction of mind and body is more subtle, but it is just as real. And the interaction of infinite mind, which is God, and the human organism, across the bridge known as prayer, is more mysterious still. But every minister and most laymen have seen unforgettable examples of it.

I remember one night when I was a young minister in Syracuse, New York, a telephone call came from a physician I knew, Dr. Gordon Hoople. He said he had a patient who was not responding to treatment. A crisis was imminent. He wanted me to come right away.

When I arrived at the home, I found Dr. Hoople and a young nurse with the patient, a middle-aged woman who seemed to be in a coma. I recognized the nurse as a member of my own congregation.

"This woman is very ill," the doctor said. "I've done everything I can for her medically, but that is not enough. I treat my patients, but it is God who does the healing. You know that and I know it. Now here we are, three believers and this woman, who is unconscious. Let us try to fill this room with the healing grace of the greatest of all physicians, Jesus Christ. Let us image her as responding to the creative life-force. Actually there is no medical reason that she should die. But her spirit seems weak. Let's put faith into that spirit."

Scripture Reaches Into Unconscious

I remember we sat down by the bedside. First I prayed. Then Hoople prayed. Then the young nurse prayed. Then we began to quote Scripture passages. It was a strange and moving experience. I felt as if there were two contending forces in the room, one regenerative, the other destructive, and that by praying and affirming faith through Scripture, we were adding strength to the life-force. I found that I could summon to mind almost any Bible passage I wanted and could recite it verbatim, even though ordinarily I could not have done this. Later, Hoople and the nurse told me they had the same experience.

Hours passed. Nothing changed. Then, all at once, the patient opened her eyes, smiled at us faintly, and fell into a quiet sleep. I remember how Hoople reached out and felt her pulse with his sensitive fingers. "It's all right now," he said. "This crisis is over. Our prayers and our affirmative faith have pulled her through." And she did indeed get well.

A less dramatic incident, but one which I remember vividly, happened some years ago when I was driving from Dayton, Ohio, to the little village of Bowersville, where I was born. The town was celebrating its one hundredth anniversary, and I had been invited, as a native son, to give the centennial address.

As I drove along, my ear began to ache. I hadn't had an earache since childhood, but now I had one that grew worse and worse. By the time we reached Bowersville, I was in agony. I asked Ruth to go into the hall where I was scheduled to give my talk and tell the people in charge that I was indisposed, that they would have to delay the talk, that perhaps I couldn't deliver it at all.

When Ruth was gone, I sat holding my head in my hands, hardly able to believe the amount of pain that could be generated by one misbehaving ear. As I sat there, I heard a tap on the window of the car and a stranger spoke to me. I remember he was a big man with a calm, kindly face. He evidently knew who I was, for he spoke my name. "You're not well?" he asked. I assured him that I was far from well. "I'm a believer," he said, "and I have the gift of healing. I'd like to give you a faith treatment. I think it might help."

I was suspicious. "What does it consist of?" I wanted to know.

"I'll put my hands on your ears," he said, "and offer a prayer of healing. I'll tell the Lord that you are needed here tonight. It is the town's birthday and people are waiting to hear you. I'll ask Him to take away the pain."

"What do I have to do?" I asked.

"Just believe," he said, "and picture yourself as healed of this pain that is tormenting you."

So I agreed. While he prayed, with his hands covering my ears, I tried to hold in mind an image of myself with two good, healthy, nonaching ears. And, to my astonishment, almost instantly the pain began to subside. It didn't vanish in one split second, but it began to diminish steadily. The man had told me to believe and visualize and I had tried, but the relief was so remarkable that I could hardly believe it. I tried to thank the man, but he simply smiled and moved away.

A moment later, Ruth came back. She had found a medical doctor and had him with her. I told them what had happened. By now the pain was perhaps 60 percent gone.

"Well," said the doctor, "that's fine, but I would like to give you a shot of antibiotic anyway."

So, at Ruth's urging, I let him give me the shot, and I'm sure it had good effect, also. Anyway, the pain continued to subside, and soon after that I was able to give my talk with almost no discomfort. Who healed me? Was it the faith healer or the doctor? Both, perhaps, plus the power of the creative image. However it may be explained, I have had no further earaches to this very day.

How can we explain the spiritual power when it is called upon that way? We can't explain it, but we know it is there. We know it works. When a prayer chain is organized for someone who is sick, with dozens or perhaps hundreds of people praying for the same result, that collective imaging of the patient's improvement can release enormous curative powers. I have seen it happen over and over again.

Belief in the power of prayer and in spiritual procedures should in no way diminish our respect and gratitude for medical science. Both are gifts from God and both, in my opinion, should be used to the utmost when needed. But science has limits. However, the power of prayer is limitless to the degree that it enables us to make contact with God, who made our bodies. I remember how my old friend Dr. Smiley Blanton handled one difficult psychiatric case. The doctor tried every possible medical approach. Nothing worked. Finally the famous psychiatrist, then an old doctor, handed the man a Bible. "Here," he said. "Take this. Go away and read it. Then just do whatever Jesus says. See yourself as a well, normal, healthy person. If you just do that, you'll be all right."

How I Stopped Having Colds

Holding a strong mental image of yourself as a healthy person definitely reduces your susceptibility to illness. I used to have the annoying habit of getting a bad cold every February. (I tried not to get it on a Sunday, because that would have interfered with my preaching.) It always went through the same cycle: sniffling, achiness, sore throat, then the vocal cords would close up and all I could do was croak unintelligibly. Finally, about four years ago, I said to myself, "This is ridiculous. It is all in your head. You expect to get a cold when February comes. You image it and so you get one. Now put that image out of your mind. Forget it. Instead, image yourself *not* having a cold in February and see what happens." So I did—and I haven't had a cold since. Ruth says dryly that she began making me take more vitamins at about that time, and perhaps she did. But I think the changed image in my mind was the main thing.

I remember one unusual case where negative images were put to a positive use. The man involved was prominent in literary and publishing circles in New York. He was very successful professionally, but he was an alcoholic. Sober, he was brilliant and charming, but drunk he was an obnoxious boor who embarrassed his friends, humiliated his wife, wrecked his automobiles, and in general was very bad news indeed.

This man would go without drinking for weeks, sometimes months. Then he would convince himself that the problem was licked, that he could handle a drink or two. But he never could. Once he took the first drink, he couldn't stop. He would drink until he passed out, sometimes in a bar, sometimes in the street, usually after creating some dismal scene.

When he came to himself after these binges, he was always filled with remorse, self-loathing, and disgust. He would vow never to touch another drop of alcohol. But then, as the memory faded, he would take the first fatal step and go through the whole sordid cycle again. Nothing seemed to break the pattern. He tried Alcoholics Anonymous, but even that powerful rescue system could not help him.

One morning he woke up in Bellevue Hospital after another binge. He was sick, trembling, miserable, filled with guilt and self-condemnation. All around him were the sights and sounds and smells of a hospital ward filled with human wreckage of every description. *I'm in hell*, he thought, *and I put myself here. If I could just remember exactly how I'm feeling now, how ashamed I am, how utterly horrible all this is, I would never take another drink.*

If I could just remember. . . . After he was released and entered into another period of sobriety, he kept hearing echoes of that phrase, and the thought came to him that if once a day he would just image himself in the alcoholic ward, recall every sordid aspect of it, and relive every gruesome detail, the revulsion would be so strong that he would not take a drink that day.

So he decided that every day when the *idea* of alcohol presented itself to him for the first time—a whiskey advertisement in the morning paper, a beer commercial on the radio, the casual mention of a cocktail party, anything—he would stop whatever he was doing for one minute and image, as vividly as possible, the horrors he had undergone (and put others through) each time he took that first drink.

He made this ironclad rule for himself, and he stuck to it rigidly. Even if he was having a telephone conversation and the subject of alcohol was mentioned, he would excuse himself, promise to call back, and then for one full minute picture himself back in the alcoholic ward— sick, miserable, remorseful, and ashamed.

And it worked. He never took another drink—a remarkable example of the positive power that can emerge from a negative image.

I believe the greatest health insurance a person can carry is to see himself, proudly and humbly, as a creation of God. God, who is infinitely gifted and infinitely wise, does not do bad work. If He created you in His image, and He did, that means that His perfection, His excellence, His craftsmanship are built into you. It follows then, does it not, that the best way to keep His handiwork in good running order is to stay close to Him.

The other day in a town where I had made a speech, a man filled with high spirits, zest, and goodwill greeted me with, "I still have the faucet."

I was baffled. "What do you mean, faucet?"

"Oh," he said, "don't you remember? You gave me the faucet idea." He went on to remind me of a talk I had given some twenty years ago, and presently I remembered the illustration he was referring to. At the time, I had been reading T. E. Lawrence's book *The Seven Pillars of Wisdom*. Lawrence was the great desert fighter of World War I who identified himself with the Arabs and became one of their leaders in their revolt against the Turks.

After the war, Lawrence took a few of his Arab friends from the burning sands of the desert to the boulevards of Paris. He put them up in one of the most elegant hotels. He showed them all the sights: the Champs Élysées, the Eiffel Tower, the tomb of Napoleon. But they were only mildly interested in these things. The one object in Paris that fascinated them was the faucet in the bathtub in their hotel. Lawrence would find them gathered around the tub turning on the faucet with exclamations of delight, and watching the strong stream of water which they could control at will. They kept saying, "Isn't this marvelous? All you do is turn a little wheel and you get all the water you want!" It was amazing to men who had lived all their lives on the hot and arid desert sands.

"You foolish fellows," Lawrence said to them. "Don't you know that this faucet is attached to a pipe, which leads to a network of pipes, which lead to great conduits, which lead to vast reservoirs? And don't you know that those reservoirs are so located that the melting snows and the rains from the mountains come surging into them? You cannot get water from a faucet unless it is connected to a source of water."

So the man who had heard me tell this story said, "That little parable got through to me somehow. I realized that I badly needed a faucet attached to the vast reservoirs of God's power. I decided to go with Jesus Christ as the directing force in my life." He went on to say that he had stopped doing some things he had been doing, and where, before there had been no flow of power in his life, now it came surging through and had been flowing ever since.

So if your health isn't what it should be, if your life isn't what you want it to be, if you have not reached the level of attainment that you desire, then you can do what so many happy, successful people have done: get yourself attached to the flow of spiritual power. You can attach yourself to this incredible power by wanting to be attached; you can attach yourself by believing, by imaging, and by following the Word.

Then, once you are attached, you will live with the power coursing through you. This power is no fantasy. It is reality, absolute reality, and one of incredible strength. It can and does enter into believing persons and thereby into situations in a way so astonishing that it should convince anyone, however skeptical, that imaging the power of God can affect persons, even situations, under the most difficult circumstances.

Miracle of Imaging in New Zealand

For example, I received a letter from a man in Auckland, New Zealand, stating that he has written a book and asking permission to use certain quotations from our writings. Of his own book he said, "I have tried to make it a practical guide to a healthy self-image, as well as finding fulfillment in life through the use of a Master Picture Plan." The book is titled *The Greatest Sale You'll Ever Make—and How to Make It.* But this author points out that "while it [his book] is primarily designed for salesmen, the same techniques can be used by anybody."

But it was the P.S. to his letter that gave testimony to the amazing power of imaging faith. The P.S. reads:

> I have been blind, but now through the power of Jesus, together with the inspiration provided by you, and the skill of a surgeon, I have got back sight in the left eye. When the local doctors said that nothing could be done, I refused to accept it, telling them, "There must be someone, somewhere in the world who can help." In a wonderful way I was guided to a specialist in Melbourne, Australia, and had pioneer operations in Royal Melbourne Hospital. I took your booklet, *"You Can Overcome Any Problem,"* with me, and used to finger it day and night. I was sent home, heavily drugged, and for two years was not allowed to work and then only for short periods.
>
> The day came when I could slowly read the title *You—Can—Overcome—Any—Problem,* but the rest was blank. I kept on praying and holding your booklet and the day came when I could read your name. Finally, praise God, the time came when I could read what is inside. The piece I want permission to quote on P. 17, "So never let any problem overawe you . . ." to me is one of the greatest passages in the booklet. In the NAME OF CHRIST I refuse to be intimidated. Thank you Dr. Peale, thank you.
>
> Bruce G. Hardie

The message is indeed impressive: "In the Name of Christ I refuse to be intimidated." Image the power, the wonder-working power, as healing, restoring. What you can image, you truly can be.

(If you would like a free copy of the booklet, "You Can Overcome Any Problem" referred to by Mr. Hardie, you may have it by writing to the Foundation for Christian Living, Pawling, New York, 12564.)

Actually, the creative healing effect of such mental attitudes and practices as positive thinking, faith, prayer, and imaging are underscored if not verified by the point of view of scientists.

In an article in the *Reader's Digest* for September 1980, Laurence

Cherry describes the work of Dr. Lewis Thomas, president of the famed Memorial Sloan-Kettering Cancer Center in New York City, whom he quotes as saying: "The natural tendency of the human body is toward health—we are amazingly tough and durable." Dr. Thomas, it seems, takes an optimistic view of the basic health of the individual. "I believe fervently in our species and have no patience with the current fashion of running the human being down. On the contrary we are a spectacular, splendid manifestation of life. We matter. We are the newest, youngest, brightest thing around." So says Dr. Thomas in his book *The Medusa and the Snail*.

Dr. Thomas is of the opinion that most germs are either friendly, like the ones in our body that help digestion, or simply not interested in us. The few germs that do attack us are usually soon annihilated by the body's white blood cells.

"As for diseases whose care is unknown at the present time, Dr. Thomas believes that science will soon learn how to eradicate them," says Laurence Cherry, adding that "in the not very distant future Dr. Thomas predicts we will be able to live out our life span without worrying about illness. Many of the disablements considered an inevitable part of age are actually the result of a disease process, probably involving viruses. There is no reason why these, too, shouldn't ultimately be eliminated," he says.

Since the most creative element in our person, the superior factor in our entire entity, is the mind, such scientific findings as those of Dr. Lewis Thomas and other outstanding thinkers would certainly seem to support the thesis that mental activity, imaging or picturing health is a valid and productive process. It validates the affirmative belief that what you can image you can be.

So visualize and picturize your own well-being. See yourself whole, healthy, and energized. Practice creative imaging—the key to health.

10

THE WORD THAT UNDERMINES MARRIAGE

WE AMERICANS SHOULD BE good at imaging because we are an optimistic people. We think mistakes can be corrected. We believe obstacles can be overcome. We like to dream big—and what is dreaming, when it is focused intensely, but a powerful form of imaging?

It has always been this way in this country. The great nineteenth-century explorer, John C. Frémont, wrote of nights spent beside a flickering campfire on the great plains, listening to the coyotes howl and dreaming of mighty cities that someday would stand in the vast emptiness around him. Frémont's dreams must have seemed like the wildest fantasies at the time. But today, there the cities stand.

One of our most beloved patriotic songs, *America the Beautiful*, reflects this soaring optimism:

> O beautiful for patriot dream
> That sees, beyond the years,
> Thine alabaster cities gleam
> Undimmed by human tears!

Hardly a reality, you may say. Ah, but what a vision! Alabaster cities gleaming somewhere down the shining road of the future. Poverty and disease conquered. War abolished. People living joyous lives of work and play and service, no tears. If Frémont could dream his impossible dreams and have them realized 150 years later, who knows what may happen to our own dreams and images in another century or two?

But there are some pressing problems that we have to solve first. And one of these concerns the ancient and honorable estate known as matrimony. Let us devote this chapter to a discussion of marriage and where it stands today.

Everyone knows that the divorce rate in this country has risen to the point where, in some states at least, one out of every two marriages winds up as a failure. This is a deeply disturbing state of affairs, because marriage is the glue that holds the family together—and the family is the basic unit of society, indeed of civilization itself. Cicero said, "The empire is at the fireside."

What is the matter with modern marriage, anyway? I think the answer is that there is nothing wrong with marriage. What is wrong is the concept—that is to say, the image—of marriage that has prevailed in the last two or three decades, especially among our young people.

The other day, on a shuttle plane between Boston and New York, I found myself sitting beside an affable stranger. When I casually asked him what took him to New York, he said that he was going down to attend his daughter's wedding that afternoon.

"Well, congratulations," I said. "That's wonderful."

He gave a wry little laugh. "Yes, a bit monotonous, though. This is her third."

"Oh!" I said, not knowing what else to say.

"She's a bright girl," he told me. "She has a very good job. But here she is, at the age of twenty-four, trying matrimony for the third time. Two down, one to go. I hope this time it works."

"I hope so, too," I said.

"But you know," he went on a bit grimly, "I don't know why it should. This fellow she is marrying seems nice enough. But so did the other two young fellows whom she divorced. This one's been divorced himself, and he's only twenty-five. I don't know what is happening to the institution of marriage, really. Young people nowadays seem to regard it as a kind of game of musical chairs." He stared out the window at the carpet of clouds below us and shook his head slowly. "It is a funny feeling to be going to your daughter's third wedding and saying to yourself, 'Maybe it'll work and maybe it won't.' "

"Maybe," I said dryly, "that is where the trouble lies—in that word *maybe*."

And it does, you know. Let me explain.

Having been completely and happily married for a lot of years, I know I tend to look at marriage from a point of view that must seem pretty old-fashioned to some members of the younger generation. I believe in monogamy, fidelity, total commitment to a married partner. I believe in these things because the Word of God Himself tells us that that is the way human beings are supposed to live. And He certainly knows the score.

Ruth and I know from firsthand experience that the rewards of living that way are so great that any deviation seems just plain senseless. To us, marriage is a compact sealed with love that cannot be broken. It is a promise between two consenting adults to join their lives and stick together through thick and thin, good times and bad, until life comes to an end. No *maybe* about it for us. None whatsoever.

But in the last two or three decades that word has crept into the American concept of marriage until it is the word most often used.

The Fatal *Maybe* Attitude

"I'm getting married, and I hope it works, but maybe it won't. And if it doesn't, maybe I can just cancel out and look for another partner. Why not? That is what everybody's doing."

"I am married, but maybe I've made a mistake. Maybe I've married a bit beneath me. Maybe I'm still growing and my partner has stopped growing. Maybe our sex life isn't what it ought to be. Maybe I'd be happier married to someone else. Maybe I'd be happier not married to anyone. . . ."

Maybe. Maybe. Maybe. Every single one of those *maybes* is a form of negative imaging. They represent images of marital failure. They leave an escape hatch always open. And the more they are thought about, or toyed with, or dwelled upon, the stronger is the possibility that the escape hatch will be used.

Two or three years ago, a young woman came to me saying that her husband was neglecting her. He was a brilliant young medical student, but she complained that he studied day and night. He never took her out to a play or a movie. He never took her dancing. They seldom went to a restaurant. They barely had enough money for necessities, and none for luxuries. He had his nose in a book all the time.

She went on whining like this for several minutes. Finally she said, "I don't know why I married Tom. There was another boy named Gerald who wanted to marry me, too. I turned him down for Tom, but maybe I made a mistake. Maybe I should have married Gerald—"

"Stop," I said to her. "Stop right there. Your husband isn't neglecting you, young lady; you're neglecting him. He is working his heart out trying to prepare for a life of helping people. He needs all the support he can get from a loyal, loving wife, not sulks and tantrums from a spoiled little fluffy kitten. So my advice to you is this: Go back to your husband. Thank God every day of your life that you are fortunate enough to be married to a man like that. Put all these ridiculous *maybes* out of your mind. The one *maybe* you can use would be to say to yourself, 'Maybe I can think of a new way to be loving and supportive of Tom today.' "

Harsh words? Perhaps. But she needed to hear them. She went away looking very pensive, and evidently some of the words got through to her, because she is still married to Tom, not to Gerald or anyone else, and Tom is about ready to start a successful medical career. Parenthetically I suggested to Tom that he knock off once in a while and at least go to McDonald's for a Big Mac. He did, and they both had fun.

Young people are not the only ones who have a flawed concept of marriage these days. Ruth and I receive a great deal of mail from older people struggling with marital difficulties, and a remarkably high percentage deals with a phenomenon that we sometimes refer to as the

Walkaway Husband Problem. In letter after letter, bewildered, unhappy, heartbroken women report that after fifteen, twenty, even thirty years of marriage their life partner has suddenly walked out on them. Sometimes another woman is involved; sometimes not. Sometimes the husbands give an explanation; sometimes they don't. The net result is the same: The husband, often the chief breadwinner, is suddenly no longer there, leaving a wife and often children to struggle as best they can to rebuild their lives, or even to survive.

Again it seems plain to me that behind this grim and increasingly frequent state of affairs lies a faulty image of marriage. To the walkaway husband, marriage has become the symbol of a relationship full of drudgery, monotony, and unrequited sacrifice. He sees himself as the plodding, patient, long-suffering bearer of endless financial burdens. *All these years*, he tells himself, *I've been pulling this load. Ninety-five percent of my earnings have gone to support this wife and these children. But what about me?*

What does he have to show for all this effort? A wife who's overweight physically and underweight mentally. Children who are leaving the nest, who have their own lives to lead. As time goes by, he and his wife have less and less in common, less and less to talk abut. Here he is, at age fifty, or fifty-five. He probably has a couple of pretty good decades left. He thinks, *Why don't I get out from under these burdens and live a little? Maybe I'll meet some woman who is physically more attractive and mentally more stimulating.* Who knows, instead of being totally dependent on him, she might be a strong person who could help him to cope with problems—a partner instead of a drag! "Anyway," he says, "I've had it. I've done my duty. I've served my time. I'm getting out!"

And to the consternation of everyone—wife, children, friends, neighbors—out he goes.

The sad thing about these cases is that I'm sure they never happen overnight. Almost always the discontent of the husband (or of the wife if the situation is reversed) has been growing over a long period of time, and the discontented partner has been giving warning signals of all kinds. "For heaven's sake, Agnes, stop nagging me about going to church!" "Harold, why don't you talk to me anymore? All you do is come home and drink beer and stare at the television!"

The signals are clear enough. But they are ignored. Communication fades away. Neither partner is willing or able to look realistically at his or her own performance, or share the blame for the slow deterioration that is taking place. And so they pass the point of no return and slide faster and faster down the slope that ends in desertion or divorce.

Now, what is the remedy for all this? What can be done to prevent such dismal endings to once-bright hopes and dreams? What can people whose marriage is in trouble do about it?

I think the main thing they can do is try to revive and recapture the image of marriage as a triumphant, rewarding, lifelong partnership where the pluses outweigh the minuses by an overwhelming margin. I think they have to stop focusing on the worst aspects of their lives together and reach out for the best—expect it and hope for it and pray for it and work for it and image it until it once more becomes a reality.

I sometimes think it would help if ministers who marry starry-eyed young couples would urge them to project themselves into the future, see themselves raising a happy houseful of kids, visualize themselves working out problems together as a team in human service, supporting each other, loving each other, being faithful to each other. They should be encouraged to visualize their later years, with grandchildren coming along and a great and satisfying marriage partnership growing ever closer and more loving. They should be urged to paint this dream as vividly as possible, and they should be assured that the reality would follow the dream if they imaged it and worked for it and prayed for it hard enough.

Imaging? Of course. But it really does create a climate in which an ever-deepening relationship can grow and flourish.

Experiment Saved a Marriage

Imaging can also be a healing influence in marriages where cracks have appeared. Some years ago a couple I had married wrote to me saying that things were going badly and that they were on the verge of divorce. They thought that since I had married them, they should let me know.

In my reply I urged them to carry out a week-long experiment that I said might save their tottering marriage. I told them to find an alarm clock, one with a loud tick, then each morning go into a room with two chairs and spend twenty minutes in uninterrupted silence.

In the first ten minutes, I wanted each of them to visualize in vivid detail (it was imaging, but I didn't call it that) what their lives would be like after the divorce. The effect on the children. The loneliness. The guilt. The sense of loss and broken dreams. The financial strains and dislocations. The side taking among former friends. The whole dreary aftermath.

Then in the second ten minutes, I urged them to recall as vividly as possible some of the happiest, most loving times they had known together. Imaging again: the memory of past happiness can point the compass of the unconscious mind toward the goal of similar happiness in the future.

I told them, finally, that if they would listen carefully to the loud, rhythmic tick of the clock, they would find it repeating the word that was at the bottom of all their troubles: *self, self, self, self!* I urged them both to ask the Lord to come into their hearts and remove that most universal of all sins: selfishness. If they would do that, I told them, they would be praying together. And I added that never in all my experience had I known any couple to get a divorce who had prayed together.

Well, you know, it worked. And imaging had a lot to do with it.

I remember other cases, too, where imaging saved a shaky marriage. In World War II, many marriages underwent severe strains when there were long separations, wives alone at home, soldier-husbands far away overseas. In one fairly typical case, a young husband stationed in England fell in love with an American Red Cross girl who was also stationed there. When the war ended, the soldier came back to his wife and told her that he was sorry, but he had met another girl, they had fallen in love, they were sure they were made for each other. He said he felt very badly about the way things had worked out, especially since he and his wife had two small children born before the war, but he wanted his wife to give him a divorce. He was sure that, under the circumstances, she would.

But the wife had had a Quaker upbringing, which meant that she had a quiet inner strength. She did not panic. She did not fly into a jealous rage. She told her husband that she knew him better than he knew himself. He was, she said, basically a good father and a good husband. That side of him would reassert itself someday. Until that day, she would simply wait. She would not give him a divorce.

The husband argued, he pleaded, he told the wife that he no longer loved her, that he loved the Red Cross girl. He said that by refusing to let him go, she was making them all miserable. He added that, being young and attractive, his wife would undoubtedly marry again. She replied that she already had a marriage. It was going through a difficult period, she admitted, but sooner or later it would come out the other side, stronger than before. She could see that day clearly in her mind. She visualized the two of them going on with their lives, raising their children, and perhaps having more. She imaged them in love again, this whole dark interlude forgotten. She said serenely that she believed this was God's plan for them. Therefore, she could not give him a divorce.

The husband departed, angry and frustrated. He went back to the Red Cross girl, who was waiting for him in her hometown. He told her that his wife would eventually stop being so stubborn. It was just a matter of time. He was in a difficult and humiliating position. All they had to do was wait.

So they waited. And waited. And waited. And gradually it became apparent to the Red Cross girl that *she* was the one who was in the humiliating position. Finally she told her lover that she was tired of waiting for the stubborn wife to step aside. The glamour was gone from their situation. She wanted a husband of her own, not a man anchored to another woman. She told him to get lost.

By this time the husband was beginning to have second thoughts himself. As his wife had said, there was a part of him that recognized his obligations to her and the children. And he also became increasingly conscious of deep emotional ties that he knew existed. He was impressed that his wife was really a great woman. Finally, sheepishly and contritely, he came back home. His wife welcomed him quietly. She was not surprised. It was all working out just the way she had imaged it. There were no recriminations. She took him back. And that marriage went forward successfully, saved by the emotional balance and good sense of a real woman who imaged her way through an ugly situation and came out triumphantly on the other side.

I remember another case in a small town where a woman was married to a man who was a notorious philanderer. He was very attractive to women, and whenever temptation crossed his path he followed Oscar Wilde's advice to get rid of the temptation by giving in to it. Small towns being what they are, his affairs and escapades were common knowledge, and from time to time certain ladies of the community, pillars of society themselves, of course, would decide that it was their duty to tell the wife about the misdeeds of her husband.

She Imaged Her Marriage to Success

But they never got much satisfaction when they did. The wife would smile and shake her head and say that she knew they meant well, but they were mistaken. She knew her husband. She trusted him. She knew he loved her. It was impossible for her to conceive of any such disloyalty on his part. Her informants were simply misinformed. The informants would go away baffled and frustrated, because they knew very well that they were right.

Now, was this wife actually imaging a husband who was a model of marital fidelity, or was she just being remarkably patient and wise? Being a mere man, I can't answer that question. All I know is that gradually the amorous adventures of the husband began to be less frequent. Finally they ceased altogether. And when a close friend asked him, in considerable amazement, what had happened, the husband said, "Well, you know, when my wife trusted me and refused to believe what people told her, even when it was true, I began to feel more and more like a low-down, no-good skunk. If she loved me that much, then the least I could do was to try to live up to her concept of me. And that's what I'm going to do from now on."

In other words, the man responded to the image of himself that he saw reflected in his wife's eyes—and began behaving like a man-sized husband instead of a heel.

Even when a clear, steady image of successful marriage is kept in mind, it is a relationship that must be constantly monitored, adjusted, and nourished. Here are seven suggestions that Ruth and I recommend to marriage partners who want to keep the flame alive.

1. *Try to have a mature concept of what love really is.* For too many Americans, love is a breathless romantic glow in which they expect to have their own emotional needs gratified. Some people, especially young people, are really little more than receiving stations for this kind of supportive attention from a member of the opposite sex. They are addicted to it. They have to have it, and they sulk if they don't get it.

But this is dependency, not love. It is shallow, not deep. It is a feeling, not a commitment, a feeling that can change as moods or circumstances change—and if the feeling vanishes, even temporarily, then it is easy to decide that love has ended.

Romantic love doesn't really change anyone. Mature love has a spiritual dimension that alters a person profoundly, and changes him or her from a self-oriented person to an others-oriented person. In mature love, the beloved's welfare and happiness becomes more important than your own; as someone said, real love is the accurate estimate and supply of another's needs. Another definition: Love is what comes from living through difficulties together. These concepts are a long way from the romantic, sex-saturated depiction of love that is so prevalent and so popular in our American culture. But they are far closer to the truth.

Some people never learn that love is not just a pleasant feeling; it is a way of regarding another person and treating that person. A young woman sitting stony-faced in my office not long ago said to me, "I don't love my husband anymore."

I said, "How do you know that?"

She said, "I don't feel loving toward him, that's why. I don't feel anything."

I said, "Love is more than a feeling. If for one month you will simply do the loving thing where your husband is concerned, do it regardless of how you feel or don't feel, perhaps the affection you once had for him will come back. Act as though you love him, whether you think you do or not. The important thing right now is how you act, not how you feel. If you will make yourself do the loving thing, if you will simply treat your husband with kindness and consideration, you may be able to salvage your marriage."

To act in this way is not deception. It is the dramatization, really, of a hoped-for image of things to come. In this case, that woman is still trying, and successfully, too, for the marriage is still alive.

2. *Work on communications constantly.* No matter how long you have been married, you can never take your lines of communication for granted. They need to be constantly used, tested, and if necessary repaired.

If a husband and wife are separated during most of the day, as many couples are, it is wise to set aside a specific time, perhaps early in the morning, perhaps before going to bed, to talk about plans and problems, grievances or misunderstandings, all or any aspect of living together. That way, difficulties can be dealt with while they are still molehills, not mountains. Once the habit of sharing things verbally is established, the marriage becomes much more resistant to the stress and strains that surround it.

The truth is, marriage is a contract that needs to be renegotiated constantly, with compromises and concessions and common sense. You have to watch for areas where you are *not* communicating (for example, can each partner discuss in-laws frankly and openly?) and try to get a dialogue going.

There are many forms of communication in marriage. Sometimes sympathetic listening is the best form; sometimes just knowing when to be silent. Sometimes it is working together; sometimes it is shared play. Sometimes it is a casual, affectionate touch; sometimes just a glance. Sometimes shared laughter. Sometimes the joy of sexual reunion. Whatever form it takes, it is the heartbeat of marriage. When it ceases, the marriage dies.

3. *Learn how to defer gratification.* This is a combination of self-control and patience. Both marriage partners have to be willing at times to put off or forgo immediate pleasures or satisfaction in order to obtain greater benefits in the future. This may sound obvious, but I have seen the failure to do this wreck many marriages. Some people cannot bring themselves to save money, or put it to work for them in long-range plans or investments. Others refuse to work overtime, even when overtime work will ultimately bring them significant rewards. They're too interested in having their pleasure or their recreation right now.

Imaging helps here, too, because if you image a desired goal vividly enough, if you visualize the rewards of patience and self-discipline clearly enough, you can often supply the motivation that otherwise might be missing.

I often think that if quarreling couples on the brink of divorce would just defer *that* gratification for a few weeks or months, they might wind up with a stronger marriage than before. They might learn that difficulties or even pain can be a trigger to growth. They might even realize, upon reflection, that escaping out the back door of marriage is not likely to change the basic problems they are facing; those problems will probably go right along with them into the next relationship that they try to establish.

4. *Take responsibility.* Accept the truth that marriage is going to be what you and one other person make it, no better and no worse. Face up to the fact that in any disagreement or controversy you are not going to change your partner very much, if at all. The only person you can really

change is yourself. But when you do change yourself, by accepting blame occasionally, by apologizing sometimes, by compromising now and then, the whole human equation changes and things often work out the way you want after all.

A man said to me not long ago, "I prayed about my wife's drinking problem."

"Has she stopped drinking?" I asked.

"No," he said, "but I've stopped nagging her. I've stopped thinking about leaving her. I think I've found the strength to go on living with her and loving her no matter what. I believe I have found the patience to lead her to the help she needs. And someday I think she will change."

I think so, too. As some wise person said, "Prayer doesn't necessarily change things for you, but it changes you for things."

5. *Learn to compromise.* Compromise doesn't mean giving in. It just means that you recognize that there are two (or more) sides to every question. Sometimes it helps to trade a bit, in a good-humored way. If the husband will go to church on Sunday instead of playing golf, the wife will stop smoking. If he will stop leaving the ice trays unfilled, she will stop squeezing the toothpaste tube in the middle. That sort of thing.

When Ruth and I first bought a place in the country over thirty years ago, she loved the house but I was bothered by the fact that across the road was a huge barn that cut off a part of our view. Ruth kept telling me how picturesque it was, but it still bothered me. It bothered me, in fact, for the next twenty-one years. Then another house became available one-half mile away where there was nothing to obstruct the view. By now Ruth was devoted to the house we had, but she knew how I felt about that barn. She felt that she had had her "druthers" for twenty-one years; now it was time for me to have mine. And so, gracefully, she agreed to move. Compromise—lubricating oil in the machinery of marriage! Footnote: She now loves the house we moved to.

6. *Practice the art of appreciation.* Everybody cherishes a word of praise. Some psychologists believe that the desire for approval is one of the strongest human traits, maybe even *the* strongest. So why not master the art of the casual compliment, the little unforeseen gesture that says, "I think you're wonderful just the way you are"? An unexpected bouquet of flowers. A love note in a pocket or under a pillow.

It was Arnold Bennett, I believe, who remarked (in his bachelor days) that it seemed to him that marriage nearly always resulted in the death of politeness between man and wife. But that doesn't have to be the case. Try complimenting your wife or your husband just once a day. The resulting rush of affection will surprise you. If they don't die of astonishment first!

7. *Strive always to increase the spiritual dimension of your life together.* Marriage is a difficult and demanding relationship; people in it need all

the help they can get. A simple and extremely practical rule is to keep Christ in the center of your life, and decisions will be sounder, joys will be greater, troubles will be more bearable, burdens will seem lighter. One businessman said a surprising and unexpected thing to me: "When I'm away from home, I call my wife long-distance every night. And when I do, I try to visualize God as a third person listening in, sharing our problems, understanding our needs, watching over both of us. It is a kind of prayer, I guess. Anyway, we both get a lot of good out of it."

Of course they do. And so do married couples who pray together, go to church together, read the Bible together, believe together. There is a Bible passage that sums it up: "Except the Lord build the house, they labour in vain that build it" (Psalms 127:1).

I once heard a wise marriage counselor compare marriage to the base camp that mountain climbers establish when they plan the conquest of some mighty peak like the Matterhorn or Mount Everest. The mountain represents life itself. The base camp of marriage is the place where the climbers—the marriage partners—keep the supplies and equipment that are essential to their assault on the mountain.

The base camp really represents survival; if at a temporary camp at higher elevations something goes wrong, the climbers can always retreat to the base camp to find food and warmth and shelter, to renew their strength for another attempt. There is liberty for each of the climbers to go forth and try different routes to the summit. But the base camp is where communication takes place, where plans and decisions are made. Unless the base camp functions as it is intended to function, the expedition will fail.

So if you are married, or if you ever intend to be married, hold in your mind the image of a base camp well and truly chosen, equipped with love and companionship, warmed by loyalty and faith and trust. And never forget to ask God's blessings on all comings and goings. Then venture forth with confidence to climb the highest peaks that life can offer.

11

THE HEALING POWER OF FORGIVENESS

USUALLY, WHEN IT COMES time on Sunday morning for me to speak, I have gone over the material so often and so carefully that it is pretty well fixed in my mind. By the time church begins at 11:15 A.M., this process of preparation is supposed to be over. But one Sunday morning recently I was having trouble with a talk as late as 10:45 A.M. I needed an illustration for a certain point, and I didn't have one, and I couldn't think of one, and the clock was ticking, and I was getting more and more uneasy.

Sitting at the desk in my study, I happened to look up at the top of the bookcase, and there was a little toy coal scuttle filled with miniature lumps of toy coal. That coal scuttle, complete with toy shovel, had been sitting there for at least thirty years, and I had ceased to be aware of it. But there was the illustration I needed!

Thirty years ago I was called to see a patient in a hospital. This woman had had a lot of misfortune in her life. Some people had treated her very badly. They had cheated her and lied to her and almost ruined her, and she hated them. This hatred darkened all her thoughts and colored them a deep, funereal black. And this in turn had begun to affect her health. She told me that she was in and out of hospitals all the time which, under the circumstances, was not surprising. She wanted me to help her.

Well, I tried, but didn't have much success. I told her that she would have to forgive the people she believed had wronged her, but she said she couldn't do this. Her feelings of anger and resentment had gained such a grip on her mind that it was impossible to displace them. Even when I told her that these thoughts were probably the cause of all her health problems, she seemed unable to relinquish them. She just went on seething with anger. She said it was justifiable anger, and maybe it was, but it was destroying her nevertheless.

One day, looking for Christmas presents for my own children, I happened to see the little toy coal scuttle, and at once this woman and her problems came to mind. So I bought the coal scuttle and took it around to her at the hospital. "Here is a present for you," I told her. "But it is more than a present, it is a prescription that may help you overcome all these health problems. I know you hate the people who wronged you, but hate is a boomerang and some of it is circling back and hurting you."

I took the toy shovel and scooped out some of the toy coal. "Those hate thoughts are as hard and black as these little lumps of toy coal," I said. "So, whenever one of these ugly thoughts comes into your mind, take this little shovel and lift out a little black lump of coal and throw it under the bed, out of sight. As you do this, visualize the dark thought being cast out of your consciousness. The more black thoughts you throw out of your mind, the sooner your mind will return to its original coloration, which is not black, but clean and white. And once your mind is normal and healthy, your body will become normal and healthy, too."

I remember she looked at the little toy coal scuttle and laughed. "You must be joking," she said. Then she added slowly, "But the way I've been feeling is no joke, is it? All right. I'll try it."

"Fine," I said. "And when the lumps of coal are all gone, have your nurse sweep them up, and start all over again."

She did, and apparently was able to make the transference between this simple symbolic act and the deeper healing process that she needed so badly, because gradually she began to get better. She no longer spent time in hospital beds. She became a well woman, a strong, practicing Christian who lived without the poison of hate in her mind or heart. Finally, she gave me back the little coal scuttle, saying that it had done its job. I put it up on the bookcase, and there it stayed until I needed it for my sermon that morning, which was on the healing power of forgiveness.

One of the most important lessons that people can learn as they move through life is how to forgive. Our Lord told us to forgive our enemies, not once, not seven times, but seventy times seven. Maybe He smiled as He said it, but the fact that He talked about forgiveness in such terms shows that He recognized how hard forgiving someone who has wronged you can be. It is difficult, hideously difficult, yet over and over again Jesus stressed how important it is. He even said that if you have a quarrel with someone, it is useless to bring a gift to God's altar and ask for blessings unless you first go and seek reconciliation with that person. Anger, resentment, and hatred set up barriers that deprive a person of spiritual power. Chronic malevolence, smoldering anger, or some terrible and long-lasting grudge are not unlike cancerous growths.

So forgiveness is not just a nice praiseworthy virtue that one ought to display because it is the Christian thing to do. Forgiveness is a needed protection for yourself. It is an antidote for poisons that can corrupt the body and damage the soul.

Compassionate Judgment

How do you set about becoming a forgiving individual? First you decide by an act of will that you are not going to be a judgmental person. The Bible says quite clearly, "Judge not . . ." (Matthew 7:1), and the reason behind this prohibition is plain: We never have all the information that would enable us to make an absolutely just judgment. There are always some things that are hidden from us, things known only to God. So it is better to leave the judging to Him. If punishment is necessary, let Him take care of it. "Vengeance is mine; I will repay, saith the Lord." In any case, none of us is so perfect that we can afford to be harsh and totally unforgiving of people whose actions hurt or displease us.

I will admit that it takes a good many years of living before you begin to see this clearly. People sometimes ask Ruth and me if our approach to helping people with their problems has changed much over the years. Well, not a great deal, but I do think we are a little more tolerant, a little more compassionate than when we started out. We know that human beings are going to make mistakes, because they are just that—human beings. And besides, we make a few mistakes ourselves. We have also learned that each of us is a tremendously delicate and complicated piece of machinery, subject to all sorts of hidden strains and stresses, and when you look at all the factors in a given case you can't help wondering how, by and large, people do as well as they do.

Some months ago, for example, I found myself talking with a woman who had consulted me because she was in deep trouble. She worked for an insurance company, and she had been stealing money from the company by falsifying insurance claims. By forging the names of doctors and inventing medical events that never happened, she had swindled the company out of almost fifty thousand dollars. She was terrified that company officials would become suspicious and start an investigation. Remorseful and frightened, she turned to me for help.

Now the woman was a thief, no doubt about that. Confession was inevitable. Restitution had to be made. And yet I think my own reaction was a bit different from what it might have been thirty years ago. Then I might have reacted mainly with righteous indignation. "You've stolen money," I might have said. "We had better go to the authorities right now. Right is right and wrong is wrong. You have stepped over the line and now you must bear the consequences."

But through the years I have learned to listen more and judge less. This distracted woman, I learned, had had a hysterectomy at twenty-six, an early age, thereby losing her capacity ever to become a mother. I began to see that her compulsive desire to acquire material things—which in turn had led her to defraud her own company—was a pathetic attempt to compensate for the children she could never have. I didn't excuse what she had done. But I did feel sorry for her.

So, after talking it over with Ruth, I called up a good friend of mine in the insurance business, described the case to him, and asked him what he thought we should do. He said that in his opinion the woman should go to the president of her company, or the highest official she could reach, confess what she had done, and ask for forgiveness and the chance to repay the money bit by bit. "I think they may be fairly lenient with her," my friend said. "The sum that seems so large to her is not that large to them. From what you say, this woman is truly sorry and wants to make amends. It may be that civil authority will not have to be brought into it."

So that was the course we followed, and in the end it did work out the way my friend predicted. The point is, a young woman who made a bad mistake was spared a criminal record because Ruth and I had learned to be more tolerant and—I hope—more understanding over the years.

A sense of compassion, then, and a conscious refusal to be a judgmental person are the first steps toward acquiring a capacity for forgiveness. Even so, it remains a difficult attitude to achieve when you think you are wronged. The instinctive, animalistic reaction is to fight back, to inflict hurt because you have been hurt. But this is precisely the response that Jesus was trying to eliminate from our hearts when He told us to love our enemies and "do good to those who despitefully use you" (*see* Matthew 5:44).

He told us that because He knew that forgiveness liberates enormous healing powers in both the forgiver and the forgiven. Recently I heard of a doctor in New York, a cancer specialist, who is very highly regarded in his field. When a new patient comes to him, before he starts any kind of treatment this doctor tries to find out all he can about the patient's background, especially relationships with parents, brothers and sisters, and any close relative or very close friend. He believes that emotional factors play a large part in a person's susceptibility to cancer, and makes a point of trying to understand the emotional climate in which the disease began.

One of the things this physician does is summon all members of the family to a session which he calls the Hour of Forgiveness. In this rather extraordinary meeting, each person is asked to express openly any grievance or resentment that he or she may have been carrying toward the patient, or even toward one another. Then, when these hidden animosities are brought out, the owner of them is asked quite simply to forgive the offender, or the fancied offender. In these sessions, amazing things come to light and often are resolved then and there.

Once these hidden grievances are neutralized by the power of forgiveness, the doctor calls for one more session called the Hour of Love, in which everyone involved expresses affection and concern for everyone else. First forgiveness. Then love. The result, this remarkable doctor feels, is an atmosphere in which the healing forces he intends to apply will work most effectively. And I think this must often be the case.

How does imaging come into all this? In a variety of ways. If you are at odds with a friend, it certainly helps to visualize that quarrel ended, the old relationship restored, the sense of pain and alienation eliminated. If you can fix that image in your mind, you have taken a tremendous first step.

If the feelings of anger and resentment go very deep, sometimes it may help to image clearly and vividly the face of the person who has wronged you, then picture the face of Jesus as you imagine it looks, then superimpose that image of Christ on top of the other image and say out loud, "I forgive you in the Name of Jesus. Amen." This is a healing prayer and a powerful one. The *Amen* at the end means "so be it," and it is really a command to your own subconscious to let go of the negative, punitive thoughts that have sunk their roots so deep into your mind. Pull them out, throw them away for good.

Prayer is necessary because sometimes forgiveness is so difficult that we simply cannot do it alone. It assuredly requires the grace of God to come into our mind and change it before we can even begin to change ourselves. But when God's power and love are allowed to act as a solvent, even the deepest bitterness can be washed away. And this is a fact, believe me.

Inspiring Story of Two Families

A few years ago in Pennsylvania, there was a sturdy farming family consisting of Jay, his wife, Ruth, and three fine sons, the youngest a cheerful, freckle-faced schoolboy named Nelson. His teachers called him "Sunshine" because he had such a lovable disposition and such a sunny smile. One day when Jay and Ruth were waiting for Nelson to come home from school, the school-bus driver came running, frantic and white-faced, up the lane. Nelson had been hit by a car as he was getting off the school bus. An ambulance was summoned, but it was too late. Nelson was dead.

The driver of the car was an off-duty policeman from New York City. With his wife he had been driving through the tranquil Pennsylvania countryside. The school bus had stopped; its warning lights and stop sign were functioning. But somehow this driver ignored them. He tried to pass the bus. And little Nelson was killed.

Jay and Ruth were devastated. So were their other sons. Their neighbors were enraged; they wanted the harshest penalties invoked. School authorities wanted to make an example of the guilty driver, an outsider, a big-city stranger.

The days went by in a blur of grief and anguish. An insurance adjuster came to discuss settlements. He had also been in touch with the policeman and his wife, and something prompted Jay to ask how they were.

"They seem broken up," the insurance man told him.

Broken up. Ruth and Jay knew what those words meant; they meant the other couple was miserable, too. They thought about it, talked about it, prayed about it. Finally they decided to ask the New York couple, whose names were Frank and Rose Ann, to come to their house for dinner. And they came.

It was awkward, of course. But the four grieving people sat down and broke bread together. Ruth and Jay learned that Frank had been a policeman for eight years and had a spotless record. The accident, he said, might cost him his job. He and Rose Ann, like Ruth and Jay, had three children. They had sent them to Rose Ann's parents because they were fearful of facing their neighbors. Both Frank and Rose Ann looked terrible. There were dark circles under their eyes. They had lost a great deal of weight.

After they left, Ruth and Jay sat down at the kitchen table and faced each other. They faced something else, too: the fact that Frank and Rose Ann were suffering almost as much as they were. The truth became plain that only through compassion, only through applying the kind of love that their religion stood for, only through forgiveness offered and accepted, could all of them find peace. And so when the trial was held, Jay decided not to press charges. Except for a traffic fine, Frank was free.

Forgiveness. What is it, really? Perhaps it is no more than the opportunity to try again, to do better, to be freed from the penalties and shackles of past mistakes. Whatever it is, it's something we all need and long for. That is why our hearts are touched and our eyes grow misty when we encounter truly great examples of it.

I remember a remarkable story of forgiveness told more than twenty years ago by Bob Considine, the famous Hearst newspaper reporter. It concerned a government warehouse worker named Karl Taylor and his wife, Edith. The Taylors had been married for twenty-three years, and they seemed a devoted couple. Whenever Karl's job took him out of town, he would write Edith a long letter every night and send small gifts from every place he visited.

In 1949 the government sent Karl to Okinawa for a few months to work on a warehouse there. Left alone in the little Massachusetts town of Waltham, Edith made the best of it as the slow months went by. She kept herself busy buying a little unfinished cottage and trying to get it completed as a surprise for Karl when he came home.

But Karl kept delaying, and letters became fewer. Finally, after weeks of silence, a note came from Karl: "Dear Edith, I wish I knew of a kinder way to tell you that we are no longer married. . . ." Karl had written to

Mexico for a divorce. He had obtained one by mail. He told Edith he was going to marry a young Japanese girl named Aiko, a maid who had been assigned to his quarters. She was nineteen. Edith was forty-eight.

Edith had every reason to be embittered and crushed. By all the laws of human nature, she should have hated the Japanese woman and despised Karl. But somehow this didn't happen. Perhaps Edith was so full of love for Karl that she simply could not hate him. In any case, she was able to understand what had happened. A lonely man, far from home, who sometimes drank too much. A penniless, vulnerable girl.

Even in her grief, Edith tried to find something good in Karl's behavior. At least he had had the honesty to get a divorce and marry the girl. He hadn't abandoned Aiko. Edith didn't really think the marriage would work out. There was too much dissimilarity in age and background. Someday Aiko and Karl would discover this. Then perhaps Karl would come home. She sold the little cottage she had worked on so long and so hard. She never told Karl about it. She kept on working at her factory job. And she waited.

But Karl never came home. He wrote to Edith saying that he and Aiko were expecting a baby. Marie was born in 1951, then another girl, Helen, in 1953. Edith sent the children little presents. She went on with her factory job in Waltham, but the real focus of her life was on Okinawa.

Then one day a terrible letter came: Karl was dying of lung cancer. The letter was full of fear, not so much for himself as for Aiko and the two children. His medical expenses were draining away his savings. What would become of them?

Edith knew, then, what she wanted to do. Her last gift to Karl could be a measure of peace of mind. She wrote and told him that she would take the two children to live with her in Massachusetts.

Aiko was their mother, and she didn't want to let them go. But what could she offer them, except poverty and hopelessness? In 1956 she finally agreed. The children were sent to Edith. They adjusted quickly to American ways, and Edith was happier than she had been for many years.

But Aiko, alone on Okinawa, was miserable. She wrote pathetic notes to Edith: "Aunt. Tell me now what they do. If Marie or Helen cry or not." Finally Edith knew that there was one more thing her love for Karl would require. She would bring the children's mother to her home, too.

It was not easy. Aiko was still a Japanese citizen and the immigration quota was full, with many waiting. But Edith Taylor wrote to Bob Considine, asking his aid. He told the story in his newspaper column. Others helped. Finally, in 1957, Aiko was permitted to enter the United States.

Here is how Bob Considine described the meeting that took place:

As the plane came in at New York's International Airport, Edith had a moment of fear. What if she should hate this woman who had taken Karl away from her?

The last person off the plane was a girl so thin and small Edith thought at first it was a child. She did not come down the stairs, she only stood there, clutching the railing, and Edith knew that if she had been afraid, Aiko was near panic.

She called Aiko's name and the girl rushed down the steps and into Edith's arms. In that brief moment, as they held each other, Edith had an extraordinary thought. "Help me," she said, her eyes tight shut. "Help me to love this girl, as if she were part of Karl, come home. I prayed for him to come back. Now he has—in his two little daughters and in this gentle girl that he loved. Help me, God, to know that."

I'm told Edith and Aiko Taylor still live together today, having raised Karl's two children, who are now fine young woman. Why does this story of selflessness and forgiveness touch us so? Because there is a kind of divinity in it. "Father, forgive them . . . ," said Jesus on the cross (Luke 23:34). That is the model, the perfect example that is always before us. But only a very few, like Edith Taylor, come close to living up to it.

If, then, you want to experience the happiness, relief, and well-being that come from the practice of forgiveness, remember these five steps:

1. *Resist the temptation to be judgmental.* Remember, only God knows all the circumstances. Leave the judging to Him.

2. *Learn to be compassionate.* The best method is to use your imagination, put yourself in the other person's shoes, ask yourself whether the fault is entirely the other person's or whether there is some blame on your own part that needs to be honestly faced.

3. *Image the whole problem in terms of reconciliation.* Visualize the broken relationship healed. See yourself freed of the poisons of resentment and anger. Let your imagination suggest hopeful things you will accomplish with the increased energy that will come to you.

4. *Pray for the person who has offended you.* If this is difficult (and it will be), pray for God's grace to come into your heart to give you the strength to do it. Remind yourself that the act of forgiveness will benefit you more than the other person.

5. *End your prayer with the Lord's prayer.* Give special thought and emphasis to the part that asks God to forgive us our debts as we forgive our debtors.

Do these five things and you will be amazed at the healing power of forgiveness. If you let it, it can change your life.

12

IMAGING THE TENSENESS OUT OF TENSION

WHAT IS THIS THING called tension, this painful feeling called tension? It is not easy to define. Fear can cause it, but it's not exactly fear. Worry can cause it; so can guilt, hate, or frustration. One thing is sure: We all know the dismal feeling that comes when tension digs its claws into us. The sense of strain. The feelings of inadequacy. The pessimism. The low boiling point. "My nerves are shot," we say. "I'm uptight. I'm ready to climb the walls."

Certainly there is too much tension, too much uptightness in our lives; the prevalence of high blood pressure and the astronomical sales of tranquilizers attest to that. But a little of it can be a stimulus, even a good thing. Dr. Hans Selye, the famous Canadian authority on this problem, has proved beyond doubt that prolonged stress can cause all sorts of illness in rats—and in people. Yet even Dr. Selye admits that some stress is inevitable and even desirable if an organism is to meet the challenges of its environment successfully.

I know this from my own experience. Every time I deliver a sermon or make a speech, I feel some tension. Maybe it is a throwback to my old inferiority-complex days; maybe it is some dim recollection of that small boy being dragged into the parlor to reluctantly recite poetry to visiting relatives. Whatever the cause, it's painful and I don't like it. And yet I know it is a kind of spur, goading me to give my best effort. Without tension, most of us would never rise to the potential that the good Lord put into us.

In this chapter I am not going to talk about this normal and desirable level of stress or tension. I'm going to talk about the kind of tension that hurts and cripples and limits people—and what can be done about it.

Years ago, I ran across a remedy for acute tension that I have been using and recommending ever since. It is a three-part remedy, and one of those parts involves imaging, although that word was not in use at the time.

Coming home one evening, tired and tense and uptight, I fell into my favorite chair and glanced at the table alongside the chair where my loving wife has a habit of leaving books or magazines or pamphlets that she thinks might interest me. This time she had left, among other things, an insurance brochure. I remember it had the word *you* on the cover in big red letters, and a picture of a hand with an accusatory finger pointing right at the reader. "You ," it said, "are full of tension! You are uptight! You are just about ready to explode!" *Well,* I thought, *that is a pretty good description of the way I'm feeling, all right. Maybe I'd better see what else they have to say about uptightness.*

The pamphlet went on to say that to get rid of excess tension you had to do three things. The first was to practice relaxation of the physical body. "Sag back in your chair," it said. "Start relaxing every muscle, beginning with your toes. Stretch out your legs, flex your ankles, try to push your toes right off your feet, then let everything go limp. Let your head fall back. Roll it around so that your neck muscles are loosened up. Let each hand fall on your knee and rest there as limp as a wet leaf on a log. Open your eyes wide, then pretend invisible weights are attached to your eyelids, slowly pulling them shut. Imagine a soft, gentle hand lightly touching your face, smoothing the tension lines away. Picture the tension draining out of your body, leaving it calm and peaceful and relaxed." This is what Smiley Blanton called relaxing muscle tensions.

"Now you are ready for the second stage, which is the relaxation of the mind. This requires an effort of concentrated imagination. See yourself alone in the north woods of upstate New York on a perfect summer's day. You are sitting with your back against a tree; you can feel the rough bark through your shirt. All around you is a forest of fir, spruce, and hemlock. The air is scented with balsam. You can hear a gentle wind sighing in the treetops. In the far distance, blue hills are outlined against a tranquil sky. That sky is mirrored in a gleaming lake whose unruffled surface is broken only by the occasional leap of a fish. The ripples spread outward and are gone. The warm sun falls on your face like a benediction. Somewhere a bird calls and another answers. In the silence that follows, the healing beauty of God's creation surrounds you. Your uptightness fades away, smaller, smaller, until it is completely gone. Tension is no more. You are at peace. . . ."

The pamphlet called that kind of mind relaxing an exercise in concentrated imagination. And so it was. But it was also a good example of imaging.

The third part of the remedy involved a deliberate attempt to refresh the soul by recalling and meditating upon great passages and great promises from the Scriptures. I have often found that one of the best antidotes for uptightness is simply to recite aloud the Twenty-third Psalm. "Yea, though I walk through the valley of the shadow of death, I will fear no evil: for thou art with me; thy rod and thy staff they comfort me" (verse 4). They do indeed!

The more you read your Bible, the more you memorize parts of it, the more you let these fragments of ancient wisdom sink down into the depths of your being, the less vulnerable you will be to the fears and uncertainties and perplexities that are the causes of tension.

There are so many of these mighty spirit lifters! "Let not your heart be troubled: ye believe in God, believe also in me. In my Father's house are many mansions . . ." (John 14:1, 2). "Peace I leave with you, my peace I give unto you . . ." (verse 27). "Thou wilt keep him in perfect peace, whose mind is stayed on thee" (Isaiah 26:3). "Fear thou not; for I am with thee: be not dismayed . . ." (Isaiah 41:10).

The three-pronged message of that insurance brochure was plain: Somehow, no matter how much stress or tension surrounds you, you have to try to maintain an inner equanimity, an imperturbability that cannot be shaken by external circumstances, no matter how trying or painful they may be.

The poet Edwin Markham once wrote, "At the heart of the cyclone tearing the sky is a place of central calm." We don't have cyclones (the modern word is tornado) up in Pawling, New York, where Ruth and I have our old farmhouse. But we do have line storms, fierce tempests that sweep up the coast in late August or September and come raging over Quaker Hill where our house stands, howling like ten thousand furies.

Storm on Our Farm

I remember one such night when Ruth and I were sitting by the fire in our quiet family room. Outside a line storm was raging. The wind would seize the house and shake it the way a terrier shakes a rat. Everything would creak and groan. Then there would be a lull in which we could hear the old Seth Thomas clock on the mantel ticking away the seconds.

Finally the wind became so furious that I was afraid some of our big maples would blow down. Taking a flashlight, I staggered out into the gale. Pointing the beam of the flashlight upward, I could see the great branches writhing and twisting and flailing about. It was terrifying; I wondered if the roof might blow off the house. I fought my way back inside and said to Ruth: "This is a killer storm. I know we're going to lose some trees. If the wind gets any worse, this whole place could blow down!"

Ruth said nothing for a few seconds. Then she said calmly, "Listen to the clock."

So I did listen to the clock. *Ticktock*, it went. *Ticktock*. Unhurried. Unconcerned. *This old house has been here for 150 years*, it seemed to be saying. *It has weathered storms like this in the past, and it will weather others in the future. What are you so upset about? Everything's okay. Ticktock*. Okay. *Ticktock*. Okay. *Ticktock*. . . .

It is a little strange to think you can be handed peace of mind by a clock, but that is what happened to me that night.

Years ago, when stress or tension began to build up in me, sometimes

I would take the family and escape to Atlantic City for a day or two. It was a restful place then, with nothing very strenuous to do. People would walk on the boardwalk or on the beach. If it was wintertime, solicitous hotel attendants would wrap you up in a blanket and put you in a steamer chair facing the ocean so that all you could see was the majestic surge of breakers rolling in and all you could hear was the sound of the surf and the sea gulls crying as they wheeled on white wings over the restless water.

I remember thinking on one occasion, *Why do I have to come back here to find this kind of tranquility? Why can' t I take it away with me in my mind and summon it up whenever I need it—a week from now, or a month, or six months, or a year.* And I would try to do just that when the pressures of New York became unbearable. Imaging, that's what it was. The kind of imaging that enables you to reach out and touch tranquility in the midst of stress.

I wonder sometimes just when all this sense of strain and hurry, all this uptightness, took over the nation. I don't remember it as a boy growing up in the Midwest. People had problems, of course, but nervous tension was seldom one of them. There was something soothing about the tempo of life, the horse-drawn wagons and the early automobiles, the placid shops and the quiet restaurants (no fast-food places, no drive-ins), the little country churches with the corn ("corn knee-high by the Fourth of July") reaching almost to the front door and then stretching away like an emerald ocean to the horizon, the clouds like fat, white sheep grazing across the blue pastures of sky, and silence so deep that you could hear a cricket chirp.

Today if you try to walk to work in New York City as I sometimes do, sirens split your eardrums, flashing lights dazzle your eyes, trucks roar and smoke like dragons, the air has a barely sublethal level of carbon monoxide, the streets are paved with debris, and harried-looking people pour in and out of subway cars so begrimed and besmeared with graffiti that they resemble trolleys from hell.

Psychologically, the tension is increased by the stridency of the media and their preoccupation with gloom, doom, crime, disaster, murder, mayhem, flood, famine, pornography, perversion, inflation, taxation, and every other unpleasantness known to man.

In the olden days they used to say that bad coinage would drive out good, meaning that if inferior coins were circulated, people would hoard the good coins and refuse to spend them. This was known as Gresham's law. Well, there seems to be a kind of Gresham's law for the news media, in which bad news drives out good. If you don't believe me, go through the local newspaper sometime and hunt for good news. You'll see what I mean.

People set up defenses against this sort of environment as best they can. My dentist in New York, Dr. Arthur Merritt, is a wise man. He works hard, on his feet all day, the hum and roar of the great city just outside. But on the wall of his office he has hung a picture of an old covered bridge in Vermont, spanning a lovely rural stream where he used to swim as a boy. He can see it every time he looks up. It is so peaceful that it almost makes the patient feel peaceful—quite a trick when you are in a dentist's chair. It's a powerful aid to imaging, which is what it is meant to be.

Peace in a Tense Ball Game

Tension invades every area of our lives if we let it, even in athletics. Coaches are finding now that it is counterproductive, as they say, to scream at their players or exhort them to frenzied efforts. This is more likely to damage performance than improve it, because it heightens tension.

The great former Dodger baseball pitcher Carl Erskine is a good friend of ours. He told Ruth and me about a crucial game where he was the pitcher. It was the fifth of October, the fifth game of the series, the fifth inning, and it also happened to be Carl's fifth wedding anniversary. The Dodgers had a four-run lead when the Yankees came to bat. They put men on bases, brought in two men, and then, with two men still on base, someone hit a home run, bringing in a total of five runs within minutes, putting the Yankees one run ahead. Carl was in trouble.

The fans were howling vociferously, urging Charles Dressen, the Dodger manager, to remove Erskine and put in another pitcher. Erskine felt as if his nerves were stretched to the breaking point. His confidence in himself was being drained away by tension. It grew worse as he saw Charlie Dressen come out of the dugout and walk slowly to the mound.

Dressen held out his hand for the ball. Carl gave it to him. Seventy thousand fans watched breathlessly. Would Dressen summon a right-hander or another southpaw? Erskine waited. Dressen looked up reflectively at the sky. He asked mildly, "Isn't this your wedding anniversary, Carl?" Erskine nodded, astonished. "What are you doing tonight?" Dressen went on. "I hope you're taking Betty out to dinner." Erskine thought, *Seventy thousand fans watching me, and Charlie is asking about my wedding anniversary!* Dressen slapped the ball back into the pitcher's glove as he said, "You're my man, Carl. See if you can get the side out before dark." And he walked back to the dugout.

The Dodgers tied the score in the seventh inning and scored again in the top of the eleventh. Erskine got nineteen consecutive outs and the Dodgers won the game and eventually the series.

In another game, Carl told us, he felt his control slipping. The familiar, paralyzing tension began to build up in him. Tension is really a muscle spasm in the mind that can interfere with the smooth functioning of the muscles of the body. Carl knew he had to head it off somehow.

He backed off the mound, picked up the resin bag, flung it down. He turned his back on the plate, groping in his mind for something that would neutralize the tension. He prayed for help, and suddenly he remembered a trip he had taken some time before with another Dodger pitcher whose nickname was "Preacher" Roe. Carl and Preacher were out fishing when they heard, from across the lake, hymns being sung at a camp meeting.

As Carl stood beside the pitcher's box, he imaged that peaceful, pastoral scene and the words of one of those hymns came back into his mind:

> Drop Thy still dews of quietness,
> 'Till all our strivings cease;
> Take from our souls the strain and stress,
> And let our ordered lives confess
> The beauty of Thy peace.

Quietness. Peacefulness. Ordered lives. Beauty. The tranquil power in those words drove the tension out of Erskine's mind, and as soon as it was gone from his mind it was gone from his body. He turned back to the mound and began firing strikes past the batters.

Buried in a Thirty-Foot Snowdrift

There are, of course, crises much more crucial than a baseball game. But even when a situation seems hopeless, a calm, resolute imaging can hold off despair. Last winter I read a newspaper story about a truck driver in a midwestern state who was caught in a roaring blizzard. His wife had begged him not to make the run that night, for the radio was forecasting a snowstorm of major proportions. But he had a load of steel wire that had to be delivered, so he didn't listen to her. Halfway to his destination, the howling storm swept down on him. When driving conditions became impossible, he pulled the big truck off the road and went to sleep.

When he woke up, everything was dark. Although he didn't know it, the truck was buried in a snowdrift thirty feet deep. The truck was completely covered; no part of it was visible from the highway. The driver could not open the doors. He was trapped. On his CB radio, he could dimly hear the voices of state police and other rescue teams, but he could not communicate with them. His CB could receive but could not transmit through all the snow.

For five days and nights he stayed in his icy tomb. He had no food.

To quench his thirst he ate snow. Five days and nights. One hundred twenty endless hours. But he didn't panic. He didn't despair. He waited, calmly and stoically, to be rescued; and finally he was.

I was so impressed when I read his story that I called him on the telephone and told him how much I admired his courage and stamina. "Weren't you afraid?" I asked.

"No," he said. "I knew my brother would be looking for me. I knew he wouldn't rest until he found me. In my mind I could see him searching, searching all up and down that highway, never getting discouraged, never giving up. I could see him just as plain as day, finally locating the drift I was buried in. And as long as I could see him like that, I wasn't afraid. It was just a question of when he'd find me, not if he'd find me. And finally he did."

There was a classic use of imaging: a man in deep trouble vividly seeing a desired goal or outcome, holding it resolutely in his mind until it became a reality. He might have visualized himself starving, or frozen, or suffocated, but he didn't. He saw himself being rescued, and that image held the wolves of fear and panic at bay.

Among the useful imaging techniques for tension control that have come to my attention is a unique procedure outlined by Jo Kimmel in her book *Steps to Prayer Power*. She suggests a process of imaging in which one visualizes all the unhealthy mixture of thought which causes tension as flowing out of the body through the toes and fingers, until an emptying of stress is achieved.

The emptying procedure is followed by a refilling process in which a healthy mixture of thought, composed of serenity, wholeness, joy, and peace is imaged as being poured into the body to circulate throughout the entire being. The result is a feeling of relaxation and rest, a diminution of tension.

Let me end this chapter by giving you a remarkable example of the power of imaging, backed by faith. I came across it in a story I read recently by a North Carolina schoolteacher named Marilyn Ludolf. For almost sixteen years her life had been full of tension and misery because of an unsightly rash across her face. It ruined her appearance; it gave her terrible headaches; it made her desperately unhappy. Apparently nothing could be done about it. She consulted doctors and dermatologists; she tried every kind of lotion and skin preparation; she ate vitamins; she went on countless diets. Nothing helped.

Mrs. Ludolf was a Sunday-school teacher, and one day while she was teaching her class, the story flashed into her mind of the woman who touched the hem of Jesus' robe and was cured of a disease that, like her own, had plagued her for years. She realized suddenly that she had tried everything except turning to God, *really* turning to Him with faith that He could and would heal her.

So she decided to go into training, like an athlete, in an effort to strengthen her faith. She knew her faith needed strengthening because she hadn't been using it, and like an unused muscle it had become flabby and weak. She took a Bible with a concordance, and she looked up all the verses to be found under the headings of *healing*, *health*, and *faith*. She found thirty-five of them scattered throughout the Bible. She wrote them down, word for word "as sort of a training manual for my faith." (They are listed at the conclusion of this chapter.)

Then she began to carry these Scriptures everywhere she went. When her car stopped at a red light, at spare moments in the classroom, while doing housework, at night before falling asleep, she read the verses and meditated on them. This became her constant routine. And gradually the thirty-five passages slowly sank into the core of her being. She began to believe, really believe, that she could be healed.

Finally Mrs. Ludolf took a decisive leap of faith. She picked a certain day a few weeks away, and ringed it on the calendar. "Lord," she prayed, "this is the day I'm asking for complete healing."

Then she began one last exercise: visualizing her skin as clear and soft as a baby's. This was hard, because the terrible red rash and the painful headaches continued. "But after a while," she wrote, "this image, like the Scriptures, began to sink into the deep, believing places of my life." (There is a great phrase for you: "the deep, believing places of my life"— a poetic and accurate way of describing her subconscious mind.) She also began to thank the Lord fervently for healing her, although as yet there was no evidence that He had.

In the meantime, she kept on reading her dog-eared Scripture verses, although she had long since memorized them. Day after day went by. Day after day she meditated and affirmed and prayed. Gradually her rash began to fade and the painful headaches grew less frequent. And on the final day, the day she had marked on the calendar, she looked into the mirror through eyes brimming with tears, because the mirror told her that her affliction was gone.

"According to your faith be it unto you" (Matthew 9:29). Believe, pray, image, give thanks—and tension can be eliminated from your life.

Mrs. Ludolf did it.

You can do it, too.

Here are the thirty-five Scriptures Mrs. Ludolf used:

Proverbs 4:2–22
Romans 10:17
Matthew 7:7, 11
Matthew 8:7, 13
Matthew 9:29, 35
Matthew 14:14

Matthew 15:30
Matthew 17:20, 21
Matthew 19:2
Mark 1:34
Mark 5:34
Mark 10:52
Mark 9:23
Mark 11:22–24
Luke 6:19
John 14:13, 14
Acts 10:38
Galatians 3:13
John 10:10
3 John 2
Hebrews 13:8
Malachi 4:2
Matthew 4:23, 24
Psalms 91:9, 10
Proverbs 3:7, 8
Exodus 15:26
James 5:15
1 Peter 2:24
Psalms 42:11
Psalms 6:2
Psalms 41:4
Psalms 103:2, 3
Isaiah 53:4, 5
Jeremiah 17:14
1 John 4:4

13

HOW TO DEEPEN YOUR FAITH

IN THE HUNDREDS OF letters that come to Ruth and me from people with problems, one of the most constant and recurring themes is lack of faith.

"I don't seem to have much faith," the unhappy refrain goes. "I try to believe, but my beliefs are shaky."

"Other people seem to have more faith than I do; what can I do to be like them?"

"Everybody tells me I should have faith, but nobody tells me how to acquire it."

"Why isn't my faith stronger? What can I do to deepen it?"

Month after month, year after year, the letters keep coming.

I sympathize with these seekers after faith, but really they are blocking themselves. When you *see* yourself as a person of inadequate faith, when you *accept* the idea that you are limited in this crucial area, when you *project* this image of yourself to others, you are really notifying your unconscious mind that you are the plaintive possessor of a permanent spiritual deficiency. If your unconscious mind accepts that image, as ultimately it will, it will program itself—and you—to perpetuate this unhappy state of affairs. That is why people tend to be, and to remain, what they keep telling themselves they are.

So the first thing the person who wishes to deepen his faith must do is change that negative image of himself as a faithless person to something else.

One way to accomplish this change is by using a powerful imaging technique that consists of just three words: *act as if.* So you think you don't have much faith? No matter: act as if you did. Act as if the whole of the gospel story, the good news proclaimed by Jesus that God loves us and cares for us, the marvelous promise He gave us that He would never abandon us, His assurance that we could have forgiveness of sins if we repented of them, His pledge that if we obeyed and believed we would have life eternal—act as if it were all true. Never mind if you feel it is too good to be true; never mind if your doubts seem overpowering; *act as if you believed.*

If you do, your unconscious mind will respond. It will say to itself, "Here is this person acting like a believer, so I am going to program him or her toward faith instead of away from it." And once your unconscious mind takes hold of that idea, you will find yourself being swept along by a current flowing ever more strongly from the arid deserts of doubt to the green fields of spiritual certainty.

Another thing: while you act as if, give thanks that this change in your life is actually taking place now. Even when you can't see it happening, even when you don't know for sure whether it is happening, give thanks, because the act of giving thanks for as-yet unglimpsed benefits is in itself a powerful form of faith.

Great men have always known this. Someone once asked the famous composer Joseph Haydn how he managed to create such marvelous music. "When I decide to compose," he replied, "I pray and thank God that it has been accomplished. Then I do it. If it doesn't come the first time, I pray again. Then it comes!" There is a classic example of the prayerize-visualize-actualize sequence, strengthened and fortified by giving thanks in advance. Perhaps the event hasn't transpired yet, but the image of it exists in the mind of man and, when prayer is involved, in the timeless mind of God as well. Giving thanks under those circumstances is an expression of pure faith, and faith is the fuel in the tank of the invisible psychic engine that makes wonderful things happen.

Act as if was the favorite advice of an old friend of mine, Dr. Samuel M. Shoemaker. Whenever some skeptic asked him how to live a faith-filled life, that is what he urged them to do. Dr. Sam also had a technique called the "six *X*'s" that he liked to recommend. He said they made a very logical progression for the faith seeker, and they went like this:

Exposure
Explanation
Experiment
Experience
Expression
Expansion

The first step, *exposure*, is essential. How are you going to acquire faith, or deepen faith, unless you make contact with it, unless you go where it is?

This means going to church, because the atmosphere of a church, conditioned by prayer and sanctified by ceremony and ritual, is the place where faith is most likely to be found. The best place to know and understand a person is in that person's home. Likewise, it is easier and more natural to believe in God when you are in God's house. You have the reinforcement of other people's beliefs; your prayers mingle with their prayers. You have the conditioning of the surroundings: the architecture, the sacred music, the familiar passages from Scripture or prayer book, a whole backdrop that has evolved through the ages, all designed to direct and focus the mind on God. So if you want to strengthen your faith, you can hardly do without church attendance.

Another form of exposure is Bible reading; what better way to understand God than by reading His Word? Yet another form of exposure is associating with people who have a deep spiritual side to their nature, observing them, watching how faith illuminates their lives. Their faith may rub off on you! And nowadays there are lots of such people. You can find them everywhere, people who are enthusiastic believers.

Explanation comes next, because there are many aspects of religion that need explaining. The plan of salvation is a logical framework of thought so solid that it has survived for almost two thousand years, but much of it needs to be explained to the inquiring mind. Bible-study classes, small prayer groups, religious books and lectures, even sermons can be a part of this explaining process. And it is a process that never ends. Vast numbers of people are studying the Bible today, more than ever before, I'm sure.

You take the third step when you begin to *experiment* with what you have learned. Perhaps you start keeping a prayer diary, and look back after a month to see how many of your prayer requests have been answered. (You'll be astonished, I assure you!) Or perhaps you decide to experiment with tithing, or with forgiving someone who has wronged you. There are great spiritual benefits to be derived from these things, but you have to experiment with them before you can be convinced.

The fourth step comes when you actually begin to *experience* these benefits or perhaps when you have a life-changing spiritual encounter of some kind that would have been impossible without your growing faith.

The fifth stage comes when you feel ready and eager to give *expression* to your deepening convictions, witnessing to the power of Jesus Christ in your own personal experience and the joy that knowing Him has brought you.

And the sixth stage, as your spiritual growth continues, is where the love of God *expands* until it fills your whole consciousness and directs your whole life.

Dr. Sam's six-point formula has helped many people. Another powerful way to strengthen your faith is to image Jesus Christ coming into your life and dealing with some problem that may be troubling you as if it were actually, literally taking place.

Recently I read a book by a physician, Dr. David L. Messenger, titled *Dr. Messenger's Guide to Better Health.* Dr. Messenger, a strong Christian, believes in what he calls "Wholistic Medicine," which means treating the patient as a whole—body, mind, and spirit, not just focusing on one set of symptoms or one particular complaint.

Before he attempts to treat the physical body, this brilliant doctor tries to locate areas of emotional hurt and relieve them. Dr. Messenger writes, in a vivid metaphor, that the octopus of anger and its internal tentacles of resentment, hatred, hostility, and bitterness have negative chemistry effects. In another place he tells us that people who "think well" tend to stay well, and people who "think sick" tend to get sick more often. I've been advocating these same ideas for years, so naturally I agree with Dr. Messenger. The Bible says it, too: "Heaviness [anxiety] in the heart of man maketh it stoop [weighs it down]" (Proverbs 12:25).

Your Greatest Hurt

But to get back to imaging: Dr. Messenger often asks a patient, "What is the biggest hurt that ever happened to you?" When he asked a woman patient that one day, she began to weep and told him that her biggest hurt was the constant bitter fighting and quarreling between her father and mother that finally resulted in her father's leaving home for good. She said the worst memory of all was of a scene where her mother became so enraged that she seized a butcher knife and tried to stab her father.

Dr. Messenger told the lady to relax, close her eyes, and visualize that scene again, just as it had happened twenty-five years earlier: the terrified child (herself), the enraged adults, the light gleaming on the deadly knife as her mother snatched it from the kitchen table. He urged her to relive all the painful emotions: the fear, the dread, the terror. Then he said to her, "Be aware of the presence of Jesus—the warm, loving, kind presence of the Person of Jesus. Now watch that scene and let Jesus do what He wants to do. When you're done, tell me about it."

After a few minutes, the woman opened her eyes and described how Jesus had walked over and gently taken the knife away from the mother. Then He had put His arm around both the mother and the father, and by the power of His infinite love had brought an end to their hatred and bitterness. Then He had picked the little girl (herself) up in His arms and had soothed and comforted her. And that simple but intense use of imaging, Dr. Messenger said, brought about a healing of the painful memories and was the first step in a physical healing for the patient as well.

That sort of imaging is close to prayer, and prayer itself is probably the surest and most direct way to strengthen your faith. If you meet someone who is attractive and appealing, and you want to know that person better, what do you do? You talk to him or her, don't you? You try to communicate. You offer yourself in what you hope will be an ever-increasing exchange of ideas and affection and intimacy. Well, that is exactly what prayer is—an exchange between you and the great Father that created all life, including yours. It is awe inspiring and almost incredible that this vast Being, this infinite Power, is available for such an exchange. But He is. That is the marvelous truth, the good news of the Gospel, the message that Jesus Christ Himself brought to us.

If you doubt that truth, you are opening the door to negative imaging. If you say to yourself, "Well, I'm not all that sure there is a God, or even if there is, I don't feel any certainty that I can communicate with Him," then you are letting doubt triumph over faith, and this uncertainty will run like jangling discord through all the major areas of your life.

If you let doubt become dominant, you probably won't even try to pray, and when you don't pray you are cutting yourself off from a tremendous source of peace and power. I know about this from firsthand experience, because I try to talk to the Lord all through the day. Nothing very formal or fancy. I just talk to Him as I would to a dearly loved friend who is always by my side. This is as close as I can get to the biblical injunction to "pray without ceasing" (1 Thessalonians 5:17). That injunction, of course, is hard to carry out in our busy, fragmented lives. But when you do find time to pray for any sustained length of time, remarkable things happen, especially when your prayers are directed toward the needs of others, not your own needs.

Wide Awake at 3:00 A.M.

Not long ago, for example, I woke up at 3:00 A.M. on a Sunday morning. I had gone to bed early, as I always do on a Saturday night when I have to preach the next day, but here I was, all of a sudden, wide-awake. I tried every known device to go back to sleep. I said the Twenty-third Psalm half a dozen times. I counted sheep (a pretty weak form of imaging, I'll admit!). But still I could not get back to sleep. Finally I got up at four o'clock, went into my library, and picked up one book and magazine after another. Nothing held my interest.

Some years ago in Switzerland, I purchased a large and beautiful eagle carved from a single block of wood, and brought it back to my library. Made by one of the old-time Swiss wood-carvers, it is really a work of art. The eagle has his wings spread and is taking off from some high eminence. I sat looking at the eagle and remembering when I bought it, and the old man who made it, and then, naturally, I began to say aloud a passage of Scripture: ". . . they shall mount up with wings as eagles; they shall run, and not be weary; and they shall walk, and not faint" (Isaiah 40:31).

This in turn led to a thought about a friend, a pastor who says that occasionally, when he needs spiritual help, he goes into the church and walks the aisles. He places his hand on the pew where a certain person sits and prays for that person by name. And he repeats the process at various pews in the empty church. The pastor says that this procedure always brings great blessing to him as well as to the persons he prays for. So, motivated by my friend's example, there alone in the early morning, I started to visualize everyone I should pray for.

The first person was my wife, Ruth. Then I prayed for our three children and their spouses, then for our eight grandchildren. I prayed for all the relatives I could call to mind. Then my mind went to the church and I prayed for the other ministers. I prayed for all the secretaries. Then one by one I prayed for all the elders and all the deacons. Finally I began to visualize the congregation at the church and prayed for everyone I could think of by name. Then I prayed for the doormen in the apartment house and for all the people with whom I am associated in any way.

Actually, I must have prayed for five hundred people by name. By this time it was 6:00 A.M. All of a sudden I felt better than I had felt in a long time. I was full of energy, and boundless enthusiasm surged within me. I wouldn't have gone back to sleep for anything. I was ravenously hungry and went and awakened my wife.

"Get up! It's 6:00 A.M.," I said. "I'm hungry, and let us have no piddling breakfast. I want bacon and eggs, the whole works!" And I ate a big, man-sized breakfast.

I went to the church and delivered a sermon and shook hands with hundreds of people. Then I went to a luncheon and gave a talk, and on to an afternoon engagement, and at eleven o'clock that night I was still going strong. I was not even tired! Such an excess of energy was mine as to astound me, and with it came a tremendous new feeling of love for life.

Now, I'm not psychologist enough to explain exactly what happened. I guess I got outside myself. Consciously, even subconsciously, I completely forgot myself in loving all those other people and praying for them and taking their burdens on myself. But this didn't add any weight, either. It added wings! And it left me happy and joyous, revitalized, reborn. Actually, I rose up "with wings as eagles."

So now, whenever I feel enervated or depressed, I repeat that prayer process. And I offer this experience as a suggestion of how you, too, may not only help others by prayer but also find marvelous new life for yourself.

Prayer has always been the most effective way to get close to the Lord. Sometimes when Ruth and I are in England, in the Lake District, we return to the place where Wordsworth is said to have written his poem "The Daffodils." Wordsworth tells us that in such beautiful spots it was his custom to imagine (image) Jesus as actually being close beside him. He would quote some words of the Savior, then reflectively say, "I wonder what the tone of Jesus' voice was when He said that?" He would "listen" to what the voice might have sounded like—the tonal quality, the depth of feeling. And then he would ask, "I wonder what the expression on His face was like when He said those words?" By imaging Jesus so vividly, lovingly filling in all those details, the poet felt the reality of His actual presence.

Nothing is more faith strengthening than to pray and have your prayer answered. In our counseling work, Ruth and I have learned, when a human problem is brought to us, to put it into a spiritual dimension by praying about it. Once that is done with sincerity and humility, we often find that mighty forces come to our aid.

God's Guidance Always Works

One time, for example, we found ourselves involved in one of those difficult human problems that arise when a person with excellent qualifications and abilities just doesn't happen to fit into the particular niche where he finds himself. In this case, it was a young minister of splendid character and great talent with a most attractive family, who had joined the staff of a church. But things had not worked out as hoped. He was greatly troubled as we, his friends, were about where he would go and what he would do.

In one discussion, the young minister said a bit disconsolately that an ambition he and his attractive wife had had for years now seemed more remote than ever. When pressed to reveal what this was, he said that he had always dreamed of starting a religious community in the mountains, a kind of retreat where young skiers might be attracted in winter and summer tourists might come in warm weather. He even knew of such a place that had a rustic building the owner might be persuaded to sell. "But of course," he said, "that is just a dream. Maybe in five years. . . ." His voice trailed off dejectedly.

Ruth had been praying hard for a solution for this young couple, and she kept turning over their dream in her mind. Finally she said to them, "Why wait five years? Why don't you try to get started on it now?"

"We'd love to," they said. "But we don't have the money. It's as simple as that."

We all nodded gloomily. No money. Too bad.

But the Lord had heard Ruth's prayers, and He was not going to let us get away with this negative, downbeat attitude. So in the middle of the night He put into Ruth's head an idea so simple and startling that she sat up in bed and began to shake me. "Norman," she said, "wake up! I've got an idea!"

"Can't it wait till morning?" I mumbled.

"No, it can't! You know those books of yours that were sold through *Guideposts,* the ones you can't accept any royalties from because you're the president of a nonprofit organization?"

"Ruth," I moaned, "are you waking me up in the middle of the night just to remind me of money that I've earned and can't have?"

"That's right," she said. "The money is there, and you can't have it for yourself. We have been holding it to donate to some worthwhile cause. Why don't we use that money to help our friends buy that building and start living their dream now?"

It was amazing how the Lord worked things out. The building has been converted into the religious center that the young couple had dreamed of for so long.

The moral seems clear: When you put an apparently unsolvable problem into the spiritual dimension by praying about it, watch out—because things are going to start happening! Good things. Abundant things. Astonishing things. What you image can really happen.

Sometimes, I think, people refuse to believe that prayer brings such quick solutions. They say, "Oh, that's just coincidence!" or "Oh, well, that would probably have happened anyway." This is negative imaging that can only serve to dilute what little faith the person may have to begin with.

But sometimes the cause and effect of prayer is so quick and so powerful that it converts a person into a total believer for the rest of his life. Not long ago I was in a taxi and noticed that the driver had a Dutch-sounding name. When I asked him about it, he said that he was indeed from Rotterdam. So I told him that I was a minister of the church which the Dutch established in New York way back in 1628, and we had a friendly chat.

As we drove along he asked, "Have you time to let me tell you a little story? It is about the first time I really met God, and it shows how good God is. I have great faith, sir, and I know that I can never get outside the care and love of God.

"It was close to the end of World War II. I was a little boy in Holland. Our country had been ravaged. The Germans had been driven out, but we were left absolutely destitute. We had ration stamps, but they weren't any good, for we had no food at all. There was no food in the warehouses or in the stores or in the country districts. Holland had been swept clean. There was nothing left.

"We were reduced to eating beets out of the fields and it was a kind of beet that is dangerous to eat without long cooking—and even then, if you don't accompany it with other food, a chemical reaction will bloat and distend the stomach. Some people died from that chemical reaction." He shook his head and was silent for a moment. Then he continued, "You know how beautiful Holland tulips are? We dug the bulbs out of the ground and ate them. That was all we had. We were desperate."

Again he was silent. I could tell he was deeply moved by those memories. Finally he went on. "A notice from our pastor went around, telling us that there would be a meeting in the church. He said that since there was no other hope, we would have a meeting and pray to God and tell Him we were His children and ask Him to feed us. It was the only thing we could do. The big church was packed; two thousand people were present. There was no sermon. We just prayed, hour after hour. The pastor prayed. People prayed aloud all over the church. We sat there huddled together, praying to God.

"I was only a little boy, but all of a sudden I became aware that God was right there with us. His presence was so strong that I was almost frightened. I could feel Him in my heart. I knew that He was there and I knew that somehow He was going to take care of us poor, starving people.

"Then we sang one of those great old Dutch hymns of faith and we went out to the streets and to our homes. With gnawing, empty stomach I went to bed and fell asleep. Early the next morning we were awakened by the roar of a tremendous armada of allied airplanes over Rotterdam, and there began an unbelievable shower of food. The sky was full of big packages, dangling from parachutes, that came floating down to the streets of Rotterdam, filling the avenues with good food. And we ate. And we were saved."

He glanced back at me from the driver's seat as he said, "As long as I live, I will believe that God heard those prayers and out of His big heart of love He fed His children."

I do believe it. And I am sure you do, also. How could anyone doubt a soul-stirring story like that? Why try to analyze it or question it or explain it away? Why not let it move you and strengthen your faith?

And be thankful.

14

IMAGING IN EVERYDAY LIFE

So FAR IN THIS book, imaging has been presented as a powerful device to achieve major goals and objectives. And so it is. But imaging can be used in many lesser ways to smooth out the minor wrinkles of living. For example, my friend Dr. Charles L. Allen, the popular minister-writer, tells a story in his book *Perfect Peace* about a woman who suffered from insomnia. Nothing very unusual about that. But her solution to the problem was interesting. She was a lover of flowers, and a skilled arranger of them. And so, when sleep didn't come easily, lying there in the dark she would visualize a table with a handsome flower vase on it and two dozen long-stemmed red roses lying beside it. She would hold the scene in her mind until it became almost real: the rich grain of the wood in the tabletop, the flowing curves of the vase, the pale green rose stems, the ruby petals glowing with velvety color.

Then she would see herself slowly picking up the roses, one by one, and arranging them in the vase. First she would visualize the vase with one tall flower, then two, then three—each carefully placed for artistic effect. Each time she added a flower, she would move back a few paces and study the composition. And according to Charles Allen, she never was able to complete the arrangement with all twenty-four flowers, because she always fell asleep!

Suppose you would like to redecorate a room in your house, or buy new furniture for the patio. Suppose, as is so often the case, you don't think you can afford to do it right away. What is to prevent you from imaging that room or that patio just the way you would like to have it? Fill in all the details—the color of the curtains, the pattern of the carpet, the kind of mirror you want above the mantelpiece—see it all in your mind's eye. It is a lot of fun, it doesn't cost a thing, and the more vivid the image, the better chance that someday it will become a reality.

When James Whistler, the great American painter, was first married, he and his wife were so poor that the only furniture they had was a bed. But this did not discourage them. In every empty room of their modest house they sketched with chalk, on the floor, the outline of each piece of additional furniture that they intended to have someday. Inside the outline they added a detailed description of what it would look like. They imaged their dream house furnished just as they wanted it to be. And the time came when that vision became a happy reality. Why? Because they pushed beyond the fuzzy, indistinct yearnings that many people settle for and *focused* their wishes with great intensity of imaging. Those chalk marks and detailed descriptions on the floor gave a substance and a reality to the dream that otherwise it would never have had. And their unconscious minds went to work instantly, providing the energy and the drive and the confidence that the young couple needed to reach their goal.

Suppose you would like to travel. Do you want to visit England or Italy, or see the Grand Canyon, or go flying down to Rio? Don't just sit and vaguely wish. Go to a travel bureau. Get some brochures. Better still, get some maps and trace the route you would like to follow. Go to the library and take out some history books. Learn all you can about the place you want to visit, its history, the people who are living there. Then image yourself against that background.

If your dream is visiting the Holy Land, visualize yourself standing in Bethany at the spot where Jesus raised Lazarus from the dead. See yourself on the shores of Galilee where He commanded the wind and the waves to be still.

Tell yourself that the same waves and the same wind are still there, waiting for you to visit them. Imagine yourself in Jerusalem, putting your hand on the olive trees in the Garden of Gethsemane or at the tomb where the stone was rolled away. Don't let negative considerations like lack of money creep in, because your unconscious mind will seize upon a negative signal just as readily as it will react to a positive one.

Does this kind of dreaming, which is just another form of imaging, guarantee that someday you will find yourself in Rio or in the Holy Land or in England or Italy? No, it doesn't: life doesn't hand out ironclad guarantees. But it raises the probabilities so enormously that it is foolish not to take advantage of it.

The thing to remember is that an image vividly conceived and stubbornly held has a reality of its own. Once a young man spoke to me after I had made a speech in Los Angeles on the subject of positive thinking. He had a dream of going into electronics, building a small factory, and he described it in detail. He had it all worked out in his mind. "But," he said, "I don't have capital and I don't have any credit. I don't know if I will ever get it built."

"But it is built," I told him. "You have already created this factory. It exists—in your mind."

"It is just a vision," he said, "just a dream."

"That's great," I said. "That is the first step and the most important step. Never tell yourself that your factory doesn't exist, because it does. You have already built it. It is there, imaged in your consciousness. The next step is to get it out of your head and onto a piece of ground somewhere. And you'll take that second step as surely as you took the first. It is just a matter of patience and persistence and determination and time."

First Built by Imaging

"You mean it's built?" he said incredulously. "You mean I have already built it? Gosh, that is an exciting idea!"

"First the dream," I told him. "The dream or image worked out in detail. The image so vivid that you can see it like a three-dimensional picture glowing in your mind. Then the hard work and the discipline and the willingness to take risks and the refusal to let go of the dream or let it fade. Put those elements together and you can't miss. You can't fail. You'll see."

He went away, and I suppose I really never expected to see him again. But about a year later, when I was greeting people after a service at Marble Collegiate Church in New York, he came along in the line. "Remember me?" he said. "Just wanted to say two words to you. It's built!"

"Wonderful!" I said to him. "But remember, it was built all the time!"

Great athletes use imaging constantly, sometimes consciously, sometimes without being fully aware of what they are doing. Have you ever watched a champion high jumper just before he makes his jump? Usually he stares at the ground for a long moment before he begins his run. And in that moment he is visualizing himself sailing across the bar. He is flinging his image over the bar, you might say, and if his body fully accepts that image, it is probably going to follow.

Years ago I heard a story about Jim Thorpe, the great American-Indian athlete whose legendary feats in sports are still revered and remembered. With the rest of the American team, Thorpe was on his way to Europe by ship to compete in the Olympic Games. Each day the athletes would work out on the ship's deck, some running, some jumping, some lifting weights. The scene was one of furious activity. One of the coaches was astonished, therefore, to come upon Thorpe one day sitting on the deck, leaning back against a lifeboat, eyes closed, not even in his track suit.

"Thorpe," the coach said sharply, "what do you think you're doing?"

The big, bronzed athlete opened one eye. "I'm watching myself win the decathalon," he said. And closed it again.

Imaging. Thorpe had never heard of the word, but he had adopted the technique and he knew it was more valuable than any amount of mere physical preparation. He was seeing himself win the decathalon *in advance*. And when the event finally took place, the image became the reality.

Well, you may say, suppose two or three other athletes from England or France or Germany had employed the same technique—what then? In that case, I would say, the contestant with the greatest physical endowments and the most vivid image of himself being victorious would win the event. But if the physical endowments were equal, then the owner of the strongest will to win, as reflected in that self-image of being the winner, would come away with the prize.

My friend W. Clement Stone, a well-known Chicago insurance man, founded a magazine called *Success Unlimited*. Not long ago it carried a fascinating article about a young graduate student named Steve DeVore. Steve, a psychology student, was reading a textbook on biofeedback one wintry afternoon and at times idly watching a TV program about championship bowling. Steve was an occasional bowler whose highest score was an unspectacular 163. But now, watching the champion bowlers reel off strings of strikes, he began to wonder if he might not somehow use the images on the TV screen to program his own mind and possibly increase his bowling skills.

So, blocking out all other thoughts and making himself as relaxed as possible, he tried to impress on his memory the images of the top bowlers making their very high scores. When the program ended, he played the images back in his mind, just as if he had a video tape inside his head. Finally, still concentrating intensely, he went out to a nearby bowling alley. There again he replayed his mental tape, telling his mind to direct and control his body and telling his body to become an instrument of his mind.

Steve DeVore then proceeded to bowl an unheard-of nine strikes in a row for a score of 286 out of a possible 300. In his second game he bowled seven strikes. Then his concentration faltered, and his game began to slide downhill. But DeVore was so impressed with what imaging could do that he started his own company, called Sybervision, to market a system of thought to athletic teams and individuals. The results, according to some professional coaches who have tried it, are nothing short of amazing.

Imaging can reach far beyond sports into almost every aspect of daily life. Suppose you are carrying a burden of guilt for some past mistake or transgression. Suppose you have tried the time-tested remedies—acknowledging your fault, making restitution, asking God to forgive you—and still feel unworthy and troubled. This load of unresolved guilt is draining strength and purpose from you. Can imaging help?

Perhaps it can. Try visualizing a blackboard with a jumble of disconnected words and phrases, or a tangle of scrawled mathematical problems with wrong answers—in short, a sorry record of mistakes.

Then image a shining figure, the Lord Himself, sweeping a sponge or a damp cloth across that blackboard, wiping it clean, preparing it for another, stronger, better effort. The Lord has forgiven your sins and mistakes. Then forgive yourself, for if you don't, the old guilt circle will repeat itself. Run this total picture sequence over and over in your mind. What you are imaging is forgiveness and acceptance, and if the vision is vivid enough, a great sense of peace and well-being will follow.

Suppose you are a victim of depression. Picture that doleful word spelled out in a gigantic electric sign on a mountaintop, with letters ten feet tall. It can be seen at night for miles. Then image the first two and the eighth letters suddenly extinguished. What's left? Two positive and vigorous words: *press on!*

Picture Yourself as Confident

Are you facing some challenge in your job where you doubt your ability to cope? Image yourself meeting the challenge, solving the problem—and give thanks for that solution in advance. Picture yourself filled with a surge of confidence and energy that sweeps away doubts and fears. Image your mind coming alive with fresh, new energy, crackling with new concepts, teeming with new ideas.

If you paint these images vividly enough, they may affect not only you but also the person or persons you are dealing with. In Australia a couple of years ago, Ruth and I met a dynamic and attractive woman named Lorraine St. Clair. She was the Australian representative for a company that specialized in reproductions of antique jewelry. Lorraine had conceived the idea of displaying these items in a real antique breakfront where prospective customers could look through the glass and see pieces of jewelry on black or red velvet—the effect was stunning.

Later Lorraine came to visit us in New York. She was very interested in our church and in the way we lived our lives. She said she had no spiritual training herself, and she wanted to find out more about such things. Ruth told her about tithing and the spiritual rewards it brings; this seemed to fascinate Lorraine and she became a tither herself.

She told us that her company wanted her to go to Europe and try to establish a market there for the jewelry. She had no connections or contacts there, but someone had told her that if she could persuade one of the principal stores to take this merchandise, others would follow.

So Lorraine fixed this goal in her mind. She began to image herself meeting the key marketing people and persuading them to carry the line of jewelry. She focused on this vision with great intensity before she left Australia and while she was flying to Europe.

Upon arriving, she called a man who was a chief buyer for a well-known store. She told him that she had studied his merchandising techniques (this was true) and admired them very much. She also told him about herself and said that she had a line of jewelry that she hoped to establish. To her amazement, the man said that he would see her. Result? Just as she had imaged it. Instant success.

Now how often would the chief buyer from a great store respond to an unknown vendor of jewelry and look at her samples? Not very often. But Lorraine had imaged precisely that outcome. Had something reached out and influenced the man on the other end of the telephone wire? Again, who can say?

Imaging can help in many other ways. Suppose you are torn with grief because a loved one has died. Surely it helps to image or visualize a future reunion with that person in the "land that is fairer than day." If the person was old or frail or feeble, picture him as vigorous and vital, as he was in the prime of life. Image the wonderful conversations and activities you will share when you are with him once again. Picture his eyes full of joy and happiness because he is reunited with you—forever.

Once or twice I have had a vision of my father and later one of my brother, Bob, after they had left this earthly life. In both instances, they looked vibrant and youthful and happy. They seemed to know that I could see them, too, because they raised their hands in the old familiar gesture of greeting and affection as if to say, "Don't worry about us. Everything is all right. We'll see you later." Those experiences, I think, were a form of imaging carried one step further into a reality we are seldom allowed to glimpse. But that reality is eternally there.

Image of a Country Home

There are other areas of imaging where things happen that are equally hard to understand. You may recall the clairvoyant vision of Mary Crowe that I described in the first chapter of this book.

Something similar happened years ago to some good friends of mine, Dr. William S. Bainbridge and his mother. Dr. Bainbridge's mother, a widow, grew tired of life in New York City and decided she wanted a place in the country. She had very definite ideas about the kind of place she wanted. She said she could visualize it clearly in her mind, right down to the last detail. But she and her son were unable to find one that suited her or that was like the place she imaged.

Finally they started praying about the problem, reading the Bible and asking for guidance. Meanwhile, the image in Mrs. Bainbridge's mind remained as clear as ever. As she was reading Scripture one day, a certain passage seemed to leap out at her: "And let us arise, and go up to

Bethel . . ." (Genesis 35:3). She felt that it had great significance for her. Her son could think of no place in the New York area called Bethel, but Mrs. Bainbridge said there must be one. Furthermore, she felt a strange conviction that the house she was seeking was there.

Finally they discovered that there was indeed a town named Bethel in Connecticut, near Danbury. But when they drove up there and Mrs. Bainbridge described her dream house to a realtor, he shook his head. "There's no place like that around here that I know of," he said.

"It's got to be here," Mrs. Bainbridge insisted.

The realtor was sympathetic but firm: there was no such house in Bethel. So the Bainbridges went back to New York.

Three days later the realtor called them. "I was wrong," he said sheepishly. "There is such a house after all, just as you described it, that I wasn't aware of. But it is not for sale."

Back went the Bainbridges to Bethel. When they saw the house, they were astounded, it matched Mrs. Bainbridge's image exactly. Furthermore, the owners said that within the past forty-eight hours a sudden change of jobs had made it necessary for them to leave town. Mrs. Bainbridge bought the house and lived in it happily for many years.

"And let us arise, and go up to Bethel." Was it all just coincidence? Who can say?

One thing seems certain: The mind has unexplored powers, and most of the time such powers remain unused. In our day-to-day activities, we are not using more than a fraction of our brain capacity. I have experienced this extra and normally unused power of the mind on various occasions myself.

One night in a southern city, for example, I was getting ready to make a speech and needed a certain person's name. I just couldn't remember it. I looked through all my papers and couldn't find it. I was to go onstage in five minutes. I had to have this name, or at least I thought I did. I remembered that some psychiatrist had said that if you relax and call upon your deeper mind, which never forgets anything, your deeper mind will deliver what you need.

It so happened that this talk was being given in a theater, and I had noticed an old rocking chair behind the curtain. I asked the chairman about the program and he said, "A lady is going to sing two songs before you are introduced."

"Have her sing three," I said. "I am going around behind the curtain and sit in that old rocking chair."

So I went around back and sat in the rocking chair. "Now," I said, addressing my subconscious mind, "I understand that you never forget anything, and everything I ever did, thought, read or heard is stored down inside of you somewhere. I need this name. I know there is greater capacity in you than I normally use, and I have not called on you very often for a special favor. But now, subconscious mind, I want this piece of information and I want it right away. I've got to have it and I believe you are going to deliver it to me."

After I said that, I sat back and relaxed. I could literally feel the subconscious mind down inside of myself going into high gear. I could almost hear the wheels spinning around. And when I came out from around the curtain, the name popped up like toast from the toaster. I went out on the platform and tried to tell my subconscious mind to deliver me some more material, but that was all it would give me that evening.

What a strange tapestry this imaging is! So many patterns. So many threads. All interconnected in ways that sometimes seem to defy logical interpretation. But I am convinced that the basic premise is true: as Emerson said, "The soul contains the event that shall befall it."

Which is just another way of saying that if you image something strongly enough, you help to make that something happen. Imaging *does* affect future events. But the decision to do the imaging is yours.

Finally, may I point out that imaging has its own formula: 1) the goal, 2) the purpose, 3) prayer activity, 4) thoughtful planning, 5) innovative thinking, 6) enthusiasm, 7) organized hard work, and 8) always holding the image of success firmly in mind. If this formula is faithfully carried out, the desired results will be achieved despite all difficulties or setbacks.

I was asked to be the speaker at a big rally in Columbus, Ohio, on behalf of World Neighbors, a service organization engaged in helping deprived people abroad. The meeting was organized and directed by Dr. Roy Burkhardt, an enthusiastic, dedicated, and able leader. He was also a confirmed positive thinker.

When I arrived at the Columbus airport at three o'clock in the afternoon, it was in an almost torrential rainstorm accompanied by high winds that drove the rain in sheets. But there to welcome me with a big smile was Roy. "The hall is full!" he cried. "The hall is full!"

Mystified, I replied, "Why Roy, it is only 3:00 P.M. and the meeting is scheduled for 8:00 P.M. Certainly the hall cannot be filled five hours ahead of time."

"Oh, yes, the hall is full," he insisted. Then it dawned upon me. He was visualizing the hall as full. He was imaging it packed to capacity, and it was a large auditorium at that.

He took me to the hotel and the rain continued in a drenching downpour all afternoon and evening. Finally at eight o'clock, when Roy and I and ex-governor John W. Bricker walked onto the stage, that big hall was indeed full and people were standing.

What accounted for that packed house? The imaging formula is the answer. A goal, a purpose, lots of prayer, planning, thinking, enthusiasm, organization, and always intense, continuous imaging. This overcame every adverse condition, including one of the worst rainstorms I have ever experienced.

"The hall is full." Life is full, also, and always will be if you so image it and forever keep God in it.

15

THE IMAGING PROCESS IN MAKING AND KEEPING FRIENDS

How do you conduct your life so that people are drawn to you? How do you get people to have a favorable attitude toward you? How do you persuade people to love you or—perhaps just as important—like you?

These are important questions for every one of us. William James, the great psychologist, said that one of the deepest drives in human nature is the desire to be appreciated, which is just another way of saying that everyone wants to be liked.

We all have this desire, and yet you know as well as I do that some people have more success in this area than others. These people seem to win friends easily and readily. They are popular. They are considered attractive, or charming, or helpful, or likable. People in trouble turn to them. Even their in-laws like them!

But there are other individuals who are not like that. Something seems to block them off from other people—and other people from them. They don't attract; they repel. And this is often a sad and painful thing, because they feel isolated and friendless without quite knowing why.

I was giving a talk not long ago at a convention of men who were executives in the automotive industry. At the luncheon preceding my speech, I was seated at a table with several men. One was a man of considerable intellectual brilliance. His mind was sharp and perceptive, his conversation incisive and stimulating. Yet there was a certain something that kept me from really being drawn to him.

Later I asked one of his associates about him. "Poor Bill," the associate said. "He is without question one of the most able men I've ever done business with. But not long ago he came to me and said, 'Charlie, would you please tell me something? Why is it people don't like me? I seem to get just so close to them and then a barrier goes up that I cannot penetrate. What is the trouble?' "

"And what did you tell him?" I asked.

He was silent for a moment. "I really didn't tell him anything," he said at last, "because I didn't know how. But did you happen to notice those two scholastic-achievement keys hanging from his watch chain? I think somehow, unconsciously perhaps, Bill projects the impression that he considers himself superior to the person he's dealing with. It is a very subtle thing, but it is there. Instead of saying, 'I care about you,' something in his manner says, 'I think I'm a little smarter than you.' And maybe he is. But all the same, it turns people off."

"You should have told him what you just told me," I commented. "You would have been doing him a favor. He might have put those academic keys away and started projecting a different image. So if you ever get another opening. . . ."

"You're right," he said thoughtfully. "I will keep it in mind."

Suppose you feel that someone dislikes you and that therefore you have grounds for disliking him—what should you do about it?

The first and most advisable thing to do is take a long, dispassionate look at yourself. Two thousand years ago, Jesus Christ put the essence of the whole thing into one short sentence: You must love your neighbor as yourself. Are you hypersensitive, suspicious, quarrelsome, wary, hostile, aggressive, contentious? You will never like your neighbor, because you don't like yourself. Are you quick-tempered, jealous, demanding, complaining? Same problem. If you want to associate on a good, friendly, normal, creative level with other people, you have to do a job on yourself—until you like yourself.

Imaging can help, because you can zero in on a character flaw and then picture yourself acting in the opposite manner. Take anger, for example—an extremely unpleasant characteristic, almost guaranteed to cause you to lose friends and make enemies. Suppose you know you have a quick temper—a short fuse, as they say. When something ignites it, hold a picture in your mind of yourself calmly extinguishing it. Or if you can't completely extinguish it, at least delay it. Very often the best cure for anger is delay.

Some years ago, I was asked to serve on a committee that was set up to study ways in which religious organizations could further the cause of world peace. A meeting was held, and it was certainly the most unpeaceful committee meeting I have ever attended. Several of the members had very firm ideas about the subject of peace, and if those ideas weren't accepted, they got very hostile about it. It became a super-heated meeting. Voices were raised. Tables were pounded. Then one man rose and, with an air of great deliberation, took off his jacket, undid his tie, and lay down on a couch that was there in the office. Discussion ceased abruptly as we all stared at the man. Somebody asked, "What's the matter? Aren't you feeling well?"

"I'm feeling fine," the man said. "I just noticed I was getting mad, that's all. And I have found that it is difficult to get mad lying down." He went on to give a little lecture on how keeping the body relaxed keeps emotions under control. He spoke in a very low voice.

"Speak up!" somebody said. "We can't hear what you are saying."

"That is the trouble with this meeting," the man on the couch said. "Too much speaking up too loudly. You can't argue in a whisper." Then he drew attention to his hands, which were resting limply with fingers spread and relaxed. He said, "I've noticed that when I get mad my fingers get tense, and before you know it I've clenched my fist. So I picture myself like this, with my fingers uncurled. With my fingers relaxed, it is very hard to get mad."

Well, I never did forget that man. He imaged himself out of a state of hostility and aggressiveness, and he carried the rest of us right along with him.

Another unlovely and unlovable quality is irritability, which often seems to be a combination of exasperation and impatience. The other day, while waiting to make a telephone call in a crowded airport where all the phones were in use, I noticed a distinguished-looking, silver-haired man in one of the booths, trying to put through a call. He got a busy signal half a dozen times. And what did this great executive do? He slammed the phone down so hard that it bounced off the hook and ricocheted around the booth on the end of its wire, an exhibition of plain, unadulterated infantilism.

We're all subject to exasperating happenings, from a broken shoelace to a friend who forgets a lunch date with you. There is a text, the twenty-first chapter of Luke, verse nineteen, that I like to repeat to myself under such circumstances: "In your patience possess ye your souls." If you practice spiritual patience you can rise above these inevitable annoyances. You can block them out, bring them under mental control. You have to decide who is going to call the shots: you or the annoyance. Patience through prayer and a quiet attitude is the best way.

When Someone Rubs You the Wrong Way

What if some person rubs you the wrong way? Here again, it is possible to learn to have an objective, scientific, dispassionate attitude. If you practice the two principles of spiritual patience and objective observation when someone does something to annoy you, you are not going to become irritated or angry. You are going to react as a scientist. A scientist is an objective, disciplined person who wants to know the causes behind circumstances. He reacts dispassionately, that is, without heat. So, acting as a scientific observer of the person whose actions annoy you, you will say to yourself, "I wonder what emotional conflict he has? What trouble is there in his life? Is he driven by some frustration or defeat?" Your reaction will be scientific and objective rather than emotional. You may even find yourself trying to help him solve his problem instead of resenting him.

I'll admit this requires greatness of spirit, because the natural tendency is to hit back. But it is a wonderfully satisfying experience when you have learned to study another person objectively and thereby avoid personal resentment.

Suppose you're having a disagreement with your wife, as we all do from time to time. Suppose she is being a real problem, or so you think. Try sitting and looking at her in a calm and pensive manner. This may be difficult, because if she is very annoyed with you she will say, "Why are you looking at me that way?"

"I'm studying you," you will say. "You used to be the greatest, sweetest girl. You were always so kind to me, and I loved you for it. Now you are upset and irritable, and I'm wondering why. Maybe it is my fault. Perhaps I'm just no good."

Do you know what she will do? She will start to defend you against yourself. "You're all right and I love you," she will firmly declare.

So there you are; the situation has been eased. You have dealt with her on a basis of spiritual psychology instead of simply reacting emotionally to her emotional state.

You will find that this principle holds true in dealing with your children, your business associates, and your friends in general. "I will study this person objectively," you say to yourself when conflicts or difficulties arise. "He has a soul, so I will treat him spiritually." You can get along with almost anybody, peacefully and without irritation, if you will refuse to be hurt and if you will look at the other person from a dispassionate and scientific point of view.

A visitor once asked Robert E. Lee, the great Confederate leader, what he thought of a certain individual.

"I think he is a very fine gentleman," Lee replied.

"He goes around saying some very uncomplimentary things about you," the visitor told the general. "What do you think of that?"

"You didn't ask me what he thought of me," Lee replied calmly. "You asked me what I thought of him."

The great general was too big to stoop to pettiness. That is why even his adversaries admired and respected him.

"Love your enemies . . ." Jesus Christ told us. ". . . bless them . . . pray for them . . ." (Matthew 5:44). It sounds hard. It is hard. But if you can bring yourself to do it, it will banish hate and anger from your heart and often turn an enemy into a friend. Christ is really telling us to let go of ill will, to image a reconciliation taking place. If you can force yourself to do this, the rewards are very great.

I remember a big, rough, tough, aggressive businessman who came to me after church services one day and said he wanted to acquire the spiritual power I had been preaching about. It sounded good to him. How could he get it? I listed the conventional answers to such questions and he went away, saying he would do as I suggested.

But a few weeks later he reappeared, saying that nothing worked. He prayed, he had read the Bible, he had cleaned up some dubious areas of his life, but he still had no feeling of spiritual power and he wanted to know what was wrong.

This time I talked to him in depth, and gradually it became apparent that his mind was full of hate and resentment for some of his business competitors. He was a big man and it was a big hatred. As a spiritual doctor I knew what he had to do if he wanted to have the power he was seeking, but I also knew that he was going to balk at the prescription, and he did. Our conversation went approximately like this: "There is an answer, if you want it and have what it takes to go for it," I said.

"Of course I want it. What is it?"

"You have to love these competitors of yours."

"What?"

"You have to love them."

"Are you crazy? Did you ever see those fellows?"

"No, I never saw them. But the Bible says you have to love your enemies."

"That is asking too much! It's impossible!"

"I thought you wanted spiritual power."

"I do!"

"I thought we agreed that I was the doctor."

"You are!"

"All right, I prescribe that you love them."

"How do I love them if I hate them?"

"I'll tell you what to do, and it won't be easy. Every day, three times a day, you have to ask the Lord to help those fellows and love those fellows and give them a bigger year in business than you have yourself."

"I refuse to do it!" he shouted.

"Well," I told him, "if you want to have spiritual power, you've got to do it."

I knew one thing about this man: If he made a promise, he would keep it, and he finally assented grudgingly. About ten days later, he came back and told me what happened. "I went home," he said, "and tried to pray for those so-and-so's and I just could not do it. When I got up the next morning I couldn't do it, and I couldn't do it at noontime. But that night I knew I had to do it or break my promise to you. So I knelt down and said, 'Lord, bless those fellows'—and I named each one—'and give them a bigger business this year then You give me.' Then I stopped and looked up and said, 'Lord, don't pay any attention to me, I don't mean a word of it!' "

I could hardly keep from laughing out loud; I knew the Lord must like a fellow like this one.

"But," he went on, "I finally said, 'Okay, Lord, I don't mean it, but I wish You would make me mean it.' So I struggled on all week like that, and finally last night a wonderful thing happened. While I was praying, all of a sudden it seemed as if a great hand came down and took away from my mind this heavy weight that has been there, and I want to tell you that today I am bursting with happiness!"

Of course he was! He did what the Lord told us all to do, and the result was real and wonderful happiness!

Help People to Like Themselves

That man finally made friends with himself. And when that happened, he could love his neighbor. So that is the first step in making friends and keeping them—get yourself straightened out. And what is the second step? It is helping your neighbor think more highly of himself. If you can just do that, you will never have to look around for friends. They will come to you. They will flock to you. You will need a stick to keep them away!

Lord Chesterfield, that wise Englishman, knew this. In his famous letters to his son he said something like this: "My son, here is the way to get people to like you. Make every person like himself a little better and I promise that he or she will like you very much."

That is profoundly true. Do you remember that earlier in the book I told about the professor at college who reprimanded me so severely and told me to improve my performance? Why do I remember him after all these years and love him still, although I was angry at the time? Because he saw a better "me" inside me, and proceeded to drag it out. He made me perform better, and when I did, I liked myself better, and I came to love the man who was responsible, even though it was a rough process. Emerson put it well in one of his memorable sentences: "Our chief want in life is someone who shall make us do what we can." That is indeed the function of a friend.

Do you lack friends? Take an acquaintance, or several acquaintances, study them a bit, then select their best attribute and praise them for it. This doesn't mean fulsome or insincere flattery. It means a fair and friendly recognition of something worthwhile in them. That recognition will increase their self-esteem. And they will eagerly give their friendship to the person who does that for them.

Everywhere you go you will find people who are not living up to the best in themselves. People love to have this best element recognized and coaxed out of them. Sometimes, to be sure, they resist. It is a paradox: they want the best drawn out of them and yet they don't. I see this quite often when I'm preaching (and what is preaching but an effort to draw the best out of people?). Some members of the congregation come to church because they know they need to be improved, and yet they hold back as if saying, "Well, get it out of me if you can!" Finally, if their lives are improved, it isn't the minister who does it. It is Jesus Christ, whose servant the minister tries to be. And that is one of the many reasons people love Jesus. He brings the best out of them and is therefore their best friend.

Another simple but basic way to make friends is to help people, not just when they ask for help but also when you see that they need it. I remember reading a newspaper story about a filling-station operator named Sam. With winter coming on, somebody sold Sam a snowplow, the kind you attach to the front of a car. When the first heavy snow came, he used it to clear the snow away from his gas pumps. It took only a few minutes. He looked across the street and saw a man's driveway all snowed in. The man was vainly trying to get his car out. Sam went over and cleaned his driveway. Then he went on to the next house. Soon he had cleaned out the driveways of twenty-nine houses.

Now where to you think all those people went the next time they needed gas? They went to see their friend Sam, of course. Later on, the story said, the Small Businessman's Association had a meeting in Washington to study methods and techniques of successful salesmanship. They had heard about Sam, for by this time he was cleaning the driveways of several hundred homes each winter. Not only that, but anyone in the community who had a problem or wanted an errand done would call on Sam because he would take on anything from baby-sitting to delivering groceries to shut-ins. The Small Businessmen's Association heard that Sam was selling more gasoline than anyone in his area, so they asked him to come and give his magic formula. Sam, to their astonishment, simply told them he got his formula out of the Bible, where it says, "Love one another" (John 15:17).

Indeed, that is the most practical, sensible, hardheaded advice in this world! Businessmen used to come around and complain to me about Christianity's being theoretical. It is theoretical, all right. It is the soundest kind of theory, because it works. I promise you that any business run by people who love their employees and love the people they serve, and who treat them all with loving-kindness, will have black figures, not red ones, in its ledgers. It is a law as inexorable as the law of gravity.

So there are really four steps you must take if you want to make friends and keep them, First, you must examine yourself and get rid of the characteristics that alienate other people. Second, you must make a conscious and deliberate effort to help other people find greater self-esteem. Third, you must go to their aid and assist them over the rough spots in the road of life. Fourth—and most important of all—you must love them, genuinely love them.

People Love You When You Love Them

Human beings always know when you love them—and they respond with love. That is the ultimate basis of friendship. That is what binds people together and holds them together. One of our most beloved entertainers, Will Rogers, used to say he never met a man he didn't like, which guaranteed him endless friends, because no one could be found who didn't like Will Rogers.

I once knew a quiet and likable man named Charlie who ran a grocery store in Pawling, New York, the small town where Ruth and I own an old 1830 farmhouse. Pawling has a population of maybe four thousand people. Charlie ran a chain grocery store for about twenty years, and then the company withdrew from the town. Charlie spoke to me and asked, "Do you think I could run a store on my own? I don't have much capital, but the company said I could have the equipment, and they would give me an inventory to start with."

"Sure you can," I said. I knew that Charlie loved people, and that people loved him. So he took the store, and the day after it opened I went in, and Charlie and I went into one of the back rooms and sat there among the cracker barrels and cartons, and Charlie said, "I want to dedicate this store to God." So he and I had a prayer of dedication.

Later, I used to watch him wait on people. One afternoon a woman came in looking tired and worn. Charlie said to her, "Mary, I'm glad you bought some of that cheese. That is a great New York State cheese, and I know what a good cook you are. Your husband and children are going to have a wonderful supper tonight. Macaroni and cheese cooked by loving hands . . . you can't beat that!" The woman stood up straighter and a wonderful smile came over her face. She picked up her groceries and went out, strengthened by the knowledge that the man who had sold them to her was interested in her as a person.

A year or two later one of those big, modern supermarkets opened up only a short distance from Charlie's little store. He asked me, "Do you think I can survive the competition from this big, new supermarket?"

I said, "Just go on loving people, Charlie. You'll be all right."

Well, he was. And when Charlie finally died, his was one of the biggest funerals Pawling ever saw. It seemed as though the whole town turned out to pay tribute to a quiet grocer who loved his fellow human beings.

Never forget it: The way to friendship and the way to happiness is through the wisdom of the wisest Man who ever lived, the Man who said, "A new commandment I give unto you, That ye love one another . . ." (John 13:34).

Follow that principle and you will find fulfillment for one of the deepest needs of human nature, the desire to be esteemed, and liked, and loved.

16

THE MOST IMPORTANT IMAGE OF ALL

THROUGHOUT THIS BOOK, I'VE talked about the value of imaging in many of the key areas of living. But there is one image that is more important than all the other images combined: the image that you have of yourself.

"As a man thinketh in his heart," the Bible says, "so is he" (*see* Proverbs 23:7). In other words, as you see yourself, so you are.

If you firmly image that you are a person destined for success, success is what you ultimately will have. If you are convinced that you will fail, failure will stalk you no matter where you go. If you think scarcity, it will befall you. If you image abundance flowing to you, it will flow.

The universe is like a great echo chamber: sooner or later what you send out comes back. If you love people, that love will be reflected back to you. If you sow anger and hatred, anger and hatred are what you will reap. If you think mainly of yourself and your own interests, people will never be drawn to you. If you put others first and yourself last, everyone will be your friend.

If you have a mental picture of yourself as an inferior person, you *will* be inferior, because you will act in a timid and ineffective manner. If you go to a meeting convinced that all others present are brainier or better informed than you are, you will sit there and never open your mouth, although quite possibly you have good ideas and worthwhile contributions to make. You will be tongue-tied by your own low opinion of yourself.

On our last trip to Hong Kong, Ruth had an appointment with a dressmaker, which left me with some time on my hands. Walking through the narrow side streets of fascinating Kowloon, I came upon a tattoo parlor run by an elderly Chinese practitioner of this ancient and venerable art. In the window of his shop were displayed the various decorations that could be imprinted on your skin if that sort of embellishment appealed to you: flags and patriotic slogans, anchors and daggers, skulls and crossbones, mermaids, and so on. But the one that caught my eye was a somber phrase: *Born to lose.*

This interested me so much that I went into the shop and asked the proprietor if he spoke English, which he did to some extent. Then I asked him about the *Born to lose* tattoo. Did people really ask to have that permanently imprinted on themselves?

Yes, he said, occasionally they did. The last customer who wanted it had had it emblazoned on his chest.

"Why on earth," I asked him, "would anyone want to be branded with a gloomy slogan like that?"

The old Chinese man gave an oriental shrug. "Before tattoo on chest," he said, "tattoo on mind!"

How true, I thought, *and how sad*. The born loser was not *born* that way at all. But if he permitted a sense of inferiority to take possession of his mind, if he allowed his self-image to become tinctured with the dye of inadequacy and failure, then a loser is what inevitably he would be.

How does a person gain and keep a strong, serene, confident concept of himself or herself? That is a big question, and there is a twofold answer. You do certain things that enhance and strengthen that image, and you avoid certain things that damage it. Let us take a look at the latter first.

There are three deadly emotions that rob a person of the normal degree of self-esteem that is so important. Those grim, unwelcome visitors are fear, guilt, and doubt. If any one of them becomes dominant in your life, your self-image is going to suffer. Let us take a look at each one and see what can be done to neutralize their baleful power.

There is an old Russian proverb that says, "A hammer shatters glass but forges steel." The hammers of life are bound to hit each of us, sooner or later. And one of these hammers is that ancient problem of the human spirit known as fear.

From the time when they are little children afraid of the dark, people have to wrestle with this adversary, and the battle continues all through life. Sometimes fear is so great that it shatters people. They lose their confidence, they withdraw from life, their image of themselves shrinks to the point where they no longer believe they can cope with hardship, or illness, or economic problems, or whatever is threatening them. And once their belief in their own competence is lost, it is hard to get it back.

But other people facing the same kind of difficulties react differently, because they have faith. When the hammer of fear hits them, they don't shatter. On the contrary, they are forged into stronger human beings. Through such forging it is possible to become a person who can stand firm, look any fear in the eye, and say, "In the name of God, I am no longer afraid."

What a glorious status to attain! And how is it done? How do you maintain a self-image that enables you to handle fear? The secret lies in a single word: *trust*. Suppose you come to a point where you no longer believe you have what it takes to deal with a situation. Your self-image is weakened. You are afraid you may lose your conviction of competence. What do you do? Well, you relinquish the frightening situation to God. You put it in His hands. You leave it with Him. And you trust Him absolutely, because you remember that He said, "Fear thou not; for I am with thee: be not dismayed; for I am thy God: I will strengthen thee; yea, I will help thee . . ." (Isaiah 41:10). That is the solemn promise of Almighty God. He made it so that we fearful human beings would believe it, and accept it, and be strengthened by it.

Complete trust—it is the most protective and sustaining emotion that the human mind can feel. We experience it as small children when a nightmare terrifies us or a thunderstorm crashes around us in the dead of night. What do we do? We get up, panic-stricken, and scurry to our parents' room, where mother or father lets us into bed, comforts us with encircling arms and soothing words, and finally takes us back to our own room, calmed and reassured and ready to go on with the business of living. They don't turn away and they don't make fun of our fears. They offer love and support until the danger and the terror are past.

And God, the Father of us all, is like that. A simply analogy, yes, but that is the essence of most profound ideas: they are simple.

Sometimes complete trust produces results that are beyond the grasp of human understanding. Not long ago I was reading a collection of stories written by members of our armed forces—army, navy, and air force veterans telling of extraordinary experiences they had had.

Adrift in the Pacific

One of the stories was by a navy machinist's mate named Pete Mesaro. Pete was on a P T boat far out in the Pacific Ocean. The sea was rough. Somehow, in the early hours of the morning, while it was still dark, he was hurled against a stanchion, felt great pain in his leg, and toppled into the ocean. No one saw him go overboard. When he came to the surface, the P T boat was racing away from him. He was alone in a vast expanse of the sea.

Finally the first faint streaks of dawn lighted up the sky and slanted across the waters. His leg pained him; it was bleeding. Then, to his horror, he saw the black, triangular fin of a shark break the surface not thirty feet away. It was making a slow circle around him. His body went so tense with fright that he could hardly breathe. He knew that the blood escaping from his leg had attracted the shark—and would attract others.

Pete was a sincere Christian boy. He prayed—not to be saved, because he didn't think that was possible. He just prayed to God to make the end come quickly and then take his soul to heaven.

"But as I prayed," he wrote, "a strange thing happened." His mind went back across the years to the classroom in the Sunday school he had attended as a child. There was a life-size cardboard cutout figure of Jesus in the corner of that room, and under it in large print were the words BEHOLD, I COME QUICKLY: BLESSED IS HE THAT BELIEVETH (*see* Revelation 22:7). But now he realized that the figure wasn't cardboard at all. It was Jesus Himself, actually speaking those words and coming toward him across the waters with outstretched arms. Indescribably elated, Pete began to swim toward Jesus.

Incredibly, the shark seemed to retreat as Pete swam forward. Then a second shark appeared, and both came at him from converging angles. But the hope that the image of Jesus had given him was stronger than his fear of the sharks. He lashed out at them, splashing and kicking like a madman.

Then the unbelievable thing happened. An American destroyer had come over the horizon. A lookout saw the frantic splashing and realized something was amiss. At flank speed the destroyer came up and lowered a boat with riflemen who drove the sharks away. Pete barely remembered strong arms lifting him into the boat. But before passing out from shock and exhaustion, he saw again the figure of Jesus with arms outstretched.

A miracle? What is a miracle? It is a wonderful occurrence beyond the reach of our analytical understanding. I believe that in this instance, a man completely lost himself in an ecstatic realization of the love and protective presence of God. Had he died, he would have died at peace. But now he lives at peace, knowing that there is nothing in life to be afraid of, so long as we trust God.

Trust really does drive out fear. The other night Ruth and I were coming back to New York from Albuquerque via Dallas. The Texas weather was good, but as we flew on toward New York it became worse and worse. Impenetrable cloud vapor enveloped our plane. It rocked and shuddered from violent wind gusts. We were told to prepare for landing at La Guardia, and we buckled our seat belts, but we could see nothing. Suddenly the swirling mist parted for a moment, and I saw below us the lights of one of New York's great bridges. The tall towers looked close enough to touch. Then suddenly the plane zoomed upward. The pilot had been told by the control tower to go around and make another approach. The cabin was very quiet. Nobody said anything, but you could feel the strain in the air. The faces of the flight attendants were tense.

Now, I am no hero in the sky. But this time, in a situation that certainly was nerve-racking, to say the least, strangely enough neither Ruth nor I felt any fear. We prayed silently for the pilot, asking that he be given calmness and good judgment. We prayed for the men on the ground who were guiding us by the invisible beacon of radar. I remember thinking that it was amazing how many unseen people we trusted—the designer of the airplane, the maintenance crews that serviced the great engines, the hydraulic systems, the communications networks, the weather forecasters . . . we trusted our lives to all of them, almost without thinking.

The pilot made another approach. Again he pulled up sharply. This time he told us, in a calm, almost laconic fashion, that at the last moment he had spotted another aircraft on the runway where we had been cleared to land. Tension in the cabin mounted even higher, but still Ruth and I were not afraid. We felt that we were in the hands of the Lord, and that those strong, loving, capable hands would put us down in a safe landing on the third attempt. I believed that. I trusted that it would happen. I imagined it happening. And so neither of us felt fear.

On the third attempt, the captain set his big bird down with a barely perceptible jolt. The whole cabin burst into heartfelt applause! Later I met the husband of one of the flight attendants and he told me that his wife said those first two attempts at landing were the most hazardous and terrifying moments of all her ten years in the air.

Perhaps, as we grow older, we begin to lose our fear of dying, which is certainly one of the most basic and universal of all fears. It is a fear that to some extent is kept alive by the paganism of the world, which regards death as the end of everything. Certainly I am in no hurry to leave this world. I enjoy life enormously. I'm having a wonderful time. It is a lovely world, and very few of us want to exchange it for death, which so often has been associated in our minds with gloom and sadness.

But trust can overcome even this most elemental of all fears. Can you believe that a God who has given us this beautiful world would, when we die, put us in a place of ugliness? Can you believe that the God who gives us such precious experiences here on earth would suddenly extinguish us like a candle flame? Do you believe that a God whose every manifestation here is of life and vitality and creativity will suddenly change and consign us all to death and destruction? I have never seen any sign that God is so capricious. The very orderliness of the universe belies it. The seasons follow one another in absolute regularity. The stars come out in the skies nightly in the same old wonderful patterns. Even those heavenly bodies that come only periodically return on the stroke of the minute. When I was a child I saw Halley's comet. It had been predicted many years before that it would come back at that precise time, and it did. And in a few years now it will come again. On time. To the split second.

Can you believe that a God of such exquisite order will suddenly become a God of disorder, that He will be kind to you at one time and cruel to you at another? There is no logic in such thinking. Faith rejects it, also. Faith as well as reasoning says a great *No* to any such proposition. The mystical experiences of life deny it. The longer I live, the more I think about death, the more convinced I am that when we finally come to it, death will be just another expression of God's unbounded love and beauty.

So don't let any kind of fear wrap and shrink the image you have of yourself. "Lo, I am with you always," said Jesus, "even unto the end of the world" (Matthew 28:20). With an assurance like that, we need never be afraid.

Damaging Effect of Guilt

The second image-damaging emotion, not as common as fear but still common enough, is guilt. How can you possibly think well of yourself if your own conscience condemns you? You can't. Even when you try to stifle the voice of conscience (and many people try to persuade themselves that they can do just that), the sense of wrongdoing will take its toll one way or another. Sometimes in the form of a physical affliction. Sometimes in a change in mental faculties. Sometimes in a deep, unacknowledged sickness of the soul: loss of vitality, of enthusiasm, of self-confidence. You can't avoid it any more than you can avoid the law of gravity.

People were more aware of this a generation ago than they are now. The church saw to that. When I was a youngster growing up in the heartland of America, there was a lot of talk from the pulpit about sin. Preachers didn't pussyfoot around. They didn't invent fancy theological terms for wrongdoing that watered it down to a comfortable level. They called sin by its rightful name, and when they banged on the Bible and said that the wages of sin is death, everybody knew what they were talking about. Adultery. Fornication. Drunkenness. Dishonesty. Deceitfulness. Selfishness. Greediness. Lust. Laziness. The list was long and it was specific. If you gave in to any of these things, you were a sinner, and the word came down, tough and uncompromising, that you had better straighten up and do better or else you were in danger of losing your immortal soul. You would go straight to hell, was the blunt way it was told.

Through the years, I have seen many physical manifestations of a hidden sense of guilt. I remember one woman who suffered from a terrible rash and itch every time she attended a church service. Why? Because these were merely external manifestations of a deep spiritual malady inside of her, mainly guilt for certain transgressions that she was trying to repress and hide. Coming to church triggered and heightened that sense of guilt. Only by confession and repentance was she able to cure the internal problem. When she did, the rash disappeared.

I remember another case years ago in Syracuse. One of my close friends, an ear, nose, and throat specialist, told me of a woman who suffered greatly from a sinus condition that no medical treatment seemed to alleviate. The doctor was astute enough to suspect that some spiritual dislocation lay behind this physical problem, and he asked me if I would help with the case. After several conversations, it became evident that the woman hated her mother, who was long since deceased. In a way, she had a valid reason for hating her mother. When another child in the family—her mother's favorite—died, the mother screamed at this daughter, "Oh, why wasn't it you? I wish it had been you!" A dreadful, hurtful thing. But the guilt the woman felt for hating her mother was so strong that it showed up as an infection in her sinuses! Once we per-suaded her to forgive her mother, to under-stand that the grief-racked woman was not entirely responsible for what she had said, the chronic sinus condition began to subside.

If you are a creative person, your self-image is of crucial importance. If you are a writer, you must believe that your thoughts and ideas are worthy of respect and attention. But if you lose your respect for yourself, you begin asking yourself why anyone else should pay attention to you. You begin to think your work is not worthy of being read. The result can be paralysis of the creative faculty.

A few years ago, a very well-known writer who was an acquaintance of mine called me up. "Norman," he said, and his voice was hoarse with tension, "I have to see you. I'm in great trouble."

I asked him what he meant by that, but he wouldn't give me any explanation. He just kept saying that he had to see me right away. He lived in a nearby town, so I finally told him to come on over to our farm-house in Pawling.

When he arrived, I was shocked at the change in the man. He was haggard and grim. He looked sick—and indeed he was sick, with a soul sickness that went very deep. He told me that he could no longer write. This had produced financial problems so acute that he could no longer sleep. I had the feeling that he was carrying an enormous load of guilt, that he had been carrying it for years, and that it had finally caught up with him. "You'd better get it off your chest," I told him. "For the moment, at least, I'm your pastor. So come clean [I used that phrase deliberately] with me. But," I warned him, "you can't hold anything back, or you will be wasting your time and mine. You will have to get it all out, whatever it is."

I took him out to a little room over our barn, where we wouldn't be disturbed. And he began to talk. He poured out a torrent of poisonous memories, mostly of sexual misconduct, that went back for years. It was a grim recital. I wondered how his image of himself as a writer had sur-vived as long as it had. Now that image was shattered, and it would require exorcising to rebuild it.

So we began the process, using the old, time-tested techniques of confession and repentance, followed by the promise of forgiveness. I made him kneel on the rough floorboards of the old barn, and I knelt with him while he poured out, before Almighty God, his guilt and misery and his desire to change. I told him that God was faithful to forgive sins where there was true repentance and that, as God's representative, I could assure him that he had that forgiveness. It was a moving and exhausting experience for both of us, but there was a new light on his face, and I knew that he would make a new start and eventually recover his lost creativity.

And so he did. But how much pain could have been avoided if he had just had the good sense to know that moral laws cannot be broken with impunity—not if you want the self-image that determines your course in life to remain strong and confident.

The third great stumbling block to a serene and confident self-image is doubt. Doctor Charles Mayo, of the famous Mayo Clinic, said, "I have never known a man to die from overwork, but I have known many to die of doubt."

Doubt is the enemy of faith. People who have developed real faith have a strong hold on an actual life-force. Faith channels into you the mysterious power that recreates and reproduces health, vitality, and energy.

But doubt can block this flow of power. A skeptic puts himself outside the magic circle. If you repudiate the reality and power of God, you are really repudiating everything, including your own importance and the reason for your own existence.

The value of achieving the absence of doubt and going on to success is illustrated by the brilliant career of a famous big-league baseball pitcher. Following is a story about him from the Baltimore *Sun:*

In the aftermath of the best season of his career, one in which he won 25 games for the Baltimore Orioles and a Cy Young Award for himself, Steve Stone was asked: "How do you explain going from an 11-7 record in 1979 to a 25-7 record in 1980?"

"I knew I had to realign my thinking about pitching," said Stone. "I knew I had to become a positive thinker in the highest form. I had heard about positive thinking, and that most people only paid it lip service. But what did it really mean? It was not enough just to win tonight. I had to take a philosophy and put it into a system I could work with, something that would hold for the rest of the season and the future. It's an easy thing to bring out; it all depends on the price you're willing to pay."

The input to this new philosophy were "creative visualization, positive thinking and meditation." And to this day, Stone can't offer a better practical explanation, than, "I just seemed to concentrate more on the mount. Instead of hoping I can get somebody out, I know I can get him out.

"It starts with almost bragging to yourself," he said. "You tell yourself things, almost to the point you laugh at yourself and say, 'Yeah, sure.' But then you have to erase all the negatives you have dealt with over the years and start replacing them with positives. It's almost like a brainwashing situation. You have to relearn the task, and relearn how to deal with it physically, psychologically and emotionally. I have reached the point now that I know I'm a winning pitcher, and I'll be a winning pitcher as long as I'm in the game."

If you are a doubter, you cannot really answer the basic questions of life: Who am I? Where did I come from? Where am I going? What am I doing here? And, naturally, if you are a skeptic, your unconscious mind gets a little confused and discouraged. "If this person doesn't know what he is doing here," it says to itself, "why should I bother to help him move in this direction or that? It makes no difference anyway, so I don't think I'll bother."

So, lack of faith can set up a profound existential uneasiness. An exceptionally strong personality may struggle on regardless, but it takes tremendous effort, and if such a person does achieve any significant success it is in spite of himself, because his self-image has no solid, unshakable base.

Even when faith is present, many people suffer from acute self-doubt. Sometimes I think such people should pray at least once a day the prayer attributed to some old Scotsman: "Oh, Lord, give me a higher opinion of myself." I don't mean we should be arrogant or conceited. I mean we should be aware of the enormous potential the good Lord has put into each of us, and move forward with the kind of assurance and confidence that He wants us to have. Sometimes when I sense a kind of gloom or despondency in people, I feel like shouting at them, "Wake up! Cheer up! You are greater than you think! Get rid of self-doubt! Replace it with faith—faith in God, faith in yourself, faith in the future. And nothing shall be impossible for you!"

When your self-image is weakened by doubt, you have a strong tendency to exaggerate the size of the difficulties facing you. Have you heard the story about the little boy who was plagued at school by an overgrown bully who lived on the same street he did? One day this boy was sitting on his front porch with a new telescope his father had bought him, but he was looking into the large end of it.

"Bill," his father said, "that is not the way to use a telescope. Use the other end. That makes the object you are focused on look bigger."

"But I'm looking at Harry," the boy explained, "and I don't want him to look bigger. This way I'm making him look small, and I'm not afraid of him."

The best way to look at difficulties is with hope and confidence. How sad it is to hear people going around saying, "Oh, my! How sick I am! How old I'm getting! How much trouble I have!" If they would just adjust their spiritual telescopes by getting their minds filled with faith and the love of God, they would be saying, "I have been sick, but I'm getting better fast! I'm not old; why, I feel better than I did ten years ago! There are a lot of troubles facing me, sure, but I have the wisdom and strength to overcome them!"

Do you recall the story of the little locomotive that we all had read to us when we were children? I think it was called *The Little Engine That Could*, and it is quite a profound parable, as children's stories often are. The little engine was called upon to pull a heavy train of cars over a steep hill. His brothers and sisters all decided the effort was too much for them; they gave up or refused to try. But the little engine had a different image of himself. He hitched himself to the train and began to pull. "I think I can, I think I can, I think I can," he puffed, slower and slower, as he labored up the hill. And when he reached the crest and started down the other side, he huffed triumphantly, faster and faster, "I thought I could, I thought I could, I thought I could!" He imaged himself as an overcomer of obstacles—and so he was!

Eight Ways to a Better Self-Image

Well, suppose your self-image is not all it should be. Can you do something about it? Of course you can! A weak self-image is not a natural state of mind. You weren't born with it. A newborn baby has a perfectly sound opinion of himself. No, you acquired it as you went along. You acquired it the way you acquire any other characteristic, good or bad: you *practiced* it. You practiced it into your mind, and what you practice *in* you can practice *out*. So here are eight suggestions designed to help you do just that.

1. *See yourself always as a child of God.* This is the greatest of all antidotes to fear. "If God be for us, who can be against us?" said Saint Paul (Romans 8:31). It is a question that calls for no reply, because the answer is obvious.

Of course, to see yourself as a child of God requires faith that God exists, that He did create you, and that He cares about you. And how do you get such faith? You make up your mind that you want it, you need it, and you are going to have it. Then you go after it.

You can take faith in, like medicine, in various ways. Through the eye, for instance. You can read the Bible and let its great messages of faith and healing drive out the doubt thoughts and the fear thoughts. Or through the ear. You can go to church and listen to the stirring hymns and anthems. You can hear the reading of the Scripture. You can listen to a sermon. You can also take in faith simply by observing the miracles of creation that surround you. The starry heavens, the vast and restless ocean, the mighty mountains, the flowers in springtime—can anyone believe they all happened by accident or by chance? "Be still," the Bible says, "and know that I am God" (Psalms 46:10). In your quiet moments, see yourself as His creation, as His child, and your self-image will have a foundation that will never be shaken.

2. *Stand in front of the mirror and take a good look at yourself.* First check your external appearance. Do you look discouraged or defeated? Make yourself stand straight and tall. Put a smile where that frown was. If your clothes seem drab or forlorn, do something about them. Your appearance reflects and affects your image of yourself; if you improve one, you will begin to improve the other.

Then look at the inner person. Do you lack energy and confidence? Are you convinced that your major goals are beyond your reach? Do you doubt your basic ability to cope with life? If you have such qualms or uncertainties, admit that you have them—but also tell yourself that with God's help, you are going to do something about them. Say a quick prayer, asking that a normal degree of self-esteem and self-confidence may be yours. Remind yourself that a weak self-image can be changed into a strong self-image at any stage of life. It is never too late—and the time to begin is now. Image yourself with an improved self-image! Believe that you will get results, and you will.

3. *Decide to treble your capacity for imaging.* If you consistently picture the best—not the worst—happening to you, powerful forces will work to bring about the thing you are visualizing. This is the central theme and message of this book, and it is true, but you will never know it is true until you have experimented with it yourself. Agnes Sanford, the famous healer, wrote in her book *The Healing Light,* "One way to understand a hitherto unexplored force of nature is to experiment with that force intelligently and with an open mind." Exactly so.

Never doubt it. What is imaged in your mind tends to actualize itself in fact. The pyramids of Egypt, the Parthenon, Saint Peter's in Rome, the great soaring bridges of New York, all exist in fact. But once they existed only as an idea in somebody's mind—and that is when their real existence began. Somebody imaged them—and eventually those images took on form and substance. That is the sequence: first the germ of the idea, then the image of the idea, then the energy and determination to clothe it with reality, and finally the triumphant reality. Put that sequence to work for you, and your self-image will expand and grow.

4. *Practice what you do well, and then learn from your successes.* Nothing builds confidence—and with it a strong self-image—like the repetition of superior performance. All good athletes know this: a crack golfer doesn't choose to remember or dwell on the unsuccessful shot. He holds in his mind the image of the spectacular shots he has made in the past, knowing that that memory will help him repeat them in the future.

If you have a skill—and everyone has something they do well—seize every opportunity to exercise that skill. If you bake good cookies, bake them every chance you get. If you don't need them, give them away: the thanks and praise you get will strengthen your self-image. After a somewhat shaky start many years ago, I have become a reasonably proficient public speaker. Now I draw strength and reassurance from reaching an audience, feeling people respond. It reinforces my image of myself as a person whose purpose is to help people over the rough spots in life.

So practice what you do well—and draw strength and confidence from your successes.

5. *Condition your unconscious mind with spiritual power principles.* The best way to do this is to memorize key Bible passages and repeat them over and over until they sink down into your unconscious mind and become part of it. If your unconscious mind accepts these principles, tremendous energies can be released—energies that may change your life and your self-image completely.

At a Rotary Club luncheon in Hong Kong a year or two ago, I heard a Chinese businessman give a remarkable talk. He had come to Hong Kong as a penniless refugee from Red China, with a wife and eight children. They had no money, no possessions, no friends; just the ragged clothes on their backs.

But these people were strongly believing Christians. The man had in his pocket a frayed copy of the New Testament. And in that little book was a line of Scripture that he had committed to memory, a line written nineteen hundred years ago by Saint Paul: "I can do all things through Christ which strengtheneth me" (Philippians 4:13).

That Chinese refugee believed those words because he had imprinted them on his conscious mind. And his unconscious mind had accepted them, too. He believed that with Christ as his ally and guide he could do anything—not just some things, but *all* things. And so he saw himself succeeding in Hong Kong despite all the odds against him. He imaged himself rising out of poverty to modest prosperity and finally to affluence. He even designed a kind of verbal-mathematical formula that he passed along to his hearers at the luncheon. It went like this: I believe plus I can plus I will equals I did.

That triumphant formula, added to that powerful assertion from Saint Paul, erased all doubts from that refugee's mind. And when doubt was banished from his self-image, he was able to move ahead with giant strides.

6. *Sensitize yourself to the beauty and variety and excitement of living.* Don't just take it all for granted. Are you ever fascinated by the infinite variety of form and color, light and shadow, that surround you? Do you ever walk out at night just to feel the charm and mystery of the stars? Are you thrilled when you see a crescent moon appearing through the branches of a tree or over a shadowy rooftop? Do you get excited about

the wonderful discoveries and happenings going on in the world? Do you reach out for new books as they come off the press, searching for the thoughts and wisdom of the leaders of our generation? Do you follow with keen interest the political, international, and sociological movements of today? In other words, are you alive? Surely something is wrong if you are not! Life is so thrilling that it should seem to us like an ever-changing, wonderful play.

And what has this to do with self-image? A great deal. If you feel you are a vital part of the marvelous tapestry of living, aware of it, immersed in it, then you are going to think and act with enthusiasm and confidence and assurance. If you see yourself merely as a bystander, an onlooker, a hesitant observer, rather than a participant, your self-image will reflect that concept.

Life is a marvelous gift. Accept it. See it, hear it, touch it, smell it, taste it . . . live it!

7. *Control your emotions.* If you don't, they may push you into situations that could seriously damage or weaken the image you have of yourself.

They can also damage you physically. Take anger, for example. There is a saying in one of the South Sea Islands—Tahiti, I think—that goes like this:"Man who gets angry quickly, gets old quickly."

If you let your emotions dominate your reason, you may be led into situations that can be devastating to your self-esteem—that is, your self-image. I remember the case of a woman whose husband went out to look for employment on the West Coast. He left her, with their small child, on the East Coast until he was sure he had the right job. Three or four months went by. She was lonely and unhappy, and when an old admirer asked her to go out for dinner she accepted. Emotions took over and she found herself drawn into an affair.

Then, unexpectedly, her husband sent word that he had a good job and wanted her to come to him and bring their child so that the family could be reunited. Suddenly she realized she would have to face her husband, and her self-image began to fall apart. She was guilty. She was afraid.

Almost immediately she found herself unable to talk. She lost her voice and could speak only in a faint whisper. It was as if her mind was trying to help her out by making it impossible to confess to anyone what she had done.

The husband was notified that his wife had some kind of throat trouble, and would have to be examined by specialists. The specialists could find nothing wrong, no growth or tumor, only that the young woman's vocal cords were slightly separated so that when she tried to speak almost no sound came through.

The doctors concluded that the trouble was psychological, not physical, and they were right. The prospect of rejoining her husband filled the wife with such guilt and terror that she was literally scared speechless. In the end, when she finally brought herself to confess her sin and seek forgiveness, the vocal cords came together again. It was not easy to restore her self-image as a loving, faithful, upright person. But finally she accomplished it.

So it is wise to watch over your emotions, to guard them and control them. Image yourself as a person always in command of yourself, and thus greatly improve the chances that that is the kind of person you will be.

8. *The last and most important suggestion I have to make is simply this: Stay close to Jesus Christ always.* Commit your life to Him. He was the first to teach the power of imaging. He told His disciples, quite plainly, that what they pictured with faith would come to pass. Now, after more than nineteen centuries, scientists and psychiatrists and psychologists are at last beginning to proclaim what the faithful knew all along: He was right.

Christ does not change; He is the same yesterday and today and forever. And the truth of His teaching doesn't change, either. You can count on it, indeed. You can stake your life on it.

The most wonderful thing that can happen to any of us is to have that most profound of all experiences—to know Jesus Christ personally. You can hear about Him all your life and never really know Him. You can believe that He lived and respect Him and honor Him as a great historical figure and still only know Him academically.

But when at last you find Him and experience His reality, when for you He comes out of the stained-glass windows and out of history and becomes your personal Savior, then you can walk through all manner of darkness and pain and trouble and be unafraid. With Him by your side, you can have the most sublime of all positive images and achieve a sure victory in this life and the next.

TREASURY OF JOY
AND ENTHUSIASM

ACKNOWLEDGMENTS

GRATEFUL ACKNOWLEDGMENT IS MADE to the following authors, agents, publishers, and other copyright holders for the use of the material quoted in this book. Every effort has been made to locate copyright holders and, if any material has been used without proper permission, the editor would appreciate being notified so that proper credit can be given in future editions.

ABINGDON PRESS, for material from *A Feast for a Time of Fasting* by Louis Cassels and for material from *Abundant Living* by E. Stanley Jones.

STANLEY ARNOLD, for his quotation, "Every problem contains within itself the seeds of its own solution."

FRED BAUER, for his poem "for quiet I like unspeaking trees," from his book *For Rainy Mondays and Other Dry Spells* (Prometheus Press).

ERNEST BENN LTD., for world rights outside the United States and its dependencies and Canada to use excerpts from "The Spell of the Yukon" and "The Three Voices" from *Songs of a Sourdough* by Robert W. Service.

BRANDT & BRANDT LITERARY AGENTS, INC., for material from *Our Town* by Thornton Wilder. Copyright © 1938, 1957 by Thornton Wilder.

BRUCE F. CLIFFE, for material from *Let Go and Let God* by Albert E. Cliffe, copyright © renewed 1979 by Albert E. Cliffe.

COLLINS PUBLISHERS, for material from the book *More Prayers for the Plain Man* by William Barclay.

CONTEMPORARY BOOKS, INC., for the poem "It Couldn't Be Done" by Edgar A. Guest. Reprinted from *Collected Verse of Edgar A. Guest*, © 1934 with the permission of Contemporary Books, Inc., Chicago.

V.A.P. CRONIN AND READER'S DIGEST for permission to reprint A. J. Cronin's article "The Turning Point in My Career."

DR. DONALD CURTIS, for his affirmation beginning, "I move serenely forward. . . ."

RALPH S. CUSHMAN, for his poem "The Secret" from his book *Spiritual Hilltops*.

DEVORSS & COMPANY, for material from *You Try It* by Robert A. Russell. Published by DeVorss & Company, Marina del Rey, California.

DODD, MEAD & COMPANY, for excerpts from "The Spell of the Yukon" and "The Three Voices" by Robert Service. Reprinted by permission of Dodd, Mead & Company, Inc. from *The Collected Poems of Robert Service.* Copyright 1907, 1909, 1912, 1916, 1921 by Dodd, Mead & Company, Inc. Copyright 1940 by Robert W. Service.

DOUBLEDAY & COMPANY, INC., for "In the Garden of the Lord" by Helen Keller, from *Masterpieces of Religious Verse,* edited by Charles L. Wallis, copyright 1948 by Harper and Brothers; excerpt from *Only in Alaska* by Tay Thomas, copyright © 1969 by Mary P. Thomas; excerpt from *Great Possessions* by David Grayson, copyright 1917 by Ray Stannard Baker; excerpt from *The Greatest Book Ever Written* by Fulton Oursler, copyright 1951 by Fulton Oursler; for material by Arnold Bennett. All selections reprinted by permission of Doubleday & Company, Inc.

WILLIAM B. EERDMANS PUBLISHING COMPANY, for excerpt from *C. S. Lewis—Images of His World* by Douglas Gilbert and Clyde S. Kilby.

EVANGELICAL PUBLISHERS, for the poem "What God Hath Promised" by Annie Johnson Flint.

GUIDEPOSTS MAGAZINE, for material from "Fragile Moments" by Phyllis I. Martin. Copyright 1973 by Guideposts Associates, Inc. Used by permission from *Guideposts Magazine.*

HARPER & ROW PUBLISHERS, INC., for "Joy," pp. 77–78 in *A Gift for God* by Mother Teresa, copyright © 1975 by Mother Teresa Missionaries of Charity; for specified excerpts from *On Happiness* by Pierre Teilhard de Chardin, English translation copyright © 1973 by Wm. Collins Sons Ltd; for "I Shall Be Glad," p. 149 in *Poems of Inspiration and Courage* by Grace Noll Crowell, copyright 1938 by Harper & Row, Publishers, Inc.; renewed 1966 by Grace Noll Crowell; for material by Margaret Applegarth from her book *Heirlooms;* for specified excerpt p. 81 from *Our Town* by Thornton Wilder, copyright © 1938, 1957 by Thornton Wilder. All selections reprinted by permission of Harper & Row, Publishers, Inc.

HOLT, RINEHART AND WINSTON, PUBLISHERS, for material from *The Raft* by Robert Trumbull. Copyright 1942, © 1970 by Robert Trumbull. Reprinted by permission of Holt, Rinehart and Winston, Publishers.

HOUGHTON MIFFLIN COMPANY for material from the works of John Burroughs, reprinted by permission of the publisher, Houghton Mifflin Company.

I DARE YOU COMMITTEE and DONALD DANFORTH, for material by William H. Danforth.

BRYSON R. KALT, for material related by his mother, Mrs. Bryson Kalt.

ART LINKLETTER, for his secret of happiness.

LITTLE, BROWN AND COMPANY, for material from *Good-bye, Mr. Chips* by James Hilton. Copyright 1934 by James Hilton. Copyright © 1962 by Alice Hilton. Used by permission of Little, Brown and Company in association with the Atlantic Monthly Press.

MRS. VINCENT LOMBARDI, for quotation by Vincent Lombardi.

MRS. KATHLEEN MARKHAM, for the poem "Outwitted" by Edwin Markham.

MCGRAW-HILL RYERSON LTD. for material from *The Collected Poems of Robert Service*. Reprinted by permission of McGraw-Hill Ryerson Limited.

ROD MCKUEN, for material from *An Outstretched Hand,* © 1980 by Rod McKuen and Montcalm Productions, published by Harper & Row, Inc.

MOREHOUSE-BARLOW COMPANY, INC., for material from *God Wants You to Be Well* by Laurence H. Blackburn, copyright © 1970. Used by permission of Morehouse-Barlow Co., Inc.

JOHN MURRAY PUBLISHERS, LTD., for excerpts from *The Spirit of St. Louis* by Charles Lindbergh. Reprinted by permission of the publisher.

GERALD L. NEES for special material.

THOMAS NELSON, INC., for material from *Today Makes a Difference* by Margueritte Harmon Bro, published by Thomas Nelson publishers.

W. W. NORTON & COMPANY, INC., for material from *Anatomy of an Illness as Perceived by the Patient* by Norman Cousins, published by W. W. Norton & Company, Inc.

MISS THEO OXENHAM, for poems "God's Sunshine" and "Are You Lonely, O My Brother?" by John Oxenham. Used by permission of T. Oxenham.

PENGUIN BOOKS LTD. for excerpts from *Our Town* by Thornton Wilder, from Thornton Wilder: Our Town & Other Plays (Penguin Plays, 1962), Copyright © Thornton Wilder, 1938, 1957. Reprinted by permission of Penguin Books, Ltd.

PRENTICE-HALL, INC., for material from *How to Turn Failure Into Success* by Harold Sherman, copyright © 1958 by Prentice-Hall, Inc.; from *Let Go and Let God* by Albert E. Cliffe, copyright © renewed 1979 by Albert E. Cliffe; from *How I Raised Myself From Failure to Success in Selling* by Frank Bettger, copyright © 1977 renewed by Frank Bettger; from *Benjamin Franklin's Secret of Success and What It Did for Me* by Frank Bettger, copyright © 1960 by Prentice-Hall, Inc.; from *Pathways to Personal Contentment* by Frank Kostyu, copyright © 1960 by Prentice-Hall, Inc. All selections published by Prentice-Hall, Inc., Englewood Cliffs, N.J.

THE PUTNAM PUBLISHING GROUP, for material from *Alone* by Richard E. Byrd. Reprinted by permission of G. P. Putnam's Sons. Copyright 1938; renewed 1966 by Richard E. Byrd.

READER'S DIGEST, for excerpts from "Wise Animals I Have Known" by Alan Devoe, *Reader's Digest*, July 1954.

PAUL W. REUTER for poem "Then Laugh" by Bertha Adams Backus and anonymous poem beginning "Give me the gift of laughter."

FLEMING H. REVELL COMPANY for material from *I Am—I Can* by Daniel Steere, copyright © 1973 by Fleming H. Revell Company; from *Finding the Way* by Dale Evans Rogers, copyright © 1969, 1973 by Fleming H. Revell Company; from *Where He Leads* by Dale Evans Rogers, copyright © 1974 by Fleming H. Revell Company; from *The Charles L. Allen Treasury* edited by Charles L. Wallis, copyright © 1970 by Fleming H. Revell Company; from *The Sermon on the Mount* by Charles L. Allen, copyright © 1966 by Fleming H. Revell Company. All selections used by permission.

MARIE RODELL-FRANCES COLLIN LITERARY AGENCY, for material from *Hill Country Harvest* by Hal Borland, published by J. B. Lippincott Co. in 1967. Reprinted by permission by Barbara Dodge Borland, Executor of the Estate of Hal Borland. Copyright © 1967 by Hal Borland.

CHARLES SCRIBNER'S SONS, a division of the The Scribner Book Companies, Inc., for excerpts from *The Spirit of St. Louis* by Charles Lindbergh. Copyright 1953 by Charles Scribner's Sons. Reprinted by permission of the publisher.

SIMON & SCHUSTER, for excerpt from *Your Prayers Are Always Answered* by Alexander Lake, copyright © 1965 by Alexander Lake. Reprinted by permission of Simon & Schuster, a Division of Gulf & Western Corporation.

DALE L. SINGER, for excerpts from his article quoting psychologist Thomas W. Allen on holistic medicine.

W. CLEMENT STONE, for material covering the secret of enthusiasm.

THE TOLEDO BLADE, for material from an editorial written by Grove Patterson.

DR. HAROLD BLAKE WALKER, for material from his article "Command the Morning."

EMORY WARD, for his statement on enthusiasm.

CONTENTS

1   BY WAY OF INTRODUCTION:
    THE IMPORTANCE TO YOU OF JOY AND
    ENTHUSIASM   257
2   LIFE CAN BE A JOYOUS ADVENTURE   274
3   THE GIFT OF LIFE   289
4   MORE POWER TO YOU   303
5   FAITH AND SUCCESSFUL LIVING   315
6   THE VALUE OF A POSITIVE ATTITUDE   328
7   LIFE WITH A SPIRITUAL UPTHRUST   340
8   KEEP YOUR SPIRIT BUILT UP   352
9   JOY AND ENTHUSIASM IN A WORLD OF BEAUTY   365
10 DARE TO BE HAPPY   380

*This book
is dedicated
in loving memory
to
Anne B. Boardman*

1

BY WAY OF INTRODUCTION: THE IMPORTANCE TO YOU OF JOY AND ENTHUSIASM

WHAT DO YOU WANT beyond all else? Life, of course. And not merely existence, or the physical ability to breathe and function. All of us desire a particular quality of life, a combination of interest, zest, excitement, achievement, satisfaction and peace of mind. Indeed, we want to enjoy the world and the society of other people. Every individual desires to experience beauty and the highest emotions, and to possess the energy and vitality necessary to meet daily responsibilities with vigor to spare. Our hope is to live on a high level of physical strength, mental interest and spiritual meaning. And to enjoy life of this superior quality, we will discover that *joy* and *enthusiasm* are important factors in the total process.

The rationale for a book with the joint themes of joy and enthusiasm is that these two qualities are basic ingredients of the good life. And I am always interested in helping people find the good life.

By the good life, I mean one that is intensely interesting, even exciting. It is a life that is full of meaning and rich in satisfaction. Such a life is not free of difficulties or problems; of course not. But it does possess the power to overcome them and to attain victorious levels of experience.

The good life is based on a definitive value system in which joy and enthusiasm serve as both cause and effect. Desirable values are stimulated—in fact, to a considerable extent produced—by the practice of joy and enthusiasm. And, in turn, effective life-style principles definitely result in a joyous and enthusiastic manner of living. In this book, therefore, I shall present my personal treasury of joy and enthusiasm. These are incidents from thought, experience and literature, drawn from many sources, which have contributed to my own joy and enthusiasm. My purpose in assembling this material is that it may be of pleasure and value to you, and aid in developing and maintaining a positive attitude of happiness.

Those persons who consistently live by the joy and enthusiasm pattern of thinking seem to achieve a remarkable mastery over circumstances. Often I have been impressed by this fact in my relations with people.

Living the Joy Way

Many recollections come to me of persons who combined joy and enthusiasm into a quality of life that is both impressive and motivational. For example, there was the popular radio personality who invited me to be a guest on her show. It was an interview format, and I was told that the conversation would cover many subjects and be quite fast-paced.

I had never met the interviewer, but advance information revealed that she was brilliant, charming and noted for the unusual force of her personality. Accordingly, my mind envisioned a so-called glamour girl—young, beautiful and vivacious. At the radio studio I met a plain-looking woman of some sixty-plus years, walking with a decided limp (the result of a childhood disease, I later learned). She was not at all the type of person I had envisaged. She greeted me in an offhand manner and gave the impression of a rather ordinary individual. I soon became aware, however, of a strength of personality, a liveliness that was very impressive.

When we went on the air, the personal qualities of this middle-aged and handicapped woman became spectacularly evident. She exuded joy, excitement, life and enthusiasm. Her pithy comments were laced with insights and decorated with happiness. She had an infectious laugh and actually seemed to bubble over with joy. One had the impression she lived with joyous excitement and delighted in life itself.

Our conversation on the air was lively and our exchange was sheer pleasure. Finally this charming emcee said, "Well, all things come to an end, and our time has about run out, but haven't we had fun? You know something," she confided, "you and I have it made, for we live the joy way. We have enthusiasm, and with enthusiasm and joy together you really have life in full measure." So saying, she signed off her program. I have always gratefully remembered that dynamic lady who, because she "lived the joy way," had developed an indepth enthusiasm that never ran down. As a result, she was able to take in stride all the difficulties that came her way and carry on—not only joyfully—but victoriously as well.

Joy as a Therapy

The fact that this woman triumphed over physical disability underscores an important fact all too generally ignored—that the practice of joy and enthusiasm can contribute physically to therapeutic and healing benefits. The wisdom of the Bible, of course, long predated our modern psychosomatic medicine. The words "A merry heart doeth good like a medicine: but a broken spirit drieth the bones" (Proverbs 17:22) were written many generations ago. When a serious physical situation arises, the negativist glumly says, "You can't laugh that off." But perhaps you can indeed literally laugh it off by the scientific practice of joy and positive faith, joined with a deep desire to live and be well.

A thought-provoking substantiation of this point of view is impressively brought forward by Norman Cousins, a well-known editor, in his book *Anatomy of an Illness as Perceived by the Patient.* This author, who enjoys impeccable intellectual credentials, was stricken with a serious collagenic illness, a disease of the connective tissues. It was marked, so he reports, by difficulty in moving his limbs. Nodules appeared on his body like gravel under the skin, and his jaws were almost locked. A specialist gave him one chance in five hundred for full recovery. The disease may have been based on an allergy or on Cousin's inability to tolerate a toxic situation which he had experienced. The result was mental and physical tension and exhaustion. To get the adrenal glands restored to proper functioning seemed part of any possible cure. But how was Norman Cousins to get those adrenal glands, and the endocrine system in general, working well again so that health might be restored, despite the medical odds against it?

Healing Through Laughter

Cousins was familiar with Dr. Hans Selye's great book *The Stress of Life*, in which the famous Canadian physician showed that adrenal exhaustion could be caused by emotional tension such as frustration, suppressed rage and overstress. Dr. Selye, whose conclusions and findings have received international acclaim by medical and scientific leaders, detailed the effect of negative emotions on body chemistry. So the question arose in the sick man's mind: *If negative emotions produce negative chemical changes in the body, wouldn't positive emotions produce positive chemical changes?* He was unconsciously reaffirming the position stated twenty years earlier by Dr. John A. Schindler, author of *How to Live 365 Days a Year*, that what are called the "good" and "bad" emotions have corresponding effects upon physical manifestations.

Then Cousins was led to ask, "Is it possible that love, hope, faith, laughter, confidence and the will to live have therapeutic value?" Some writers had been saying for a long time that these positive factors do have such value, but they had been looked upon askance and labeled by intellectuals as superficial. But now, even though this distinguished writer knew that the turning on of positive thoughts is no simple matter, he produced a convincing corroboration of the power of the positive emotions to affect physical states. His analysis set in motion a dramatic renewal of his health and well-being.

Mr. Cousins worked out a program of laughter stimulation by watching humorous movies and reading joke books. He "made the joyous discovery that ten minutes of genuine belly laughter had an anesthetic effect and would give me at least two hours of pain-free sleep." As further proof of the healing power of self-induced joy, the patient and his physician took repeated sedimentation readings which registered scientifically that the laughter-joy procedure produced five-point drops in the sedimentation rate, and the decrease not only held but was cumulative. "I was greatly elated," concludes Mr. Cousins, "by the discovery that there is a physiological basis for the ancient theory that laughter is good medicine." And, as previously pointed out, that "ancient theory" was first referred to in the Bible: "A merry heart doeth good like a medicine: but a broken spirit drieth the bones."

Norman Cousins's experience underscores the teaching that I have been advocating for nearly half a century: that the religion of the Bible is basically scientific. It enunciates principles of mind and action which constitute formulas that will inevitably work under appropriate conditions. Indeed, Christianity may in an important sense be regarded as an exact science, for its teachings, when practiced, produce definitive results. If, for example, you hate, you will produce hate. The application of love produces love. Negative thinking brings about negative results, while positive thinking results in positive outcomes.

The human being is a mental and spiritual entity operating in a physical body. Thomas A. Edison once remarked that the basic use of the body is as a mechanism to house the brain, through which its functioning may be accomplished. It is in the brain that we consider, analyze, decide, remember, dream, aspire, believe and achieve. This being true, the rational conclusion is that the body is under the control of thinking, emotion and faith, and that this marvelous and complex physical instrument with its many involved and interlocking parts may be vitally affected by positive thinking, positive belief, positive joy and enthusiasm.

Power of Positive Thinking in Healing

United Press International released an article by Dale Singer in which he quoted psychologist Thomas W. Allen, who believes "the power of positive thinking is stronger in fighting disease than all of the technology of modern medicine." Professor Allen, of the faculty of Washington University in Saint Louis, says Singer, "preaches holistic medicine—the treatment of a patient as a whole person rather than treatment of specific symptoms of a disease." "Our thoughts reverberate in our bodies," declares psychologist Allen, who has pioneered in the use of imagery to change the way the body acts. The views of Dr. Allen and others have been supported by experiments. Cancer patients taught to use imagery techniques lived longer and better lives than their doctors had thought possible. A key point in the use of imagery to fight cancer is recognizing that cancer cells are not overpowering invaders but can be conquered. Patients who use imagery picture their immune system as victoriously aggressive and the cancer cells as relatively weak and confused. That is why radiology works; the body is bombarded and the cancer cells are overwhelmed.

Personally, I do not in any sense minimize the science of medical practice, for I believe that the doctor is a servant of God in healing. As a famous physician once said: "We treat the patient; God heals him." But I also believe it is a fact that the application of joyful, enthusiastic and positive thoughts, long and deeply held, can "bombard the body," breaking down systemic disease and helping to free the system to enjoy vitality and health.

To Feel Better, Practice Joy

The therapeutic effect of Christianity is indicated in the words of Jesus, "These things have I spoken unto you, that my joy might remain in you, and that your joy might be full" (John 15:11). Again, the Bible says, "Rejoice in the Lord always: and again I say, Rejoice" (Philippians 4:4).

Why does the Bible teach these things? Because it is known that the best way to clear the cobwebs from the mind, to gain relief from pain, to get the blood circulating and the heart acting properly, and to keep blood pressure normal is to get joy pulsing throughout the body.

Dr. John A. Schindler said that thousands are suffering from a malady which he calls the "CDTs": *cares, difficulties* and *troubles*. Another name for it is *psychosomatic illness*—the effect on the body of mental states. He writes that many people are sick or below par because of an impenetrable blanket of gloom resting on their minds. When they are lifted mentally for only a few minutes daily into an area of pure joy, they can become well. No doubt that is why Jesus tells us that a way to be healthy is to cultivate joy.

"Little Bill" Miller, who coached the Cincinnati Reds, the Chicago Cubs and other teams, taught that being happy resulted in enhanced rhythm, which of course is important in athletic performance. Teaching a tense and uptight man to play golf, the coach suggested, "Walk around the tee and sing a song." The man did so and he became relaxed and rhythmic in movement. Then he stepped up to the ball, still singing, and hit a beautiful drive.

Perhaps we do not fully realize what our religion can do for us. If you are gloomy and depressed, consciously seek God's joy. This will send a new sense of well-being coursing through your body.

Joy, flowing through the channels of consciousness, seems to affect the blood that flows to the arteries and veins. Indeed, it appears that joy effectively contributes to improved circulation. The birds are the most joyous of creatures, and they have a blood circulation that completes its circuit every two minutes. Joy steps up the chemical activity of the human body and helps pale red cells become deep red again. It is a preventive against anemia. It is amazing how many cases of illness are corrected, if not healed, by the simple application of joy. Anemia tends to be present where there is a shortage of happiness; high blood pressure where there is an overabundance of that which reduces happiness—monotony, anger, worry.

The more we deliberately let God shoulder the heavy responsibilities of life, the more we take life calmly and with patience, the more we can check or relieve ailments. Man, it is said, is as old as his arteries. A contributing cause of arteriosclerosis is the thinking of old defeat or frustration thoughts. A preventive, and often a help in a cure, is the inflow of new thoughts, especially light-bringing thoughts of peace, happiness and enthusiasm. Long-held hate thoughts, fear thoughts, unhappiness thoughts and other negative thoughts tend to take the spring out of life. To be healthy, it is advantageous to be religious, if the religion is love- and happiness-oriented.

Jesus said we could have joy like His own, and fullness of joy at that (John 15:11). That may be one reason why there is a significant upsurge of spiritual faith and practice today; why people are reading religious literature as never before; why increasing numbers of churches are thronged with enthusiastic people. There is, for a fact, health, vitality, new life and radiant happiness in the practice of inner joy.

And How Does One Practice Inner Joy?

It is important, first, to deal with old habit patterns. If you are a habitual negative thinker, to feel better you will need to learn to practice inner joy and thereby develop more positive attitudes. We have physical setting-up exercises; we also need spiritual setting-up exercises.

When you arise in the morning, look at yourself in the mirror; look at your face. Then for two minutes deliberately pass happy thoughts through your mind. We exercise our bodies, toning them up. Similarly, it is important to exercise the mind, just as muscles are exercised. It is in the mind that the issues of life are decided, so it must be alive and vital.

Another suggestion is to sing at least two songs every day. It has been felt by many that the best songs are religious ones, for they are positive in spirit. Learn a few hymns and sing them. As you do so, throw back your shoulders and sing with gusto. It will do you good, not only spiritually, but mentally and physically as well.

Every morning while taking your shower or bath, sing. As you wash yourself on the outside with soap and water, "wash" yourself on the inside with a spiritual song. It will stimulate cleanness and zest of mind and so contribute to your health and happiness.

To Have Enthusiasm, Practice It

Enthusiasm is one of life's greatest qualities, but it must be *practiced* to become a dominant factor in one's life.

What is the outstanding characteristic of a small child? It is enthusiasm! He thinks the world is terrific; he loves it; everything fascinates him. Thomas Huxley said that the secret of genius is to carry the spirit of the child into old age, which, of course, means never to lose your enthusiasm. But too few persons retain this excitement, and a reason is that they let enthusiasm be drained off. If you are not getting as much from life as you want, examine the state of your enthusiasm.

My mother was one of the most enthusiastic persons I ever knew. She got an enormous thrill out of the most ordinary events. She had the ability to see romance and even glory in everything. She traveled the world over and was always bursting with enthusiasm. I recall one foggy night when we were crossing from New Jersey to New York City on a ferryboat. To me, there was nothing particularly beautiful about fog seen from a ferryboat, but my mother exclaimed, "Isn't this thrilling?"

"What is thrilling?" I asked.

"Why," she replied, "the fog, the lights, the ferryboat we just passed! Look at the mysterious way its lights fade into the mist."

Just then came the sound of a foghorn, deep-throated in the heavy, padded whiteness of the mist. My mother's face was that of an excited child. I myself had felt nothing about this ride, except that I was in a hurry to get across the river.

Mother stood at the rail that night and eyed me appraisingly. She said gently, "I have been giving you advice all your life, Norman. Some of it you have taken; some you haven't. But here is a suggestion I want you to take. Realize that the world is athrill with beauty and excitement. Keep yourself sensitized to it. Love the world, its beauty and its people." I do believe that anyone trying consistently to follow that simple advice will be blessed with abundant enthusiasm and have a life full of joy. I know, for I took her advice, to my great good fortune.

"Miss Nobody"

It works for others also. For example, one night I met "Miss Nobody." After I spoke in a West Coast city, a young woman gave me a limp handshake and said in a small, timid voice, "I thought I'd like to shake hands with you, but I really shouldn't be bothering you. There are so many important people here and I'm just a nobody."

"Please remain for a few moments," I replied. "I'd like to talk with you." Later I said, "Now, Miss Nobody, let's have a little talk."

"What did you call me?" she asked in surprise.

"I called you by the only name you gave. You told me you were a Nobody. Have you another name?"

"Of course," she said. "You see, I have quite an inferiority complex. I came to hear you hoping you might say something that would help me."

"Well," I answered, "I'm saying it to you now: You are a child of God." And I advised her to draw herself up tall each day and say aloud, "I am a child of God." I outlined some techniques for practicing enthusiasm and self-confidence.

Recently when I spoke in the same area, an attractive young woman approached me. "Do you remember me?" she asked. "I'm the former Miss Nobody." Her enthusiastic manner and the light in her eyes showed a dramatic change.

This incident underscores an important fact. You can change! Anybody can change! And even from a dull Nobody to an enthusiastic Somebody—through the practice of joy and enthusiasm.

Try the "As If" Principle

You can deliberately make yourself enthusiastic. To change yourself into whatever type of person you wish to be, first decide specifically what particular characteristic you desire to possess and then hold that image of yourself firmly in your consciousness. Then proceed to develop it by acting *as if* you actually possessed the desired characteristic, and repeatedly affirm that you are in the process of self-creating the qualities you wish to develop. In this way you are making effective use of the "As If" principle.

Often called the father of American psychology, William James (who taught this principle) said, "If you want a quality, act as if you already had it."

Shakespeare tells us in Act III of *Hamlet*, "Assume a virtue, if you have it not."

Frank Bettger, a highly successful insurance man, made effective use of this principle, as you will see in chapter 5.

Tell Yourself Good News

In developing enthusiasm, you can condition the day in the first five minutes after you awaken. Henry Thoreau, the great American writer, used to lie abed in the morning, telling himself all the good news he could think of. Then he arose to meet the day in a world filled with good things, good people, good opportunities. The practice of spiritual motivation at the start of each day will infuse you, as it did him, with new zest.

The late William H. Danforth, a prominent business leader, said: "Every morning pull yourself up to your full height and stand tall. Then think tall—think big, elevated thoughts. Then go out and act tall. Do that and joy will flow to you."

Go on spreading enthusiasm all day, and at night you will have a deposit of joy full to overflowing.

Read your Bible, for it is full of enthusiasm generators. What greater motivators, for example, are there than: ". . . all things are possible to him that believeth" (Mark 9:23), and ". . . whatsoever ye shall ask in prayer, believing, ye shall receive" (Matthew 21:22)? Saturate your mind with great passages from the Bible.

Then pray to God for guidance and get going!

(For forty life-changing Bible passages, write to the Foundation for Christian Living, Pawling, New York 12564 and ask for a free copy of my booklet *Thought Conditioners*.)

Love Life and People to Be Enthusiastic

One magic formula for successful and enthusiastic living is stated in six powerful words: *Find a need and fill it*. Every enterprise that has achieved success has been predicated on that formula.

Find people's needs; fill them. Love people. Love the sky, the hills and valleys. Love beauty, love God. The person who loves inevitably becomes enthusiastic. If you are not enthusiastic, deliberately begin today to cultivate the love of living.

Consider Fred, for example, who runs a little eating place in a big city. I went there for a late evening snack.

Resting big hands on the counter, he asked, "Okay, brother, what'll you have?"

"Are you Fred?" I asked in return.

"Yep."

"They tell me you have good hamburgers here."

"Brother, you never ate such hamburgers."

"Okay, let me have one, please."

At the counter sat an old man who looked extremely miserable. He was hunched over; his hands shook. After Fred had put my hamburger in front of me, he placed his hand in a friendly way on that of this old fellow. "That's all right, Bill," he said, "everything is all right. I'm going to fix you a bowl of that nice hot soup that you like." Bill nodded gratefully.

Another old man shuffled up to pay his check. Fred said, "Mr. Brown, watch the cars out there on the avenue. They come pretty fast at night." And he added, "Have a look at the moonlight on the river. It's mighty pretty tonight."

When I paid my check, I couldn't help remarking, "I like the way you spoke to those old men. You made them feel that life is good."

"Why not?" he asked. "Life *is* good. Me, I get a kick out of living. They're pretty sad old guys, and our place is sort of like home to them. Anyway, I kind of like 'em."

Believe in yourself and in your life. Practice the principles of enthusiasm. *Find needs and fill them.* Believe that your job and, indeed, your whole life performance can be improved. Believe that you can be better than you think you are. And remember—if you think you can, you can! Bring new and bona fide enthusiasm to your life-style, for enthusiasm always makes a difference—a big difference—in your life.

The Power of Affirmation in Enthusiasm

An important technique in changing your outlook is that of affirmation. In fact, you can make almost anything of yourself by affirmation. Suppose, for example, you are full of fear. Affirm, "I'm not afraid. 'With God all things are possible.' " (Matthew 19:26). The immediate effect may seem unnoticeable, but by such affirming you will have taken the first step toward courage. And if you affirm it persistently enough, your conscious mind will accept the affirmation.

If you have been apathetic and to overcome this you start affirming enthusiasm, presently it will begin to show in your new vitality. This requires self-disciplinary determination; it requires perseverance. But you can achieve a new and positive attitude. *To become* enthusiastic, *act* enthusiastic.

A help in this process of change is to develop the habit of expressing only hopeful, enthusiastic ideas. Deliberately look at the best side of things and it will become natural to expect the good, the positive. You will automatically find within yourself the enthusiasm you desire. Express enthusiasm freely and upon all occasions, and your life will strongly tend to become joyful and enthusiastic.

Walter Chrysler once said, "If I am trying to decide between two men of fairly equal ability and one man definitely has enthusiasm, I know he will go further, for enthusiasm has self-releasing power and carries all before it."

Certainly! And a person who has enthusiasm always wants to learn, so he gives the job complete interest and attention. The enthusiastic individual constantly releases maximum potential because of the outgoingness that accompanies enthusiasm.

This type of person develops spiritual and mental resources equal to his problems. This does not mean that the enthusiast will not have hard moments. He or she will even fail at times. But even so, that person will learn from failure ("failing forward," as "Boss" Charles Kettering once said) and will use failure creatively in the direction of eventual success.

Doubtless you have heard the familiar expression "If life hands you a lemon, make lemonade of it." This is another way of saying "Turn the crisis to advantage; fail forward." Enthusiasm helps you to avoid allowing problems to become overwhelming.

H. W. Arnold tells us: "The worst bankrupt is the person who has lost enthusiasm. Let one lose everything but enthusiasm and that person will again come through to success." To keep your mind and spirit full of enthusiasm, keep your intake of thought energy greater than the outgo. If you are tense and uptight, the constant tension depletes your energy and with it your enthusiasm. Therefore, utilize the spiritual and practical technique of "letting go and letting God." Ask for wisdom and guidance, and then give to your job your very best. And ". . . having done all . . . stand" (Ephesians 6:13). Leave the outcome to the Lord, trusting in His providence. In doing this calmly and confidently, you will find renewal, new energy, new enthusiasm.

Enthusiasm Changes Job Situations

Enthusiasm makes all the difference in work performance. Expose your daily occupation to apathy and your job will become difficult and tiresome. No job will go well for the person who considers it just another dull chore.

Perhaps you may say, "But my job *is* dull and there is just no future in it." But might it be that you have a dull attitude toward it? Try enthusiasm and watch it change. And see how you change with it. Enthusiasm changes a job because it changes the jobholder. When you apply enthusiasm to the job, that job comes alive with exciting new possibilities. So if you wish for a new job, try instead to apply enthusiasm to your present one and perhaps it will make that job new.

For example, ask yourself what someone else might see and do in your present job. Imagine what action he would take if suddenly he took over your job. How do you think he would react toward it? What fresh and innovative changes would he make to put new life and achievement into what you consider a dull job? Then *you* apply those ideas.

An employer told me he was going to fire an employee "out of the business." I asked, "Why not fire that person *into* the business?" He did, and the employee presently became very important to the organization. This individual was fired but not out. Enthusiasm fired him to new participation. A new personality bloomed in this worker: successful, happy, creative. Try enthusiasm on *your* job. The result can be amazing.

Enthusiasm Works Miracles in Problems

Enthusiasm is no simple or easy concept. It is a strong, rugged mental attitude that is hard to come by, difficult to maintain—but powerful.

The word *enthusiasm,* from the Greek *entheos,* means "God in you," or "full of God." So when we say that enthusiasm contains the power to work miracles in solving problems, we are actually saying that God Himself in you supplies the wisdom, courage and faith necessary to deal successfully with all difficulties. We need only to discover how to apply efficiency and right thinking enthusiastically to our problems.

Attitudes Are More Important Than Facts

Enthusiasm helps work what people describe as "miracles" in solving problems. This is because enthusiasm is an attitude of mind, and the mental attitude in a difficult situation is an important factor in its solution. Indeed, attitudes are more important than facts, for enthusiasm changes the mental outlook from fearing facts to the solid assurance that there is an answer.

These eleven words by Stanley Arnold can make an amazing difference in your thinking: *Every problem contains within itself the seeds of its own solution.*

A woman came to me at a national business convention and asked, "How may one practice what you call the magic of believing and gain the positive power of enthusiasm?"

"You might invent a method of your own for practicing that," I suggested. "You will find that it works and your enthusiasm will grow."

Here was her solution: Like many executives, she had on her desk a receptacle for incoming mail and other papers, and a second one for outgoing material. To these she innovatively added a third receptacle labeled WITH GOD ALL THINGS ARE POSSIBLE. In this she placed all papers for which she did not yet have answers. Then she added memos on problems for which no solution had been determined. To use her own phrase, she held these matters in "prayerful thinking." She said, "I surround the problems in that box with the magic of believing and the results are amazing." I was impressed by the uniqueness and workability of this ingenious method for problem solving.

Use Self-Motivators

W. Clement Stone, well-known business leader, is genuinely enthusiastic and I asked the secret of his enthusiasm.

"As you know," he answered, "the emotions are not always immediately subject to reason, but they are always immediately subject to action, mental or physical. Furthermore, repetition of the same thought or physical action develops into a habit which, repeated frequently enough, becomes an automatic reflex.

"And that's why I use self-motivators. A self-motivator is an affirmation that you deliberately use to move yourself to desirable action. You repeat a verbal self-motivator fifty times in the morning and fifty times at night for a week or ten days, to imprint the words indelibly in your memory.

"Some self-motivators are:

For a serious personal problem: *God is always a good God!*
For a business problem: *You have a problem . . . that's good!*
Within every adversity there is a seed of an equivalent or greater benefit.
What the mind can conceive and believe, the mind can achieve.
Find one good idea that will work and . . . work that one idea!
Do it now!
To be enthusiastic . . . act . . . enthusiastically!"

The Contagion of Enthusiasm

"Enthusiasm, like measles, mumps and the common cold, is highly contagious," says the writer Emory Ward.

But, unlike measles and mumps and colds, enthusiasm is good for you. Hope you catch it—and good.

When contagious, enthusiastic faith in yourself releases you from the self-built prison of your mind, then you begin to change, and as you change, your whole life also changes. You are set free to live on a level never before experienced.

Perhaps you are being overwhelmed by problems. When they have you disorganized and confused, remember there is Someone concerned about you. The Lord will help you to turn about, rethink clearly and overcome. Your victories will fill you with enthusiasm and joy. Your problems will give way before enthusiasm and positive faith.

One night Mrs. Peale and I were invited to dinner in a very fashionable apartment on New York's Park Avenue. In fact, we were told that our host was one of the richest men in the world. I never did learn whether that was so, but the home was indeed palatial. One walked on thick carpets; the decorations were exquisite, the hangings lovely. All kinds of jade and vases and Chinese art were displayed. However, my chief interest (because finally it was getting close to nine o'clock) was the dinner. At long last, the hostess, with some embarrassment, announced to the twenty guests that the cook had become indisposed, and therefore there wasn't going to be any dinner served there. But she had made arrangements with a nearby restaurant, and we would all go there.

So we all piled into taxicabs and went. The restaurant turned out to be one of those gloomy, dark (but high-class) places where you have to grope your way to a table through flickering candlelight. I had never been in this place before, in fact I had never heard of it. As we were being seated I asked my wife, "What is this joint?" In a whisper she said, "Don't show your ignorance. This is a night club."

Well, my acquaintance with night clubs is very limited, but the dinner must have been satisfactory. I couldn't see what I was eating but suffered no ill effects. After dinner it was announced that a floor show was coming on. I said to my wife, "Let's get out of here."

She replied, "You can't; it wouldn't look right."

"But," I persisted, "they wouldn't even see us if we left."

"Well," she said, "you've got to stay and say good-bye to your hostess in a proper way."

I suggested, "I'll leave her a note."

But my wife was firm. "No. Stay here with me."

And I am certainly glad that I did remain, because a woman came on to sing. I became deeply impressed by this woman. She wore a long, black dress that had no shape to it; she had no jewelry or any other kind of adornment. And she wasn't very beautiful (at least she wasn't so beautiful you would write home about her). She was a very plain person and I figured her age at about fifty to fifty-five. I said to my wife, "I thought they had only young-appearing glamour girls in these places."

She replied, "This woman is supposed to be one of the greatest."

"Well," I remarked, "she has to prove it to me."

Then she started to sing. She was French, and she sang some of her songs in French and others in English, the latter with a delightful French accent. She captivated everyone. She seemed to sort of reach out and hug all those people to herself with love. She threw herself, body, mind and soul, into her singing. She sang as if it were the last time on earth she would ever sing. She sang as though that was the greatest thing in the world, and she lifted me right out of my seat. Here was a woman who loved what she was doing; who didn't particularly care how she looked. Now, maybe that's good or maybe it's bad, but it doesn't make all that much difference. She rose above appearance; she was a believer in life. She loved life, and she made everybody else love it. She was filled with enthusiasm and a joy that is unforgettable to me now, years later, as I write about it.

Zest for Life

It is important to live with zest even in the midst of life's troubles.

In the office of a large business organization, the head of the firm radiated exuberance and confidence. When I arrived, he was in conference with his chief assistant. As they discussed a problem, I could do no other than listen to their conversation. The talk was positive and enthusiastic. It was a refreshing, stimulating and upbeat treatment of a problem.

I asked, "How do you explain your zest and positive thinking? You two are alive, really alive, and you have confidence that you can handle a tough problem."

One of them leaned across the table and said, "Remember those words, 'I can do all things through Christ who strengthens me'? [Philippians 4:13 NKJB]. Well, we believe that. We don't talk about it, but that is the source from which we derive faith in ourselves and our ability to handle our problems."

"And so you are joyful and enthusiastic. Is that it?" I asked.

"That's it," said both of them. They had zest and enthusiasm and so they attracted zest and enthusiasm. Life does give back in kind.

"Let Enthusiasm Take Hold!"

I knew the late Vince Lombardi, the famous football coach. When he went to Green Bay, he faced a defeated, dispirited team. He stood before the men, looked them over silently for a long time, and then in a quiet but intense way said, "Gentlemen, we are going to have a great football team. We are going to win games. Get that. You are going to learn to block. You are going to learn to run. You are going to learn to tackle. You are going to outplay the teams that come against you. Get that.

"And how is this to be done?" he continued. "You are to have confidence in me and enthusiasm for my system. The secret of the whole matter will be what goes on up here." And he tapped his temple. "Hereafter, I want you to think of only three things: your home, your religion, and the Green Bay Packers, in that order! Let enthusiasm take hold of you—beginning now!"

The players sat up straight in their chairs. "I walked out of that meeting," said the quarterback, "feeling ten feet tall!" That year the team won seven games—with virtually the same players who had lost ten games the year before. The next year they won a division title and the third year the world championship. Why? Because, added to hard work and skill and love of the sport, enthusiasm made the difference.

What happened to the Green Bay Packers can happen to an individual. What goes on in the mind is what determines the outcome. When a person gets real enthusiasm, it can be seen in the flash of the eyes, in an alert and vibrant personality. You can observe it in the spring of the step. You see it in the verve of the whole being. Enthusiasm makes the difference in attitude toward other people, toward the job, toward the world. It makes a big difference in the joy of human existence.

Are you vibrantly alive? Do you possess contagious enthusiasm? God the Father wants to give you the Kingdom, so that you will have joy in life. Jesus said, ". . . because I live, ye shall live also" (John 14:19). And He meant life abundant and overflowing.

Joy and Enthusiasm Can Remake Your Life

The kind of living that makes life good is as exact as a science, and not something that you muddle through without rules. Life responds to certain precise methods and procedures. Your life can be either a hit or a miss, empty or full, depending on how you think and act. The enthusiast knows and draws upon valid resources. He plays it cool and straight. Such a person believes there is nothing in life so difficult that it can't be overcome; that faith can indeed move mountains. It can change people. It can change the world. It can help you survive all the great storms in your life.

However, joy and enthusiasm are qualities that must be affirmed and reaffirmed, practiced and repracticed. Donald Curtis suggests that you affirm each morning:

I move serenely forward into the adventure of life today. I am filled with inspiration and enthusiasm. I am guided and protected by the Infinite in everything I say and do. I project confidence and authority. I am sure of myself in every situation. With God's help, I am filled with the strength and energy to be what I am and to do what I have to do. . . .

Walk in Newness of Life

Activate your mind so that it becomes alive and vital. Heed the Bible, which tells us to "walk in newness of life" (Romans 6:4). That is a powerful thought. We are not to think old, dead, dull and desultory thoughts. Walk in newness of life, in a quality of life that is new every morning and fresh every evening—always exciting and joyful.

The Bible glows with excitement and enthusiasm. It is well called the Book of Life. "And be renewed," it says, "in the spirit of your mind" (Ephesians 4:23)—not merely on the surface of your mind, but in the deep spirit that activates your thoughts.

Joy and enthusiasm can remake your life! This book was assembled to help you think and live the joy way, the enthusiasm way.

Ten Steps to a Joyful and Enthusiastic Life

Since thinking has much to do with what your life becomes, you might consider the following suggestions:

FIRST Stop depreciating yourself. There is a lot that is *right* in you. Empty your mind of failure thoughts and mistakes and start seeing yourself as a competent person.

SECOND Eliminate self-pity thoughts. Start thinking of what you *have*, instead of dwelling on what you may have lost. List your assets of personality and talent.

THIRD Quit thinking constantly of yourself. Think of *others*. Actually go out and look for someone who needs the kind of help you can give, and then give it freely. You will not maintain a continuing flow of abundance if your thoughts are only of yourself.

FOURTH Remember the words of Goethe: "He who has a firm will molds the world to himself." Almighty God put a tough power into human beings called the *will*. Use it.

FIFTH Have a *goal* and put an achievable timetable on it.

SIXTH Stop wasting your mental energy on gripes and post-mortems, and start thinking about what to do *now*. Amazing things happen when you think constructively.

SEVENTH Every morning and every evening articulate these words aloud: "I can do all things through Christ who strengthens me."

EIGHTH Every day say three times: "This is the day the Lord has made. I will rejoice and be glad in it" (adapted from Psalms 118:24).

NINTH Think and practice joy every day.

TENTH Get enthusiasm; think enthusiasm; live enthusiastically!

2

LIFE CAN BE A JOYOUS ADVENTURE

LIFE CAN BE A JOYOUS adventure every day all the way. The word *adventure* suggests something rather big and special, but life as a joyous adventure need not be "a big deal." It can move forward daily in the simple things that comprise most of our life experience.

Henry van Dyke states the matter quite well, I think. The great writer and preacher says:

> To be glad of life, because it gives you the chance to love and to work and to play and to look up at the stars; to be satisfied with your possessions, but not contented with yourself until you have made the best of them; to despise nothing in the world except falsehood and meanness, and to fear nothing except cowardice; to be governed by your admirations rather than by your disgusts; to covet nothing that is your neighbor's except his kindness of heart and gentleness of manner; to think seldom of your enemies, often of your friends and every day of Christ; and to spend as much time as you can with body and with spirit, in God's out-of-doors—these are the little guide-posts on the footpath of peace

These "little guideposts on the footpath of peace," practiced daily, add up finally to a totality of joy and enthusiasm. Both of these desirable qualities are developed through a constant cultivation of goodness, appreciation and love. Add to this the habit of consciously living with God, and joy wells up within your heart and your mind bursts with enthusiasm. The joy of life has become yours.

Mother Teresa of Calcutta, who received the 1979 Nobel Peace Prize for her selfless devotion to India's teeming multitudes of the poor, is considered by many a living saint. In her book *A Gift for God*, she shows how joy is simply to try to carry out God's will in the common way of daily experience:

> Joy is prayer—Joy is strength—Joy is love—Joy is a net of love by which you can catch souls. She gives most who gives with joy.

The best way to show our gratitude to God and the people is to accept everything with joy. A joyful heart is the inevitable result of a heart burning with love.

We all long for heaven where God is but we have it in our power to be in heaven with Him right now—to be happy with Him at this very moment. But being happy with Him now means:

loving as He loves,
helping as He helps,
giving as He gives,
serving as He serves,
rescuing as He rescues,
being with Him for all the twenty-four hours,
touching Him in His distressing disguise.

When one loves and gives and helps and serves in the manner so touchingly suggested by Mother Teresa, then joy deepens and enthusiasm for God's world and its people measurably increases. And the result is that life becomes good—very good indeed. Its meaning and purposes are enhanced. One rejoices to be alive.

And God's sunshine will keep going, as John Oxenham describes it in a charming poem:

GOD'S SUNSHINE

Never once since the world began
    Has the sun ever stopped his shining.
His face very often we could not see,
And we grumbled at his inconstancy;
But the clouds were really to blame, not he,
    For, behind them, he was shining.
And so—behind life's darkest clouds
    God's love is always shining.
We veil it at times with our faithless fears,
And darken our sight with our foolish tears,
But in time the atmosphere always clears,
    For his love is always shining.

If we pass through every day with the thought of joyous adventure, if we are activated by decent motives, and at all times treat people in a kindly manner, we will feel good about ourselves and the love of life will grow. As Rod McKuen says:

I measure success by how well I sleep on a given night. If I have not had to question my motives for any particular action I might have undertaken, or knowingly caused another human being trouble or discomfort, then I am at peace with my God and myself and I fall asleep easily.

If sleep comes hard, then I know the day has been a personal failure.

I have personally put Rod's principle to the test by letting my mind run over the day as I lie down to sleep. If I can honestly feel that I have been motivated by right purposes and that my relationships with my family, friends and all others I have met have been loving and caring, then it is amazing how fast I can go off to sleep and what a good night I have. And this has much to do with starting off the next morning on another adventure of joyous living.

Of course I realize that life in its course brings us face to face with hardship, pain, illness and difficulties of one kind or another. This is the way our years on earth are made. The wise Creator, it appears, wants to make strong people of us, and no one can become strong without struggle with adversity, resistance and problems. Struggle makes us strong, and in the process of overcoming, we achieve happiness. We learn thereby how, despite everything, life can become a joyous adventure.

Let me tell you about a husky, active fifteen-year-old high school athlete in Indiana who dove into a pond and broke his neck. He was pulled from the water but has not walked since. The swimming accident paralyzed his arms and legs and confined him to a wheelchair, perhaps for the rest of his days.

Needless to say, life almost stopped for this hitherto vigorous and very alive boy. In a situation like that it could be easy to settle for defeat, to give up in despair. But Gerald Nees was not made of weak stuff. He was strong in mind and strong in character.

One thing he was determined to do was to graduate from high school. Needing just one credit to complete the requirement, he told his mother he planned to take an art course.

"But how will you do that?" she asked. "Your hands cannot move." Undaunted, he showed her how he could draw with a pencil between his teeth. Being a strong mother of a strong son, she encouraged him to take the course, and a new life began for him.

Becoming seriously interested in art, Gerald was granted a partial art scholarship by the University of Minnesota. Then he received a full scholarship from the Famous Artists School in Connecticut, where he learned to work with oils. With infinite patience, he paints the things of beauty he sees around him, holding a brush in his mouth. Many of his paintings depict the farmland scenes of his home. Living with his mother on a fifty-acre farm worked by his brother-in-law, he helps to support the family through his paintings.

Gerald has exhibited in a number of one-man art shows. His first one was sponsored by W. Clement Stone, who purchased fourteen paintings himself. We had some of Gerald's paintings on display at the Foundation for Christian Living in Pawling, New York, and as I looked at them I myself was inspired by this remarkable man.

It is amazing how a person, no matter how handicapped, can create and release dynamic forces that turn back defeat. Gerald Nees's rebound capacity, his faith in God, his comeback power, his ability to stand up to his adversity, brought him through the crisis. Loving life, he refused to take defeat, and he is putting a lot into life every day.

"I guess I'm kind of ornery," says Gerald. "I don't like pity and I don't give it. I like living and I want to live as long as I can, because I don't want to miss anything. I feel good—I feel happy."

There are two possible attitudes to take when things go hard. One is to let it throw you, to become discouraged, even hopeless, to give up and to let go the feeling that you can do something about it. That attitude is, of course, disastrous. For if you admit—even to yourself—that you do not have what it takes to cope with adversity, your personal resources will not come into action. And these personal resources are amazing in their potential.

Almighty God put into each one of us that power called *spiritual resource*, and, if we keep it alive, cultivate it, activate it, step it up, when the crisis comes, we may draw upon it. Therefore, in addition to never giving up, the secret is to draw hard and deep on your inherent spiritual resources.

The person who possesses a strong faith in God is the most fortunate of all people, for that individual has resources to depend on.

> The Lord is good, a strong hold in the day of trouble; and he knoweth them that trust in him.
>
> *Nahum1:7*

Actually, though stormy weather may be less than pleasant, storms are not all that bad if we know how to meet them—and even turn them to our advantage. And of course the best and simplest method is just to stand up to them with courage and dogged persistence added to the faith that you are never alone. Or as Rod McKuen says:

> Never fear being alone, because you never are.

I like the story and the philosophy of storms expressed by a rugged old-time cowboy who said he had learned life's most important lesson from Hereford cows. All his life he had worked cattle ranches where winter storms took a heavy toll among the herds. Freezing rains whipped across the prairies. Howling, bitter winds piled snow into enormous drifts. Temperatures might drop quickly to below-zero degrees. Flying ice cut into the flesh. In this maelstrom of nature's violence, most cattle would turn their backs to the icy blasts and slowly drift downwind, mile upon mile. Finally, intercepted by a boundary fence, they would pile up against the barrier and die by the scores.

But the Herefords acted differently. Cattle of this breed would instinctively head into the windward end of the range. There they would stand shoulder to shoulder facing the storm's blast, heads down against its onslaughts. "You most always found the Herefords alive and well," said the cowboy. "I guess that is the greatest lesson I ever learned on the prairies—just face life's storms."

The lesson is a valid one. Do not attempt to evade things you are afraid of, or difficulties; don't go drifting with the wind, trying to keep away from them. Every human being has to decide again and again, and still again, whether to meet fearsome difficulties head-on or to try running away.

Actually, you can never outrun fear; nor can you outrun adversity. Try that unequal race and you will run yourself down, a pathetic victim of the inevitable. Try a better way. Stand up to your troubles and stormy times, remembering always that they are removable.

In this day when walking, jogging, running and bicycle riding are popular with a nation of health-conscious citizens, the philosophy of a bicycle rider says something about how to think when the going gets hard and thereby to keep the joyous adventure spirit in one's mind:

> Those who ride bicycles say that it is easier to ride up a hill at night than it is during daylight. Hills that are practically impossible of ascent may be negotiated at night. At night the cyclist can see but a few feet in front of him, and the faint light of his lantern gives him the illusion that the hill is either level or not steep. He feels that he can go the few feet more than his light shows, and in this manner keeps on and on, while in the daytime he sees the whole hill, the whole problem, and it seems so steep to climb that his courage fails him.

AUTHOR UNKNOWN

It is a fact that joy comes out of difficulty, perhaps even more certainly than out of fortuitous circumstances. As I think of the truly joyful people I have known, almost without exception the happiest are those who found their joy either in spiritual experience, or in difficulty, or in both.

Harold Blake Walker tells it truly:

> Trouble is no disaster when we know we can manage it. Indeed, the joy of Jesus came not from the absence of difficulty, but from a conviction of

power to triumph. What a day it is for a boy learning to swim when he comes up from a ducking with a sputtering shout: "Look, Dad, I'm swimming!" It isn't the absence of problems that brings joy to a man struggling to build a little business on Main Street; it is the grateful assurance of capacity for victory affirmed in the gleeful word to his wife: "Honey, we're solvent."

What brings joy to the morning isn't the thought that today will be free from problems, or difficulties or troubles, but rather the knowledge that "I can do all things in him who strengthens me." A man I know in the hospital understands that. He is a tonic when I see him, snared as he is with arthritis and a bad heart. He greets me with a grin that stretches from ear to ear and even when he feels the worst he has some cheerful word. He knows from long years of comradeship with God that he is spiritually adequate for anything that may come.

The well-known writer Margueritte Harmon Bro gives us some good, ancient Japanese wisdom:

> One of the most famous of the sixteenth-century shogun rulers of Japan, Tadaoki Hosakaw, was asked one day by his senior statesman, "What sort of man do you call an able man?"
>
> "An able man is like an oyster in the Bay of Akashi."
>
> "You are right," the senior statesman said, pleased at his master's wisdom.
>
> The men around them looked blank. One of them said, "We really cannot comprehend the oyster which seemed to satisfy your highness."
>
> The statesman explained: "The Bay of Akashi is one of the most stormy of all bays, so that fierce waves toss and toughen the oyster shells until it is known that the best shells come from that bay of violence. So, in the world of men, the best men have been tried in continual storms of adversity."

One of the great sources of joy in the adventure of life is the wonderful feeling that we have what it takes to overcome—our fears, our problems, our adversities, even pain and death.

Life is out there, shouting at you what it is going to do to you. Face it, love it, live it! Just remember who you are—you are a child of the eternal God; you are a disciple of Jesus Christ. And stand up to death, knowing that nothing can ever destroy you, for you have life that is forever new. So go forward with confidence.

We cultivate joy in the experience of trouble. We also may cultivate it by practicing it, by learning to laugh and be glad. We finally become what we think and what we do. Therefore, if we want to live a joyous life, we will do well to act joyfully. And one way to do so is just to laugh.

Bertha Adams Backus gives some good advice about laughter as a way to joy:

THEN LAUGH

Build for yourself a strong box,
 Fashion each part with care;
When it's strong as your hand can make it,
 Put all your troubles there;
Hide there all thought of your failures,
 And each bitter cup that you quaff;
Lock all your heartaches within it,
 Then sit on the lid and laugh.

Tell no one else its contents,
 Never its secrets share;
When you've dropped in your care and worry
 Keep them forever there;
Hide them from sight so completely
 That the world will never dream half;
Fasten the strong box securely—
 Then sit on the lid and laugh.

A poet whose name I do not know prayed for the gift of laughter in the midst of trouble. And to have the ability to live joyously is to make life an exciting adventure regardless of how many dark valleys we must traverse.

Give me the gift of laughter, oh, I pray,
 Though tears should hover near;
Give me the gift of laughter for each day—
Laughter to cast out fear.

With hope to greet the coming of each dawn,
And faith that never dies;
Give me the gift of laughter, oh, I pray—
 Laughter instead of sighs.

But I would like to reiterate that the ability just to hang in there, to stick with it through storm and hard going, is to come out with joy. I have the pleasure of knowing the famous writer A.J. Cronin, and I admire him greatly as an author who has entertained and inspired millions. But he got his training the hard way. The joyous adventure of life for him came down some rough roads. If life goes hard for you, read the following. I have read this story for my soul's good half a hundred times or more:

THE TURNING POINT OF MY LIFE

I was 33 at the time, a doctor in the West End of London. I had been lucky in advancing through several arduous Welsh mining assistantships to my own practice—acquired on the installment plan from a dear old family physician who, at our first interview, gazed at my cracked boots and frayed cuffs, and trusted me.

I think I wasn't a bad doctor. My patients seemed to like me—not only the nice old ladies with nothing wrong with them, who lived near the Park and paid handsomely for my cheerful bedside manner, but the cabbies, porters and deadbeats in the mews and back streets of Bayswater, who paid nothing and often had a great deal wrong with them.

Yet there was something . . . though I treated everything that came my way, read all the medical journals, attended scientific meetings, and even found time to take complex post-graduate diplomas . . . I wasn't quite sure of myself. I didn't stick at anything for long. I had successive ideas of specializing in dermatology, in aural surgery, in pediatrics, but discarded them all. While I worked all day and half of most nights, I really lacked perseverance, stability.

One day I developed indigestion. After resisting my wife's entreaties for several weeks, I went casually to consult a friendly colleague. I expected a bottle of bismuth and an invitation to bridge. I received instead the shock of my life: a sentence to six months' complete rest in the country on a milk diet. I had a gastric ulcer.

The place of exile, chosen after excruciating contention, was a small farmhouse near the village of Tarbert in the Scottish Highlands. Imagine a lonely whitewashed steading set on a rain-drenched loch amid ferocious mountains rising into gray mist, with long-horned cattle, like elders of the kirk, sternly munching thistles in the foreground. That was Fyne Farm. Conceive of a harassed stranger in city clothes arriving with a pain in his middle and a box of peptonizing powders in his suitcase. That was I.

Nothing is more agonizing to the active man than enforced idleness. A week of Fyne Farm drove me crazy. Debarred from all physical pursuits, I was reduced to feeding the chickens and learning to greet the disapproving cattle by their Christian names. Casting around desperately for something to do, I had a sudden idea. For years, at the back of my mind, I had nursed the vague illusion that I might write. Often, indeed, in unguarded moments, I had remarked to my wife, "You know, I believe I could write a novel if I had time," at which she would smile kindly across her knitting, murmur, "Do you, dear?" and tactfully lead me back to talk of Johnnie Smith's whooping cough.

Now, as I stood on the shore of that desolate Highland loch I raised my voice in a surge of self-justification: "By Heavens! This is my opportunity. Gastric ulcer or no gastric ulcer, I will write a novel." Before I could change my mind I walked straight to the village and bought myself two dozen penny exercise books.

Upstairs in my cold, clean bedroom was a scrubbed deal table and a very hard chair. Next morning I found myself in this chair, facing a new exercise book open upon the table, slowly becoming aware that, short of dog-Latin prescriptions, I had never composed a significant phrase in all my life. It was a discouraging thought as I picked up my pen and gazed out the window. Never mind, I would begin. Three hours later Mrs. Angus, the farmer's wife, called me to dinner. The page was still blank.

As I went down to my milk and junket—they call this "curds" in Tarbert—I felt a dreadful fool. I recollected, rather grimly, the sharp advice with which my old schoolmaster had goaded me to action. "Get it down!" he had said. "If it stops in your head it will always be nothing. Get it down." And so, after lunch, I went upstairs and began to get it down.

Perhaps the tribulations of the next three months are best omitted. I had in my head clear enough the theme I wished to treat—the tragic record of a man's egoism and bitter pride. I even had the title of the book. But beyond these naive fundamentals I was lamentably unprepared. I had no pretensions to technique, no knowledge of style or form. I had never seen a thesaurus. The difficulty of simple statement staggered me. I spent hours looking for an adjective. I corrected and recorrected until the page looked like a spider's web, then I tore it up and started all over again.

Yet once I had begun, the thing haunted me. My characters took shape, spoke to me, laughed, wept, excited me. When an idea struck me in the middle of the night I would get up, light a candle, and sprawl on the floor until I had translated it to paper. At first my rate of progress was some 800 labored words a day. By the end of the second month it was a ready 2000.

Suddenly, when I was halfway through, the inevitable happened. Desolation struck me like an avalanche. I asked myself: "Why am I wearing myself out with this toil for which I am so preposterously ill-equipped?" I threw down my pen. Feverishly, I read over the first chapters which had just arrived in typescript from my secretary in London. I was appalled. Never, never had I seen such nonsense in all my life. No one would read it. I saw, finally, that I was a presumptuous lunatic, that all I had written, all that I could ever write was wasted effort, sheer futility. Abruptly, furiously, I bundled up the manuscript, went out and threw it in the ash can.

Drawing a sullen satisfaction from my surrender or, as I preferred to phrase it, my return to sanity, I went for a walk in the drizzling rain. Halfway down the loch shore I came upon old Angus, the farmer, patiently and laboriously ditching a patch of the bogged and peaty heath which made up the bulk of his hard-won little croft. As I drew near, he gazed up at me in some surprise: he knew of my intention and, with that inborn Scottish reverence for "letters," had tacitly approved it. When I told him what I had just done, and why, his weathered face slowly changed, his keen blue eyes scanned me with disappointment and a queer contempt. He was a silent man and it was long before he spoke. Even then his words were cryptic.

"No doubt you're the one that's right, doctor, and I'm the one that's wrong. . . ." He seemed to look right to the bottom of me. "My father ditched this bog all his days and never made a pasture. I've dug it all *my* days and I've never made a pasture. But pasture or no pasture," he placed his foot dourly on the spade, "I canna help but dig. For my father knew and I know that if you only dig enough a pasture can be made here."

I understood. I watched his dogged working figure with rising anger and resentment. I was resentful because he had what I had not: a terrible stubbornness to see the job through at all costs, an unquenchable flame of resolution brought to the simplest, the most arid duties of life. And suddenly my trivial dilemma became magnified, transmuted, until it stood as the timeless problem of all mortality—the comfortable retreat, or the arduous advance without prospect of reward.

I tramped back to the farm, drenched, shamed, furious, and picked the soggy bundle from the ash can. I dried it in the kitchen oven. Then I flung it on the table and set to work again with a kind of frantic desperation. I lost myself in the ferociousness of my purpose. I would not be beaten, I would not give in. I wrote harder than ever. At last, toward the end of the third month, I wrote *finis*. The relief, the sense of emancipation, was unbelievable. I had kept my word. I had created a book. Whether it was good, bad or indifferent I did not care.

I chose a publisher by the simple expedient of closing my eyes and pricking a catalogue with a pin. I dispatched the completed manuscript and promptly forgot about it.

In the days which followed I gradually regained my health, and I began to chafe at idleness. I wanted to be back in harness.

At last the date of my deliverance drew near. I went around the village saying good-by to the simple folk who had become my friends. As I entered the post office, the postmaster presented me with a telegram—an urgent invitation to meet the publisher. I took it straight away and showed it, without word, to John Angus.

The novel I had thrown away was chosen by the Book Society, dramatized and serialized, translated into 19 languages, bought by Hollywood. It has sold millions of copies. It altered my life radically, beyond my wildest dreams . . . and all because of a timely lesson in the grace of perseverance.

But that lesson goes deeper still. Today, when the air resounds with shrill defeatist cries, when half our stricken world is wailing in discouragement: "What is the use . . . to work . . . to save . . . to go on living . . . with Armageddon round the corner?" I am glad to recollect it. The door is wide open to darkness and despair. The way to close that door is to go on doing whatever job we are doing, and to finish it.

The virtue of all achievement, as known to my old Scots farmer, is victory over oneself. Those who know this victory can never know defeat.

A. J. CRONIN

And, I might add, they also know the joyous adventure of life.

Knowing Dr. Cronin's strong Christian faith, I am sure he was buttressed in his struggles by great words like those found in Deuteronomy 31:6, words that will see you through most difficulties:

Be strong and of a good courage, fear not, nor be afraid of them: for the Lord thy God, he is that doth go with thee; he will not fail thee, nor forsake thee.

One thing that must be overcome if your life is to be a joyous adventure is fear and its components of worry and anxiety. A medical doctor asked me recently how often, during a year of sermons and speeches, I gave a talk against fear. He added that if he were a speaker or writer he would be out there fighting fear most of the time. "If we could cut down the incidence of fear, worry and anxiety, I could get in a lot more games of golf, for fear is basically what keeps my office filled up with patients," he said with a smile.

The late Dr. Smiley Blanton, famous psychiatrist, said: "Anxiety is the great modern plague." But he added that anxiety can be eliminated by the practice of healthy thinking and by developing a strong faith. Indeed, Dr. Blanton and I together once wrote a book entitled *Faith Is the Answer*. So never minimize fear, worry or anxiety. The English word *worry* is derived from an old Anglo-Saxon word which meant to strangle or to choke. Long-held worry, on the basis of this definition, results in a strangulation of life. And therefore life can hardly be a joyous adventure if it is based on a mental attitude of fear.

Here is what some thinkers have to say about fear:

There is perhaps nothing so bad and so dangerous in life as fear.

JAWAHARLAL NEHRU

Fear is the most devastating of all human emotions. Man has no trouble like the paralyzing effects of fear.

PAUL PARKER

The only thing we have to fear is fear itself.

FRANKLIN D. ROOSEVELT

Fear is the sand in the machinery of life.

E. STANLEY JONES

They can conquer who believe they can. He has not learned the first lesson of life who does not every day surmount a fear.

RALPH WALDO EMERSON

Fear makes the wolf bigger than he is.

GERMAN ADAGE

Faith in yourself and faith in God are the key to mastery of fear.

HAROLD SHERMAN

And to all of these wise statements about fear as a chief enemy of joyous adventure, let me add an even greater one:

> For God hath not given us the spirit of fear; but of power, and of love, and of a sound mind.
>
> *2 Timothy 1:7*

What a combination: power—love—a sound mind. With a life so constituted, you can walk under the sun and the stars unafraid. And have the time of your life all your life.

I rather like the "sound mind" attitude expressed by Frank Bettger, one of America's greatest salesmen:

> I wrote an article on "When You Are Scared, Admit It!" in 1944 for *Your Life* magazine. Shortly after it was published I was thrilled to receive the following letter:

> *Somewhere in the Pacific*
> *September 11, 1944*

> *Dear Frank Bettger:*
> *I have just finished reading and thinking over an article by you in the September issue of* Your Life *magazine. You entitled your article "When You Are Scared, Admit It!" and I have been thinking over just how good that advice is—especially out here as a soldier in a combat area.*
> *I have naturally had experiences similar to those you relate. Public speeches in high school and in college; conferences with employers before and after obtaining a job; the first serious talk with that certain young woman—all these have caused me to be scared, and greatly so.*
> *Well perhaps you wonder why I write to you from out here to second your statements because certainly I'm not giving public speeches or asking for a job. No, I'm not subjected to ordeals from that direction, but believe me I do know what fear is and how it affects a person. And also, we have found that your advice, "Admit it!" is absolutely just as appropriate and right when you are facing a Jap demon assault.*
> *It has been proven time and time again out here that the men who fail to admit their fear are the ones who crack in battle. But if you admit you are scared, damned scared, and don't try to fight it down, then you are on the right road to overcoming your fear in most cases.*
> *And now, thank you for writing that article, and I sincerely hope that those lucky students and workers who have the opportunity to make use of your advice will certainly do so.*
>
> *Sincerely,*
> CHARLES THOMPSON

This letter from out there in the firing line was certainly written under the most dire circumstances, yet, there are probably people right now, reading this chapter, who have walked up and down time and time again in front of a man's office door, trying to get up enough courage to go in. Are you one of them? Big men—their wives don't tremble in their presence! You pay a big compliment to a man when you tell him you are scared in his presence.

There is no disgrace in admitting you are scared, but there is disgrace in failing to *try*. So whether you're talking to one person, or a thousand if that strange demon fear, public enemy number one, suddenly steals up on you, and you find yourself too scared for words, remember this simple rule:

When You're Scared, Admit It.

I once gave a sermon in a church in London and told the congregation how in-depth faith can cast out fear. The late British industrialist Arthur Rank was present and afterward asked me if I knew of his "Wednesday Worry Club." I replied that I had heard of it but would he tell me more about this ingenious device.

Lord Rank pointed out that Christianity is a commonsense teaching, one that works when worked. Therefore we can outwit fear by innovative procedures. For example, he told me that there were thirteen steps from the ground level to his office. Every morning he would "say a little prayer" on each of those steps as he mounted them.

Daily some worry or anxiety would arise. Instead of permitting the worry to disturb him then, he wrote it on a slip of paper and deposited it in a box to be worried about on Wednesday at 4:00 P.M. When that time came, the "Wednesday Worry Club" would meet and he would open the box, only to find that practically all of the worries collected there had been handled or were no longer important. "In fact," he declared, "I would find that about ninety-two percent of my worries had failed to materialize."

"But what did you do about the eight percent?" I asked.

"Oh," he laughed, "I just put them back in the box to be worried about next Wednesday afternoon."

Ralph Waldo Emerson had the same sensible understanding:

> Some of your hurts you have cured,
> And the sharpest you still have survived,
> But what torments of grief you endured
> From evils that never arrived!

Laurence H. Blackburn, my longtime friend, for whom life was always a joyous adventure, gives some good advice about handling fear effectively:

Everyone is afraid of something, either admitted or unconfessed. Some fears have been brought out into the open and recognized for their universality, as well as the damage they do. There is the fear of any unsettling situation that may make us less sure of ourselves; a rut is so comfortable, after all! And what if we should be exposed for the person we really are? Then there might come disregard or humiliation or ridicule. Some find it unbearable to contemplate any change within or without. The fear of failure makes us inadequate to meet the tests of life; the fear of poverty keeps us poor; the fear of people fends off those who would be our friends; the fear of dying fills every living hour with the haunt of death. Add to these scores of others, like the fear of old age, the fear of the dark—as well as your own pet fears.

What shall we do about our fears?

Instead of denying them, or hiding them, or running away from them, why not face our fears to see what they really are?

Direct action is recommended as a most effective remedy, too. If you handle your fears one by one with decisiveness and courage, you will find that they will shrivel into less significance. You will be the master over them. You will be free. How wise were Emerson's words: "He has not learned the lesson of life who does not every day surmount a fear."

The cure for fear is Faith.

Make use of great affirmations. Put them on your desk, your mirror, or over the kitchen sink. Keep them in your mind. Repeat them at every odd moment during the day. Say them over and over before you go to sleep. You know many to use, but here are some suggested affirmations. Make your own list and use them daily as adversaries of fear:

The Lord is my shepherd (Psalms 23:1).

When I am afraid, I put my trust in thee (Psalms 56:3 RSV).

I sought the Lord, and he answered me, and delivered me from all my fears (Psalms 34:4 RSV).

The world will make you suffer. But be brave! I have defeated the world! (John 16:33 TEV).

By practice you can develop your faith into assurance. Put your fears into God's hands—and leave them there! His care of us in our yesterdays gives us faith that He will take care of us today.

Dr. W. R. Maltby describes the disciples of Jesus Christ, who, knowing the score about life's tough realities, were also victoriously joyous:

In the Sermon on the Mount, Jesus promised his disciples three things—that they would be entirely fearless, that they would be absurdly happy, and that they would get into trouble. They did get into trouble and found, to their surprise, that they were not afraid. They were absurdly happy, for they laughed over their own troubles and only cried over other people's.

Let us sum up this matter of fear and worry by the two following quotations from the wisest of all books, the Bible:

Do not worry about tomorrow; it will have enough worries of its own. There is no need to add to the troubles each day brings.

Matthew 6:34 TEV

For I the Lord thy God will hold thy right hand, saying unto thee, Fear not; I will help thee.

Isaiah 41:13

With those ideas as guiding lights, any one of us can go far toward making life a joyous adventure.

Perhaps this down-to-earth poem says it all:

WORRY

Ain't no need to worry
    about the things to come
Forget about your problems
    and face them one by one.
Ain't no need to worry
    about what might have been
Just trust the Heavenly Father
    and let that be the end.
Ain't no need to worry
    about things unknown to you
Have faith in God and rest assured
    that He will see you through.

                    EARLINE ROSS COLE

3

THE GIFT OF LIFE

I HAVE OFTEN WONDERED why certain writers, speakers and leaders are remembered forever. For their ability, leadership qualities and achievements, of course, but one important reason is their boundless enthusiasm and the joy they took in life and in the world.

Moby Dick, for example, is an unforgettable story, and its author, Herman Melville, whose life span was from 1819 to 1891, is an unforgettable character. His imagination seemed to tingle with life and with the charm and fascination of the world. Here is an example of his extraordinary ability to express his enthusiasm:

> Standing at the masthead of my ship during a sunrise that crimsoned sky and sea, I once saw a large herd of whales in the east, all heading towards the sun, and for a moment vibrating in concert with peaked flukes.
>
> As it seemed to me at the time, such a grand embodiment of adoration of the gods was never beheld, even in Persia, the home of the fire worshippers.
>
> As Ptolemy Philopator testified of the African elephant, I then testified of the whale, pronouncing him the most devout of all beings. For according to King John, the military elephants of antiquity often hailed the morning with their trunks uplifted in the profoundest silence.

Sensitivity to life in all its varied and incredible forms is to be expected, especially when amazement and wonderment are awakened. But sensitivity to the marvelous privilege of responding to life's simple things is perhaps a more profound indicator of joy and enthusiasm.

One March morning I went to breakfast in a motel in a midwestern city. The coffee shop was crowded and I stood in the doorway surveying the room for a vacant table. Then I noticed a table for two by a window where a stranger was seated. He waved to me to come over and invited me to sit with him.

He was a very pleasant person and had a remarkably cheerful attitude for a dark, dreary, windy, rainy March morning. In fact, he was quite enthusiastic. A gust of wind drove a hail of raindrops against the window and the rain ran down in fast-moving rivulets on the windowpane. "I get a great kick out of March," he observed, "with its wild winds. They seem to sigh around the house whispering mysteriously. And just look at those big raindrops hanging like jewels on the bare branches of that bush out there."

Then he noticed the steam rising from the coffee. "Don't you like to see steam coming up from food on a table?" he asked. "It's like home, somehow. Anyway, it's great to be alive, and what a day we're going to have."

"My friend," I said, "you are full up with poetry, romance, aliveness and enthusiasm, and that is what I like to see in a person. But how did you get this way?"

He told me he was in a serious automobile accident and hung for some weeks between life and death. Once, from seemingly afar off, he heard an attendant in the hospital say of him, "I don't think this one will make it." Then, what seemed long ages later, a kindly man in a white coat looked down at him and said quietly, "You are going to live; you are going to get well and be okay."

"You cannot possibly imagine the delicious sense of life that surged in me at those words," said my table companion. "Like a condemned prisoner, I had a reprieve; the sentence of death was lifted. And ever since I've had a sharp and distinct awareness of the wonder and glory of the simple things—like wind, and rain, and steam, and sunlight."

I sat entranced by this wonderful man who thrilled me with a new joy and enthusiasm for that great gift—the gift of life—and for the beautiful world with its dear old, simple, everyday blessings.

Thomas Curtis Clark writes of them with sensitivity:

GOD GIVE ME JOY

God give me joy in the common things:
In the dawn that lures, the eve that sings.

In the new grass sparkling after rain,
In the late wind's wild and weird refrain;

In the springtime's spacious field of gold,
In the precious light by winter doled.

God give me joy in the love of friends,
In their dear home talk as summer ends;

In the songs of children, unrestrained;
In the sober wisdom age has gained.

God give me joy in the tasks that press,
In the memories that burn and bless;

In the thought that life has love to spend,
In the faith that God's at journey's end.

God give me hope for each day that springs,
God give me joy in the common things!

And David Grayson (pen name for Ray Stannard Baker) gets the common glory even more down to earth:

Blessed is the man who can enjoy the small things, the common beauties, the little day-by-day events; sunshine on the fields, birds on the bough, breakfast, dinner, supper, the daily paper on the porch, a friend passing by. So many people who go afield for enjoyment leave it behind them at home.

Great Possessions

Of course we would expect wise Ralph Waldo Emerson to have something good to say on this subject, and he does. The following quotation is given to every person who appears on "The Alan McGirvan Radio Show" in Brisbane, Australia. Alan gave one each to my wife and me when we were guests on his sprightly program recently:

To laugh often and much;
to win the respect of
intelligent people and the
affection of children;
to earn the appreciation of honest
critics and endure the betrayal of
false friends;
to appreciate beauty;

to find the best in others; to leave
the world a bit better, whether by
a healthy child, a garden patch or
a redeemed social condition;

to know even one life
has breathed easier because
you lived.

This is to have succeeded.

Life, even with all its woes, frustrations and difficulties, is still a wonderful experience.

Part of the problem concerning our attitude toward life is, perhaps, that we tend to shut our eyes to its qualities of beauty and excitement. Our senses may be dulled to the excitement all about us every day, wherever we may be. Simply to be able to hear and see the glory in the everyday is one of the most unused yet important of all skills.

Lorado Taft says it pointedly:

> We are living in a world of beauty, but few of us open our eyes to see it!
> What a different place this world would be if our senses were trained to see and to hear!
> We are the heirs of wonderful treasures from the past: treasures of literature and of the arts. They are ours for the asking—all our own to have and to enjoy, if only we desire them enough.

I often think of Saint Francis of Assisi when reflecting on insensitivity to the beauty and wonderment in common things. This saint in his youth was the rather roistering son of a nobleman. But later he had a profound spiritual awakening and as a result became one of the most lovable characters of history.

I seem to recall a story about him that says a lot about the type of person he was. One day, so the story goes, he said to a monk, "Let us go to the village square and preach." But instead of talking, he patted a dog in the town, helped a poor woman across a street, stopped to comment on the beauty of a weed. He spoke most kindly to all the people they passed in their walk around the square and then the two headed for home. "But, master," said the monk, "we came to preach."

"We have done so, my son," said the saint. "We just went about loving people, and dogs, and life. That was of itself a sermon."

In fact, it is said of Francis that, so happy was he, he was known to "preach" to the cattle and the birds, telling them how wonderful life is and how much God loved them as well as all of us. This sheer delight in the wonder of life is reflected in the following prayer in which he hails the sun as his brother and the moon as his sister:

> O Most High, Almighty, Good Lord God, to Thee belong praise, glory, honor and all blessing.
> Praised be my Lord God, with all His creatures, and especially our brother the Sun, who brings us the day and who brings us the light: fair is he, and he shines with a very great splendour.
> O Lord, he signifies us to Thee!
> Praised be my Lord for our sister the Moon, and for the Stars, the which He has set clear and lovely in the heaven.
> Praised be my Lord for our brother the Wind, and for air and clouds, calms and all weather, by which Thou upholdest life and all creatures.
> Praised be my Lord for our sister Water, who is very serviceable to us, and humble and precious and clean.
> Praised be my Lord for our brother Fire, through whom Thou givest us light in the darkness; and he is bright and pleasant and very mighty and strong.

Praised be my Lord for our mother the Earth, the which doth sustain us and keep us, and bringeth forth divers fruits and flowers of many colors, and grass.

Praised be my Lord for all those who pardon one another for love's sake, and who endure weakness and tribulation: blessed are they who peacefully shall endure, for Thou, O Most High, will give them a crown.

Praised be my Lord for our sister, the Death of the Body, from which no man escapeth. Woe to him who dieth in mortal sin. Blessed are those who die in Thy most holy will, for the second death shall have no power to do them harm.

Praise ye and bless the Lord, and give thanks to Him and serve Him with great humility.

This wonder of life, which we sense in the simple things all about us, is further demonstrated in another marvelous thing that we often take for granted as ordinary. The human body, which we use every minute in life, is likewise one of the world's wonders, as is pointed out by Margaret Applegarth:

Here you sit, held together by a fabulous interweaving of flexible muscles and tendons and cartilages, all comfortably tucked inside an enormous envelope called skin, which in turn is made up of literally billions of cells, each busy every blessed second wearing out, eliminating, and then building up.

Yet you take your incredible body for granted, unless something goes wrong.

Even the Psalmist centuries ago noticed. "I am fearfully and wonderfully made."

Part of the wonder is that you have so little fear. Rarely do you remind your pulse: "For heaven's sake, beat!" Or your heart: "Did you pump? Did you count it? How often per minute? Five quarts a moment, I hope. Seventy-five an hour, remember!" Or to each little drop of blood: "Are you taking your exciting excursion trip through 169 miles of my canal-ways and blood vessels in three minutes?" Or to your eyelids: "Did you blink? And are my tear ducts sluicing off the dust from my eye-balls regularly?"

Best of all, how blest you should feel that instead of making you embarrassingly tall to contain the thirty-five to forty feet of tubes inside your intestinal and kidney tracts, your Creator cleverly looped them into a neat little twenty cubic inches.

It might be well, therefore, to say to your brain, "Ponder!" For your body is a temple made for worship and thanksgiving, and you have much for which to be profoundly grateful every moment of every day that you dare live so carefree of all these details.

So even those things, and even people who annoy and situations that frustrate and irritate, may be put in proper perspective as we contemplate the beauty and wonder of life and the world and God.

The following anonymous verse says it quite well, I think:

> God—there are things in my life I don't like,
>   Folks I can't bear;
> But there are more things I would hate to change,
>   Friends I can't spare.
> So when you hear me complaining aloud,
>   Just turn away;
> Deep inside my ungracious heart, I am
>   Grateful each day. *Amen.*

As we hope to grow in wisdom while walking along the pathway of life, we may acquire the basic philosophy and faith expressed by Margaret E. Sangster:

> To bluest skies that arch the way
> I lift my thankful eyes to-day.
> The sunlight pours a golden tide
> O'er airy forest, green and wide;
> Pure odors drift the morning through,
> And God has led me hitherto.
> What bliss to take His guiding hand
> To trust, if not to understand;
> To rest through change and toil and tears
> On Him whose grand eternal years
> In ever living youth are new
> And cry, "He leads me hitherto."

That philosophy and faith may stand us in good stead in times of crisis. And crisis may come when least expected, which makes the development of faith all the more important:

HE'S WITH ME

Storm clouds and strong gusts of wind had come up suddenly over Columbus, Ohio. The Alpine Elementary School radio blared tornado warnings. It was too dangerous to send the children home. Instead, they were taken to the basement, where the children huddled together in fear.

We teachers were worried too. To help ease tension, the principal suggested a sing-along. But the voices were weak and unenthusiastic. Child after child began to cry—we could not calm them.

Then a teacher, whose faith seemed equal to any emergency, whispered to the child closest to her, "Aren't you forgetting something, Kathie? There is a power greater than the storm that will protect us. Just say to yourself, 'God is with me now.' Then pass the words on to the child next to you."

As the verse was whispered from child to child, a sense of peace settled over the group. I could hear the wind outside still blowing with the same ferocity of the moment before, but it didn't seem to matter now. Inside, fear subsided and tears faded away.

When the all-clear signal came over the radio sometime later, students and staff returned to their classrooms without their usual jostling and talking.

Through the years I have remembered those calming words. In times of stress and trouble, I have again been able to find release from fear or tension by repeating, "He's with me now."

PHYLLIS I. MARTIN

Nature, its varied aspects and moves, its grandeur and pastoral serenity, has an enormous influence on life as an experience of peace, inspiration and wonder. Some of our encounters with nature are memorable and, indeed, unforgettable. For example, I remember a time years ago in the China Sea. The ocean was smooth, even limpid, and the ship glided almost silently save for the far-off rumble of the engines and a wash at the stern. A mist lay over the vast deep and the silvery moon rays filtered through what seemed a gossamer curtain. Life may be said to be a collection of such jewel-like memories fastened on the string of the years.

Another memory is of dusk at an observation point on the rim of the Grand Canyon, when the slanting, sinking sun quickly changed the reds and golds of the peaks and minarets of the canyon into purple shadows and night fell across the desert. Meanwhile, in a chance encounter there, the greatest authority on the Grand Canyon, John C. Merriam, discussed the antiquity and still-continuing evolution of the vast abyss.

Still another memory that will linger across the years is a leisurely ramble I took through the noble aisles and arches of Sherbrooke Forest in Victoria, Australia. Dwarfed by the aged and enormous eucalyptus trees that soared perhaps two hundred feet, we wandered in a silence almost primeval. And yet it was not absolute silence, for presently the ear became tuned to the immense activity of the forest as it went about its designed functioning. But the long shafts of sunlight, occasional clouds floating high above, the smell of the good earth, the buzz of insects, the profound serenity, left a healing memory of the wonder of the world.

When I think of these things my mind goes to Robert Service, the poet of the Alaska ice peaks, of the Yukon's turbulent blue waters, of the great silences of the lofty mountains. Here are lines from his compelling poem, "The Spell of the Yukon":

I've stood in some mighty-mouthed hollow
That's plumb-full of hush to the brim;

> I've watched the big, husky sun wallow
>   In crimson and gold, and grow dim,
> Till the moon set the pearly peaks gleaming,
>   And the stars tumbled out, neck and crop;
> And I've thought that I surely was dreaming,
>   With the peace o' the word piled on top.

Everything in the great northland of the continent was dear to Robert Service. Its beauty charmed and thrilled him; its rugged power inspired him. Its effect was almost beyond words, but still his glorious speech caught and held this wonder of life:

> The summer—no sweeter was ever;
>   The sunshiny woods all athrill;
> The grayling aleap in the river,
>   The bighorn asleep on the hill.
> The strong life that never knows harness;
>   The wilds where the caribou call;
> The freshness, the freedom, the farness—
>   O God! how I'm stuck on it all.

All my life long I have read and quoted Robert Service. In a bookshop in New York on February 20, 1925, I bought a little book by William L. Stidger called *Giant Hours With Poet Preachers*, and in that volume I first met Service. I've traveled to Alaska and to the Yukon and on starlit nights have read again his inspired words from the poem "The Three Voices":

> For the stars throng out in their glory,
>   And they sing of the God in man;
> They sing of the mighty Master,
>   Of the loom his fingers span,
> Where a star or a soul is a part of the whole
>   And weft in the wondrous plan.
>
> Here by the camp fire's flicker,
>   Deep in my blanket curled,
> I long for the peace of the pine gloom,
>   Where the scroll of the Lord is unfurled,
> And the wind and the wave are silent,
>   And the world is singing to world.

And Service also is a devotee of the simple, strong, beautiful things that mark the glory of the world, the wonder of life. For he writes in praise of them: "The simple things, the true things, the silent men who do things. . . ." He was a gold seeker, as many were in those far-back, heroic days of America's youth. But he found a fairer gold even than shining metal. He found gold tinged with glory:

> There's gold, and it's haunting and haunting;
>   It's luring me on as of old;
> Yet it isn't the gold that I'm wanting
>   So much as just finding the gold.
> It's the great, big, broad land 'way up yonder,
>   It's the forests where silence has lease;
> It's the beauty that thrills me with wonder,
>   It's the stillness that fills me with peace.
>
>   *The Spell of the Yukon*

Despite all the pain, difficulty and tragedy of human existence, life—just plain life itself—remains a wonderful thing. So much so that with the Psalmist we may say:

> O praise the Lord, all ye nations: praise him, all ye people. For his merciful kindness is great toward us: and the truth of the Lord endureth for ever. Praise ye the Lord.
>
>   *Psalms 117*

And to make it truly great, I have long advocated my own practice of quoting every morning aloud these dynamic, life-stimulating words:

> This is the day which the Lord hath made; we[I] will rejoice and be glad in it.
>
>   *Psalms 118:24*

None of the things we have said must be taken to indicate that life, wonderful as it is, will be altogether sweetness and light. There are in its structure not a few disappointments, troubles and sorrows. But the person who believes in life in its totality and in its various aspects will be one who shares the faith expressed by Ella Wheeler Wilcox:

FAITH

> I will not doubt, though all my ships at sea
>   Come drifting home with broken masts and sails;
>   I shall believe the Hand which never fails,
> From seeming evil worketh good to me;
>   And, though I weep because those sails are battered,

> Still will I cry, while my best hopes lie shattered,
>   "I trust in Thee."
>
> I will not doubt, though all my prayers return
>   Unanswered from the still, white realm above;
>   I shall believe it is an all-wise Love
> Which has refused those things for which I yearn;
>   And though, at times, I cannot keep from grieving,
>   Yet the pure ardor of my fixed believing
>   Undimmed shall burn.
>
> I will not doubt, though sorrows fall like rain,
>   And troubles swarm like bees about a hive;
>   I shall believe the heights for which I strive,
> Are only reached by anguish and by pain;
>   And, though I groan and tremble with my crosses,
>   I yet shall see, through my severest losses,
>   The greater gain.
>
> I will not doubt; well anchored in the faith,
>   Like some stanch ship, my soul braves every gale,
>   So strong its courage that it will not fail
> To breast the mighty, unknown sea of death.
>   Oh, may I cry when body parts with spirit,
>   "I do not doubt," so listening worlds may hear it
>   With my last breath.

Life can indeed be wonderful and replete with joy and enthusiasm when you have a positive and reasonable attitude toward yourself and your job. A bit of solid philosophy by an old-time big league baseball player has long struck my fancy. It is by Bobby Doerr, one-time Boston Red Sox star and also a member of nine All-Star teams and a participant in the World Series:

> It seems to me that what any man's beliefs are depends upon how he spends his life. I've spent a good part of mine as a professional baseball player and the game that I play for a living is naturally a very important thing to me. I've learned a lot of things on the baseball diamond about living—things that have made me happier and, I hope, a better person. I've found that when I make a good play and take my pitcher off the hook, it's just natural for me to feel better than if I made a flashy play that doesn't do anything except make me look good for the grandstands. It works the same way off the ball field, too. Doing a good turn for a neighbor, a friend, or even a stranger gives me much more satisfaction than doing something that helps only myself. It's as if all people were my teammates in this world and

things that make me closer to them are good, and things that make me draw away from them are bad.

Another belief very important to me is that I am only as good as my actual performance proves that I am. If I cannot deliver, then my name and reputation don't mean a thing. I thought of this when in the spring of 1951 I told my team that I would not play in 1952. I reached this decision because I realized that I wouldn't be able to give my best performance to the people who would pay my salary by coming through the turnstiles. I don't see how anyone can feel right about success or fame that is unearned. For me, most of the satisfaction in any praise I receive comes from the feeling that it is the reward for a real effort I have made.

Many ball players talk a lot about luck and figure that it is responsible for their successes and failures, on and off the field. Some of them even carry around a rabbit's foot and other good-luck charms or they have little rituals that they go through to make sure of things going the way they want them to. I've never been able to go along with people who believe that way. I've got a feeling that there's something much deeper and more important behind the things that happen to me and whether they turn out good or bad. It seems to me that many of the things which some people credit to luck are the results of divine assistance. I can't imagine an all-wise, all-powerful God that *isn't* interested in the things I do in my life. Believing this makes me always want to act in such a way as to deserve the things that the Lord will do for me.

Maybe that's the most important thing of all. Doing good in order to deserve good. A lot of wonderful things have happened to me in my lifetime. I've had a long, rewarding career in organized baseball. The fans have been swell to me and I've always liked my teammates. But what really matters is that I've got just about the best folks that anyone could ask for. Doing what I can to make things more pleasant for my father and mother and for my wife and our son has been one of the things I have enjoyed most because it seems to be a way for me to pay back something of what I owe them for all the encouragement and pleasure they've given me.

I guess the best way to sum it all up is that I'm happy to be around and I'd like to be able to make other people glad of it, too.

To enjoy the wonder of living and to experience true pleasure, we must never give up, never falter, but always keep on keeping on. Many years ago Frank L. Stanton wrote a poem called "Keep a-'Goin' " and to do that is to keep joy and enthusiasm alive:

> If you strike a thorn or rose,
>   Keep-a-goin'!
> If it hails or if it snows,
>   Keep a-goin'!
> 'Taint no use to sit an' whine
> When the fish ain't on your line;

> Bait your hook an' keep-a-tryin'—
>   Keep a-goin'!
> When the weather kills your crop,
>   Keep a-goin'!
> Though 'tis work to reach the top,
>   Keep a-goin'!
> S'pose you're out o' ev'ry dime,
> Gittin' broke ain't any crime;
> Tell the world you're feelin' *prime*—
>   Keep a-goin'!
>
> When it looks like all is up,
>   Keep a-goin'!
> Drain the sweetness from the cup,
>   Keep a-goin'!
> See the wild birds on the wing,
> Hear the bells that sweetly ring,
> When you feel like singin', sing—
>   Keep a-goin'!

The amazing power inherent in human beings to keep going despite disaster is poignantly illustrated in the life experience of Elena Zelayeta. I was a guest for dinner in her home in San Francisco and it was a delightful evening. The dinner itself would have made the evening memorable, but the sparkling personality of our hostess was the truly memorable experience.

There were many courses, each one a masterpiece, in this typical Mexican dinner. As each course came on, its history and how it was made was explained to us, for Elena is an expert in Mexican cooking. She had cooked this dinner herself—and she is totally blind.

This amazing woman once ran a beautiful and very successful restaurant in San Francisco. As she was sitting alone at home one day the telephone rang. She groped her way to it to hear a voice saying: "Your husband has been in an accident. I must tell you that he is dead."

Blind—and now suddenly her husband had been taken. Struggling in her darkness, she reached for the help of Almighty God. She told me that one day in that darkness she felt as though a great hand took hold of her own and lifted her up. She began to live a wonderful life. She traveled the West Coast speaking to audiences, demonstrating her cooking on the stage, cooking with the senses of taste and smell and touch. "After all," she says, "that is what cooking is about. You don't need to see."

That night I asked her, "What is your secret?"

Her answer was priceless: "Always act as if the impossible were possible."

Years ago I found a little book entitled *I Dare You* by William Danforth. It seems that when Danforth was a young boy he was in delicate health and it was supposed he would not live long, that he wouldn't be able to keep going. The story of how he developed positive faith and lived to a great age has long impressed me.

One day at school a teacher who frequently gave the boys some strong talk on health singled out young Danforth and said to him, "I dare you to become the healthiest boy in this class." Now practically every boy in the class was a real husky compared with Will. But the teacher said to him: "I dare you to chase those chills and fevers out of your system. I dare you to fill your body with fresh air, pure water, wholesome food and daily exercise until your cheeks are rosy, your chest full and your limbs sturdy. I dare you to become the healthiest boy in this class."

Will Danforth took the dare—and he developed a splendid, robust physique. Seventy years after that time, in the lobby of the Jefferson Hotel in Saint Louis, where I had a little visit with him, I asked, "Mr. Danforth, just what did you do to get strong?" And so enthusiastic was he that despite his age he proceeded to show me all his exercises right there in the lobby of the hotel and insisted that I follow the exercises myself!

We soon had an audience of about twenty-five people around us. He said to them, "Everyone can be strong." And they believed it. And I believe it. He told me that he had outlived every member of his class. Dare to be strong! And determine to keep going!

Mr. Danforth tells about a salesman named Henry. This salesman came to him one morning and said, "Mr. Danforth, I've had it. I never can be a salesman. I haven't got the nerve. I haven't got the ability. You shouldn't be paying me the money I receive. I feel guilty taking it. I'm quitting right now."

Mr. Danforth looked at him and said, "I refuse to accept your resignation. I dare you, Henry, to go out right now today and do the biggest sales job that you've ever done. *I dare you.*"

He writes that he could see the light of battle suddenly blaze up in the man's eyes—the same surge of determination which he himself had felt when that teacher years before dared him to become strong and healthy. The salesman simply turned and walked out. That evening he came back and laid down on Mr. Danforth's desk a collection of orders showing that he had, in fact, made the best record of his life. And the experience changed him permanently. He surpassed his own record many times in the years that followed. Positive faith can always keep you going with joy and enthusiasm, living life at its best.

Finally, in talking about the fact life is wonderful, I just want to say that I think people are wonderful. I once asked Art Linkletter the secret of his happiness, for he is truly a happy man. His answer was "Interest and curiosity." He said, "Will Rogers said he never met a man he didn't like. I have never met a person who didn't interest me." Thornton Wilder would agree:

> Now there are some things we all know . . . We all know that *something* is eternal. And it ain't houses, and it ain't names, and it ain't earth, and it ain't even stars—everybody knows in their bones that *something* is eternal, and that something has to do with human beings. All the greatest people ever lived have been telling us that for five thousand years and yet you'd be surprised how people are always losing hold of it. There's something way down deep that's eternal about every human being.
>
> *Our Town*

4

MORE POWER TO YOU

"MORE POWER TO YOU," said a man whom I casually encountered in an airport. It was said only in passing and is a remark frequently heard. But for some reason, I continued to reflect upon it and what possible meaning it had for me. That we do need more power is obviously a fact: power to do the job, to keep going, to stand up to and rise above difficulties. Without such power, life can be pretty bleak and discouraging. But with inner power of mind and spirit it can be quite the contrary. Life will then take on victorious results and accordingly joy and enthusiasm.

I well recall one of the first times I experienced the relationship of power to joy and enthusiasm. As a very young minister in Brooklyn, New York, I was asked to give a brief invocation at a meeting scheduled to be held in Prospect Park on Memorial Day. I prepared the few sentences of a short prayer. On arrival at the speaker's stand I looked out at a crowd estimated at fifty to sixty thousand people. Examining the printed program, I was astonished and aghast to note that I was listed not for an invocation but rather for an "address." Immediately I was overcome with fear and the strong negative thought that no way could I meet this unexpected assignment. I was prepared only for a short prayer, not for an address to such a large crowd. Nervously I went to the presiding official, the late Brigadier General Theodore Roosevelt, Jr., son of President "Teddy" Roosevelt, and timidly called his attention to the error. He looked at me speculatively. "You *are* a minister, aren't you?" I nodded.

"What's the matter, son? You surely are not afraid." He pointed toward a section of the crowd reserved for the mothers of service men and women who had died. "As a representative of God I know you have something to say to those sad and grieving mothers. You can do it. More power to you."

The way in which he talked to me and his encouraging punch in the chest did something to me, and while the program was in progress, I put together a talk designed especially to comfort and strengthen those mothers. When I sat down after my speech General Roosevelt said,

"What did I tell you? You rang the bell. You had the power going for you." Well, I knew full well that my ringing of the bell was pretty faint but all of a sudden I was full of happiness—and new enthusiasm for reaching and helping people welled up within me. And, needless to say, I loved General Roosevelt until the day he died on the beaches of Normandy.

Power is available to meet difficult situations. And this power is built into us by the Creator. It is there waiting to be called upon, to be summoned forth, and it can help us through many a crisis. This fact should give rise to joy and stimulate an abounding enthusiasm.

Victor Hugo gives a bit of wise advice:

> Be like the bird
> That, pausing in her flight
> Awhile on boughs too slight,
> Feels them give way
> Beneath her and yet sings,
> Knowing that she hath wings.

One of the greatest of all spiritual principles is expressed in the phrase, "Let go and let God." He is the basic, the true Power. The principles is to do all you can about a problem in the way of thought, study, discussion and prayer. Then, as Saint Paul says, ". . . having done all . . . stand" (Ephesians 6:13). When you have done all that you possibly can, what more can be done by you? It is then that one is wise to let God take over. Trust Him to handle the situation, for He has the know-how, and since He is deeply interested in you as His child, He will produce for you a good result. And it will surely be a good result, for He Himself is good and does all things right and well.

One of the great spiritual writers of the past hundred years was a devout and gifted woman by the name of Hannah Whitall Smith, whose book *The Christian's Secret of a Happy Life* is a classic. One section of the book deals with the matter of leaving your burdens with the Lord:

> I knew a Christian lady who had a very heavy temporal burden. It took away her sleep and her appetite, and there was danger of her health breaking down under it. One day, when it seemed especially heavy, she noticed lying on the table near her a little tract called "Hannah's Faith." Attracted by the title, she picked it up and began to read it, little knowing, however, that it was to create a revolution in her whole experience. The story was of a poor woman who had been carried triumphantly through a life of unusual sorrow. She was giving the history of her life to a kind visitor on one occasion, and at the close the visitor said feelingly, "Oh, Hannah, I do not see how you could bear so much sorrow!" "I did not bear it," was the quick reply; "the Lord bore it for me." "Yes," said the visitor, "that is the right way. We must take

our troubles to the Lord." "Yes," replied Hannah, "but we must do more than that: we must *leave* them there. Most people," she continued, "take their burdens to Him, but they bring them away with them again, and are just as worried and unhappy as ever. But I take mine, and I leave them with Him, and come away and forget them. If the worry comes back, I take it to Him again; and I do this over and over, until at last I just forget I have any worries, and am in perfect rest."

My friend was very much struck with this plan, and resolved to try it. The circumstances of her life she could not alter, but she took them to the Lord, and handed them over into His management; and then she believed that He took it, and she left all the responsibility and the worry and anxiety with Him. As often as the anxieties returned, she took them back, and the result was that, although the circumstances remained unchanged, her soul was kept in perfect peace in the midst of them. She felt that she had found out a practical secret; and from that time she sought never to carry her own burdens, nor to manage her own affairs, but to hand them over, as fast as they arose, to the Divine Burden-bearer.

This same secret, also, which she had found to be so effectual in her outward life, proved to be still more effectual in her inward life, which was in truth evermore utterly unmanageable. She abandoned her whole self to the Lord, with all that she was and all that she had, and, believing that He took that which she had committed to Him, she ceased to fret and worry, and her life became all sunshine in the gladness of belonging to Him. It was a very simple secret she found out: only this, that it was possible to obey God's commandment contained in those words, "Be careful for nothing; but in everything by prayer and supplication, with thanksgiving, let your requests be made known unto God"; and that in obeying it, the result would inevitably be, according to the promise, that the "peace of God which passeth all understanding shall keep your hearts and minds through Christ Jesus."

And when that deep peace of God that passes understanding comes to us, then we do indeed have great joy and enthusiasm.

The effect of faith applied to the problems of life is astonishing—amazing—in its power. In a newspaper column about interesting phenomena I read of a professor who performed an amazing demonstration. His equipment consisted of a board, a large nail, a bottle and a very small fleck of carborundum. He took the bottle in his right hand—it was a big, thick, heavy bottle, one of the thickest, heaviest bottles obtainable—and he used it as a hammer. With a series of powerful strokes of the bottle he drove the nail into the board. This did not fragmentize the bottle, break it, crack it or chip it—so strong was that bottle. Then the professor took the tiny fleck or carborundum, which is one of the hardest of the solids, and dropped it into the glass bottle, which instantly shattered into many pieces. It wasn't size or amount that did it; rather, it was essence.

So it is with the problems and difficulties of this life. Suppose you bring to bear against your difficulties all the force and power that you can muster, all the struggling that you can manage, all the resisting of which you are capable, but it isn't effective. Then take a mustard-seed pinch of faith and drop it with confidence into the problem. The problem shatters, breaks apart; all the elements of the problem are revealed and you can put it together for a solution.

Faith of the in-depth variety that goes beyond mere intellectual assent produces joy and enthusiasm that no adversity or trouble can diminish. The late Governor Charles Edison of New Jersey told me of the resilient, undefeatable spirit of his father, the famous inventor Thomas A. Edison.

On the night of December 9, 1914, the great Edison industries of West Orange were virtually destroyed by fire. Thomas Edison lost 2 million dollars that night and much of his life's work went up in flames. He was insured for only $238,000, because the buildings had been made of concrete, at that time thought to be fireproof.

Thomas Edison's son was twenty-four; Thomas was sixty-seven. The young man ran about frantically, trying to find his father. Finally he came upon him, standing near the fire, his face ruddy in the glow, his white hair blown by the December winds.

"My heart ached for him," Charles Edison told me. "He was sixty-seven—no longer a young man—and everything was going up in flames. He spotted me. 'Charles,' he shouted, 'where's your mother?' 'I don't know, Dad,' I said. 'Find her,' he bade me. 'Bring her here. She will never see anything like this again as long as she lives.' "

The next morning, walking about the charred embers of all his hopes and dreams, Thomas Edison said, 'There is great value in disaster. All our mistakes are burned up. Thank God we can start anew."

And three weeks after the fire, his firm delivered the first phonograph. That is the story of a man who faced the inevitable hazards of human existence with fortitude, courage, faith. He knew that sixty-seven years meant nothing, that the loss of money meant nothing, because he could always build again.

There is generally someone about who always will say, "But Thomas A. Edison was a very unusual man. He could take it that way. I couldn't."

Yes, Edison was unusual. But I have seen many people, unknown to fame and fortune, who were also unusual in the same way; people who thought right, acted right and believed right under the adversity which comes to every human being. Through faith you can be victorious over anything this world can do to you. The Bible promises that. ". . . In the world ye shall have tribulation: but be of good cheer; I have overcome the world" (John 16:33). And you can too, if you have positive faith.

Never let anything get you down, no matter how difficult, how dark, how hard it is, how hopeless it may seem, how utterly depressed you may become. Whatever the nature of the circumstances involved, never let anything get you down. Always there is help and hope for you.

In Switzerland I was having dinner with some friends in an ancient inn called the *Chesa Veglia*, at Saint Moritz in the Upper Engadine Valley. This inn is some four hundred years old. The Swiss and Germans have a curious custom of carving interesting sentiments on the interior walls of such places. And some old chalets have inspiring legends carved or painted on the outside walls. On the dining room wall in the *Chesa Veglia* I saw this inscription written in German:

> *Wenn du denkst es geht nicht mehr,*
> *Kommt von irgendwo ein lichtlein her.*

In English this reads:

> When you think everything is hopeless,
> A little ray of light comes from somewhere.

That wise saying is about four hundred years old. When you think everything is hopeless, always remember, a little ray of light comes from somewhere.

Where is this somewhere? Inside your own mind, of course. You may feel hopeless—but Almighty God has established Himself in you, and nothing is hopeless.

A great poet wrote, "Hope springs eternal in the human breast." Whenever you feel that things are getting you down, remember, there is a little ray of hope, of light, that comes from somewhere. It comes from God, of whom it is said, "With men this is impossible; but with God all things are possible" (Matthew 19:26). And Jesus also said, "Remember, I will be with you forever" (Matthew 28:20 paraphrased). So, if darkness has settled in your mind, just open it up and let in that little ray of light that comes from somewhere.

Edison, it would seem, as he viewed that fire, was the kind of person Joseph Addison had in mind when he wrote:

> The grand essentials to happiness in this life are something to do, something to love, and something to hope for.

There is a curious thing about happiness and enthusiasm in that these qualities can exist and grow and dominate, even in the midst of trouble and difficulty. This interesting thought is expressed by William George Jordan:

Happiness is the greatest paradox in Nature. It can grow in any soil, live under any conditions. It defies environment. It comes from within; it is the revelation of the depths of the inner life as light and heat proclaim the sun from which they radiate. Happiness consists not of having, but of being; not of possessing, but of enjoying. It is the warm glow of a heart at peace with itself. A martyr at the stake may have happiness that a king on his throne might envy. Man is the creator of his own happiness; it is the aroma of a life lived in harmony with high ideals. For what a man *has*, he may be dependent on others; what he *is*, rests with him alone. What he *obtains* in life is but acquisition; what he *attains* is growth. Happiness is the soul's joy in the possession of the intangible. Absolute, perfect, continuous happiness in life is impossible for the human. It would mean the consummation of attainments, the individual consciousness of a perfectly fulfilled destiny. Happiness is paradoxical because it may coexist with trial, sorrow and poverty. It is the gladness of the heart, rising superior to all conditions. . . . Man might possess everything tangible in the world and yet not be happy, for happiness is the satisfying of the soul, not of the mind or the body.

I am reminded of a vigorous man just past middle age who had some trouble that led to the amputation of one of his legs. But he took it cheerfully and very soon was back leading an active life again. Ten years later, the other leg had to be removed. I went to see him in the hospital. Inquiring my way to the right ward, I told the nurse in charge that I wanted to see Mr. Weiss.

"Oh, Mr. Weiss," she replied. "That man is the life of this hospital. He is the most joyful and enthusiastic patient we ever had. We just love him here."

She told me that a few days before, a drunken man—in a state of real inebriation—had come in carrying a big bunch of flowers, saying he was looking for a friend of his. The nurses didn't want to irritate the fellow if they could help it, so they let him walk through the ward, but he couldn't find his friend. Finally he said, "Okay, my friend isn't, here. I will give my flowers to somebody else. I am going to give my flowers to the happiest person in this ward. I've got to go around and look at everyone." So he walked around staring at each face in turn. He said, "I never saw such a gloomy bunch of people." But then he came to Mr. Weiss. And through the fumes of alcohol his mind registered and he said, "You are a happy man. I can tell it. Here are the flowers. You are my friend."

As I talked with this man who had now lost both legs, I said, "They tell me you are the happiest, most enthusiastic man in the hospital. Where do you get all this happiness and enthusiasm? Let me in on the secret."

He pointed to the little table beside the bed. There was a Bible on it. "When I get to feeling a little low I read some of those wonderful words.

Then I become lighthearted and life seems good." His secret was that he had learned one of the most difficult things there is to learn in life—one learned only by simplicity and by faith. He had learned to hold God's hand and trust Him. ". . . whoso trusteth in the Lord, happy is he" (Proverbs 16:20). The person who has faith in God's providence has a reserve of serenity deep inside even when things are very tough.

Upon leaving, as I shook hands with my inspiring friend, I said, "More power to you."

With a crushing handclasp and a big smile he responded, "The same to you—and we know where that power comes from, don't we?"

Here is a thought from Charles Dickens that may motivate us to develop joy and enthusiasm:

> Cheerfulness and content are great beautifiers and are famous preservers of youthful looks.

The wise David Grayson suggests a source of joy that needs underscoring:

> Joy of life seems to me to arise from a sense of being where one belongs. . . . All the discontented people I know are trying sedulously to be something they are not, to do something they cannot do. . . .
>
> Contentment, and indeed usefulness, comes as the infallible result of great acceptances, great humilities—of not trying to make ourselves this or that (to conform to some dramatized version of ourselves), but of surrendering ourselves to the fulness of life—of letting life flow through us.

And the Bible reminds us of a basic way in which joy may be found:

> But when the Holy Spirit controls our lives he will produce this kind of fruit in us: love, joy, peace, patience, kindness, goodness, faithfulness, gentleness and self-control. . . .
>
> *Galatians 5:22, 23 TLB*

And when joy and enthusiasm are developed spiritually, we have a power greater than anything the world can do to us, as illustrated by this early Christian testimony quoted in Margaret Applegarth's book *Heirlooms:*

> *Pliny:*   I will banish thee.
> *Christian:* Thou canst not, for the whole world is my Father's house.
> *Pliny:*   I will slay thee.
> *Christian:* Thou canst not, for my life is hid with Christ in God.
> *Pliny:*   I will take away thy treasurers.

Christian: Thou canst not, for my treasure is in heaven.
Pliny: I will drive thee away from men, and thou wilt have no friend left.
Christian: Thou canst not, for I have a Friend from whom thou canst never separate me.

It must have been a person like that whom Henry Wadsworth Longfellow had in mind:

> None but one can harm you,
> None but yourself who are your greatest foe;
> He that respects himself is safe from others:
> He wears a coat of mail that none can pierce.

Such persons as these had faith, the quality of faith that releases power. They believed—wholeheartedly believed—and power came, and with it often comes healing, as the following story by Frank Kostyu illustrates:

> One day a poet and an artist were looking at a picture by the great French painter, Poussin, representing the healing of the two blind men at Jericho. Said the artist: "What seems to you the most remarkable thing about this picture?"
> "Well," the poet replied, "everything is excellently painted, the figure of Christ, the grouping of the individuals, the expressions on their faces."
> "But," said the artist, "look." And he pointed to the steps of a house shown in the corner of the canvas. "Do you see that discarded cane lying there?"
> "Yes, but what about it?"
> "Why," the artist replied, "on those steps the blind man sat with the cane in his hand, but when he heard Christ come he was so sure he would be healed that he let the cane lie there, and went to Christ as if he could already see."
> The Master made one demand on those who sought to be healed by him. It was belief. He understood the blocks that prevented the healing influence from working in the sick body or soul. So time and time again, he stressed the matter of belief. It was a primary prerequisite to being healed.

Actually joy is a lubricant for belief. It frees the mind and unlocks the muscles. It puts us into rhythm. A truly joyful person is in God's rhythm the same as the heavenly bodies are in His rhythmic processes.

Your internal system of blood and heart and organs constitutes a rhythm. And rhythm is another word for harmony, and harmony is another word for joy. Therefore, when you are joyful, you are in rhythm.

This is true of great athletes. In his book *The American Diamond,* perhaps the classic work on the game of baseball, Branch Rickey says that Honus Wagner was the greatest shortstop in baseball history. Mr. Rickey recalls how Wagner's whole body responded in such perfect rhythm that he scooped balls up from either side, he picked them out of the air, he reached for them wherever they were. And it is said that the reason for his vast ability was that he was a happy man. He loved the game and he loved life. Therefore, because of this joy, he was in harmony and he was in rhythm.

I once knew a tennis instructor who always emphasized the importance of joy and harmony in the game. Whenever he got a stiff pupil who did not have flexibility, his solution was to have him sing as he played.

One day he was instructing a girl who had real potential, but there was no harmonious flow in her game, despite her technical perfection. He asked her whether she knew "The Blue Danube Waltz." "As we play tennis," he said, "I want you to time your strokes to the rhythm of 'The Blue Danube Waltz.'"

As she played, she hummed the tune and her strokes began to increase in rhythm and symmetry. Afterward, her face aglow, she said, "I never felt the joy and thrill of this game before. For the first time in my life I feel I can master it." And similarly, joy and enthusiasm produce rhythm in the game of life, so that we can master it also.

I feel it should be pointed out that always in life, joy and enthusiasm are intermixed with pain, suffering, disappointment and other forms of trouble. But the joy and enthusiasm remain because we have the power through faith in God to see it through, to hang in there, to overcome. Annie Johnson Flint philosophizes factually:

WHAT GOD HATH PROMISED

God hath not promised
Skies always blue,
Flower-strewn pathways
All our lives through;
God hath not promised
Sun without rain,
Joy without sorrow,
Peace without pain.
But God hath promised
Strength for the day,
Rest for the labor,
Light for the way,
Grace for the trials,
Help from above,

> Unfailing sympathy,
> Undying love.

And Isaiah tells us in an immortal sentence (40:31) just how we keep going always with the power and the joy and the enthusiasm and the victory:

> But they that wait upon the Lord shall renew their strength; they shall mount up with wings as eagles; they shall run, and not be weary; and they shall walk, and not faint.

Rufus M. Jones, a Quaker and a great spiritual leader, was one of the most thoughtful men of our time. He had experienced joy and sorrow. And he had spiritual power in full measure. Thinker that he was, he stated a profound fact:

> The real test of a happy life is to see how much pain and loss of frustration can be endured and absorbed without spoiling the joy of it.

Life has been described in many ways; as a journey, a game, a battle, an adventure. But call it what you will, the one who lives must have the power. And that power working in his mind will give him the victory.

This book has as its purpose to help you, the reader, to grasp life now and know it in all its fullness. What better way to illustrate this than with a thought from that master of insight into human nature, William Shakespeare?

> There is a tide in the affairs of men,
> Which, taken at the flood, leads on to fortune;
> Omitted, all the voyage of their life
> Is bound in shallows and in miseries:
> And we must take the current when it serves,
> Or lose our ventures.
>
> *Julius Caesar*

More power to you. That phrase captions many a life story.

Some years ago I received a moving letter from a woman who told of learning to walk when it was assumed she could never do so. When I last heard from her she was in her eighties, still strengthened by the same positive faith described in her first letter:

> I'm a little old lady in my late 60's and I would like to tell you and all the ones that have no faith that with the power of faith one can achieve miracles. I'm sorry I have no education and can't even spell right, but I'm going to try

to relate to you my first great problem of my life and how I did draw on the power of faith.

I was born with dislocation of both my hips and doctors said I would never walk, but as I grew up and looked at others walk I said to myself, "Please, God, help me. I know You love me." I was six years old and my heart was broke and so one day I tryed to stand up between two chairs and down I would go but I didn't give up. Every day I'd speak to God and tryed again and again until I held myself up for a few seconds and I can't describe to you the joy in my heart being able to stand on my feet. I gave one scream to mama. "I'm up! I can walk!"

Then I went down again. I can't never forget the joy of my parents and when I tryed again my mother handed me the end of a broomstick while she held the other end and said, "Give one step forward with one foot and then another," and that is how my faith helped me to walk the duck walk, that's what the doctors call it but I have been so grateful ever since then.

Three years ago I had an accident and I broke my left ankle and was in the hospital and they took x-rays of my legs. Then the doctors came to me and said lady how did you walk? And I said God was my doctor and they said its a miracle you have no socketts and no joints on her hips how did you stand up? And memories came back to me and I have waited 60 years to find out that I have no socketts and no joints for I never knew why.

Then the doctors were afraid that with the accident and broken ankle and my age I would not walk again but God came to my rescue again and to the surprise of all I'm walking again, and still holding my job of taking care of four children of a widow mother while she works. I'm a widow too and had to work very hard to grow my children. My husband died with the spanish flu in 1919. I had two little girls and a son was born two months later. I scrubbed floors on my knees for 17 years and never was sick in my life I don't know what a headach is.

Another story, somewhat similar yet different in that the healing was mental rather than physical, has always appealed to me as one of the remarkable ways God works in human problems.

This is an incident from the experience of a man who became a news-paper editor. He was of French Canadian parentage and had been reared in Canada. He was born with a bad right leg; it was shriveled, atrophied and wouldn't bear any weight. So from infancy he wore a brace on this withered leg.

When he was a very little boy it didn't bother him overly much, but as he became older he realized that with a useless leg he couldn't com-pete. He could not run, play games, or climb trees like the other boys. So he got the impression that if he could not climb a tree, he could not climb the ladder of life. He began to develop an acute sense of being dif-ferent—a sense of limitation and of inferiority. This misery went deeply into his mind, and he brooded over it and became gloomy and fearful about himself.

His father said to him, "Son, don't worry about your leg." And he told the boy that in the cathedral there was a big pile of crutches and braces left by people who had gone to the cathedral with maladies and disabilities and had been healed. He said, "Some day I am going to take you there, when I think you have matured enough so that you can believe; then we will pray and ask the Lord to heal you so you can leave your brace on the altar." The boy was impressed.

The great day came. Dressed in their Sunday best, father and son entered the great cathedral. The sun was streaming through the high stained-glass windows. Soft organ music reverberated through the aisles and arches. The little boy looked wonderingly around. When they arrived at the altar his father said, "Son, kneel and pray and ask the Lord to heal you."

The boy prayed most earnestly, prayed with faith and asked the Lord to heal him. He had a peaceful feeling inside. Then he lifted his eyes and looked at his father. He had always loved his father and had seen his face under many different circumstances. "But always," he said in later life, "will I remember the unearthly beauty that was on my father's face at that moment. There were tears in his eyes, and shining through was the joyous, exalted faith of the true believer."

Profoundly stirred, the boy stood up. But when he looked down, there was his withered leg, the same as before. Very depressed and despondent, he started down the aisle with his father, the old brace thumping along as usual. Then as they approached the huge door of the cathedral something incredible happened:

"I felt something tremendously warm in my heart. I seemed to feel something like a great hand pass across my head. I can feel to this day the lightness and yet the strength of that touch. Suddenly I was boundlessly happy. I cried, 'Father! You are right! I have been healed! I have been healed!'! "Young as I was, I knew what had happened. God had not taken the brace off my leg, but He had taken the brace off my mind."

From then on the withered leg had no power to dismay the boy. He grew in faith and confidence and went forward into a splendid career, the power with him all the way.

5

FAITH AND SUCCESSFUL LIVING

OCCASIONALLY I AM ASKED what books have meant the most to me, and of course I could name many. But for present purposes I want to mention one. It contains a chapter "Enthusiasm," which I have read and reread for many years. The book is *How I Raised Myself From Failure to Success in Selling* by Frank Bettger, and I have mentioned it earlier in this book. While I am not a salesman, that chapter taught me an important truth about life generally. I would like to reprint the entire chapter here, but limitations of space prevent it. But I will give you in my own words the vital principle taught by Frank Bettger, for in my opinion it is important to successful living.

Bettger was a baseball player on a minor league team and, though technically a good player, he was fired for lack of enthusiasm. "Your heart just doesn't seem to be in the game, Frank," said the manager. "I'm sorry to let you go, but you're not alive enough."

Later, Bettger signed with another minor league club where he repeated the same desultory performance. A big league player who liked the young man and saw his possibilities said, "Frank, you have got to be more enthusiastic if you expect to get anywhere in baseball."

"But," complained Frank in despair, "I am just not enthusiastic. I'm not made that way. You can't go to a drugstore and buy a bottle of enthusiasm. If you haven't got it you just haven't got it."

"Oh, but you are so wrong, Frank. You can have enthusiasm by acting enthusiastic. We become what we act."

(The older player probably did not realize that he was teaching the younger man the famous "As If" principle of William James, mentioned earlier. James said that if you are a fearful person you can reeducate your mind to courage by deliberately acting *as if* you had courage. It was this same Professor James who said that a human being can alter his life by altering his attitude of mind.)

"So," said the older player, "start all over on a new club and from the first day act as if you were surcharged with enthusiasm." Frank Bettger was signed by New Haven. On his first day the temperature was over 90 degrees, but he threw the ball with such force it burned the hands of the players. He hit at everything and as a result got three hits in the game, and he ran the bases like a whirling dervish. The papers next day headlined "this ball of fire" and nicknamed him "Pep" Bettger. Soon a scout for the St. Louis Cardinals spotted him for his enthusiastic performance and he became their second baseman. Later he repeated the same "As If" principle of enthusiasm in the insurance business, becoming one of the top producers in the nation.

So, even if you feel tired and down—even sick—turn your thoughts to energy and act enthusiastic, until your subconscious mind takes over that concept. Your muscles will respond accordingly. There will be in you an amazing revitalization as you practice and keep on practicing the "As If" principle.

Among the many vital truths taught in the Bible is this one: "In him we live, and move, and have our being . . ." (Acts 17:28). Perhaps we can say it this way: *In Him we are alive and are energetic and enter fully into our being.* Sounds like being enthusiastic, does it not?

Nehemiah 8:10 says it well:

> . . . for the joy of the Lord is your strength.

Act out in your own life the joy of the Lord—*live it, speak it, think it, be it*—and the joy of the Lord will indeed be your strength.

One of our great American founding fathers, Patrick Henry, whose fervent enthusiasm for liberty ignited the Revolution, was a wise and thoughtful man who knew how the Christian religion makes life better for everyone. When he made his last will and testament he wrote:

> I have now disposed of all my property to my family. There is one thing more I wish I could give them, and that is the Christian religion. If they had that, and I had not given them one shilling, they would have been rich; and if they had not that, and I had given them all the world, they would be poor.

No doubt Patrick Henry had many things in mind when he expressed the desire to leave the Christian religion to his heirs. He wanted them to be aware of God and divine guidance, of the moral teachings of the Bible, and to accept Jesus Christ as their Savior. Judging by his own life and career, I am sure that he knew and valued the power of faith. He wanted it to be operative in the lives of his loved ones, as is suggested by the Bible verses which follow:

> If thou canst believe, all things are possible to him that believeth.
> *Mark 9:23*

What things soever ye desire, when ye pray, believe that ye receive them, and ye shall have them.

Mark 11:24

Whosoever shall say unto this mountain, Be thou removed, and be thou cast into the sea; and shall not doubt in his heart, but shall believe that those things which he saith shall come to pass; he shall have whatsoever he saith.

Mark 11:23

Be determined and confident. Study the book day and night. Make sure that you obey everything written in it. Then you will have good success. Be not afraid, for I your God am with you.

Joshua 1:7–9 paraphrased

. . . If ye have faith as a grain of mustard seed . . . nothing shall be impossible unto you.

Matthew 17:20

Dale Evans Rogers, entertainer and author, beloved by millions, points out that faith can make life successful. But, of greater value, it can make life abundant:

We rush through life so fast that we don't even know the flowers are there.

But it doesn't have to be like this. You can decide to do otherwise, to travel another way. This is *your* life. Choose ye this day. . . .

Now sooner or later in this life, like the man on the road to Jericho, we all discover that there are thieves lying in wait for us to rob us of our chance to really *live*. There are good values and bad values screaming for our money and/or our lives; there is God and the devil, and we will eventually travel with one or the other. You can't avoid it: you will have to choose between them. God cannot and will not do it for you. He gives you your years, your breath of life; you can use it either for Him or against Him.

Since I have come to know God and walk His way, the pressures and temptations that made my life so empty before I knew Him have disappeared completely. His power makes my life abundant instead of merely successful. He would do the same for you.

But faith can do even more. It can restore the lost beauty to a person and rehabilitate the misplaced or misused quality of one's nature and personality. Such a change occurred in the life story of a man who had read a book of mine. He was a very unhappy person, invariably dejected, his thinking cynical, negative and gloomy. He went on this way for several years. Then, for a while, I did not see him. Suddenly he wrote me a ten-page letter. I left it on my desk for quite a while before reading it; it looked so formidable. When finally I got into it I was amazed. Here was the lilting happy testimony of a man who at last had found himself and was telling me how happy he was. What had happened? That man had developed a five-fold program for himself, and through it had found the cure for his negativism and unhappiness. Here is how he described his program.

"*First*," he says, "I pray twenty-five times a day." If anybody will pray twenty-five times a day he will change the character of his thoughts, and so change his life.

Second, this man "soaks his mind" with Bible passages, imaging them as deeply penetrating his consciousness.

Third, he sits down with pen and paper and sees how many good thoughts he can write down about people he knows. He remarks that this was the toughest thing in the whole process. But if you think bad thoughts about people, you have a residue of unhappiness.

Next, he tells the Lord several times a day how much he loves Him.

Finally, the man tries to keep all sin out of his life.

The foregoing five-point spiritual-action program activated the power of faith to make this man over into a person of genuine joy and enthusiasm. As he himself described his new life-style, he was moving up from level to level and hoped ultimately to attain top-level life.

This man's experience reminded me of a wise insight of Pierre Teilhard de Chardin, in which he indicates that the ultimate in happiness is this moving upward to a higher state:

> Happiness has no existence nor value in itself, as an object which we can pursue and attain as such. It is no more than the sign, the effect, the reward (we might say) of appropriately directed action: a by-product, as Aldous Huxley says somewhere, of effort. Modern hedonism is wrong, accordingly, in suggesting that some sort of renewal of ourselves, no matter what form it takes, is all that is needed for happiness. Something more is required, for no change brings happiness unless the way in which it is effected involves an *ascent*.
>
> The happy man is therefore the man who, without any direct search for happiness, inevitably finds joy as an added bonus in the act of forging ahead and attaining the fullness and finality of his own self.

Faith of course is more than an intellectual belief in God. It is a closeness with God, a closeness to such degree that His loving and watchful care may be experienced in time of sorrow or crisis or danger. And this to a point where to call such care a matter of coincidence is to deny an obvious reality.

This is illustrated in a remarkable way by an event that happened in Shenkiu, in Central China's Honan Province, at the time of the Japanese invasion of China during World War II. The Japanese were approaching this city; they were very near—only two or three days away. The Chinese colonel came to the mission compound and told the pastor's wife that she had better leave, as he had received orders not to defend the city against the Japanese. The pastor, a medical missionary, had been taken to a hospital, himself ill. He was 115 miles away and would not return for perhaps a month. His wife was alone with a baby girl two months old and a two-year-old son.

An exodus from the city began. The elders of the church came and invited the missionary's wife to go with them to their villages. They were very kind and gracious people. But she had these two babies, and she knew that the village homes of these people were vermin-infested and full of germs. Western babies lacked the necessary immunity. There had been many deaths among missionaries' children exposed to conditions in the villages. Therefore, she was afraid to take her babies into those houses. So she remained in the city, alone, one American woman with two babies. The gatekeeper, her last protection, came and said that he, too, must leave. The poor woman was filled with fear. She was alone and unprotected, in bitter January weather, with the enemy approaching.

She went to the kitchen sink to fix a bottle for the baby. Her hands were cold. She shook so from fear that the bottle almost fell from her hands. Then she saw above the sink her Bible-text calendar. It was January 16, 1941, and beneath the date she read these words from Psalms 56:3: "What time I am afraid, I will trust in thee." She was astonished, but strangely comforted. All that night she kept her two little ones huddled close to her to keep them warm. She lay awake, listening to the wind rattle the paper windowpanes in the bamboo frames, praying to God, who, all the time she was afraid, would assuredly be with her. It was noon before she remembered to pull the page off the little daily calendar. The tenth verse of the Ninth Psalm proclaimed: "And they that know thy name will put their trust in thee: for thou, Lord, hast not forsaken them that seek thee." As she bowed her head over her noonday meal, she thanked God for those particular words at that moment.

When the following morning came, she realized that she was without food. All the stores were empty or closed, for there were no food supplies coming in from the countryside. All she had were the goats, but she did not know how to milk them. Once again, fear clutched at her. How would she feed the children? She pulled off the calendar page for January 17 and, believe it or not, under the date of January 18 were these words: ". . . I will nourish you, and your little ones" (Genesis 50:21). This modernly trained woman, schooled in the new thinking, asked herself, "Is this only a coincidence?"

Then came a rap at the door. It was a little Chinese woman, Mrs. Lee, a longtime neighbor. "We knew you would be hungry," she said, "and that you do not know how to milk the goats. So I have milked your goats. Here is milk for your children."

Presently another little woman came, holding a live chicken by the legs and also carrying some eggs. Once again the pastor's wife looked at the words, "I will nourish you, and your little ones."

That night her heart was full of hope. To the sound of shells bursting in the sky, she prayed that somehow God would spare the city and the gentle people whom these missionaries loved.

The next morning she rushed to the little calendar hanging on the nail and tore off the page. She read: "When I cry unto thee, then shall mine enemies turn back: this I know; for God is for me" (Psalms 56:9).

This time it seemed too much to believe! Surely a verse chosen by chance for a Scripture calendar couldn't be taken literally. And again fear clutched her. The Japanese army—what would they do with one lone, defenseless woman? She went through her husband's papers, destroying any that might be construed to incriminate her. She could hear the sound of gunfire coming closer and closer. She went to sleep that night fully dressed, prepared at any moment to meet the Japanese invaders.

She awoke in the early dawn expecting to hear rough shoes on the gravel, the sound of marching troops. But instead there was a deep quietness. Cautiously she went to the gate and watched as the streets began to fill, not with Japanese soldiers, but with townspeople coming back into the city. The colonel reappeared and said to her, "We don't understand it. The Japanese were headed for this city. They were going to take it. Suddenly they turned aside. We didn't defeat them. They just went another way and left our city unoccupied."

Was it coincidence? When you come right down to it, what *is* coincidence? Can it be an act of God in the midst of time, even modern time?

Faith, I believe, would so agree.

Many have found that reality in the glorious words of Isaiah 26:3:

> Thou wilt keep him in perfect peace, whose mind is stayed on thee: because he trusteth in thee.

Robert A. Russell writes:

> How did man get out of the Kingdom of God? How did he lose his place in it? By his negative thinking. How does he return to it? How can he find expression in a Kingdom of Good only? By using the Mind of Christ, by allying his thoughts with the Divinity within him. If we are praying or speaking the word for some greater good, we know that Christ is speaking the word through us. "In all thy ways acknowledge Him, and He shall direct thy paths." "Delight thyself also in the Lord; and He shall give thee the desires of thine heart."

And Edna D. Cheney has expressed this faith in poetry:

THE LARGER PRAYER

At first I prayed for Light:
  Could I but see the way,
How gladly, swiftly would I walk
  To everlasting day!

And next I prayed for Strength:
  That I might tread the road
With firm, unfaltering feet, and win
  The heaven's serene abode.

And then I asked for Faith:
  Could I but trust my God,
I'd live enfolded in His peace,
  Though foes were all abroad.

But now I pray for Love:
  Deep love to God and man,
A living love that will not fail,
  However dark His plan.

And Light and Strength and Faith
  Are opening everywhere;
God only waited for me, till
  I prayed the larger prayer.

According to Fulton Oursler, men like Washington, who said, "The event is in the hands of God," and Adams and Lincoln had no trouble in separating coincidence from the mighty acts of God operating in human affairs:

"It is impossible to rightfully govern the world without God and the Bible," said George Washington, and John Adams called it "the best book in the world," while Lincoln said, ". . . Take all of this book upon reason that you can and the balance by faith and you will live and die a better man."
  The Greatest Book Ever Written

I once knew a scientist who was also a great spiritual leader. Dr. Albert E. Cliffe taught every Sunday the largest Bible class in Canada. I like Dr. Cliffe's reminder that we have an intelligent God who wants us to be happy and so helps us through our faith:

God's intelligence is available to your intelligence for use, for guidance and inspiration. He wants you to be a happy, successful, healthy person, and He is ever waiting for you to use His power through Jesus Christ.

Let Go and Let God

Perhaps two of the most powerful forces in this life, which affect persons for either good or bad, are faith and fear. Indeed, the only force more powerful than fear is faith. And faith can overcome fear.

Positive faith is closely associated with common sense. Tackle a fear-centered situation with sound reason and you gain the courage to deal with it effectively.

A friend had a long bout with a disease. He attacked his illness in his usual businesslike manner. He had it—that was that—and he proceeded to fit the treatments into his daily schedule. He went on with his business, never showing any emotion. I asked him, "At any time during this experience were you afraid?"

"Yes," he replied, "there was one time when I was afraid. That was when my temperature stayed at 104 degrees for three days. The thought crossed my mind that maybe I wasn't going to make it. But I was afraid only temporarily. I just began to apply common sense, and as I did so the fever went down. All the common sense I had told me that the doctors on this case were confident that they were doing the right thing." And he added, "Beyond that, I was in good hands. When I board a plane I'm not afraid. I know the equipment is good. I know the plane has been well serviced, that the pilots and engineers know their business. I don't sit there being afraid. I apply common sense to it. I am in a scientific universe."

"Well," I commented, "you're one man who doesn't seem to have fear in the slightest degree."

"Why should I?" he replied. "I gave my mind to Jesus Christ. He freed me of fear. And when you do that you don't need to be afraid of anything."

"For God hath not given us the spirit of fear; but of power, and of love, and of a sound mind" (2 Timothy 1:7). Such is the positive faith that gave courage to this man.

Sometimes it is necessary to do battle with your fear and kill it. There are times when no lesser method will suffice. Emerson in a famous statement said, "Do the thing you fear and the death of fear is certain."

Somewhere (if I knew the source, I would gladly acknowledge it), I read a thrilling story about a man in the South African gold fields by the name of Courteney. He had started as a working miner and eventually owned a gold mine. As he was working his way up he was tough as nails, but after he acquired the gold mine he became rich and fat and soft.

One day he went down into the mine and there came a rumbling in the earth that became an underground cataclysm. The miners ran. They were lithe and lean and got away. But he was fat and slow and was trapped by falling rock. All the lights went out. Fortunately, there was a piece of metal above his head that shored up the rocks directly above him, giving him space enough to stand erect with about five inches clearance. But the rocks grating and settling all around him closed him in with just enough room to move his elbows a bit. Dust filled the air. He managed to tear off a piece of his shirt and put it over his nose to avoid suffocation.

He realized his predicament well: he was many feet beneath the surface of the earth, entirely alone, entombed by rocks. That old devil, claustrophobia, seized him. He wanted to shriek and scream. But his mind told him it would be of no avail and that he must preserve his strength. He had just enough air to sustain life for a while.

At length he heard in the silence the tap of metal on stone and knew that relief was coming. By a herculean effort of prayer and faith he controlled himself until the rescue workers reached him. Finally came cool, sweet air and he was taken out to safety.

But that night in bed it suddenly seemed as though the darkness was closing in on him again; it was as if the bedclothes were rocks falling all around him. With a cry of terror he threw back the covers, leaped from the bed and ran outside. He breathed the fresh air and looked up at the stars and the moon. The terror subsided. But he sat up the remainder of the night.

Night after night he tried to sleep, but always the terror would come over him. He knew his faith must be deepened. He prayed and asked the Lord how to handle his problem.

One day he told his friends that he was going to be gone for a little while—that he was going "to kill a devil." He went to the mine shaft and told the man who ran the lift to take him down to the fourteenth level. The man refused. "Mr. Courteney, I can't take you to the fourteenth level. It's not shored up properly down there. We haven't worked it for a long time. It's very dangerous. I can't take you down, sir."

"Look, my friend," said Courteney, "I own this mine. Take me down to the fourteenth level." Reluctantly, the man took him down. Then Courteney said, "Now take the lift up and leave me here."

The darkness crept around him and with it came the terror. He started walking down a tunnel. He could hear water dripping. He knew that this tunnel was shored up with very old timbers that had been there for many years. He heard a rumble in the earth. His heart beat faster. Cold sweat came upon his face. Terror seized him. But he prayed, "Lord, Lord, help me. I must kill this devil of fear or I will die." He stayed there in the darkness of the mine, affirming faith until the devil lay dead. Then he signaled for the lift and was taken up. He said to the lift operator, "There's a dead devil down below." He walked out into peace, in control of himself.

Kill a devil, the devil of fear, the devil that drives you and haunts you all your life. There has to come a time when your faith becomes so deep and positive that you can kill that fear, leaving it dead, finished. Only faith can kill fear. ". . . Take a heart, it is I; have no fear" (Matthew 14:27 RSV). And when a person develops power over fear, then joy and enthusiasm will be boundless. And it is faith that leads to that highly desirable mental condition.

My wife and I had lunch one cold day in a charming old restaurant in Bath, England; afterward we sat before an open fire for a while in a little parlor where on the wall was this framed ancient prayer:

> I arise today
>> in the might of Heaven
>> brightness of the sun
> whiteness of the snow
> splendour of fire
>> I arise today
> in the Might of God for my piloting
>> Wisdom of God for my guidance
> Eye of God for my foresight
> Ear of God for my hearing
>> I evoke therefore all these forces:
> against every fierce merciless force that may
> come upon my body and soul;
> against incantations of false prophets;
> against false laws of heresy;
> against black laws of paganism;
> against deceit of idolatry;
> against spells of woman, smiths, and druids;
> against all knowledge that is forbidden the human soul.
> against poison, against burning
> against drowning, against wounding,
> that there may come to me a multitude of rewards.
> Christ with me, Christ before me,
> Christ behind me, Christ in me,
> Christ under me, Christ over me.

Think of it: You can arise today in the might of Heaven, against all sorrow, defeat, against all your fears. So, when plagued by anxiety, worry, apprehension or fear, affirm that God is good, affirm that God loves you. Affirm that God is taking care of you. And the forces of fear will be driven off. Positive faith will increase your courage always.

Having faith, we can walk through this world with urbanity and courage, living successfully and with joy and enthusiasm every day all the way. The famous psychiatrist, Dr. Carl G. Jung, considered faith important to mental and physical well-being:

Among all my patients in the second half of life—that is to say, over thirty-five, there has not been one whose problem in the last resort was not that of finding a religious outlook on life. It is safe to say that every one of them fell ill because he had lost that which the living religious of every age have given to their followers, and none of them has been really healed who did not regain his religious outlook.

And Archbishop William Temple agrees:

The causes of health, as the causes of sickness, are very many, but among the forces which will tend to keep us in health will be a faith which is extended to a real expectation of God's goodness in every department of our being. That will bring us either actual health or a greater power of triumphing over ill-health, and either of these is a great blessing. Moreover, when we triumph in the way that I have described over ill-health, the result is, in fact, that our health is somewhat better than if we were merely lying passive in the grip of our disease, because owing to the exaltation of mind there is a real access of vitality which tends to combat the disease itself.

The healing power of faith is illustrated by one of America's greatest preachers, Dr. Charles L. Allen, who tells of a troubled man who came to him for help and to whom he gave a healing "prescription":

If you could look at this man who came to see me, you would think that he never had had a worry in his life.

I asked him his trouble; it was that he could not sleep at night. He told me he had not had a full night's sleep in six months.

We continued talking, and finally he said, "I have everything a man should want in life, but I am just plain scared and I do not know why I am scared."

I took a sheet of paper and wrote across the top of it these words: "HE LEADETH ME BESIDE THE STILL WATERS." I handed him the sheet of paper and told him to put it in his pocket and before he went to bed that night to write down under the quotation everything he thought it meant and whatever related thoughts it brought to mind. Then he was to put the paper in his dresser drawer. The following night he was to take out what he had written, read it over, and add whatever additional thoughts had come to him. He was to keep that up every night for a week and them come back to see me.

I wanted to saturate his mind completely with that one thought. I know that it is utterly impossible to keep fear and thoughts of "still waters" in a mind at the same time. Any good fisherman can testify to that. That is the reason that fishing is such a great medicine for so many people.

There is no nerve medicine on this earth to be compared with still waters; when we create those clear, cool, still waters on the screen of our imagination, it is wonder-working. As Longfellow put it, "Sit in revery, and watch the changing color of the waves that break upon the idle seashore of the mind."

Another bit of wisdom is to live a day at a time. Robert J. Burdette says it well:

There are two days in the week upon which and about which I never worry—two carefree days kept sacredly free from fear and apprehension.

One of these days is yesterday. Yesterday, with its cares and frets and all its pains and aches, all its faults, its mistakes and blunders, has passed forever beyond my recall.

It was mine.

It is God's.

And the other day that I do not worry about is tomorrow. Tomorrow, with all its possible adversities, its burdens, its perils, its large promise and poor performance, its failures and mistakes, is as far beyond my mastery as its dead sister, yesterday.

Tomorrow is God's day.

It will be mine.

There is left for myself, then, but one day in the week—today. Any woman can carry the burdens of just one day. Any man can resist the temptations of today.

It is only when we add the burdens of those two awful eternities, yesterday and tomorrow, that we break down.

The literature on successful living in America is vast and varied, for Americans have historically been attracted by the idea of doing the best they can with their lives. So here are eight steps to success in life by the great early American showman, P. T. Barnum:

1. Engage in a business for which you have a talent.
2. Secure a suitable locality for your business.
3. Stick to your business. Do not assume that just because you are a success in one field that you can be so in any.
4. Be economical; not parsimonious, nor stingy, but never go into debt.
5. Be systematic. No man can succeed in business who neglects the strict observance of system in his business.
6. Advertise. Have a good article and make it known in some way to the public that you have such a thing for sale.
7. Be charitable. It always pays a businessman to perform acts of benevolence.
8. Be honest. Honesty is the best policy. A man who lacks honesty will soon lack customers for his goods.

The early American preacher Jonathan Edwards comes up with similar advice:

Resolved: To live with all my might while I do live.

Resolved: Never to lose one moment of time, but improve it in the most profitable way I possibly can.

Resolved: Never to do anything which I should despise or think meanly of in another.

Resolved: Never to do anything out of revenge.

Resolved: Never to do anything which I should be afraid to do if it were the last hour of my life.

And William James joins the chorus of wisdom for successful living:

We forget that every good that is worth possessing must be paid for in strokes of daily effort. We postpone and postpone until these smiling possibilities are dead. By neglecting the necessary concrete labor, by sparing ourselves the little daily tax, we are positively digging the graves of our higher possibilities.

I like the thought expressed by Winfred Rhoades that what we become within ourselves is the true success. And to become that, faith is a vital ingredient:

Life's supreme adventure is the adventure of living. Life's greatest achievement is the continual remaking of yourself so that at last you do know how to live.

The man who is set for the building up of a self he can live with in some kind of comfort and with the hope of continued improvement chooses deliberately what he will let himself think and feel, thoughts of admiration and high desire, emotions that are courageous and inspiring. It is by these that we grow into more abundant and truer life, a more harmonious inner state and a more stalwart personality.

6

THE VALUE OF A
POSITIVE ATTITUDE

W ILLIAM ARTHUR WARD, creator of many wise sayings, reminds us that:

A cloudy day is no match for a sunny disposition.

It is also true that a positive attitude is a match for all the gloom and depression that affects so many these days. It is almost magical how a sunny disposition and joyfully positive attitude chases gloom away.
Frank Kostyu says:

In town I stopped to talk to a business friend. It was a cold, dreary day and, as might be expected, the conversation opened with some remarks about the weather.
"It certainly is a gloomy day," I said.
Then he told me an interesting thing that had happened to him on just such a dismal day. He left the house one morning dreading to go to his place of business. From the house next door, his friendly neighbor called, "Hello, neighbor! It's a great day!"
My friend looked up, observed that many trees were still in full autumn color. The air was clean to breathe.
"Yes," he answered, a little more cheerfully, "it is a great day."
He straightened his shoulders, walked down to the corner barber shop and said to the boys, "It is a great day!"
They smiled back, "It sure is!"
When he arrived at his store, he spoke to his clerks. "It's a great day!" They all looked up and smiled.
Wherever he went that day he radiated the happy spirit, and when he arrived home in the evening he said to his wife, "This has indeed been a great day. It looked dismal at the beginning, but everything seemed to turn for the better and the whole day was bright." His wife reflected his spirit. She, too, seemed happy.
A cheerful word changed the whole day.

Charles Kingsley believed that a sunny disposition has much to do with a successful career:

The men I have seen succeed have always been cheerful and hopeful, who went about their business with a smile on their faces, and took the changes and chances of this mortal life like men . . . If you wish to be miserable, you must think about yourself; about what you want, what you like, what respect people ought to pay you, what people think of you, and then to you nothing will be pure. You will spoil everything you touch; you will make sin and misery out of everything God sends you; you can be as wretched as you choose.

"But," you may say, "it's not always easy to have a positive and sunny attitude." To which we suggest the following for consideration:

I can do all things through Christ which strengtheneth me.

Philippians 4:13

And Ella Wheeler Wilcox gives us some wise counsel in her poem "Optimism":

> Talk happiness. The world is sad enough
> Without your woes. No path is wholly rough;
> Look for the places that are smooth and clear,
> And speak of those, to rest the weary ear
> Of Earth, so hurt by one continuous strain
> Of human discontent and grief and pain.
>
> Talk faith. The world is better off without
> Your uttered ignorance and morbid doubt.
> If you have faith in God, or man, or self,
> Say so. If not, push back upon the shelf
> Of silence all your thoughts, till faith shall come;
> No one will grieve because your lips are dumb.
>
> Talk health. The dreary, never-changing tale
> Of mortal maladies is worn and stale.
> You cannot charm, or interest, or please
> By harping on that minor chord, disease.
> Say you are well, or all is well with you,
> And God shall hear your words and make them true.

While we are considering the joy of a positive attitude, it may also be well to think of the contrary attitude of unhappiness. The famous writer and psychologist William James says:

The attitude of unhappiness is not only painful, it is also mean and ugly.

What can be more base and unworthy than the pining, puling, mumping mood, no matter by what outward ills it may have been engendered?

What is more injurious to others?

What less helpful as a way out of difficulty?

It but fastens and perpetuates the trouble which occasioned it, and increases the total evil of the situation.

This brings to mind the old man I heard about who was a guest on a television show with a famous emcee. It seems that this man was on the program on his ninetieth birthday because he was noted for his physical well-being and his joyful spirit. He was a marvelous raconteur and kept everyone entertained by his stories, his humorous quips and wise remarks. He really stole the show. But the emcee didn't mind; in fact, he was enjoying his guest immensely. Finally he said, "Our time is just about up, but one more question. You seem a genuinely happy man. How did you get that way?"

"Sure, I'm happy," replied the old gentleman. "You see, it's this way. Every morning when I wake up I have two choices: one—to be unhappy, or two—to be happy. And since I'm not dumb, I just choose to be happy. It's as plain as the nose on your face."

And so it is, really, but perhaps we let life awe us, actually persuading us that living is so complex and difficult that we are even under the control of circumstances; whereas actually it can be just the other way around. As Daniel C. Steere says:

Life is very manageable. It is intended to be. Life is exciting, and positive, and rewarding.

Life is the most marvelous tool God has created for you. Everything on earth has been put here at man's disposal. God intends for you to use life. He wants you to take advantage of all the things He has put here, and to use them as resources and opportunities.

There are two crucial concepts for improving self-confidence. The first is: Who you are will always be consistent with who you think you are. The second is that you are an underachiever! There are enough buried reserves of capability and talent for you to be anyone you want to be.

Add to those basic concepts of yourself a third basic truth. This fact is about life:

Most people have to overcome their awe of life before they can master it!

The famous writer Sydney Smith, back in the 1700s, stated the simple principle of choice put forward by the elderly man on the television show. He said, adding a warning:

When you arise in the morning, form a resolution to make the day a happy one to a fellow-creature.

Never give way to melancholy; resist it steadily, for the habit will encroach.

A positive attitude that is joyful and enthusiastic will, if sincerely long held, produce joyful, enthusiastic and positive results in our lives.

Dr. Albert E. Cliffe wrote a great and inspiring book called *Let Go and Let God,* in which he says:

> "He that will love life, and see good days . . . let him eschew evil, and do good."
>
> *1 Peter 3:10–11*

If we hold such negative thoughts until they dominate our minds, if we look for sin and sickness in everyone, we will certainly find it.

Every day can be a blue day to you, every night just another night of misery; you produce in your daily life these very things by constantly impressing wrong ideas upon your mind. Every person living on this earth is as he is because of the pattern of his past thinking, and if your life has been unhappy up to now, then it is time for you to change your ideas and begin to practice a Christianity that will radiate happy living into your experiences.

Many of you enjoyed, no doubt, during the last summer a wonderful vacation, going to new places, seeing new areas of nature, meeting different people all living very different lives from your own. You came back with a thoroughly different picture of life from that which you had before. You came home refreshed, after being absent for some time from your daily toil, your daily worries, the people who annoyed you. Oh, how much you enjoyed the change. You lived happily during your vacation.

Was it a miserable world to you then? Did you not enjoy every minute of it? Did you not love the beauties of the sea, the forest, the countryside, the lake shore? Was it a hell on earth to you or was it a picture of God's perfection? You had a complete change of scene and peace of mind. In those few weeks you changed the pattern of your thinking, and what did you find? In the beauties of nature you found God and you found a heaven on earth. You loved life while on your vacation, didn't you? Then why is it not possible to enjoy this happy living three hundred and sixty-five days a year?

The Bible says, "He that will love life and see good days," and this tells you very definitely that the Master, Jesus Christ, knows all about life, knows all about the good in life, all about good living, and He wants you as a child of His Father, to share that good life, to be happy with Him right now.

Can you imagine the Master, Jesus, as a sad-faced, weary, miserable-looking person, a man without personality, a negative individual thinking only of the miseries of life? Would such a man have brought Lazarus back from his eternal home to continue on such an earth if it were a place of misery? It isn't common sense.

You can make your life a happy one if first of all you will forget and forgive the past, if you will learn to live one day at a time, believing that a radiant future is yours.

Fears and diseases will follow you no more when you learn from the depths of your heart how to let go the evils of your life and let God take care of you.

There is a simple technique for living the Christian life. First of all you must believe in and accept the teachings of the Master. You must read about Him every day in the Gospels. You must make an appointment with Him every day to talk to Him. Through this simple faith you will demonstrate a life of overflowing abundance and overwhelming happiness. You will learn how to put yourself last in your life, and your fellowmen before yourself. You will then have a most powerful mental attitude towards life. This is faith, and the Bible is full of stories of what faith has done for others and what faith in a living vibrant Christ will do for you. Nothing in this world will be impossible to you.

What about the promise, "What things soever ye desire, when ye pray, believe that ye receive them, and ye shall have them"? What a marvelous promise this is, and how true you can prove it to be.

Stanley Jones says that it is much more fun being a Christian than going to the devil; one feeds a life, the other satisfies an impulse. One ends in a mess, the other in the joy of living.

Many things will happen to you when you take Jesus Christ as your guide to happiness. Many little coincidences will take place in your daily life which you had previously looked upon as good luck. But they are all part of that divine plan, for the world is created by a God who runs it on laws, and when you live up to those laws, then you *let go and let God*. The joy of living becomes a daily coincidence with you. . . .

A businessman came to see me some time ago who had failed in business. While he seemed to have good ideas, he did not have enough working capital. After discussing his life with me, we discovered he was filled with criticism and resentment of former employers and his life was dominated by these resentments. He had to ask forgiveness of his employers. He had to ask forgiveness of God. He had to seek peace and follow it; he had to surrender his life to Christ. Then he gained his answer. Several offers of capital came to him from sources he had never known before, and the more he practiced living one day at a time, the more he forgot that wicked past, and the more successful he became.

Do you believe that God wants you to live a miserable life? Do you believe that He wants you to have worries, anxieties and sicknesses? That is not the teaching of the New Testament. He wants you to be happy and to radiate that happiness.

Many people want to be happy but do not know how. They take their happiness from the material things of life; but do you often see happy faces leaving a movie or cocktail bar? Not really happy faces.

Then we have that type of Christian so proud to tell you how long he has been saved, who thinks it a crime to smile in church. I often wonder why so many Christians frown so much in their daily lives and in their jobs. They don't realize that it takes twenty-seven face muscles to form a frown, and only eight to make a smile. This kind of Christian naturally overworks his face.

The teachings of Jesus make us happy, radiant, joyful, successful. Jesus makes you glad; He makes you sing. . . .

Your guide to happiness is the Christ—His way of life.

Do you want it? There is a price to be paid. You must surrender your whole self to God through Jesus Christ. Pray for it, act on it, believe it, and you will begin at once to feel His power in you. Plant this idea firmly in your mind, affirm it every day, strive for it. Try to make yourself worthy of being a temple for His Spirit. . . . There is not a soul upon earth who cannot make his or her life a marvelous thing, a tremendous experience.

Let go those things in life which have kept you from happiness, *and let God.*

The foregoing reminds me of a charming one-liner by Janet Lane:

Of all the things you wear, your expression is the most important.

And I also like these verses by G. J. Russell, a sound, common-sense philosopher.

IT MIGHT HAVE BEEN WORSE

Sometimes I pause and sadly think
  Of the things that might have been,
Of the golden chances I let slip by,
  And which never returned again.

Think of the joys that might have been mine;
  The prizes I almost won,
The goals I missed by a mere hair's breadth;
  And the things I might have done.

It fills me with gloom when I ponder thus,
  Till I look on the other side,
How I might have been completely engulfed
  By misfortune's surging tide.

The unknown dangers lurking about,
  Which I passed safely through
The evils and sorrows that I've been spared
  Pass plainly now in review.

So when I am downcast and feeling sad,
  I repeat over and over again,
Things are far from being as bad
  As they easily might have been.

Robert Louis Stevenson's philosophy also represents a positive attitude:

As yesterday is history, and tomorrow may never come, I have resolved from this day on, I will do all the business I can honestly, have all the fun I can reasonably, do all the good I can willingly, and save my digestion by thinking pleasantly.

The famed religious leader, John Wesley, had, it would seem, a proper self-appraisal of his relationship to the universe:

He who governed the world before I was born shall take care of it likewise when I am dead. My part is to improve the present moment.

We must never lose sight of the fact that the important thing is not what happens to you but, rather, your attitude toward what happens. A friend once gave me a carved-wood plaque which I have on my wall. It reads in raised letters, ATTITUDES ARE MORE IMPORTANT THAN FACTS.

When this was first given to me I thanked my friend but disagreed with the statement. "Nothing," I said, "can be more important than a fact, for a fact is a fact and that is that."

"Nothing," he replied, "is more important than your attitude toward the fact."

He illustrated his point this way: Here is a big, hard fact. And to deal with this fact are two men, both of equal mentality, equal education, equal ability. One man approaches the fact and is awed by it. "What a huge fact," he says. "This fact is really overwhelming and tough." And as he thinks and talks the fact gets bigger and the man smaller. The result is that he is defeated by the fact.

The second man approaches the same fact and recognizes its complexity; he does not minimize it. But he is not only a realist about the difficulty inherent in the fact, he is a positive thinker and takes a positive attitude toward the fact and—what is more important—toward himself also. He reasons, "This is indeed a tough fact, but I am tougher than the fact. I'm bigger than this fact. I have the know-how or I know how to get the know-how, and with God's help I can handle this situation"—which he proceeds to do and successfully deals with the fact. Because of his attitude he demonstrates that attitudes are indeed more important than facts.

John Homer Miller agrees with this positive point of view:

COLORS

Your living is determined not so much by what life brings to you as by the attitude you bring to life; not so much by what happens to you as by the way your mind looks at what happens. Circumstances and situations do color life, but you have been given the mind to choose what the color shall be.

Even an attitude toward dark nights and storms, even toward despair, can become joyful, John Kendrick Bangs tells us:

> I never knew a night so black
> Light failed to follow on its track.
> I never knew a storm so gray
> It failed to have its clearing day.
> I never knew such bleak despair
> That there was not a rift, somewhere.
> I never knew an hour so drear
> Love could not fill it full of cheer!

And I like that poem by Robert E. Farley called "Thinking Happiness," which tells how the happiness attitude results in joy and enthusiasm:

> Think of the things that make you happy,
>   Not the things that make you sad;
> Think of the fine and true in mankind,
>   Not its sordid side and bad;
> Think of the blessings that surround you,
>   Not the ones that are denied;
> Think of the virtues of your friendships,
>   Not the weak and faulty side;
>
> Think of the gains you've made in business,
>   Not the losses you've incurred;
> Think of the good of you that's spoken,
>   Not some cruel, hostile word;
> Think of the days of health and pleasure,
>   Not the days of woe and pain;
> Think of the days alive with sunshine,
>   Not the dismal days of rain;
>
> Think of the hopes that lie before you,
>   Not the waste that lies behind;
> Think of the treasures you have gathered,
>   Not the ones you've failed to find;
> Think of the service you may render,
>   Not of serving self alone;
> Think of the happiness of others,
>   And in this you'll find your own!

The philosopher Arthur Schopenhauer points out that joy from within is the best form of happiness and that our own personal world is determined by how we look at it, or our attitude toward it:

The happiness which we receive from ourselves is greater than that which we obtain from our surroundings. . . . The world in which a man lives shapes itself chiefly by the way in which he looks at it.

The development of a positive attitude requires effort and may not come easily. We are born with a positive attitude. At least, I do not believe I ever saw a negative baby. But that same child may be born into a negative family climate. And being absorbent—a sponge of prevailing attitudes, so to speak—the child soon takes on the mental atmosphere prevalent in the family. When, later as a young person, the child now wants to become a positive thinker, he or she must begin a mental re-education process which can be long and difficult, even painful, for old thought habits die hard. To achieve a new and positive attitude may indeed, perhaps definitely will, require practice, discipline and continuous vigilance to avoid slipping back into the old negative thought pattern.

Perhaps one might work out for oneself a procedure of thought practice such as that which Sybil F. Partridge employed:

JUST FOR TODAY

Just for today I will be happy.
This assumes that what Abraham Lincoln said is true, that "most folks are about as happy as they make up their minds to be." Happiness is from within; it is not a matter of externals.

Just for day I will try to adjust myself to what is, and not to try to adjust everything to my own desires.
I will take my family, my business and my luck as they come and fit myself to them.

Just for today I will take care of my body.
I will exercise it, care for it, nourish it, not abuse it nor neglect it, so that it will be a perfect machine for my bidding.

Just for today I will try to strengthen my mind.
I will learn something useful. I will not be a mental loafer. I will read something that requires effort, thought and concentration.

Just for today I will exercise my soul in three ways.
I will do somebody a good turn and not get found out. I will do at least two things I don't want to do, as William James suggests, just for exercise.

Just for today I will be agreeable.
I will look as well as I can, dress as becomingly as possible, talk low, act

courteously, be liberal with praise, criticize not at all, nor find fault with anything and not try to regulate nor improve anyone.

Just for today I will try to live through this day only.
    Not to tackle my whole life problem at once. I can do things for twelve
hours that would appall me if I had to keep them up for a lifetime.

Just for today, I will have a program.
    I will write down what I expect to do every hour. I may not follow it
exactly, but I will have it. It will eliminate two pests, hurry and indecision.

Just for today I will have a quiet half-hour all by myself and relax.
    In this half-hour sometimes I will think of God, so as to get a little more
perspective into my life.

Just for today I will be unafraid.
    Especially I will not be afraid to be happy, to enjoy what is beautiful, to
love, and to believe that those I love, love me.

Frank Bettger went through the attitude reeducation process, which
he describes to a degree, at least, in the following:

> Soon after I started out to sell, I discovered that a worried, sour expres-
> sion brought results that were just about infallible—an unwelcome audience
> and failure.
>   It didn't take me long to realize that I had a serious handicap to over-
> come. I knew it wasn't going to be easy to change that worried expression on
> my face left by so many years of hardship. It meant complete change in my
> outlook on life. Here is the method I tried. It began to show results *immedi-
> ately* in my home, socially, and in business.
>   Each morning during a fifteen-minute bath and vigorous rubdown, I
> determined to cultivate a big, happy smile, just for that fifteen minutes. I
> soon discovered, however, that it couldn't be an insincere, commercialized
> smile, developed just for the purpose of putting dollars in my pocket. It had
> to be an honest-to-goodness smile from down deep inside, an outward
> expression of happiness from within!
>   No, it wasn't easy at first. Time and again I found myself during that
> fifteen-minute workout thinking thoughts of doubt, fear, and worry. Result?
> The old worried face again! A smile and worry simply won't mix, so once
> again I'd force the smile. Back came cheerful, optimistic thoughts.
>   Although I didn't realize it until later, this experience seems to substan-
> tiate the theory of the great philosopher and teacher, Professor William
> James of Harvard: "Action *seems* to follow feeling, but really action and
> feeling go together; and by regulating the action, which is under the more
> direct control of the will, we can indirectly regulate the feeling, which is
> not."

Let's see how starting off with a good fifteen-minute workout of the smile muscles helped me during the day. Before entering a man's office I would pause for an instant and think of the many things I had to be thankful for, work up a great big, honest-to-goodness smile, and then enter the room with the smile just vanishing from my face. It was easy then to turn on a big, happy smile. Seldom did it fail to get the same kind of smile in return from the person I met on the inside. When Miss Secretary went in to the boss and announced me I feel sure she reflected some part of the smiles we'd exchanged in the outer office, for she would usually come back still wearing that smile.

Let's assume for a moment that I had gone in looking worried, or forcing one of those rubber-band smiles—you know, the kind that snaps right back—don't you think that secretary's expression would have practically told her boss *not* to see me? Then walking into the boss's office, it was natural for me to give him a happy smile as I said: "Mr. Livingston! Good morning!"

That the positive attitude reeducation process is important in leading to joy and enthusiasm is indicated by Dr. Albert E. Cliffe:

Negative thinking will always lead to failure and nervous prostration; but positive faith—positive thinking—will lead you towards happy, healthy and abundant living.

Finally, there are always those who dolefully say, "It can't be done." These negativists and pessimists probably want others to fail, perhaps to justify their own deficiencies. It is undoubtedly wiser to listen to creative people like Edgar A. Guest who say that it *can* be done. They are the positive people who help others to achieve the best in life through joy and enthusiasm.

IT COULDN'T BE DONE

Somebody said that it couldn't be done,
  But he with a chuckle replied
That "maybe it couldn't," but he would be one
  Who wouldn't say so till he'd tried.
So he buckled right in with the trace of a grin
  On his face. If he worried he hid it.
He started to sing as he tackled the thing
  That couldn't be done, and he did it.

Somebody scoffed: "Oh, you'll never do that;
  At least no one ever has done it";
But he took off his coat and he took off his hat,
  And the first thing we knew he'd begun it.

With a lift of his chin and a bit of a grin,
   Without any doubting or quiddit,
He started to sing as he tackled the thing
   That couldn't be done, and he did it.

There are thousands to tell you it cannot be done,
   There are thousands to prophesy failure;
There are thousands to point out to you, one by one,
   The dangers that wait to assail you.
But just buckle in with a bit of a grin,
   Just take off your coat and go to it;
Just start to sing as you tackle the thing
   That "cannot be done," and you'll do it.

                           EDGAR A. GUEST

7

LIFE WITH A SPIRITUAL UPTHRUST

WITH GOOD REASON WE have been encouraged to pray and know the Bible, for in this manner we become conditioned with a *spiritual upthrust*. Joy, enthusiasm and vitality of spirit result from a mounting tide of spiritual power within the personality.

Recently a man whom I have known for many years took me to his club for lunch. The members of the club sat at a huge round table and although my host had told me that he wanted me to entertain the group, I had no chance to do so, for my host was the center of a sparkling, vivacious and positively fascinating conversation. I studied him with amazement, for I remember the time, years before, when his father came to me and said, "What can I do with my son? He fails at everything he touches. I think he is intelligent. He has had a good education. But he is so dull and apathetic and spiritually down that I despair of him." Had my friend's father been alive and at the luncheon, I'm sure he would have looked with astonishment at his son.

Naturally I wanted to know the secret, so later I asked him.

"There is no secret," he said. "All I did was to start using that idea of taking God as your partner. Now, every day of my life I read the New Testament; it is filled to overflowing with life."

The Bible is filled with life. Take a concordance and look up the words that are mentioned most often in the Bible. You will find that they are *life*, *love* and *faith*. "In him was life . . . (John 1:4). The idea is that if you really center your life in Christ, the deadness, the gloom, the apprehension, the weariness, the disgust, the tiredness will fall away.

How does one become filled with such joyous vitality? Everybody wants this. How does one acquire it?

It is the old phenomenon of a human being making actual contact with this dynamic, joyous, vital power which is in Jesus Christ. Nobody needs to be half-alive; everyone can live delightfully, with joyous vitality, if the relationship with Jesus is one of reality and is personal in nature.

To live with joyous vitality, practice is important. For if you practice being dead over a long period of time, you will be dead even while you live. If you practice being apathetic over a long period of time, you will become an apathetic personality. If you practice being unhappy, you will become unhappy.

Act as though you were filled with joy and vitality.

"Well," you might say, "that isn't honest, because I am not filled with joy."

But, yes, you are! It is below the surface of your nature waiting to be released. ". . . the kingdom of God is within you" (Luke 17:21). It is just that it has never come out. So act as though you had life and enthusiasm, as though you had health, as though you had talent, as though you had joy, and you will come to have them.

As William Barclay said:

> Prayer is not flight; prayer is power. Prayer does not deliver a man from some terrible situation; prayer enables a man to face and to master the situation.

And, of course, when one is able to master a difficult situation, he becomes joyful and life takes on brighter tones.

Proverbs are sayings that grow out of the long-accumulated wisdom of the human race. And therefore the old English proverb "Prayers should be the key of the day and the lock of the night" may be significant in that away back in time, spiritually minded people discovered that prayer gave enthusiasm for the day's work and peace filled with joy at eventide.

> Jesus has told us that when we learn to be perfect in thought, word and deed, that if we really try day after day, then we will discover God. Every good thought you have, every good deed you do, every good secret desire of your heart is a whisper from God. Take time each hour of every day to contact God where you are, get an appointment with Him for one minute hourly, and day by day you will gain faith and conviction. Your thoughts, your whole personality, will change, for you will become, as Jesus, able to overcome all things in life.
>
> Because God lives within you, then truth lives within you. His spirit is in you, His power is within you. Attend God every hour of your day, and the law of God will always work for you to bring you health, peace of mind and happiness.

The writer of the above, Dr. Albert E. Cliffe, often said that Jesus Christ is a scientist in that he teaches the workable formula of the good life, of joy, enthusiasm and peace of mind.

One of the happiest and most enthusiastic men I have ever known was Frank Bettger, whom I have quoted earlier. His joyful spirit and enthusiastic attitude derived from his profound faith, as indicated in the following story of a close call with death that he experienced.

This was written many years ago in the early days of air travel:

Out on the Nevada desert one glorious moonlight night, just below the great Hoover Dam, on Lake Meade, I saw a strange phenomenon. I was stretched out on the flat of my back, looking up at a million stars. Guests of the Lake Meade Lodge had built a huge bonfire on the beach from drift-wood . . . then I saw it! The smoke from that roaring fire was spiraling up into the sky from right to left, like the hands of a clock *turning backward*!

I had heard of this strange power caused by the rotation of the Earth; and I wondered why this same power causes smoke south of the Equator to *reverse* the action and spiral in the direction followed by the hands of a clock.

And it can never be different!

Likewise, the winds in a cyclone *north* of the Equator spiral counter clockwise; *south* of the Equator they spiral clockwise.

Lying there on the beach, gazing up at the stars and a beautiful full moon, I began wondering about the miracle of the Earth making a complete revolution—24,000 miles every 24 hours—right to the split second! "In addition to that," I got to thinking, "here we are, on the beach by this quiet lake, in perfect peace, yet this same power is carrying the Earth like a great space ship, on a complete round trip, circling the Sun every 365 days—the fantastic distance of *five hundred eighty-seven million miles every year*!"

. . . Not long afterward, I boarded a plane in Des Moines, Iowa, at seven o'clock in the morning. I was scheduled to speak that night in Toledo, Ohio. Shortly after we took off, a terrible wind and thunderstorm began tossing our two-motored plane around in the air. When we arrived over Chicago, a thick fog had blown in from the Great Lakes, bringing almost zero visibility. No incoming planes were permitted to land. After circling around more than an hour, the pilot announced that he had been instructed to go up to Milwaukee. When we reached Milwaukee, the fog was too heavy to make a landing there, so we were ordered to go on through to Toledo. But there, it was even worse, so we tried Cleveland. Same result. Great bolts of lightning flashed all around us. Violent thunderbolts shook the heavens. Our plane kept going, but no one seemed to know where.

Six o'clock that night, our pilot radioed the airport that our gas was running dangerously low. We were given the signal to descend. Everyone held his breath! Suddenly, we began bouncing on the ground, and the next thing we knew we came to a stop directly in front of the main building of the Cleveland Airport! Then, something happened in that plane I never saw happen before—nor since. Simultaneously, every one of us, twenty-four passengers, applauded! It was an applause quite different from any I ever heard before . . . I think we were all praying—not saying—"*Thank You God!*"—and "*Thank you!*" to the pilot.

I managed to get a sandwich and hot coffee at the lunch-counter. A west-bound plane came in—the fog was lifting a bit, so they put me on. I arrived in Toledo just in time for the meeting. Three men were waiting at the airport to greet me. They had been there for hours.

As we drove out to the Scott High School Auditorium, where I was to make my talk, they told me the following extraordinary story:

"Gil" Dittmer, prominent insurance executive and chairman of this meeting, was giving a five-o'clock cocktail party at his home in my honor. Naturally, I was supposed to be there. Twelve committee members were enjoying a jolly party, because the meeting was a sell-out, and these men had all worked hard for it. But, as time went on, they began receiving frightening reports from the three members waiting at the airport. "One plane over Indiana crashed!" they said, "and Frank Bettger's plane is in trouble!" Later, when rumors started that the plane I was on was reported missing, the cocktail party developed into a *Prayer Meeting*!

"Some of those prayers," they told me later, "were the most fantastic God ever listened to, but we were all convinced that God heard us all right, because He never listened to more sincere, earnest praying!" One man declared, "A few of those prayers were delivered by men who hadn't prayed in years!"

I'm not recommending "cocktail party-prayer meetings" . . . but I must admit, I'll always feel highly honored by the one that was "rounded up" for me!

. . . Now, let me tell you about some of the thoughts I had up there in that plane. I had plenty of time to think. Eleven hours of it! During the worst part of the flight, I had a little prayer-meeting all of my own! I seemed to be listening for the most part. I heard nothing. Yet, a message seemed to come to me just as clearly as if I did hear it! It was in the form of questions . . . like this:

. . . "Remember that night in Nevada on the beach at Lake Meade, how you noticed the phenomenon of the smoke spiraling into the sky from right to left? . . . And how it dawned on you that the great Power controlling the movement of that smoke is the same Power which controls and navigates the Sun, the Stars, the Earth, and all the other planets? . . .

"That God created this power, and the Laws; and is directing all things on this earth. *He* has the only *Master Plan*. And *these* laws—man can never revoke . . . Remember?

"Do you know there is another great Law—created by this same Power—controlling the destiny of man—the *Law of Right and Wrong*?—and that this is another law man can never revoke? . . .

"Unknowingly—when you hit the sawdust trail and grasped Billy Sunday's hand, you were making a decision to harness your life to this *Great Power* . . . Since that day, some miraculous things have happened to the broken down ballplayer that little mongrel brought away from the bridge in Chattanooga, Tennessee. . . ."

These were some of the thoughts that kept running through my head up there while we were being tossed around ten thousand feet in the air. Was I scared? Was I worried? Believe it or not—No! I had a strange feeling of security. I had a *job* to do. *This job*. And I believed I would be allowed to finish it. I believed this. I really did. I just *knew* I was going to get down out of that plane alive!

When I applauded *"Thank You!"* with all the other passengers, I wasn't applauding because fear had passed, and I was alive and breathing. I was saying *"Thank You!"* because I discovered my faith had been so real. I had experienced the Great Universal *Power of Faith!*

Another inspiring friend was Ralph Spaulding Cushman who wrote a poem that bubbled out of his faith-filled and joyous nature. It is called "The Secret." It is indeed a basic secret of living and one anyone can learn:

I met God in the morning
When my day was at its best,
And His presence came like sunrise,
Like a glory in my breast.

All day long the Presence lingered,
All day long He stayed with me,
And we sailed in perfect calmness
O'er a very troubled sea.
Other ships were blown and battered,
Other ships were sore distressed,
But the winds that seemed to drive them
Brought to us a peace and rest.

Then I thought of other mornings,
With a keen remorse of mind,
When I too had loosed the moorings,
With the Presence left behind.

So I think I know the secret,
Learned from many a troubled way:
You must seek Him in the morning
If you want Him through the day!

Dale Evans Rogers gives her own secret of the joy and enthusiasm which has filled her life despite some hard experiences. She says:

Prayer! I couldn't live without it; I would have died a dozen times if it had not been for my chance to talk it over with God, and gain strength in it from Him.

How can we know the mind and will of God? How can we know His plan for our daily lives? Deciding about that is most difficult, as all important decisions are difficult.

I think the best way to arrive at the right decision is to first pray about it, placing it in God's hands. Then sleep on it. The next morning, when you get up, I believe that the first solution that comes to your mind will be the right one—that is, if you have complete confidence in God's guidance. "But let him ask in faith, nothing wavering. For he that wavereth is like a wave of the sea driven with the wind and tossed" (*James* 1:6). Ask God's help in faith, and our decision will be right. I have found it unwise to make important decisions at the end of the day, when we are weary and tired. But once we have made a decision, we must not look back, like Lot's wife. We must act then on the faith that God has given us the answer—and know that only good will come out of it.

Since prayer is a basic way to deal with life's problems and a source of wisdom and peace and joy, I have practiced nine prayer steps suggested by my friend, Dr. Charles L. Allen. These nine steps will work when practiced:

To make the most of prayer, let me suggest nine prayer steps.

There are three steps to take *before* prayer:

(1) Decide what you really want. Get clearly in mind exactly what you plan to ask in prayer.

(2) Seek to determine whether or not what you want is right. Ask yourself such questions as: Is it fair to everyone else concerned? Is it best for me? Is it in harmony with the Spirit of God?

(3) Write it down. Reducing our requests to writing helps to clarify our thinking and deepen the impressions upon our mind and heart.

Then, there are three steps to take *during* prayer:

(1) Keep the mind still. Just as the moon cannot be perfectly reflected on a restless sea, so God cannot be experienced by an unquiet mind. "Be still, and know that I am God" (Psalm 46:10). At this point we must concentrate to keep the mind from wandering.

(2) Talk *with* God, and not *to* God. Instead of saying, with Samuel, "Speak; for thy servant heareth" (1 Samuel 3:10), we are prone to say, "Listen, Lord, for Thy servant speaketh." Prayer is both speaking and listening.

(3) Promise God what you yourself will do to answer your own prayer. God answers prayer, not for you, but with you. Jesus performed many of His miracles by giving the person to be helped something to do. As you pray, search for the things that you yourself can do.

Then, there are three steps to take *after* prayer:

(1) Always remember to thank God for answering your prayer. You would not pray in the first place if you did not believe God would answer. Now, confirm that belief by thanking Him for the answer, even though it has not yet come.

(2) Be willing to accept whatever God's answer may be, remembering the words of our Lord, ". . . nevertheless not my will, but thine, be done" (Luke 22:42).

(3) Do everything loving that comes to your mind. One of the objects of prayer is to bring the love of God into our hearts; and as we express that love, we make it possible for God to answer our prayers better.

And it is to our advantage to remember, especially whenever the going gets hard, some reassuring words from Psalms 145:18:

The Lord is nigh unto all them that call upon him, to all that call upon him in truth.

That reassurance will keep your faith going even when doubts tend to creep in as to whether God is there listening to you. As Helen Steiner Rice so touchingly puts it:

GOD, ARE YOU THERE?

I'm way down HERE!
You're way up THERE!
Are You sure You can hear
My faint, faltering prayer?
For I'm so unsure
Of just how to pray—
To tell you the truth, God,
I don't know what to say . . .
I just know I am lonely
And vaguely disturbed,
Bewildered and restless,
Confused and perturbed . . .
And they tell me that prayer
Helps to quiet the mind
And to unburden the heart
For in stillness we find
A newborn assurance
That SOMEONE DOES CARE
And SOMEONE DOES ANSWER
Each small sincere prayer!

Apparently human beings have always turned their thoughts and prayers to the Great Divinity which they perceived in the structure of the world, in its beauty, and in the power and majesty of nature. And from that source they drew strength and the power to live greatly. Something of these thoughts is in this prayer of a Chippewa Indian:

O Great Spirit, whose voice I hear in the woods and whose breath gives life to all the world, hear me. I am a man before you, one of your many children. I am small and weak. I need your strength and wisdom. Let me walk in beauty, and make my eyes ever behold the red and purple sunsets. Make my hands respect the things you have made, my ears sharp to hear your voice. Make me wise so that I may know the things you have taught my people, the lessons you have hid in every leaf and rock. I seek strength, O Great Spirit of my fathers—not to be superior to my brothers, but to be able to fight my greatest enemy, myself.

Make me ever ready to come to you with clean hands and a straight eye, so that when life fades like a fading sunset, my spirit may come to you without shame.

The elevated insights contained in the prayer of the Indian are also present in a medieval prayer, the author's name unknown as far as I am able to ascertain:

Almighty God, Father, Son, and Spirit, who art power, wisdom, and love, inspire in us those same three things:

> power to serve Thee,
> wisdom to please Thee,
> and love to accomplish Thy will;
> power that I may do,
> wisdom that I may know what to do,
> and love that I may be moved to do all
>   that is pleasing to Thee.

Always we find as we read in the literature of prayer and devotion that spiritual upthrust comes through, and invariably those who practice in-depth quality prayer are joyful, peaceful, enthusiastic and even radiant people. It all seems to indicate that a close relationship exists between the love and daily living with God and the quality of happiness. Rufus M. Jones, one of the outstanding spiritual leaders of our time, even goes so far as to say that communion with God is the solution of all our troubles. He states:

LIVING COMMUNION

The solution of all our troubles and problems is, I maintain, to be found in the recovery of more vital methods of living communion with God. It would be well for us to reduce the amount of talk, of words, of argument, of question-asking, reduce also what is formal and mechanical, and greatly increasing the living, silent, penetrating corporate activity of worship of which Whittier wrote those great words of his—the meaning of which he had experienced:

> "Without spoken words, low breathings stole
> Of a diviner life from soul to soul,
> Baptizing in one tender thought the whole."

And Louis Cassels writes on the same theme:

That doughty Christian, St. Theresa of Avila, speaks of "the dark night of the soul." She was referring to an experience shared by all who travel more than a few steps along the Christian way. The traditional name for the experience is "doubt." But in this context the word has a special meaning.

It does not necessarily imply that you are plunged into intellectual doubt about the existence of God. It means, rather, that you suddenly feel bereft of a sense of his presence which hitherto has been very real to you. The feeling is one of acute loss, almost of bereavement.

What brings on "the dark night of the soul"? It may be simply an expression of great fatigue—mental, emotional, or physical. It may be the result of allowing the mind to wander too far from the things that really matter and becoming too preoccupied with the cares and pleasures of everyday life. But in some cases, it seems to be God himself who deliberately withdraws the consciousness of his presence from these who are accustomed to being sustained by it.

Why does God do this? George Macdonald offered this guess: "He wants to make us in his own image, choosing the good, refusing the evil. How should He effect this if He were *always* moving us from within, as He does at divine intervals, towards the beauty of holiness?" In other words, God withdraws in order to give us the freedom of choosing anew whether we will pursue him above all else.

What can a person do when he finds his prayers bouncing back from the ceiling? Macdonald has this advice: "Fold the arms of your faith and wait in quietness until the light goes up in your darkness. Fold the arms of your faith, I say, but not of your action. Think of something you ought to do, and go do it. Heed not your feelings. Do your work."

Perhaps a reason that prayer and faith produce an upthrust of joy is the fact of their powerful working in sickness and suffering.

A passage in the Book of James (5:13–16) deals with this matter:

Is any among you afflicted? let him pray. Is any merry? let him sing psalms.

Is any sick among you? let him call for the elders of the church; and let them pray over him, anointing him with oil in the name of the Lord:

And the prayer of faith shall save the sick, and the Lord shall raise him up; and if he have committed sins, they shall be forgiven him.

Confess your faults one to another, and pray one for another, that ye may be healed. The effectual fervent prayer of a righteous man availeth much.

I have the habit of keeping stories I have read and often they have come to good use in helping others. Here is one that concerns three young fellows who discovered the upthrust of spirit that comes from prayer and the Bible. Actually their lives were saved by it. It was written by Robert Trumbull:

(*Early in 1942, Americans read with pride and admiration the short newspaper accounts of three Navy fliers who fought the sea for thirty-four days, while they drifted in a rubber raft without food, equipment, and for some time without clothes, yet survived to land, weak and bent, on a strange shore.*)

Before evening, the three of us were sitting dejectedly silent. Then Gene made a suggestion.

"It might be a good idea," he said, not meeting our eyes, "to say a prayer."

We discussed this seriously. We found that we had all been reared in some religious atmosphere, but that we had all drifted away. It had been many years since I had been inside a civilian church, but I sometimes attended Sunday services held by the chaplain aboard ship, when my duties permitted and I was not going ashore.

We all concluded that a word of prayer wouldn't hurt anything.

So we sat in the steaming little cup that our boat had become, and bowed our heads beneath the cruel tropic sun. We each mumbled a few words of our own awkward choosing, calling on our God to bless our loved ones back home, over whom we were more concerned than ourselves, and asking for a little rain.

We were all quite skeptical about the possibility of any answer to our prayer.

"Well, now we done all we could," Tony said.

"Gee, give it a chance," Gene answered impatiently. I called on my store of proverbs.

"God helps those that help themselves," I said.

"Well, come on, rain," Tony challenged. "Or maybe it ain't gonna rain no mo', no mo'."

We lifted our voices lustily at that and sang, "It Ain't Gonna Rain No Mo'," as far as we knew the words—which wasn't far—as if by our false cynicism we could put a reverse hoodoo on the elements.

At least we were all laughing again, which we hadn't done for some time.

Despite our elaborate irreverence, there was no denying that the prayer had made us feel better. Gene, who had more piety in his nature than either Tony or I, took evident satisfaction. His mind now was obviously clean of worries or self-reproaches.

That night it rained.

We had another prayer meeting that night, and every night thereafter. Each evening, after the sun's flamboyant departure left us feeling more alone in a world that suddenly lost all color, we devoted perhaps an hour to our informal service. There was a comfort in passing our burden to Someone bigger than we in this empty vastness. Further, the common devotion drew us together, since it seemed that we no longer depended entirely upon each other, but could appeal, simultaneously, to a Fourth that we three held equally in reverence.

After our halting prayers—neither Gene nor I was scholarly in formal religion, and Tony could pray only in Polish—we developed naturally the "fellowship period" familiar to those who have attended Protestant Sunday school.

We sang some popular songs, a time or two. I couldn't remember any except old ones. I hadn't been to a dance, except occasionally, in twelve or fifteen years, and popular songs go away from me. The songs that I knew, the boys had never heard. The more recent ones that they could sing, I couldn't. However, we managed to get together on a few, and that gave us a lift.

It was later that I came to realize how little we knew about the Bible. One night, after our prayer meeting, I told a Bible story. Appropriately, it was the miracle of the loaves and fishes.

The boys were tickled with it. In my youth I had been brought up in a denomination of the church that holds regular Sunday school, so I drew upon a long memory. Of course, the stories were in my own improvised words. I hadn't been to church for many years, so it's easy to imagine how good I was at recalling the stories I had learned as a youngster. I hadn't been inside a civilian church since 1923, when I was back home after my first cruise. Aboard ship, the chapel services which I occasionally attended included everything but Bible stories.

My religious training had been such that I could now recall all the favorite stories of the Scriptures, but nowhere near verbatim. Gene recalled a number of stories, but couldn't tell them. He would think of a story, and then it would be up to me to tell it.

Tony had never heard any of these things before. In his church, all the services were in Polish—or Latin. The best-known Biblical tales were all new to him. He begged me every night to tell him more and more.

Well, I didn't want to tell him everything I knew in one night, so each evening I'd tell one story. That went on until the end.

I found my recollections of the Bible very useful in the last week or ten days, when we were all exhibiting a tendency to brood over our position. One of my hazy parables would snap us out of our depression and start a flood of discussion in which our dismal outlook was momentarily forgotten.

Many a time I wished a preacher, or someone well versed in Scripture, were present. The wording I used would certainly shock a Bible student.

We finally landed on an island through a jagged and dangerous reef. The commissioner was curious as to how we had reached this particular part of the island. Had we walked there? We merely turned and pointed seaward. He was astounded. That, he said, was impossible! He could not believe we had come upon this beach from the sea. No one had ever come over that reef and lived to tell the tale!

It was our turn to be astonished. But after a surprised glance at each other, we pointed to our little raft, tied to the piling near the shack.

In all, we covered approximately one thousand miles in the raft, but actually, from the point at which we landed our plane to this island the distance was about 750 miles.

Joy is basic in the teachings of Jesus. "These things," He said, "have I spoken unto you . . . that your joy might be full (John 15:11). He knew that joy "doeth good like a medicine" (Proverbs 17:22) and He was a teacher of those attitudes and thoughts that lead to joy and enthusiasm.

So the advice of Hermas, early Christian writer and wise man that he was, deserves to be heeded:

Put sadness away from thee, for truly sadness is the sister of half-heartedness and bitterness. Array thee in the joy that always finds favour in God's sight and is acceptable with him; yea, revel thou therein. For everyone that is joyous worketh and thinketh those things that are good, and despiseth sadness. But he that is sad doth always wickedly; first because he maketh sad the Holy Spirit that hath been given to man for joy; and secondly he worketh lawlessness, in that he neither prays to God nor gives him thanks. Therefore cleanse thyself from this wicked sadness, and thou shalt live with God. Yea, unto God all they shall live who have cast out sadness from themselves, and arrayed themselves in all joy.

8

KEEP YOUR SPIRIT BUILT UP

FRANK BETTGER WRITES:

Make a high and holy resolve that you will double the amount of enthusiasm that you have been putting into your work and into your life! . . . If you carry out that resolve . . . be prepared to see astonishing results. It will probably double your income, and double your happiness.
"If you can give your son or daughter only one gift,
let it be Enthusiasm!"

—BRUCE BARTON

That is wise advice. In his day Bruce Barton, one of the nation's leading advertising executives, influenced the attitudes and therefore the lives of thousands of people through his books, articles and speeches. He knew the importance of enthusiasm as a sort of mental and spiritual fire which burns off the negative attitudes and makes it possible for positive concepts to become dominant and therefore determinative. He believed in the constant build-up and refreshing of the spirit.

And I am sure that the man who has been called the wisest American would agree with the foregoing high appraisal of the value of enthusiasm, for Ralph Waldo Emerson said:

Nothing great was ever achieved without enthusiasm.

But enthusiasm can run down lest you keep joy going strong. For enthusiasm thrives on joy. But there are always hardships, frustrations and failures ready to attack our joy and undercut enthusiasm.

Ella Wheeler Wilcox, whose poetry has delighted and inspired millions, had something to say on this problem:

Fate used me meanly; but I looked at her and laughed,
That none might know how bitter was the cup I quaffed.
Along came Joy, and paused beside me where I sat,
Saying, "I came to see what you were laughing at."

Albert E. Cliffe agrees with Ella Wheeler Wilcox when he says:

You know you sometimes think yourself into unhappiness, into a depression. Do you know that you can also think yourself into gladness? It is by such thinking that you get well, that you prosper, that your prayers are always answered. Become the master of your own thinking. Stop thinking about how tough life is to you, stop thinking about the future and the past, think of God's riches and love, try to express such thoughts from day to day. You will become whatever you think.

And I like the statement relative to the build-up of joy and enthusiasm made by Emily M. Bishop in her book called *The Road to Seventy Years Young:*

The best mental tonic for the vital processes are the habits of cheer and courage. Not "spells" of happy confidence which are more than offset by "spells" of doubt, of timidity and of poisonous fear, but *an habitually positive cheer-courage outlook*. Of course, thinking and feeling are not strictly voluntary acts, but it lies within the domain of one's volitional power to select the kind of thoughts and feelings which shall receive hospitable encouragement.

Many years ago in Cornwall there was a preacher who associated with John Wesley named Billy Bray. He was a man of powerful spiritual gifts who came out of a hard life in the tinworks of that area of England. In his own inimitable way, when he heard someone telling a long story about troubles and sorrows, his remark was: "I've had my trials and troubles. The Lord has given me both vinegar and honey, but He has given me the vinegar with a teaspoon and the honey with a ladle."

Margaret E. Sangster echoed the spirit of the Cornish miner-preacher in joyous words. She found this to be a great and wonderful world, which is a true insight that certainly vies with the so-called profundity that sees everything as bad—very bad:

This beautiful world! This joyous life! I wonder if we are as happy and light of heart as we ought to be, we children dwelling even here in our Father's house. Most of us need, after youth is past, to cultivate a mood not only of contentment but of gaiety, and to make it the dominant note of our days. . . .

Notice, the joys far outnumber the sorrows. Though the latter come in groups on occasion, they are exceptional, and whether occurring singly or together, they are offset by a long procession of calm and halcyon days, weeks, months and years, years which the Psalmist had in mind when he said, "I will remember the years of the right hand of the Most High."

Once my wife, Ruth, and I went out with a native driver onto the Serengeti plains in Africa for a period of two weeks. For that length of time we were entirely separated from newspapers, radio and television. At first we missed the news acutely, for are we not victims of the fast-paced, breathless media? But after a few days our attitude was one of "So what?" and finally even "Couldn't care less." And when, after fourteen days, we returned to a city and grabbed for a newspaper, we found that despite its big headlines and aside from a few details, the news wasn't all that different from two weeks before.

Our fortnight with the impalas, elephants, giraffes, wildebeests and lions of the Serengeti had done something deep and quiet and perhaps philosophical to us. Association with God's creatures had certainly given our inner joy and enthusiasm a definite build-up. Actually, we were not as sure as we had been just who had the best civilization—the men or the animals.

Indeed, the so-called lesser creatures may, through intuition or instinct, often come upon truth in deeper insight. Mark Guy Pearse says it in his poem "Don't Trouble Trouble":

> Don't you trouble trouble till trouble troubles you.
> Don't you look for trouble; let trouble look for you.
> Who feareth hath forsaken the heavenly Father's side;
> What He hath undertaken He surely will provide.
>
> The very birds reprove thee with their happy song;
> The very flowers teach thee that fretting is a wrong.
> "Cheer up," the sparrow chirpeth; "Thy Father feedeth me;
> Think how much He careth, oh, lonely child, for thee."
>
> "Fear not," the flowers whisper; "since thus He hath arrayed
> The buttercup and daisy, how canst thou be afraid?"
> Then don't you trouble trouble till trouble troubles you;
> You'll only double trouble, and trouble others too.

And in this connection I like "The Creed for Optimists" stated by Christian D. Larsen:

1. Promise yourself to be so strong that nothing can disturb your peace of mind.
2. Promise yourself to talk health, happiness and prosperity to every person you meet.
3. Promise yourself to make all your friends feel that there is something in them.
4. Promise yourself to look at the sunny side of everything and make your optimism come true.

5. Promise yourself to think only of the best, to work only for the best, and to expect only the best.
6. Promise yourself to be just as enthusiastic about the success of others as you are about your own.
7. Promise yourself to forget the mistakes of the past and to press on to the greater achievements of the future.
8. Promise yourself to wear a friendly countenance at all times and give every living creature you meet a smile.
9. Promise yourself to spend so much time improving yourself that you have no time left to criticize others.
10. Promise yourself to be too large for worry, too noble for anger, too strong for fear, and too happy to permit the presence of trouble.

A sure way to go about building up your joy and enthusiasm is to bypass your own troubles and get under the burdens of other people. It is surprising how the doing of that makes one glad. As Arnold Bennett so well said:

The best cure for worry, depression, melancholy, brooding, is to go deliberately forth and try to lift with one's sympathy the gloom of somebody else.

Helen Steiner Rice writes:

The more you love, the more you'll find
That life is good and friends are kind
For only what we give away
Enriches us from day to day.

So when we give away ourselves to get free of ourselves in being helpful to the less fortunate, we receive in return at least two magnificent gifts: a deep inner joy and a brand new enthusiasm for life and for people.

And I believe there is a subtle joy secret, a spiritual upthrust of happiness, in Grace Noll Crowell's lines:

I SHALL BE GLAD

If I can put new hope within the heart
Of one who has lost hope,
If I can help a brother up
Some difficult long slope
That seems too steep for tired feet to go,
If I can help him climb
Into the light upon the hill's far crest,
I shall begrudge no time

Or strength that I can spend, for well I know
How great may be his need.
If I can help through any darkened hour,
I shall be glad indeed.

For I recall how often I have been
Distressed, distraught, dismayed,
And hands have reached to help, and voices called
That kept me unafraid.
If I can share this help that I have had,
God knows I shall be glad.

It is a fact, of course, that love is a basic source of happiness and the zest for life. Whenever one is captured, that person is bound to find a whole new and exciting world and becomes capable of a new sensitivity to people, to beauty, to everything enthralling everywhere. I wonder if you remember that book of years ago *Good-Bye Mr. Chips* by James Hilton. It was read through laughter and some tears by multitudes. Mr. Chipping (Chips), the delightful master at Brookfield, an old English school, came to be loved by everyone, and it was because love made him joyful, and he in turn transmitted joy to all who came under the charm of his personality. Here are a few excerpts from this heartwarming story:

> . . . his marriage was a triumphant success. Katherine conquered Brookfield as she had conquered Chips; she was immensely popular with boys and masters alike. Even the wives of the masters, tempted at first to be jealous of one so young and lovely, could not long resist her charms. . . .
>
> But most remarkable of all was the change she made in Chips. Till his marriage he had been a dry and rather neutral sort of person; liked and thought well of by Brookfield in general, but not of the stuff that makes for great popularity or that stirs great affection . . . now came love, the sudden love of boys for a man who was kind without being soft, who understood them well enough, but not too much, and whose private happiness linked them with their own. He began to make little jokes, the sort that schoolboys like—mnemonics and puns that raised laughs and at the same time imprinted something in the mind. . . .

[Mr. Chips is called out of retirement during World War I and when the Head of Brookfield dies, he is made Acting Head of Brookfield "for the duration."]

> He was a grand success altogether. In some strange way he did, and they all knew and felt it, help things. For the first time in his life he felt *necessary*—and necessary to something that was nearest his heart. There is no sublimer feeling in the world, and it was his at last.

He made new jokes, too—about the O.T.C. and the food-rationing system and the anti-air-raid blinds that had to be fitted on all the windows. There was a mysterious kind of rissole that began to appear on the School menu on Mondays, and Chips called it abhorrendum—"meat to be abhored." The story went round—heard Chips's latest? . . .

Laughter . . . laughter . . . wherever he went and whatever he said, there was laughter. He had earned the reputation of being a great jester, and jests were expected of him. Whenever he rose to speak at a meeting, or even when he talked across a table, people prepared their minds and faces for the joke. They listened in a mood to be amused and it was easy to satisfy them. They laughed sometimes before he came to the point. "Old Chips was in fine form," they would say, afterward. "Marvelous the way he can always see the funny side of things. . . ."

[After another retirement he still keeps in touch with the current students as well as former ones. They drop in for tea and he is over at Brookfield frequently.]

About a quarter to four a ring came, and Chips, answering the front door himself (which he oughtn't to have done), encountered a rather small boy wearing a Brookfield cap and an expression of anxious timidity. "Please, sir," he began, "does Mr. Chips live here?"

"Umph—you'd better come inside," Chips answered. And in his room a moment later he added: "I am—umph—the person you want. Now what can I—umph—do for you?"

"I was told you wanted me, sir."

Chips smiled. An old joke—an old leg-pull, and he, of all people, having made so many old jokes in his time, ought not to complain. And it amused him to cap their joke, as it were, with one of his own; to let them see that he could keep his end up, even yet. So he said, with eyes twinkling: "Quite right, my boy. I wanted you to take tea with me. Will you— umph—sit down by the fire? Umph—I don't think I have seen your face before. How is that?"

"I've only just come out of the sanatorium, sir—I've been there since the beginning of term with measles."

"Ah, that accounts for it."

Chips began his usual ritualistic blending of tea from the different caddies; luckily there was half a walnut cake with pink icing in the cupboard. He found out that the boy's name was Linford, that he lived in Shropshire, and that he was the first of his family at Brookfield.

"You know—umph—Linford—you'll like Brookfield—when you get used to it. It's not half such an awful place—as you imagine. You're a bit afraid of it—um, yes—eh? So was I, my dear boy—at first. But that was— um—a long time ago. Sixty-three years ago—umph—to be precise. When I—um—first went into Big Hall and—um—I saw all those boys—I tell you—I was quite scared. Indeed—umph—I don't think I've ever been so scared in my life. Not even when—umph—the Germans bombed us—

during the War. But—umph—it didn't last long—the scared feeling, I mean. I soon made myself—um—at home."

"Were there a lot of other new boys that term, sir?" asked Linford shyly.

"Eh? But—God bless my soul—I wasn't a boy at all—I was a man—a young man of twenty-two! And the next time you see a young man—a new master—taking his first prep in Big Hall—umph—just think—what it feels like!"

"But if you were twenty-two then, sir—"

"Yes? Eh?"

"You must be—very old—now, sir."

Chips laughed quietly and steadily to himself. It was a good joke.

"Well—umph—I'm certainly—umph—no chicken."

There is still another source one can call upon to help keep the spirit built up and that is good old nature, the great mother and teacher of us all. There one can, if one will listen, and look, and meditate, find the great and loving God, the Creator of nature, who speaks to every seeking heart through His marvelous, powerful and exquisite handiwork.

Anne Frank found it so despite the tragedies:

> The best remedy for those who are afraid, lonely or unhappy is to go outside, somewhere where they can be quite alone with the heavens, nature, and God. Because only then does one feel that all is as it should be and that God wishes to see people happy, amidst the simple beauty of nature. As long as this exists, and it certainly always will, I know that then there will always be comfort for every sorrow, whatever the circumstances may be.

I believe it was Emerson who said, "The sky is the daily bread of the eyes." I recall one crystal-clear, crisp day on the far western prairie when I became acutely conscious of the vast, unobstructed expanse of the sky from horizon to horizon. I watched it for hours—the changing light and shadow, the appearance and disappearance of fleecy clouds now enormous, now small floating ships of white in a great canopy of blue. It was indeed food for the eyes and the soul.

Alfred Kreymborg has a line that is memorable and it makes one glad just to read it:

> The sky is that beautiful old parchment in which the sun and the moon keep their diary.

And John Ruskin, whose garden I have several times visited in northern England, reminds us that:

> Nature is painting for us, day after day, pictures of infinite beauty if only we have eyes to see them.

That thought about the sky being food for the soul is echoed by Luther Burbank, who said:

> Flowers always make people better, happier and more helpful; they are sunshine, food and medicine to the soul.

As a student in college I fell under the charm of the English poet William Wordsworth and have several times journeyed to Tintern Abbey, that storied and romantic ruin on the river Wye in Wales. C.S. Lewis describes it well:

> It is an abbey practically intact except that the roof is gone, and the glass out of the windows, and the floor instead of a pavement is a trim green lawn. Anything like the sweetness and peace of the long shafts of sunlight falling through the windows on the grass cannot be imagined. All churches should be roofless. A holier place I never saw.

Always at Tintern Abbey I have shared Wordsworth's feeling of joy and deeply moving inspiration which he describes in a famous sentence:

> ... And I have felt
> A presence that disturbs me with the
>   joy
> Of elevated thoughts; ...

Again and still again I have visited the poet's cottage at Grassmere and have wandered over the Lake district at daffodil time looking for the spot where he saw "a crowd, a host, of golden daffodils." And I will always believe I found the spot on that sun-swept day when, by Ullswater, I saw *my* crowd of daffodils "beside the lake, beneath the trees, fluttering and dancing in the breeze."

Man is nature's child and therefore God's child. And when he turns for a build-up of spirit to the woods and seas and waterfalls and meadows lying in the sun, the upthrust will come surging into his heart.

Faith is the great restorer of spirit. When one has faith nothing can crush him—not even death itself. For faith gives the glorious insight that life in spirit is deathless." ... because I live, ye shall live also" (John 14:19).

For years I have been recording a series of incidents which bear out the conviction that life, not death, is the basic principle of our universe. From them I have gained the unshakable belief that there is no death, that here and hereafter are one. When I reached this conclusion, I found it to be the most satisfying and convincing philosophy of my entire life. Following are the experiences which convinced me that human spirits on both sides of death live in a fellowship that continues unbroken.

H. B. Clarke, an old friend of mine, was of a scientific turn of mind, restrained, factual, unemotional. I was called one night by his physician, who expected him to live only a few hours.

I prayed for him, as did others. The next day his eyes opened and after a few days he recovered his speech. His heart action returned to normal. After he recovered strength he said, "At some time during my illness something very peculiar happened to me. It seemed that I was a long distance away, in the most beautiful and attractive place I have ever seen. There were lights all about me. I saw faces dimly revealed—kind faces they were—and I felt peaceful and happy. In fact, I never felt happier.

"The thought came, 'I must be dying.' Then it occurred to me, 'Perhaps I have died.' I almost laughed out loud, and asked myself, 'Why have I been afraid of death all my life? There is nothing to be afraid of in this.'"

"Did you want to live?" I asked.

He smiled and said, "It did not make the slightest difference. If anything, I think I would have preferred to stay in that beautiful place."

Hallucination? A dream? A vision? I do not believe so. I have spent too many years talking to people who have come to the edge of "something" and had a look across, who unanimously have reported beauty, light and peace, to have any doubt in my mind.

A member of my church, Mrs. Bryson Kalt, tells of an aunt whose husband and three children were burned to death when their house was destroyed by fire. The aunt was badly burned but lived for three years. When finally she lay dying, a radiance suddenly came over her face. "It is all so beautiful," she said. "They are coming to meet me. Fluff up my pillows and let me go to sleep."

Friends of mine, Mr. and Mrs. William Sage, lived in New Jersey and I was often in their home. Then Will Sage died. A few years later, when Mrs. Sage was on her deathbed, the most surprised look passed across her face. It lighted up in a wonderful smile as she said, "Why, it is Will!" That she saw him those about her bed had no doubt whatsoever.

The late Rufus Jones had a son, Lowell, the apple of his eye. The boy became sick when Dr. Jones was on the ocean, bound for Europe. The night before entering Liverpool, while lying in his bunk, Dr. Jones experienced an indefinable, unexplainable sadness. Then, he said, he seemed to be enveloped in the arms of God. A great feeling of peace and a sense of profound possession of his son came to him.

Upon landing in Liverpool, he was advised that Lowell had died; the death had occurred at the exact moment when Dr. Jones had felt God's presence and the everlasting nearness of his son.

A boy serving in the war in Korea wrote to his mother, saying, "The strangest things happen to me. Once in a while at night, when I am afraid, Dad seems to be with me." His father had been dead for ten years. "Do you think that Dad can actually be with me here on these Korean battlefields?"

Why not? How can we not believe that this could be true? Again and again proofs are offered that this universe is a great spiritual sounding house, alive and vital.

My mother was a great soul, and her influence on me will ever stand out in my life as an experience that cannot be surpassed. During my adult years, whenever I had the opportunity, I went home to see her. It was always an exciting experience.

Then came her death, and in the fullness of summertime we tenderly laid her body in the beautiful little cemetery at Lynchburg in southern Ohio, a town where she had lived as a girl.

It came autumn, and I felt that I wanted to be with my mother again. I was lonely without her, so I went to Lynchburg. The weather was cold and the sky overcast as I walked to the cemetery. I pushed through the old iron gates and my feet rustled in the leaves as I walked to her grave, where I sat sad and lonely. But of a sudden the clouds parted and the sun came through.

Then I seemed to hear her voice. The message was clear and distinct, stated in her beloved old-time tone: "Why seek ye the living among the dead? I am not here. I am with you and my loved ones always."

In a burst of inner light I became wondrously happy. I knew that what I had heard was the truth. I stood up and put my hand on the tombstone and saw it for what it was: only a place where mortal remains lay. But she, that gloriously lovely spirit, is still with us, her loved ones.

The New Testament teaches the indestructibility of life. It describes Jesus after His Crucifixion in a series of disappearances and reappearances. This indicates He is trying to tell us that when we do not see Him, it does not mean He is not there. Out of sight does not mean out of life.

The mystical appearances which some of us today experience indicate the same truth: that He is near. Did He not say, "Because I live, ye shall live also"? In other words, our loved ones who have died in this faith are also nearby, and occasionally draw near to comfort us.

The Bible gives other insights into the great question, "What happens when a man leaves this world?" And it wisely tells us that we know these truths by faith. The surest way into truth, says Henri Bergson, the philosopher, is by perception, by intuition; by reasoning to a certain point, then taking a "mortal leap." You come to that glorious moment when you simply "know" the truth.

Of these deep and tender matters I have no doubt whatsoever. I firmly believe in the continuation of life after what we call death takes place. I believe there are two sides to the phenomenon known as death: this side where we now live, and the other side where we shall continue to live. Eternity does not start with death. We are in eternity now. We merely change the form of the experience called life—and that change, I am persuaded, is for the better.

Recently I read a curious but fascinating dissertation called "Wise Animals I Have Known" by Alan Devoe. Animals, as I have observed them, are not tense or worried. They seem quietly and calmly to live under the protection of God. And it is wonderful how animals seem to avoid being infected by the uptightness of humans. Living with them makes its contribution to the uplifted spirit:

If I live to be 80 and still greet the morning with a praise like prayer, it will not be from anything I have read in books of philosophy. It will be because I knew animals.

They are very close, said Saint Francis, to the paternal heart of God. I think they must be. By instinct an animal puts infinite trust in life.

This morning at sunrise I watched Thomas, our cat, greet the new day. Thomas is now (in human terms) going on for 80. Every morning I share daybreak with him. It is great medicine. First there is his rush up the cellar stairs, lithe and springy as a tiger, from the place where he sleeps by the furnace. While I fix his food I watch him. He always begins with the ritual of str-*etch*-ing. Nothing trivial or hasty, mind you, but a leisurely, carefully relished luxury that does him as much good as a vacation. Left front paw, right front paw, now both hind legs, now a long bend of the back . . . *aaah!* A brisk shake; the big green eyes open wide; the ears perk up.

He dashes to the French window, rears up with forepaws on the glass, and peers out all quivering and tail twitching with excitement. Sunshine! Trees! Great heaven, there is a leaf blowing hop-skip across the lawn! Thomas has looked out through this same pane hundreds of mornings, but every time it is fresh and challenging and wonderful.

And so with breakfast. You'd think he had never seen this old chipped dish before. He pounces on his food like a man finding uranium. Then, when the last bit has been neatly licked from the plate, comes the ecstatic moment for going out to the new day.

Thomas never just goes through the doorway. (Animals don't take these moments lightly.) First he glides *half*way through, then stands drinking in the sounds, scents, sights out there. Another inch or two and he stands again. At last, very slowly, he slips over the threshold. If so much wonder were to hit Thomas all at once he could hardly stand it.

Now he rushes to the middle of the lawn and there this octogenarian performs a riotous caper. He takes a flying jump at nothing in particular, then zigzags after nonexistent mice. He leaps in the air and claps his paws on invisible butterflies. Then some quick flip-flops, rolling over and over, all four paws waving. In a minute it is finished and he steps gravely off to his day's adventures.

What better lesson in living could one have? Here is joy in every moment, an awareness of the electric excitement of the earth and all that's in it. One further lesson from Thomas: when he sleeps, he *sleeps*. He curls up in a ball, puts one paw over the top of his head and turns himself over to God.

All animals give themselves wholeheartedly to the joy of being. At dusk in my woods flying squirrels play aerial roller-coaster. I have seen an old fox batting a stick in absorbed rapture for half an hour. Children react thus simply to the world about them, before reason steps in to complicate their lives. . . .

If animals can be said to have a philosophy, it is as simple as this: When Nature says, "I give you the glory of the senses and of awareness, and the splendor of earth," surrender yourself to these things, not worrying if it looks undignified to turn somersaults at 80. When the word is "Fight!" pitch in and fight, not weighing hesitant thoughts about prudence.

"Rest," says your monitor. "Play." "Sleep." "Feed and breed and doze in God's green shade by the brookside," each in its season. Heed the voice and act. It is a simple philosophy. It holds the strength of the world.

Animals do not know worry. . . .

An animal doesn't know what brotherhood means, but when it hears the call "Help!" it answers instinctively. . . .

Not only do the wild things meet life in all its aspects wholeheartedly; they greet death the same way. "Sleep now, and rest," says Nature at the end. . . .

In animals shines the trust that casts out fear.

I have always observed that people who keep company with the natural world, who live with mountains, plains, lakes, with the sun and the wind, the moon and the stars, are peaceful, joyous men and women, and they are nourished in their souls by a spirit that can flow only from God. So John Muir writes.

> Climb the mountains and get their good tidings. Nature's peace will flow into you as sunshine flows into trees. The winds will flow their own freshness into you and the storms their energy, while cares will drop off like autumn leaves.

The greatest of all earthly mysteries perhaps lies in the astonishing potential built into a person that can be released by a change to a positive attitude. As William James said:

> The greatest discovery of my generation is that human beings can alter their lives by altering their attitudes of mind.

Finally, to help in always keeping a built-up spirit, I give you three of the great promises that lead to a joyous and enthusiastic life:

. . . In the world ye shall have tribulation: but be of good cheer; I have overcome the world.

John 16:33

Hitherto have ye asked nothing in my name; ask, and ye shall receive, that your joy may be full.

John 16:24

Jesus said unto him, If thou canst believe, all things are possible to him that believeth.

Mark 9:23

9

JOY AND ENTHUSIASM IN A WORLD OF BEAUTY

"THIS IS THE DAY which the Lord hath made; we will rejoice and be glad in it." So says Psalms 118:24.

I have recommended that one magnificent salutation to the day to thousands of people in scores of audiences across the land and in foreign nations for many years. And I can factually and gratefully report that it has changed lives wherever it has become part of the daily experience. It has helped make happy and positive individuals out of those who previously had been desultory, defeated and negative. These people have discovered that the practice of a joyous and enthusiastic attitude every day results in one's days becoming so conditioned.

For one thing, such a positive attitude puts one into harmony with this world of beauty, with nature itself. The famous London preacher who creatively touched the lives of thousands a century ago expressed this harmony in an impressive statement. Charles H. Spurgeon said:

> Doth not all nature around me praise God? If I were silent, I should be an exception to the universe. Doth not the thunder praise Him as it rolls like drums in the march of the God of armies? Do not the mountains praise Him when the woods upon their summits wave in adoration? Does not the lightning write His name in letters of fire? Hath not the whole earth a voice? And shall I, can I, silent be?

I have long been a reader of Hal Borland, who, in his *Hill Country Harvest* and other writings, has the power to lead us along familiar roads into nature's beauty with a sensitivity that opens up whole new areas of meaning:

> There are two times in the year when any person with a grain of sense, or sensitivity, can't stay indoors. One is in the spring, usually late April, when the outdoor world is on tip-toe, ready to burst into spring. That is the time when one walking along a country road or taking his time across an open meadow and along the edge of a woodland is privileged to participate in a kind of annual genesis. The other time is right after the first hard frost.

The color hasn't yet vanished, but a good deal of it is down out of the treetops. Quite a few maples and most of the oaks on my own mountainside are still full of leaves, but when I walk there I am ankle-deep in crisp gold and crimson. The roadsides are scuffing, and every breeze is full of leaves, it seems. If I pause beside a clump of sumac I am sure to be showered with color, for the sumac leaves are so loose that even my own breath will bring a few floating down. And when I stand beneath a red oak I can't believe there are so many leaves still on the tree because the ground seems to be covered with them. Which proves only that even an oak, which hasn't as many leaves as a maple the same size, has more leaves than I could count in a week.

I come to a tangle of tall weeds, mostly goldenrod and milkweed. The goldenrod is all brown stems and shriveled leaves, but the gray fluff of its seed plumes is like mist, riding every breath of air. And the milkweeds are a golden beauty, the leaves startlingly yellow, yellower than willow leaves. The pods, still gray-green, are already spilling their silken contents, and when the breeze passes it takes on the shimmer of milkweed floss.

At the roadside stands a tree that I knew in boyhood as a box elder. There's not a leaf left on it, but its twigs are loaded with brown tassels of seed, keys like those of the sugar maples in front of my house. This tree, of course, is one of the maple family, the ash-leaved maple; the keys prove it, and if there were further doubt one could tap it in early spring and make syrup from its sap. Just beyond is a barberry bush, its leaves deep purple, its berries brilliant scarlet. It stands in a fencerow, obviously planted there by the birds, as are most of the barberries that grow at the roadside. And the birds busy at this bush right now will plant still more barberries along other fencerows. Just as they have planted that golden tuft of asparagus that shines in the sunlight. I never notice how much asparagus grows wild until autumn, when the fine-cut fern foliage turns that unmistakable golden yellow, twinkling with ripe red berries.

Wild grape leaves are a rich tan. I have to stop and pluck one and feel its texture, which is almost exactly like that of a paper napkin. And while I am standing there I wonder which birds ate all the berries from the big, red-stemmed pokeweed. There's not one berry left, nothing but the wine-red splay of empty stems where the purple-black berries hung in a loose panicle two weeks ago. Those berries are mildly poisonous to people, but apparently the birds have no trouble digesting them. Glancing at the wild grape vine again I look for bunches of fruit, see only the empty stems and remember the October evening when I found a possum in a tangle of wild grape vines, stained with their juice from black nose tip to his very paws. Possums like those little grapes. So do foxes, though I never caught a fox as red-handed as I did that possum.

The asters are looking rather sad, though here and there I find a few big purples that evidently opened after the night of hard frost. They are particularly gay looking, and their golden centers look almost orange. And here is a bunch of bouncing Bet, still blooming bravely though its leaves are rather forlorn. But when I look up the hillside I see a stand of Christmas fern, its fronds as lively and green as they were in July. This fern pays little heed to the weather, though its cousins are brown as oak leaves, crisp as corn flakes.

A small flock of flickers comes swooping across the pasture, and as they go past I see the white rump patches. They won't be here much longer. As I follow their flight I know that they, too, are seeing the distant horizon as neither they nor I have seen it since last April. There it is, in plain sight through the bare branches of the trees, and those few trees still in leaf only make the new openness more noticeable.

The world has new dimensions now. It has broadened beyond summer belief. It summons the flickers to migration, and it summons me to reach and travel at least with my mind and my imagination. Valleys broaden now, and hilltops are out in the open. This is a world complete for another season, and if I do not go out and see it I am without understanding of creation itself.

Perhaps the greatest naturalist in American history was that lover of nature and teacher of its wise and healing secrets. John Burroughs writes:

If I were to name the three most precious resources of life, I should say books, friends, and nature; and the greatest of these, at least the most constant and always at hand, is nature. Nature we have always with us, an inexhaustible storehouse of that which moves the heart, appeals to the mind, and fires the imagination—health to the body, a stimulus to the intellect, and joy to the soul. To the scientist, nature is a storehouse of facts, laws, processes; to the artist she is a storehouse of pictures; to the poet she is a storehouse of images, fancies, a source of inspiration; to the moralist she is a storehouse of precepts and parables; to all she may be a source of knowledge and joy.

And John Kendrick Bangs, who evidently tried to convince someone of the presence of God, gives us a rather thoughtful poem:

BLIND

"Show me your God!" the doubter
    cries.
I point him to the smiling skies;
I show him all the woodland greens;
I show him peaceful sylvan scenes;
I show him winter snows and frost;
I show him waters tempest-tossed;
I show him hills rock-ribbed and
    strong;
I bid him hear the thrush's song;
I show him flowers in the close—

The lily, violet, and rose;
I show him rivers, babbling streams;
I show him youthful hopes and dreams;
I show him maids with eager hearts;
I show him toilers in the marts;
I show him stars, the moon, the sun;
I show him deeds of kindness done;
I show him joy; I show him care;
And still he holds his doubting air,
And faithless goes his way, for he
Is blind of soul, and cannot see!

But Emerson, with his usual sensitivity and depth of insight, saw God everywhere in the beauty of the world and it became a blessing to him:

> Never lose an opportunity of seeing anything that is beautiful; for beauty is God's handwriting—a wayside sacrament. Welcome it in every fair face, in every fair sky, in every fair flower, and thank God for it as a cup of blessing.

A world of joyousness and enthusiasm, of delight and wonder is about us on every hand, but, unhappily, even the most amazing wonders can become commonplace through constancy of repetition. As Henry Wadsworth Longfellow says:

> If spring came but once in a century instead of once a year, or burst forth with the sound of an earthquake and not in silence, what wonder and expectation there would be in all hearts to behold the miraculous change.

An unknown author describes what we may find in this glorious God's world and our world to make us happy and surcharge us with enthusiasm for life.

THE DAWN

One morn I rose and looked upon the world.
"Have I been blind until this hour?" I said.
On every trembling leaf the sun had spread,
And was like golden tapestry unfurled;
And as the moments passed more light was hurled
Upon the drinking earth athirst for light;
And I, beholding all this wondrous sight,
Cried out aloud, "O God, I love Thy world!"
And since that waking, often I drink deep

The joy of dawn, and peace abides with me;
And though I know that I again shall see
Dark fear with withered hand approach my sleep,
More sure am I when lonely night shall flee,
At dawn the sun will bring good cheer to me.

Admiral Richard E. Byrd, in the frozen world of the South Pole listening to the vast and impalpable silence, found peace and God in the frigid twilight:

I paused to listen to the silence. My breath, crystallized as it passed my cheeks, drifted on a breeze gentler than a whisper. The wind vane pointed toward the South Pole. Presently the wind cups ceased their gentle turning as the cold killed the breeze. My frozen breath hung like a cloud overhead.

The day was dying, the night was being born—but with great peace. Here were the imponderable processes and forces of the cosmos, harmonious and soundless. Harmony, that was it! That was what came out of the silence—a gentle rhythm, the strain of a perfect chord, the music of the spheres, perhaps.

It was enough to catch that rhythm, momentarily to be myself a part of it. In that instant I could feel no doubt of man's oneness with the universe. The conviction came that that rhythm was too orderly, too harmonious, too perfect to be a product of blind chance—that, therefore, there must be purpose in the whole and that man was part of that whole and not an accidental offshoot. It was a feeling that transcended reason; that went to the heart of man's despair and found it groundless. The universe was a cosmos, not a chaos; man was as rightfully a part of that cosmos as were the day and night.

Charles A. Lindbergh, always a seeker after peace, found it alone one time especially. It was on his immortal and fabulous flight in the *Spirit of St. Louis*:

It's hard to be an agnostic up here in the *Spirit of St. Louis*, aware of the frailty of man's devices, a part of the universe between its earth and stars. If one dies, all this goes on existing in a plan so perfectly balanced, so wonderfully simple, so incredibly complex that it's far beyond our comprehension— worlds and moons revolving; planets orbiting on suns; suns flung with apparent recklessness through space. There's the infinite magnitude of the universe; there's the infinite detail of its matter—the outer star, the inner atom. And man conscious of it all—a worldly audience to what if not to God?

Jesus was the greatest intellectual who ever lived. He cut through all philosophizing by asking, "You want to be happy? Then love people and trust them."

I am enthusiastic about people. One of the happiest places I ever visited is one that used to be called a Reform School for Boys. (Now they have better names for such schools.) But no one visiting there would have thought it had anything to do with delinquent boys. It might have been Hotchkiss, Taft, Deerfield, Groton—any preparatory school. Living in a cottage system, the boys were fine, radiant-looking, manly and polite.

The school was established by Floyd Starr, who got the idea for it when he was four years old. Some visitor in his home told about adopting fifty homeless boys. The story fascinated the little boy, and he told his mother he was going to adopt fifty boys when he grew up. They laughed at him, of course. But, in college, just before graduation, when a group was sitting around in the fraternity house telling each other what they were going to do after commencement, Starr said, "I am going to adopt fifty of the worst boys I can find. I am going to love them and trust them into becoming great men. I don't think there is such a thing as a bad boy." They laughed at him again and said it couldn't be done. But today his establishment is "Starr Commonwealth for Boys" in Michigan.

The courts of Michigan will give any boy brought in for committing a crime the opportunity of going to Floyd Starr's school if he wishes. These boys are adjudged bad boys. One of them, sent from New Jersey, had the reputation of being the worst boy in the state. It was claimed that nothing could be done with him. Nevertheless on my recent visit when I helped dedicate a chapel, I saw this "bad boy" from New Jersey going around snuffing out candles and dressed in ecclesiastical costume. His face was radiant.

"He is going to be an Episcopal minister," Mr. Starr explained. "I do not care what boys have done. I am only interested in what they are and what they are going to be. I never look at a case history.

He had one of these boys drive him one evening to a meeting fifty miles away. When they arrived, he gave the boy a five-dollar bill, told him to get his supper and come back and pick him up about nine o'clock. Right on the dot of nine the boy arrived and handed him the change from the bill.

On the way home the boy said, "Uncle Floyd, you trust me, don't you?"

"Certainly," Mr. Starr answered.

"Why do you?" the boy asked. "You're the first one who ever did."

"Bill," Mr. Starr explained, "I trust you because I love you and believe in you."

"But, Uncle Floyd," the boy persisted, "don't you know why they sent me to your school?"

"No, Bill," he said, "I haven't the slightest idea."

Then the boy told him. He had come home one night to find an ambulance in front of his house. His father, drunk, had stabbed his mother. They were taking her to the hospital; they didn't expect her to live.

"They were drunk and swearing all the time," the boy said. "My father is in state prison now. I joined up with a gang and got away with plenty for a long time. They sent me here for stealing cars. And tonight you let me have your own car."

Mr. Starr slipped an arm around the boy's shoulders. "You are never going to steal cars again," he said.

Once in a while you meet a man so Christlike that it moves you to the depths of your heart. Such a man is Starr. As someone remarked to me during my visit, "What makes this such a happy place is that Starr-dust gets all over you."

In some schools of this kind, rehabilitation is 34 percent. Starr's record is 94 percent. Psychiatrists have told him he is foolish not to read the case histories. I think his results justify his methods.

Doesn't it make you happy to hear me tell about this man and his work? If you want to be happy in an unhappy world, quit hating people; quit hating anybody. Just skip it. Go around loving people. Believe in them. Where all other books fail, the Bible keeps on going because it gives us the technique for happy living in an unhappy world. "In him was life; and the life was the light of men" (John 1:4). That is the avenue to the joyous and enthusiastic life.

It has been a habit of ours—of my wife, Ruth, and me—to go to the Swiss Alps for a time each year. Usually we have a writing assignment which we tell ourselves we can do best among the snowy peaks and high alpine meadows.

During this time, we work every morning until nearly noon, then go to the small symphony orchestra concerts in the village. They always play the great and inspiring masterpieces. Then we set out onto the mountain paths winding through the valleys and rising among the cliffs, along surging and foaming streams that dash swiftly down to the strong flowing rivers below. All through the summer afternoons we walk six to eight miles, until the shadows begin to lengthen. Then we return to our hotel and soak in a hot bath before dinner, and then early to bed.

For years this has been part of our annual program of work and renewal. Always it has been a source of inexpressible joy and enthusiasm for this glorious world of beauty and for the even greater beauty of the people we have known. It all seemed to be perfectly summed up one Sunday at evensong in the little chapel by the lake shore where, in the German language, the congregation was singing a hymn long known to us, one which united the beauty of nature and of man in the creative harmony of Almighty God:

FOR THE BEAUTY OF THE EARTH

For the beauty of the earth,
   For the beauty of the skies,
For the love which from our birth
   Over and around us lies,
Lord of all, to Thee we raise
This our hymn of grateful praise.

For the beauty of each hour
   Of the day and of the night,
Hill and vale, and tree and flower,
   Sun and moon, and stars of light,
Lord of all, to Thee we raise
This our hymn of grateful praise.

For the joy of ear and eye,
   For the heart and mind's delight,
For the mystic harmony
   Linking sense to sound and sight,
Lord of all, to Thee we raise
This our hymn of grateful praise.

For the joy of human love,
   Brother, sister, parent, child,
Friends on earth, and friends above,
   For all gentle thoughts and mild,
Lord of all, to Thee we raise
This our hymn of grateful praise.

For each perfect gift of Thine,
   To our race so freely given,
Graces human and divine,
   Flowers of earth, and buds of heaven,
Lord of all, to Thee we raise
This our hymn of grateful praise.

FOLLIOTT SANDFORD PIERPOINT

As the words of the old hymn of praise wafted out that evening over the sweet-scented meadows and seemed to flow in melody up the nearby mountainsides, we were filled with an indescribable love of all things and all people and with an overwhelming love of life itself. I found myself thinking of some words of Dostoyevsky, one of my favorite writers, which later I looked up again and give you here:

Love all God's creation, the whole and every grain of sand in it. Love every leaf, every ray of God's light. Love the animals, love the plants, love everything. If you love everything, you will perceive the divine mystery in things. Once you perceive it, you will begin to comprehend it better every day. And you will come at last to love the whole world with an all-embracing love.

And when one heeds that injunction, the result will be a love of the world which will manifest itself in a new and sensitized love of life itself. This in turn will activate joy and enthusiasm in full measure. Such joy, perhaps, as that which is described by John Kendrick Bangs:

TODAY

Today, whatever may annoy,
The word for me is Joy, just simple joy:
The joy of life;
The joy of children and of wife;
The joy of bright, blue skies;
The joy of rain; the glad surprise
Of twinkling stars that shine at night;
The joy of winged things upon their flight;
The joy of noonday, and the tried
True joyousness of eventide;
The joy of labor, and of mirth;
The joy of air, and sea, and earth—
The countless joys that ever flow from Him
Whose vast beneficence doth dim
The lustrous light of day,
And lavish gifts divine upon our way.
Whate'er there be of Sorrow
I'll put off till Tomorrow,
And when Tomorrow comes, why then
'Twill be Today and Joy again!

But some respond dolefully to these positive attitudes, objecting that neither joy nor enthusiasm nor excitement nor delight are possible when adversity stalks life; when one is ill or weak or blind or afflicted with multiple woes. But the great Helen Keller did not allow her handicaps to keep joy away, as she tells us exultantly:

IN THE GARDEN OF THE LORD

The word of God came unto me,
Sitting alone among the multitudes;

And my blind eyes were touched with light,
And there was laid upon my lips a flame of fire.

I laugh and shout for life is good,
Though my feet are set in silent ways.
In merry mood I leave the crowd
To walk in my garden. Even as I walk
I gather fruits and flowers in my hands,
And with joyful heart I bless the sun
That kindles all the place with radiant life.
I run with playful winds that blow the scent
Of rose and jasmine in eddying whirls.

At last I come where tall lilies grow,
Lifting their faces like white saints to God.
While the lilies pray, I kneel upon the ground:
I have strayed into the holy temple of the Lord.

Some of life's best lessons are taught by things like trees, for example. At our place on Quaker Hill in Pawling, New York, which we call The Hill Farm, our family has learned much from wise old Mother Nature.

One thing is how trees handle storms. They move with the wind as it mounts in intensity, not with fear of the tempest nor by resisting it. They just bend with it, and as the tumult and force of a line storm gale increases, the boiling of the leaves of the gigantic old maples seems as if the tree is laughing with glee in the knowledge that it can ride out the storm, which it always seems to do. Next morning the storm is over and the sun is out. The ground may be strewn with leaves and twigs and perhaps a branch or two, which was about to be discarded by the tree anyway. But the tree still stands and actually is stronger than ever, having wrestled with and overcome another storm in its long life.

This tells us something about how we human beings can also ride out our storms in life. Bend with the wind. Lean against it. Laugh with it. Rejoice in struggle. It grows you strong.

I like the way pine trees handle a big snowfall. The accumulating snows lie heavy on the supple branches, but those branches seldom break. They just yield gracefully to the extra weight of the snow. And in due course the pine tree's friends, the wind and the sun, either blow it off or melt it, and then the branches slowly—never hurriedly—come back to normal position—which isn't a bad technique for a person to learn!

And then I cannot fail to mention our cherished old apple tree. It must be at least a hundred years old. Once it was quite large for its species; perhaps three feet thick, with a wide spread of branches. But now the trunk has been reduced to a width of no more than three or four inches, and at its center is a large hole two feet long and eight inches wide. But even this reduced trunk sturdily holds up the spread of branches. The tree is in a spot protected from the main force of winds, but it gets its share of the wind, rain, ice and snow in the changing seasons.

I marvel at this tree, for it is old and reduced in structure, its youth and the vigor of its prime gone. But it does not know that it is old and weakened. Every springtime it puts out its blossoms, as it always has done, and as a matter of fact it seems to outdo the blossom business, for its branches are overwhelmingly full of pinkish-white blooms, and it is a sight to behold.

Then come the apples. We never have sprayed this old tree, but even so the fruit is crisp and juicy, apart from a few worms and rough spots. Ruth makes delicious applesauce from them. The tree demonstrates a powerful loyalty to its purpose, which is of course to put out leaves in the spring, to blossom and to produce apples in the fall; and it just continues, with fidelity to its purpose in being, to do that despite age and decrepitude. So every year, spring and fall, I go and stand beneath its spreading branches and reverently salute the old tree as my teacher, saying to it, "Dear old apple tree, I am going to keep on doing my job and I hope to do it as well as you do yours."

As long as I live and own the place, that tree will never be cut down, unless some winter gale proves too strong for it. Then I will sadly yield it to time and the elements, but cherish it forever in memory.

Henry David Thoreau, one of that small coterie of thinkers who really set the tone of early America, writes of snowflakes, and that, too, is a big part of the New England-New York State country heritage:

SWEEPINGS OF HEAVEN'S FLOOR

Nature is full of genius, full of the divinity, so that not a snowflake escapes its fashioning hand. Nothing is cheap and coarse, neither dewdrops nor snowflakes.

Myriads of these little disks, so beautiful to the most prying eyes, are whirled down on every traveler's coat, the observant and the unobservant, on the restless squirrel's fur, on the far-stretching fields and forests, the wooded dells and mountain tops.

Far, far away from the haunts of men, they roll down some little slope, fall over and come to their bearings, and melt or lose their beauty in the mass, ready anon to swell some little rill with their contribution, and so, at last, the universal ocean from which they came. There they lie, like the wreck of chariot wheels after a battle in the sky.

Meanwhile the meadow mouse shoves them aside in his gallery, the school boy casts them in his snowball, or the woodman's sled glides smoothly over them, these glorious spangles, these sweepings of heaven's floor.

And they all sing, melting as they sing, of the mysteries of the number six, six, six, six.

He takes up the water of the sea in His hand, leaving the salt; He dispenses it in mist through the sky, He re-collects and sprinkles it like grain in six-rayed stars over the earth, there to lie till it dissolves in bonds again.

And the Psalmist, with consummate descriptive skill, exalts the mighty power of God the Creator:

He formed the mountains by his mighty strength. He quiets the raging oceans and all the world's clamor. In the farthest corners of the earth the glorious acts of God shall startle everyone. The dawn and sunset shout for joy! He waters the earth to make it fertile. The rivers of God will not run dry! He prepares the earth for his people and sends them rich harvests of grain. He waters the furrows with abundant rain. Showers soften the earth, melting the clods and causing seeds to sprout across the land. Then he crowns it all with green, lush pastures in the wilderness; hillsides blossom with joy. The pastures are filled with flocks of sheep, and the valleys are carpeted with grain. All the world shouts with joy, and sings.

Psalms 65:6–13, TLB

From Tay Thomas (Mrs. Lowell Thomas, Jr.) comes a vivid description of the beauty of Alaska in autumn, from her book *Only in Alaska:*

One doesn't mind the loss of the flowers, however, when the trees and undergrowth begin to change their color. Accustomed as I was to the brilliance of New England falls, the bright, intense splash of colors here still leaves me breathless. Autumn is far too brief in the Far North—it lasts two or three weeks at the most—but nature seems determined to make up for the brevity by supplying the hues of yellows and reds in double strength. The small wild dogwood, lingonberry, and strawberry plants closest to the ground turn a deep red first, followed by the taller fireweed, wild rose, wild red currant, and rusty menziesia. Amid this bright red wild growth, the large leaves of the devil's-club turn a vivid yellow. Then the leaves of the birch and aspen become such a rich and brilliant gold that on clear days even the most unartistic person is highly tempted to reach for a paintbrush and try to capture the scene. And it isn't just the yellows and reds of the leaves—the waters of the lakes and the inlet turn an extra-deep blue, the birch bark seems whiter, and the mountains take on soft, gentle hues of red, beneath violet-colored peaks.

The blessings of life and the natural world confer upon the person of faith the healing, strengthening and hope needed to carry on valiantly day by day. As Fred Bauer tells us:

FOR QUIET I LIKE UNSPEAKING TREES

for quiet I like unspeaking trees
for cares a spirited mountain walk
for fulfillment someone to please
for laughter hearing children talk

for reassurance a hand to hold
for strength the persevering sea
for understanding a friendship old
for hope I turn to Thee

Charles A. Lindbergh, alone amidst the silent vastness of skies over the Atlantic, found the peace and greatness of God in moon flow:

I'd almost forgotten the moon. Now, like a neglected ally, it's coming to my aid. Every minute will bring improving sight. As the moon climbs higher in the sky, its light will brighten, until finally it ushers in the sun. The stars ahead are already fading. The time is 10:20. There have been only two hours of solid darkness.

Gradually, as light improves, the night's black masses turn into a realm of form and texture. Silhouettes give way to shadings. Clouds open their secret details to the eyes. In the moon's reflected light, they seem more akin to it than to the earth over which they hover. They form a perfect setting for that strange foreign surface one sees through a telescope trained on the satellite of the world. Formations of the moon, they are—volcanoes and flat plateaus; great towers and bottomless pits; crevasses and canyons; ledges no earthly mountains ever knew—reality combined with the fantasy of a dream. There are shapes like growths of coral on the bed of a tropical sea, or the grotesque canyons of sandstone and lava at the edge of Arizona deserts— first black, then gray, now greenish hue in cold, mystical light.

I weave in and out, eastward, toward Europe, hidden away in my plane's tiny cockpit, submerged, alone, in the magnitude of this weird, unhuman space, venturing where man has never been, irretrievably launched on a flight through this sacred garden of the sky, this inner shrine of higher spirits. Am I myself a living, breathing, earth-bound body, or is this a dream of death I'm passing through? Am I alive, or am I really dead, a spirit in a spirit world? Am I actually in a plane boring through the air, over the Atlantic, toward Paris, or have I crashed on some worldly mountains, and is this the afterlife?

For a moment the clouds give way, and the moon itself peers through a tremendous valley, flooding unearthly bluffs with its unearthly light, screening the eastern stars with its nearer, brighter glow, assuming mastery of the sky by night as does the sun by day.

Far ahead, a higher cloud layer is forming, thousands of feet above my level—glowing, horizontal strips, supported by thick pillars from the mass below—sculptured columns and arches to a temple of the moon. Has the sky opened only to close again? Will they finally merge, these clouds, to form one great mass of opaque air? Must I still turn back? *Can* I still turn back, or have I been lured to this forbidden temple to find all doors have closed? North, south, and west, clouds rise and tower; only the lighted corridors ahead are clear.

I've been tunneling by instruments through a tremendous cumulus mass. As I break out, a glaring valley lies across my path, miles in width, extending north and south as far as I can see. The sky is blue-white above, and the blinding fire of the sun itself has burst over the ridge ahead. I nose the *Spirit of St. Louis* down, losing altitude slowly, two hundred feet or so a minute. At eight thousand feet, I level out, plumbing with my eyes the depth of each chasm I pass over. In the bottom of one of them, I see it, like a rare stone perceived among countless pebbles at your feet—a darker, deeper shade, a different texture—the ocean! Its surface is splotched with white and covered with ripples. Ripples from eight thousand feet! That means a heavy sea.

It's one of those moments when all the senses rise together, and realization snaps so acute and clear that seconds impress themselves with the strength of years on memory. It forms a picture with colors that will hold and lines that will stay sharp throughout the rest of life—the broad, sun-dazzled valley in the sky; the funnel's billowing walls; and deep down below, the hard, blue-gray scales of the ocean.

Emerson would have understood the deep-level feelings of Lindbergh:

The man who has seen the rising moon break out of the clouds at midnight has been present like an archangel at the creation of light and of the world.

Taken all in all, the glory and wonder of this planet upon which we are permitted to live for a time brings us finally to sing with Maltbie D. Babcock that "This Is My Father's World":

This is my Father's world,
And to my listening ears,
All nature sings, and round me rings
The music of the spheres.
This is my Father's world:
I rest me in the thought
Of rocks and trees, of skies and seas;
His hand the wonders wrought.

This is my Father's world,
The birds their carols raise,
The morning light, the lily white,

Declare their Maker's praise.
This is my Father's world:
He shines in all that's fair;
In the rustling grass I hear Him pass,
He speaks to me everywhere.

This is my Father's world,
O! let me ne'er forget
That though the wrong seems oft so strong,
God is the Ruler yet.
This is my Father's world:
The battle is not done;
Jesus who died shall be satisfied,
And earth and heaven be one.

10

DARE TO BE HAPPY

THERE IS AN OLD anonymous poem which I have always liked. In a down-to-earth sort of way it describes the happiness and zest for life which comes when one just lives in a loving and caring manner:

FELLOWSHIP

When a feller hasn't got a cent
And is feelin' kind of blue,
And the clouds hang thick and dark
And won't let the sunshine thro',
It's a great thing, oh my brethren,
For a feller just to lay
His hand upon your shoulder in a friendly sort o' way.

It makes a man feel queerish,
It makes the tear-drops start.
And you kind o' feel a flutter
In the region of your heart.
You can't look up and meet his eye,
You don't know what to say
When a hand is on your shoulder in a friendly sort o' way.

Oh this world's a curious compound
With its honey and its gall;
Its cares and bitter crosses,
But a good world after all.
And a good God must have made it,
Leastwise that is what I say,
When a hand is on your shoulder in a friendly sort o' way.

Feeling toward other people in the way that poem suggests goes a long way toward giving one a sense of worth, a feeling that life is meaningful. Charles Dickens says it well:

No one is useless in the world who lightens the burden of it for anyone else.

And Leo Tolstoy says:

Joy can be real only if people look upon their life as a service, and have a definite object in life outside themselves and their personal happiness.

So it would appear that to have real joy and enthusiasm one must drop or reduce self-emphasis and become genuinely outgoing; develop the attitude of good will or perhaps make it even stronger—that of love for all kinds of people. People need love, and the person who whole-heartedly gives love to them is loved by them and that induces a deep and genuine happiness all around. I knew a famous humorist of my boyhood days who was also a man with a big heart. He was a happy man whose joy and excitement for life derived from his love of people. He wrote this poem called "Need of Loving":

Folk need a lot of loving in the morning;
　The day is all before, with cares beset—
The cares we know, and they that give no warning;
　For love is God's own antidote for fret.

Folk need a heap of loving at the noontime—
　In the battle lull, the moment snatched from strife—
Halfway between the waking and the croontime,
　While bickering and worriment are rife.

Folk hunger so for loving at the nighttime,
　When wearily they take them home to rest—
At slumber song and turning-out-the-light time—
　Of all the times for loving, that's the best.

Folk want a lot of loving every minute—
　The sympathy of others and their smile!
Till life's end, from the moment they begin it,
　Folks need a lot of loving all the while.
STRICKLAND GILLIAN

And I have personal memories of Edwin Markham in his latter years, a white-haired genial giant with whom I once spent a never-to-be-forgotten evening. Asked which of his poems he valued the highest, he answered, "How can you choose between your own children?" He did voice the opinion that his four lines called "Outwitted" might have lasting qualities because love lasts. And I had the feeling that the really deep joy of this great American poet stemmed in large measure from the genuine outgoing love the man had for his fellows:

> He drew a circle that shut me out—
> Heretic, rebel, a thing to flout.
> But Love and I had the wit to win:
> We drew a circle that took him in!

Many people are lonely in this world, and that, too, is a painful experience. Anyone who helps another person out of loneliness will make two persons joyful: the lonely one and the one who helps. As John Oxenham says:

> Are you lonely, O my brother?
> Share your little with another!
> Stretch your hand to one unfriended,
> And your loneliness is ended.

So deep and meaningful is the joy and the enthusiasm that is born in one's mind and heart by human love and helpfulness that it has the power to motivate for a lifetime.

A physician well on in years told me how he became a doctor. His story was so wonderful that I never forgot it. He told me that, as a small boy, he lived with his parents in Kansas, in a district where, in wintertime, the countryside often lay under deep drifted snow and there would be difficulty getting in and out between town and his family's farm.

One winter when he was about seven years old, his little sister got sick, ran a high fever, became delirious. By the time his father got a message over the well-nigh impassable roads to the doctor, and the doctor finally arrived, with horse and buggy breaking through the snow, the little girl was sick unto death. The doctor remained for twenty-four hours until the crisis was passed. The whole household was in anguish. No one had a minute's sleep.

Finally the little boy saw the doctor walk across the room and put his hands on the shoulders of his father and mother, and heard him say to them, "By the grace of God, I am happy to tell you that little Mary will get well." The boy, from where he stood crouching behind a chair, could see his parents' faces in that moment. He had never seen them so beautiful, so lighted up, so wonderfully happy. They had been made that way by what the doctor had said to them.

"Right in that moment," my friend concluded, "I decided I was going to be a doctor, so I could say things like that to people that would bring that light to their eyes, that joy to their faces."

You don't have to be a doctor to say or do that which puts light in a human eye and joy on a human face. Simply practice Jesus' commandment that we love one another. Go out and do something for somebody. These are the things that make happy people happy. "If ye know these things, happy are ye if ye do them" (John 13:17). Here is the one never-failing source of the joy and enthusiasm we are talking about throughout this book.

No wonder that Christianity, which teaches the way to happy life, emphasizes and underscores love. Three great words there are—*faith, hope, love;* but the greatest of the three greatest words in the English language, or, indeed, any language, is *love.* And "Love never fails ..." (1 Corinthians 13:8, NKJV).

Saint John says:

> Greater love hath no man than this, that a man lay down his life for his friends.
>
> *John 15:13*

> And this commandment have we from him, That he who loveth God love his brother also.
>
> *1 John 4:21*

And in Galatians we read:

> Bear ye one another's burdens, and so fulfil the law of Christ.
>
> *Galatians 6:2*

And those who pass on kindness and love as they journey through this life are carrying out the rules for the good and happy life, which are set like jewels in the Scriptures. This poem by Henry Burton will encourage us to pass our joy on:

PASS IT ON

Have you had a kindness shown?
    Pass it on.
'Twas not given for thee alone,
    Pass it on.
Let it travel down the years,
Let it wipe another's tears,
'Till in heav'n the deed appears—
    Pass it on.

Did you hear the loving word?
    Pass it on.

Like the singing of a bird?
　Pass it on.
Let its music live and grow
Let it cheer another's woe;
You have reaped what others sow—
　Pass it on.

'Twas the sunshine of a smile—
　Pass it on.
Staying but a little while!
　Pass it on.
April beam a little thing,
Still it wakes the flowers of spring,
Makes the silent birds to sing—
　Pass it on.

One of the happy things you can do for someone else and so bring new joy and enthusiasm to yourself is to help that person face a devastating experience and overcome it. There is a middle-aged businessman who gives me renewed zest every time I see him, for he never fails to remind me of the day he "really hit bottom" in his career, as he expresses it. He credits me with helping him to recover from a "blow that nearly finished me off." I really did not do all that much for him that day except that I cared, and happened to have at hand a little story full of human wisdom that grabbed his mind. Anyway, it turned him from failure to success.

I talked with a young man who had been fired from a good position for making a serious mistake. A bit strange, I thought, for a company to throw out a young fellow for one mistake. I knew a famous employer who would allow at least two mistakes. Around his plant were signs reading HE WHO STUMBLES TWICE ON THE SAME STONE DESERVES TO BREAK HIS OWN NECK.

I pointed out to the dejected young fellow that mistakes could originate from an error pattern in one's thinking, or from inexperience, or from carelessness. But in any event you should derive what know-how the experience contained and then don't let it throw you. Turn your back on it; look to the future; try again. I happened to have on my desk at the time an editorial from the Toledo *Blade* written by my old friend, Grove Patterson, a famous newspaper editor, for whom I once worked on a Detroit paper. It was titled "Water Under the Bridge." I read it to the crushed young man:

A boy a long time ago leaned against the railing of a bridge and watched the current of the river below. A log, a bit of driftwood, a chip floated past.

Again the surface of the river was smooth. But always, as it had for a hundred, perhaps a thousand, perhaps even a million years, the water slipped by under the bridge. Sometimes the current went more swiftly and again quite slowly, but always the river flowed on under the bridge.

Watching the river that day, the boy made a discovery. It was not the discovery of a material thing, something he might put his hand upon. He could not even see it. He had discovered an idea. Quite suddenly, and yet quietly, he knew that everything in his life would some day pass under the bridge and be gone like the water.

The boy came to like those words *water under the bridge*. All his life thereafter the idea served him well and carried him through. Although there were days and ways that were dark and not easy, always when he had made a mistake that couldn't be helped, or lost something that could never come again, the boy, now a man, said, "It's water under the bridge."

And he didn't worry unduly about his mistakes after that and he certainly didn't let them get him down, because it was *water under the bridge*.

The young man sat without a word. Then he stood up. I had a feeling the editorial had registered. "Okay," he said, "I get it. It's water under the bridge. I'll try again." And he did all right, because he learned the very great truth that no failure ever need be final. Because you failed, made a mistake, acted stupidly does not indicate lack of brains or ability. It's just that now and then anyone can stumble or even take a bad fall. But that does not mean that you are not all right yourself. Just pick yourself up mentally. Say, "Okay, that happened, but now it has passed. I'll turn my back on all of it and look confidently to the future." Keep on believing in yourself. Have confidence.

The young man made more mistakes, of course, as we all do, but thereafter he knew how to handle them, and the number and importance of his errors averaged very low. It is not at all strange that when we meet at rare intervals we are both happy and enthusiastic, as is bound to be the case between the helped and the helper.

The famous poet Emily Dickinson has something important to say on this matter of helping people:

IF I CAN STOP ONE HEART FROM BREAKING

> If I can stop one heart from breaking,
> I shall not live in vain;
> If I can ease one life the aching,
> Or cool one pain,
> Or help one fainting robin
> Unto his nest again,
> I shall not live in vain.

And so does the notable writer Henry Drummond:

THE RETURN

Instead of allowing yourself to be unhappy, just let your love grow as God wants it to grow. Seek goodness in others. Love more persons more. Love them more impersonally, more unselfishly, without thought of return. The return, never fear, will take care of itself.

George Eliot issues a warning that no day should be allowed to pass except we do something to help at least one person, that is, if we expect to live a happy life:

COUNT THAT DAY LOST

If you sit down at set of sun
And count the acts that you have done,
　　And counting find
One self-denying deed, one word
That eased the heart of him who heard;
　　One glance most kind,
That fell like sunshine where it went—
Then you may count that day well spent.

But if, through all the livelong day,
You've cheered no heart, by yea or nay—
　　If, through it all
You've nothing done that you can trace
That brought the sunshine to one face—
　　No act most small
That helped some soul and nothing cost—
Then count that day as worse than lost.

And, to further impress this important point upon our minds—that we do not forget to do the simple, nice and kindly things, I give you a poem by Margaret E. Sangster:

THE SIN OF OMISSION

It isn't the thing you do;
　　It's the thing you leave undone,
Which gives you a bit of heartache
　　At the setting of the sun.

The tender word forgotten,
　　The letter you did not write,

The flower you might have sent,
   Are your haunting ghosts at night.

The stone you might have lifted
   Out of a brother's way,
The bit of heartsome counsel
   You were hurried too much to say;

The loving touch of the hand,
   The gentle and winsome tone,
That you had no time or thought for
   With troubles enough of your own.

The little acts of kindness,
   So easily out of mind;
Those chances to be helpful
   Which everyone may find—

No, it's not the thing you do,
   It's the thing you leave undone,
Which gives you the bit of heartache
   At the setting of the sun.

My Christmas Eve discovery took place in Brooklyn, New York. I was feeling happy because things were going well with my church. As a young bachelor minister I had just had a fine visit with some friends and was saying good-bye to them on their front steps.

All around us up and down the street houses were decorated in honor of Christ's birthday. Suddenly a pair of wreaths on the house across the street caught my eye. One had the traditional red bow, bright and gay. But the ribbon on the other was a somber black— the symbol of a death in the family, a funeral wreath. It was the custom at that time and place to hang such wreaths outside a house of mourning.

Something about that unexpected juxtaposition of joy and sorrow made a strange and moving impression on me. I asked my host about it. He said that a young couple with small children lived in the house but he did not know them. They were new in the neighborhood.

I said good night and walked down the street. But before I had gone far, something made me turn back. I did not know those people either. But it was Christmas Eve, and if there was joy or suffering to be shared, my calling was to share it.

Hesitantly I went up to the door and rang the bell. A tall young man opened it and spoke pleasantly to me. I told him that I was a minister whose church was in the neighborhood. I had seen the wreaths and wanted to offer my sympathy.

"Come in," he said quietly. "It's very kind of you to come."

The house seemed very still. In the living room a wood fire was burning. In the center of the room was a small casket. In it reposed the body of a little girl about six years old. Over the years in memory I can see her yet, lying there in a pretty white dress, ironed fresh and dainty. Nearby was an empty chair where the young man had been sitting, keeping watch beside the body of his child.

I was so moved that I could barely speak. *What a Christmas Eve*, I thought. Alone in a new neighborhood, no friends or relatives, a crushing loss. The young man seemed to read my thoughts. "It's all right," he said, as if he were reassuring me. "She's with the Lord, you know." His wife, he said, was upstairs with their two smaller children. He took me to meet her.

The young mother was reading to two small boys. She had a lovely face, sad yet serene. And suddenly I knew why this little family had been able to hang two wreaths on the door, one signifying life, the other death. They had been able to do it because they knew it was all one process, all part of God's wonderful and merciful and perfect plan for all of us. They had heard the great promise: ". . . because I live, ye shall live also" (John 14:19). They had heard it and they believed it. That was why they could move forward together with love and dignity, courage and acceptance.

The young couple asked if they could join my church. They did. We became good friends. Many years have passed since then, but not one has gone by without a Christmas card from some member of that family expressing love and gratitude.

But I am the one who is grateful.

I sometimes find myself thinking of an anonymous poem I like, for it speaks of the simple kindness we should be spreading:

I SHALL NOT PASS THIS WAY AGAIN

> Through this toilsome world, alas!
> Once and only once I pass;
> If a kindness I may show,
> If a good deed I may do
> To a suffering fellow man,
> Let me do it while I can.
> No delay, for it is plain
> I shall not pass this way again.

The joy we derive and the enthusiasm we may develop by thinking of the neglected and the lonely cannot be minimized. And to receive this wonderful blessing is often all so simple. All we need do is make a telephone call or write a letter, and a chain of joyousness and gratitude is set in motion.

I once had a friend, a great big-hearted man, a college professor and minister, Dr. William L. Stidger. One Thanksgiving Day during a recession and hard times when his friends were grumbling about "nothing to be thankful for," Dr. Stidger got to thinking. And he wrote this piece:

We were a group of friends in the midst of an after-dinner conversation. Because Thanksgiving was just around the corner and prosperity wasn't, we fell to talking about what we had to be thankful for. As I look back, it seems to me the conversation was rather cynical.

One member of the group, a minister, described the outline for his sermon on the theme *Thankful for What, This Depression Year?* His approach was so negative that the rest of us began a barrage of criticism.

"All right, I'm a realist and I intended to be honest about it," he replied. "If you don't like what you call my negative approach to Thanksgiving, then give me something to talk about that is affirmative."

That started us to thinking about what we had to be thankful for. One of us said: "Well I, for one, am grateful to Mrs. Wendt, an old schoolteacher who thirty years ago in a little West Virginia town went out of her way to introduce me to Tennyson."

Then he launched into a colorful description of Mrs. Wendt, a lovely little old lady who had been his high school teacher and who evidently had made a deep impression on his life. She had gone out of her way to awaken his literary interest and develop his gifts for expression. His was a dramatic and vivid description of a simple and natural small-town schoolteacher who had taken her work seriously.

"And does this Mrs. Wendt know that she made that contribution to your life?" someone put in.

"I'm afraid that she doesn't. I have been careless and have never, in all of these years, told her either face-to-face or by letter."

"Then why don't you write her? It would make her happy if she is still living, and it might make you happier, too. The thing that most of us ought to do is to learn to develop the attitude of gratitude."

Now, all this is very poignant to me, because Mrs. Wendt was *my* teacher, and *I* was the fellow who hadn't written. That friend's challenge made me see that I had accepted something very precious and hadn't bothered to say thanks.

That very evening, I tried to atone. On the chance that Mrs. Wendt might still be living, I sat down and wrote her what I called a Thanksgiving letter. I reminded her that it was she who had introduced my young mind to Tennyson and Browning and others.

It took about a week for the Post Office Department to search for Mrs. Wendt with my letter. It was forwarded from town to town. Finally it reached her, and this is the note I had in return, handwritten in the feeble scrawl of an old woman. It began:

My dear Willie—

That introduction itself was quite enough to warm my heart. Here was a man of fifty, fat and bald, addressed as "Willie." I had to smile over that, and then I read on:

I remember well your enthusiasm for Tennyson and the Idylls of the King when I read them to you, for you were so beautifully responsive. My reward for telling you about Tennyson did not have to wait until your belated note of thanks came to me in my old age. I received my best reward in your eager response to the lyrical beauty and the idealism of Tennyson. I shall never forget the way you read aloud to me:

My strength is as the strength of ten/Because my heart is pure!

But, in spite of the fact that I got much of my reward at that time, I want you to know what your note meant to me. I am now an old lady in my eighties, living alone in a small room, cooking my own meals, lonely and seemingly like the last leaf of fall left behind; or, as the old song used to put it, "The last rose of summer."

You will be interested to know, Willie, that I taught school for fifty years and, in all that time, yours is the first note of appreciation I ever received. It came on a blue, cold morning, and it cheered my lonely old heart as nothing has cheered me in many years.

I wept over that simple, sincere note from my teacher of long ago. I read it to a dozen friends. One of them said: "I believe I'm going to write Miss Mary Scott a letter. She did something similar to that for my boyhood!"

That first Thanksgiving letter was so successful and satisfying that I made a list of people who had contributed something definite and lasting to my life and planned to write at least one Thanksgiving letter every day in November. On the list were my father and mother, my brother and sisters, my grammar-school, high-school, and college teachers, some fellow ministers, and friends who had come to my side in hours of trouble and had helped me to see light through darkness. There were more than a hundred names on the list, and I hadn't thanked one of them! I could hardly wait to write my second letter.

It went to a college friend named Louis Sherwin, now a Presbyterian minister in Chicago.

One day he had arrived at Moundsville, West Virginia. It was mid-summer and I had recently been graduated from high school. I was lying in an old barrel-stave hammock, which I had made. He sat on the steps of our porch and talked to me about going to Allegheny College. I remembered that he talked enthusiastically about the football team, the beautiful campus, and the professors who did the teaching, of course.

Then and there I decided to go to his college, whereupon he dropped the matter and pulled out of his pocket a small leather-bound copy of Robert Louis Stevenson, read to me from it for half an hour and then, just as he departed, gave that book to me. I still have it.

There was a Thanksgiving letter for Louis, asking him if he remembered that hot summer afternoon and the gift he had left behind. And in a week I had his letter back. He was then in Oil City, Pennsylvania. The last line of his letter read: "I have not had such an easy time, Bill, and I cannot tell you how your letter has really helped me."

The next summer I received from Edinburgh, Scotland, a leather-bound copy of another Stevenson book from Stevenson's own city. Louis was so grateful for my letter of thanks that, while traveling through Scotland, he had thought of me again.

The list of Thanksgiving letters sent out that November numbered fifty. All but two brought answers immediately, and those two were returned by relatives with the information that the addressees were dead. Even those letters expressed thanks for the little bit of thoughtfulness.

For ten years, I have kept up this exciting game of writing Thanksgiving-month letters. I have a special file for answers, and I now have more than five hundred of the most beautiful letters anyone has ever received. I never dreamed the response would be so satisfying. I had merely thought of building up in myself an attitude of gratitude such as my friend suggested that night.

One of the most beautiful and touching letters came from the late Bishop William F. McDowell, in whose Washington home I had found some needed rest before a speaking engagement. Seeing that I was tired out, Mrs. McDowell put me to bed to rest, and I was so grateful for that motherly thoughtfulness that I never forgot it. And yet I had never written her a letter of thanks.

When I started in on my Thanksgiving letters I remembered her and, knowing that she was gone, I wrote my thank-you letter to the bishop, going over the memory and telling him all about it. I received this in response:

My Dear Will:

Your thanksgiving letter, as you called it, was so beautiful, so real, that as I sat reading it in my study the tears fell from my eyes, tears of gratitude. Then, before I realized what I was doing I arose from my chair, called her name and started to show it to her—for the moment forgetting that she was gone. You will never know how much your letter has warmed my spirit. I have been walking about in the glow of it all day long.

A Thanksgiving letter isn't much. Only a few lines are necessary, and a stamp to mail it. But the rewards are so great that eternity alone can estimate them. Even now, in dark moments of discouragement, I go over these responses to my Thanksgiving letters, and drive away any darkness by reading a few selected at random.

I often wondered where Bill Stidger got all that joy and that enthusiasm which were so characteristic of him. And this little story lets me in on his secret.

But some people actually seem afraid to be happy. Subconsciously they feel that something bad is going to happen. They may even believe it is not right to be joyful with so much suffering in the world. But you hardly help the unhappy by acting unhappy yourself. By your happiness you can actually pick them up. And by a joyous, enthusiastic spirit you can get out there and make it a better world for everyone.

Perhaps all you need do to be happy is simply to smile and do simple good deeds and rejoice over the happiness of others. Like Charles Lamb, for example who says:

> The greatest pleasure I know is to do a good action by stealth, and to have it found out by accident.

And Archibald Rutledge has a fine idea:

> One of the sanest, surest, and most generous joys of life comes from being happy over the good fortune of others.

And I like what Robert Louis Stevenson says:

> A happy man or woman is a radiant focus of good will, and their entrance into a room is as though another candle had been lighted.

My joyous friend Frank Bettger wrote:

> I have asked thousands of men and women in audiences all over the country for a pledge to smile, just for *thirty days*, their happiest smile at every living creature they see. Easily 75 per cent of the people in each audience willingly raised their hands. What has been the result? I quote from one letter received from a Knoxville, Tennessee, man. It is typical of several letters which have come to me:
>
> > My wife and I had just about agreed to separate. Of course, I thought she was entirely at fault. Within a few days after I began to put this idea into action, happiness was restored in my home. I then came to realize that I had been losing out in business because of a sullen, losing attitude. At the end of the day, I would go home and take it out on my wife and children. It was all my fault, not my wife's at all. I am a totally different man from what I was a year ago. I'm happier because I've made others happy too. Now everybody greets me with a smile. In addition my business has shown surprising improvement.
>
> This man was so excited about the results he got from smiling, that he kept writing me for years about it!

Just having enough love in your heart for people to get out there and help them, you will experience exquisite joy and live with enthusiasm and joyous excitement.

Read this story by Alexander Lake, a newspaper reporter, and you will have a heart full of joy and with it a greater respect for what people can be:

CHRISTMAS EVE MIRACLE

One Christmas Eve, when I was a police reporter on the Seattle *Post Intelligencer*, I was idling at my typewriter in the police station press room when an overwhelming impulse sent me hurrying to Pioneer Square, three blocks down the street, where I arrived just in time to knock a loaded revolver away from the head of a man about to shoot himself.

A cold drizzle was falling, and the gun slid across the glistening path and came to rest in the grass. The little park was deserted. For an unreal moment, I stared at the illuminated hands of a clock in the window of a restaurant across the street. They read five minutes past seven.

Three or four minutes ago, I'd been half-dozing in the warm, poorly ventilated reporters' room. Now here I was at the foot of Seattle's Skid Row with a man I'd just saved from death.

Whence had come the impulse that sent me out into the dreary night? What had directed me to the exact spot where a fellow human was about to blast himself into eternity? It seemed so fantastic that I wondered if I was dreaming. However, I didn't have time to think much about it for the man suddenly dropped to his knees and began fumbling in the wet grass for the gun.

I pushed him with my foot, and he sprawled on his face. I picked up the gun and slipped it into my coat pocket. Then I helped the man to his feet. He was blubbering.

"Snap out of it, fellow," I said. "I'm here to help you. Let's go across to that restaurant and get some hot soup, or something."

He didn't answer. I put my hand on his shoulder.

"For God's sake," he said, "go away. Leave me alone." Then he covered his face with his hands.

Rain was running down the back of my neck, and I pulled up my coat collar. "Come on, Jack. Snap out of it," I said.

He looked at me. "You know me?" he asked.

"No."

"You called me *Jack*."

"Okay, Jack. Let's go someplace where it's dry. Someplace where we can talk."

He shook his head. "I don't want to talk," he said. But he did want to talk, for words began pouring from him.

"I can't go on," he said. "I can't face them. They have no food. No Christmas presents. I'm tired and sick. I'm in hell."

"Who are they?" I said.

"My family. My wife and kids. I've walked these streets for six days with that stuff," he said, pointing to a square bundle lying on the walk. "Stuff to prevent windshields fogging," he explained. "I've been trying to sell it. Six days. Know how much I've made? Seventy-five cents."

"How about that soup now, Jack?" I said.

"Yes . . . Jack," he said bitterly. "Jack Bryan—Auto Accessories. Know what? The constable locked the doors of my business last week. Didn't even let me take the money from the till. Finance company took my car. No money. No food in the house. I picked up this line of windshield stuff to sell. Six days. Seventy-five cents. Going crazy with worry. I saw that gun in a service station and stole it. No food in the house. No money for rent. Six days. . . ."

"Yes, yes, Jack," I interrupted—for he was becoming incoherent. He was cold and wet; probably hungry. I walked him across First Street to a restaurant.

We never did get that soup. Inside the restaurant, I went to a pay phone and called my city editor. He ordered me to rush over to the morgue and ride out with the "dead wagon" to pick up the body of a woman reported murdered.

Grabbing Bryan by the arm, I hurried him up an alley and into the morgue garage. Bill Corson, son of the City Coroner, was in the driver's seat. We piled in beside him and rolled out into the night.

Bryan didn't seem to know or to care what was happening. He sat there next to me, hunched and silent. I handed him two ten-dollar bills, but he pushed them aside, so I crumpled them and pushed them into the breast pocket of his coat.

Corson turned left beyond King Street station, and the wagon squished through mud and slush into Seattle's worst slum district—a section where poverty-stricken Italians lived in squalor. We pulled up before a ramshackle house overflowing with wailing, moaning neighbors. Corson and I carried the basket, and Bryan followed.

We set the basket on the floor in a small bedroom in which the body of a large, work-worn woman lay on a broken-down bed. She hadn't been murdered—she'd dropped dead at her washtub.

Corson ushered the neighbors into the yard. The woman's husband and five small children remained at the foot of the bed, clutching one another.

I'll never forget the misery in that husband's eyes. Bryan noticed it too, for as Corson and I lifted the heavy body into the basket, he walked to the man, and without a word, handed him one of the two ten-dollar bills I'd put in his pocket.

The husband sobbed, and the children began a sympathetic lament.

Corson strapped down the lid, and we carried the basket through the mob of neighbors in the yard, and lifted it into the wagon.

As the three of us settled into the front seat, Bryan said, "I've got to get home. Please—take me home. I must have been crazy. I didn't know what misery is."

Corson swung around to James Street and dropped Bryan and me off in front of a small white cottage. Bryan hurried up the steps. I followed, slowly. I paused in the little hall and watched through the kitchen door. With eyes closed, Bryan was holding his wife as if he'd never let her go. Two little girls, about three and five years old, were each hugging one of their daddy's legs.

Then Mrs. Bryan noticed me and moved out of her husband's arms. She came into the hall and shut the door. "He's been so worried and sick," she said, eyes filled with tears. "Tonight when he wasn't home by seven o'clock, I knelt down and prayed God to please take care of him, and to bring him home safely. And here he is."

I realized then, why the impulse to get to Pioneer Square had come to me at exactly seven. I felt awed and humble.

"His business went broke," Mrs. Bryan said, "but I'm not a bit worried. I've asked God to take care of that, too."

I looked into Mrs. Bryan's calm eyes and thought: It was this woman's faith in God that sent me out into this dismal night to bring her husband home to her.

I said, "I'm certain things will work out just as you want them to, Mrs. Bryan."

I told her to call me at the police station if she needed me, then stepped out onto the little porch. As the door closed behind me, I remembered that Bryan had given ten dollars to the Italian, so I turned back into the house. Father, mother, and the two little girls were kneeling at kitchen chairs, praying. I stood for a moment, then tiptoeing to the table put a few one-dollar bills on it and slipped out.

God did take care of Bryan's business. Today, automobile men up and down the Pacific Coast know him and his line of accessories.

Back at the police station press room, I picked up the phone and called the city desk. "That trip with Corson," I said.

"I'll give you a rewrite man," said the city editor.

"No—don't bother," I said. "There wasn't any story."

One of the greatest things about human beings is how they can and do so forget themselves when loving others that they will put their own lives on the line for them. And what is their reward? Not that they do what they do for reward. But there is a reward just the same, and it is joy. Beyond that, it is an inexpressible enthusiasm for life, for people and for God.

I would like to write *Finis* to this treasury of joy and enthusiasm with one of the most glorious statements ever made:

> But as it is written, Eye hath not seen, nor ear heard, neither have entered into the heart of man, the things which God hath prepared for them that love him.
>
> *1 Corinthians 2:9*